The purpose of the Junior League is exclusively educational and charitable and is to promote volunteerism, to develop the potential of its members for voluntary participation in community affairs and to demonstrate the effectiveness of trained volunteers.

*The proceeds from the sale of **Bound To Please** will be used to support the community projects of the Junior League of Boise.*

A COLLECTION OF RECIPES
FROM THE JUNIOR LEAGUE OF BOISE

Foreward by Joan Hemingway and Arthur Hart
Illustrations by Lisa Penny
Illustrations Text by Lindy High

The purpose of the Junior League is exclusively educational and charitable and is to promote volunteerism, to develop the potential of its members for voluntary participation in community affairs and to demonstrate the effectiveness of trained volunteers.

*The proceeds from the sale of **Bound To Please** will be used to support the community projects of the Junior League of Boise.*

FIRST EDITION

First Printing: 10,000 copies, September 1983
Second Printing: 10,000 copies, December 1984

SECOND EDITION

First Printing: 10,000 copies, September 1987

BOUND TO PLEASE
P.O. Box 6126
Boise, Idaho 83707

Please include $14.95 plus $2.00 postage and handling per book. For Idaho delivery please include sales tax.

Table of Contents

The History of
The Junior League of Boise

The spirit of volunteerism in America began in earliest colonial days and was carried West as our country expanded. Neighbors gathered for quilting bees, harvesting, canning and barn-raisings, accompanied by a spirit of cooperation and helpfulness between friends, neighbors and communities.

We see this tradition alive and well among members of the Junior League of Boise. Our birthday into the Association of Junior Leagues of America was March, 1928, when the energetic Boise Junior Charity League was accepted to membership with 28 charter members.

Over the decades, a fine working relationship between the community and the League grew with such projects as well-baby clinics and educational lectures in the '30s, Red Cross classes, the Idaho Concert and Artists Series and the Hospital Shop at St. Alphonsus' Hospital in the '40s. With the dawn of the '50s, the League entered into the cultural field more actively with the Civic Symphony Youth Concert, the Marionette program at the Idaho Historical Museum and Children's Art Show at the Boise Art Gallery.

Successful civic projects of the following years indicated a change toward more historical interests as well as the desire to further address the needs of women and children. Coinciding with Idaho's Territorial Centennial, an historical chapel was preserved and moved permanently to the Boise State University campus and the League founded the Boise Children's Zoo. Perhaps the most successful contribution in terms of lasting community impact was the Boise School Volunteers.

League projects have traditionally involved members in service to the community, but a new dimension, advocacy on behalf of children, has been added. Recent League involvement in the community includes: the Committee for the Prevention of Child Abuse and Neglect, the Guardian Ad Litem program where abused and neglected children going through the judicial system are assigned a trained League guardian to insure that the children's interests are protected, Alcohol Awareness program with trained members teaching sixth grade classes about the impact of alcohol and drug abuse, Crime Prevention with members establishing Block Watch Programs and finally Art in the Schools, providing art experiences for elementary school children.

New projects involving League members are The Discovery Center of Idaho, a hands-on science museum for children of all ages; a new Ronald McDonald House, to provide housing for out of town families of critically ill children; and a teen pregnancy program providing support for teenage mothers.

Throughout the years, these community-oriented projects have been funded by League fundraisers. Currently, members operate a thrift shop, Second Time Around, and have created a national market through the sale of this cookbook, first published in 1983. This brings us full circle with our predecessors, known for their dedication to community and love of fine food and gracious entertaining. The Junior League of Boise has published three previous cookbooks from which we have taken old favorites.

We have come far, we have learned much, but what we are is rooted in our beginnings and we have much to be thankful for in those who went before us. And so we offer ourselves, our heritage, our dedication and our hopes for the future which are indeed *Bound To Please.*

We would like to thank you, the Junior League of Boise, your families and friends who donated recipes, tested and tasted them in your homes, and gave so generously of your time and talents. We proudly dedicate this book to you with the hope that it is
Bound To Please.

The First Edition Cookbook Committees

Chairman
KATIE STEIN

Production Chairmen
BONNIE HUTCHINSON MARY JANE HILL
MIKEL McMURRAY ANN MURDOCH

Testing Coordinator
SUE BAXTER

Chapter Editors
TERRI TURPIN
BARBARA BARNEY THERESA CHANEY
JEANNENE BOYD ANNE OPPENHEIMER
KATHY BROMSTEAD TANYA STORTI

Menus
SUSAN SMITH

Marketing Plan
JOLENE DEWALD KANDY HEARNE
PATTY GLAISYER CAROLE SCHROEDER

Sustainer Advisor
FRAN HOPPER

The Second Edition Cookbook Committees

DONNA MATLOCK   GEMMA VANHOLE
Chairmen 1986-1987

CINDY ANDERSON	TONI PRICE
SUSY BALDWIN	SUSAN SAHLBERG
SANDY CHRISTENSEN	JAN SOLBERG
BARBARA DERBY	CAROLYN SWAN
DEBBIE JOHNSON	DEBBIE WETHERELL

CELESTE KELLER

DEBBIE JOHNSON
Chairman 1987-1988

VIRGINIA PELLEGRINI	KRISTIN HOFF
Assistant Chairman	RHONDA HUGHS
CINDY ANDERSON	CELESTE B. KELLER
SUSAN BAILOR	KAREN MANGUM
SHARON BURKETT	TERESA McLEOD
LINDA COGEN	CRISTINA DELVALLE RATHBONE
KATHY COHEN	CYNTHIA RAMSEY STIVERS
LAURIE CORRICK	COLLEN WILCOX
REBECCA GROVER	GLORIA SMITH

BARBARA DERBY, Sustainer Advisor

The Junior League of Boise gratefully acknowledges . . .

JOAN HEMINGWAY

ARTHUR HART
Foreward

LISA PENNY
Illustrator

LINDY HIGH
Writer

WILLIAM C. WIECK
Capitol Lithograph & Printing, Inc.

ARNY SKOV
Cover Design and Illustration

B & J TYPESETTING

GORDON RANDALL

GEORGIA SMITH

MARIO DELISIO

ROMAINE HON

IDAHO POTATO COMMISSION

TIMOTHY D. McGREEVY

JOHN KIRTLAND

G. W. SANDER

BARBARA SIMPSON

TIM AND ERICA CRAIG

CELESTE HARRIS

JUDITH AUSTIN

ARDYTH SCHUSTER

. . . for their expertise in the development of this cookbook.

Foreward

Good and exciting eating has been an important part of living in Idaho for as long as my family has been here. People do have their quirks though. I remember my grandfather, Ernest Hemingway, had a penchant for ham and egg sandwiches with a slice of raw onion bathed in ketchup on white bread for breakfast while traveling, even though he was a trencherman of note when it came to game dishes and a variety of exotic foods. He loved Idaho for its outdoor beauty and the basic values of its people. Probably more than anything else, he loved the hunting and the bird shooting. Game preparation has been an important part of kitchen life in Idaho.

My father, Jack, lives for fishing. While he seldom kills stream trout, we often enjoy the rich red-meated rainbows from our local reservoirs and lakes. Finding a new way to prepare these succulent fish is always a challenge . . . a challenge met deliciously with the recipes found in this book.

This collection of recipes by the Junior League of Boise will open the door for you to an important part of the culinary wealth that is Idaho.

— Joan Hemingway, Sun Valley
Co-author of *Rose Bud* and *The Picnic Gourmet*

Native Americans, in Idaho for more than 10,000 years before the first whites arrived, had their own distinctive foods. They knew how to gather and use many kinds of native plants, and how to catch the abundant fish and game with which the land was blessed.

The trappers who roamed over Idaho's rugged mountains lived much as the Indians — hunting and fishing to feed themselves. Necessity often dictated that they eat the beaver they had just trapped and skinned.

Emigrants on the Oregon and California trails passed through Idaho by tens of thousands in the 1840s, '50s and '60s. These were mostly eastern or midwestern farm folks who brought their groceries with them: flour, cornmeal, dried beans, bacon, and salt pork. Of necessity the cooking was rough and ready. The men could occasionally shoot wild game, and when Indian fishing camps were encountered, could trade for fresh salmon. Francois Payette at Fort Boise had a vegetable garden much appreciated by the weary travelers.

Prospectors and miners were the next large population to swarm over Idaho after gold was discovered here in 1860. The miners in new towns like Pierce, Florence, Elk City, Idaho City, and Silver City, created a market for all kinds of foodstuffs. Since the mines were in remote mountain country, everything had to be hauled in. Idaho's agriculture got its start because of this mountain market, and Idaho's cattle industry arose for the same reason.

Chinese miners brought their distinctive culture and cooking to the camps, and the culinary skill of these natives of the Flowery Kingdom made Chinese cooks fixtures in many early hotel, ranch and farm kitchens. Chinese restaurants opened in many communities; and even before the gold rush was over Chinese gardeners were plying their age-old farming skills to supply townspeople with fresh fruits and vegetables.

Japanese and Basque cooking came to Idaho too, both in the 1890s. These added richness and variety to a culinary tradition which already included that of German, French, and Scandinavian immigrants. Easterners on the Idaho frontier often went to great trouble to get favorite delicacies from "the states." Boise restaurants in the 1870s regularly offered fresh Baltimore oysters, shipped live across the continent by rail and stagecoach in barrels of sea water.

What is Idaho cooking? As the recipes in this book will show, it is cosmopolitan, drawn from the culinary culture of that passing parade of peoples who have called Idaho home. To join that parade, read on.

— **Arthur A. Hart**
Retired Director of the Idaho State Historical Society

Idaho cuisine at its finest is reflected in the many different types of restaurants throughout the state. From continental to country, they offer a special ambiance and distinctive style that says "Welcome to Idaho."

Our thanks to the following restaurants for sharing popular favorites as well as special secrets from their kitchens.

A MATTER OF TASTE
Ketchum

CAFE ROSE
Boise

CHRISTIANIA
Sun Valley

HAS BROUCK HOUSE
Nampa

JAKE'S
Boise, Idaho Falls, Pocatello

KOFFEE KLATCH
Boise

LA MIA CUCINA
Boise

NINA MAE'S
Boise

PETER SCHOTT'S CONTINENTAL RESTAURANT
Boise

RED ROBIN
Boise, Ketchum

SANDPIPER
Boise, Idaho Falls, Pocatello, Twin Falls

SHORE LODGE
McCall

THE KNEADERY
Ketchum

Over 2,000 recipes have been prepared and tested by Boise Junior League testing teams. Team members selected and approved over 700 recipes for **Bound To Please.** We gratefully acknowledge the many hours spent by these women and it is our sincere hope that none have been inadvertently overlooked.

Team Captains

DELPHINE ALDECOA
JAN BERGESEN
KATIE BERQUIST
JEANNENE BOYD
KATHY BROMSTEAD
JOLENE DEWALD
MARCIA DONNELLY
FRAN HOPPER
MARY HORMAECHEA
CARMELYN JOHNSON

JEANNE KING
BECKY LANGHUS
LYN McCOLLUM
NANCY McDANIEL
BARBARA MOSSMAN
DIANA NICHOLSON
SUZI PEARSON
JANIS PERRY
SHEILA ROBINSON
CAROLE SCHROEDER

KIM SCHUH
BETTY SHEILS
DIANNA SHERMAN
JUNE SMITH
SUSAN SMITH
LINDA SWANSON
JENA VASCONCELLOS
STEPHANIE WHITE
CHEROL WILLIAMS
JANE WILLIAMSON

Team Members

Jean Allan
Sally Allred
Carole Almond
Winnie Ambrose
Lody Andersen
Patty Backus
Barbara Barney
Sue Baxter
Susan Beckman
Dianne Bevis
Linda Bilow
Lorna Board
Lou Ann Boyd
Anne Brown
Miriam Burns
Jane Buser
Laura Bushnell
Theresa Chaney
Dolores Chapman
Helen Chastain
Jeanne Christianson
Robbye Clements
Sue Clemons
Betty Clifford
Darlene Code
Marcia Cogswell
Martha Coughlin
Connie Crookston
Gayle D'Alessandro
Jane Daly
Margaret Decker
Barbara Derby
Nancy Donald
Carol Elliott
Geridee Farley
Sharon Fowler
Kathy French
CeCe Gadda
Marijke Geston
Betty Gibson
Patty Glaisyer

Ellen "Tootie" Glaisyer
Marcia Glenn
Vickie Glerum
Linda Gossett
Dodie Gray
Susan Grey
Tonya Hall
Bev Harad
Kay Hardy
Jana Harris
Gail Hawkins
Kandy Hearne
Ramona Higer
Mary Jane Hill
Rosemary Hill
Dana Holstine
Romaine Hon
Cathy Hull
Bonnie Hutchinson
Mary Ann Jackson
Anna Margaret Jones
Jayne Jones
Charlene Kaufman
Mary Keto
Carolyn Kiefer
Jo King
Pauline Kluth
Kaye Knight
Diane Kreizenbeck
Sue Lambuth
Sheila Lincoln
Julie Lliteras
Carol Lloyd
Leann Logson
Karen Marmillion
Peggy Marshall
Mary Lou Martin
Terry McDaniel
Mikel McMurray
Stacy McMurray
Nancy Meadows
Meryle Kay "Mert" Michael

Donna Moore
Violet Moore
Carole Morgan
Kathy Moyer
Ann Murdoch
Sharyn Negus
Leslie Welsh
Anne Oppenheimer
Anne Peterson
Linda Pierce
Christine Poole
Bitsy Quinn
Phyllis Richardson
Vicki Risch
Carole Schroeder
Ardyth Schuster
Alice Serrao
Marilyn Sharp
Penny Simons
Linda Squyres
Catherine Stein
Katie Stein
Margie Stevens
Ernestine Stivison
Vicki Stoppello
Tanya Storti
Nancy Streff
Jean Sullivan
Joan Sullivan
Cynthia Thoreson
Terri Turpin
Susan Van Engelen
Mary Lou Wagner
Jan Way
Mary Katherine Wenske
Karen Wetherell
Chris Whitcomb-Smith
Muriel Williams
Barbara Wilson
Judy Witt
Liz Zemlicka

Bound to Please: Sun Valley Serenade

Union Pacific Railroad wanted a winter attraction for its western rail lines, and W. Averell Harriman was intrigued by the growth of European ski resorts. He hired Count Felix Schaffgotsch to find the perfect place, and in 1936 the Austrian skier chose what is now Sun Valley. Railroad engineers designed the ski resort and gave it the world's first chairlift.

In the decades since, Sun Valley has played host to thousands of visitors. It was here Ernest Hemingway wrote "For Whom The Bell Tolls," here that hunters and hikers watched the changing autumn colors along the Wood River, and here that the Sun Valley Center for the Arts and Humanities attracts musicians, artists, and writers. A resort for all seasons, Sun Valley has justified Harriman's dreams.

Superbowl Party

BARBECUED SAUSAGE BALLS

COCKTAIL QUICHES

BROCCOLI AT ITS BEST WITH FRESH VEGETABLES

HOMEMADE SALAMI   SWEDISH RYE BREAD

~~~

FRENCH MINT PIES

FINGER CHEESECAKE BARS

~~~

SPICED WALNUTS

Everybody You Owe Cocktail Party

TEQUILA PUNCH

~~~

CHORIZO-FILLED WON TONS

SHRIMP CHAFING DISH

CONTINENTAL PATE   STEAK TARTARE

SPINACH-STUFFED MUSHROOMS

HOT CLAM DIP IN A SHELL

MUSHROOM-DEVILED EGGS   COCKTAIL MEATBALLS

OYSTER/CREAM CHEESE ROLL

DIVINE CRAB   EASY CAVIAR DIP

TAOS SALSA AND TORTILLA CHIPS

Halloween Party
for Costumed Crowd

MIXED GREEN SALAD WITH OIL AND VINEGAR DRESSING

~~~

WORLD FAMOUS CHILE CON CARNE

PAIN DE MENAGE

~~~

CREAM CHEESE POUND CAKE

Easter Brunch

SHERRIED CLAM CHOWDER

~~~

STUFFED FILLET OF SOLE WITH MUSHROOM SHERRY SAUCE

WELSH CASSEROLE AU GRATIN

ASPARAGUS SUPREME

BANANA-CARROT BREAD

~~~

DOUBLE WHAMMY FROZEN CHOCOLATE CREPES
WITH VANILLA SAUCE

Sunday Morning Brunch

GUAVA-RUM PUNCH

~~~

HAM-CHUTNEY MUSHROOMS

CHEESE-SPINACH ROLL

ROQUEFORT-STUFFED TOMATOES

FRESH FRUIT SALAD WITH HONEY FRENCH DRESSING

~~~

KUCHEN

Father's Day Brunch

BLOODY MARYS

~~~

CURRIED FRESH MUSHROOM SOUP

CRAB-STUFFED POTATOES

BROCCOLI HELENE WITH LIME SAUCE

WHEAT GERM MUFFINS

~~~

WHITE CHOCOLATE ICE CREAM

ROCKY ROAD

Saturday Fun Run Brunch

SUNRISE FRUIT SMOOTHIE

~~~

COTTAGE QUICHE

FRESH SPINACH AND BACON SALAD WITH CHUTNEY DRESSING

~~~

ORANGE ROLLS

Pre-Golf Brunch

BELL PEPPER SOUP

~~~

CHEESE SOUFFLE BRUNCH

HOT CRAB SANDWICHES

HOT DILL PICKLES

APPLE-SPINACH SALAD

~~~

HOOTENHOLLER WHISKEY CAKE

Book Review Luncheon

SUPER SEAFOOD

~~~

HOT VEGETABLE CASSEROLE

LEMON MUFFINS

~~~

FROSTED CHOCOLATE COOKIES

Ladies' Spring Luncheon

CURRIED CRAB AND AVOCADO PIE

BERMUDA SALAD

PINEAPPLE-BRAN MUFFINS

~~~

PRETZEL COOKIES

Bridge Luncheon

CURRIED OLIVE APPETIZERS

~~~

SALMON CREPES

SPINACH IN PASTRY

BUTTER LETTUCE SALAD WITH HEARTS OF PALM

~~~

CHOCOLATE THUMBPRINTS

Poolside Luncheon

PINA COLADAS

~~~

COLD CUCUMBER AND SPINACH SOUP

CHINESE CHICKEN SALAD

WHOLE WHEAT SESAME CRESCENTS

~~~

ALMOND-POTATO TORTE

HAWAIIAN ICED COFFEE

Greenbelt Biking Picnic

ORANGE JULIUS

~~~

PICKLED ASPARAGUS

GARDEN SALAD SOUP

DELUXE CHICKEN SALAD SANDWICHES

BROCCOLI-CAULIFLOWER SALAD

~~~

PERFECT SUGAR COOKIES

BASQUE SANGRIA

Tailgate Picnic

HOT MULLED WINE

~~~

TOMATO BISQUE

POTATO-ONION ROLLS

VERMICELLI-SEAFOOD SALAD

BRIE EN CROUTE WITH FRESH FRUIT

~~~

CHOCOLATE-CARAMEL CLUSTERS

Ladies' Luncheon

GARDEN SALAD SOUP

~~~

CHICKEN-PINEAPPLE SALAD

LEMON TEA BREAD

~~~

DELICES AU CHOCOLAT

Italian Patio Picnic

ITALIAN FRIED CHICKEN   PICNIC PIZZA

ROTELLE SALAD

MARINATED VEGETABLE SALAD

~~~

CHOCOLATE-DIPPED STRAWBERRIES WITH ORANGE CREAM

Menus

New Year's Eve Dinner

CHICKEN LIVERS SAUTEED WITH ROSEMARY

~~~

LAMB CHOPS WITH ROQUEFORT CHEESE

IDAHO POTATOES ANNA

SPINACH CREPES

~~~

CHOCOLATE RING

Valentine's Sweetheart Dinner for Two

BAKED CLAM APPETIZERS

~~~

STEAK BENEDICTINE

DILLED NEW POTATOES

BEETS AND MUSHROOMS VENETIAN STYLE

SALAD OF CELERY ROOT IN MUSTARD MAYONNAISE

~~~

FRENCH PEAR PIE A LA CREME

40th Birthday Dinner

CRAB CANAPES

~~~

STUFFED FILLET OF SOLE WITH MUSHROOM-SHERRY SAUCE

POPPY SEED POTATOES   CARROTS PIQUANT

~~~

CHOCOLATE RUM TORTE

Potluck Pasta Party

AVOCADO APPETIZER

~~~

ITALIAN MINESTRONE

ITALIAN BREADSTICKS

SEAFOOD LASAGNA

ZESTY ITALIAN SPAGHETTI AND MEATBALLS

SPINACH NOODLES WITH GORGONZOLA SAUCE

~~~

AMARETTO CHEESECAKE

SERBIAN COFFEE

Curry Fare

EAST INDIAN CHEESE BALL

~~~

INCOMPARABLE SHRIMP CURRY

BENGAL SALAD

RICE

ALMOND BAVAROIS

CAFE MARRAKECH

Sit-Down Seasonal
Spring Dinner

ASPARAGUS MOUSSE

~~~

MARINATED SALMON STEAKS

RICE PILAF

PEA PODS AND WALNUTS WITH ZUCCHINI

GOUGERE

~~~

STRAWBERRY MOUSSE WITH RASPBERRY SAUCE

Summer Buffet Supper

SUMMER PARTY WINE

CONTINENTAL PATE

MOLDED ROQUEFORT CREME

~~~

POACHED SALMON WITH SHERRIED CAPER SAUCE

POTATO AND ROAST BEEF SALAD

MARINATED CARROT SALAD

GOURMET PARISIAN BREAD

~~~

FRESH COCONUT CAKE

Mexican Feast

FROZEN MARGARITAS

~~~

MEXICAN HAYSTACK

TORTILLA SOUP

ENCHILADA CASSEROLE

FIESTA CHILE BAKE

MEXICAN CORN

~~~

JAMOCA WHIZZ

CAFE MEXICANO

Backyard Barbecue

EASY CAVIAR DIP WITH FRESH VEGETABLES

~~~

SHISH KEBAB

RICE

BEER BREAD

SHRIMP-WALNUT SALAD   MUSSEL AND POTATO SALAD

~~~

MILE HIGH ICE CREAM PIE

Summer Pasta Buffet

MARINATED MUSHROOMS

CHICKEN WINGS AS HORS D'OEUVRES

~~~

MINESTRONI DI SPINACI

SEAFOOD AND PASTA SALAD PESCARA

PASTA PUTTANESCA CON VONGOLE

SEAFOOD FETTUCINI

ITALIAN TOMATO PIE

CLASSIC CAESAR SALAD

FOOD PROCESSOR FRENCH BREAD

~~~

CHOCOLATE-KAHLUA CHEESECAKE

AMARETTO

Autumn Soup Dinner

SPINACH SALAD WITH CELERY SEED DRESSING

~~~

OKTOBERFEST SOUP

BRAIDED SQUASH BREAD

~~~

CHOCOLATE-MINT SQUARES

Dog Day Dinner

COLD CUCUMBER AND SPINACH SOUP

~~~

NO FAULT SALAD

REFRIGERATOR CRESCENT ROLLS

~~~

SOUR CREAM ``FALLING DOWN'' CAKE

Game Dinner

CRANBERRY CHUTNEY WITH CREAM CHEESE

~~~

PHEASANT AND SHERRY

CARROTS IN ORANGE SAUCE   WILD RICE CASSEROLE

~~~

PERSIMMON PUDDING WITH SAUCE

Chinese Banquet

CHINESE CHICKEN WINGS

~~~

OO SOUP

SHRIMP LO MEIN   SWEET AND SOUR BEEF

TROUT ORIENTAL

STEAMED RICE

~~~

PINEAPPLE SHERBET

Christmas Day Dinner

TRADITIONAL TOM AND JERRYS

DEVILED CRAB

~~~

PRIME RIB SUPREME

SPINACH-STUFFED ONIONS

NEW POTATO GRATIN   YORKSHIRE PUDDING

~~~

CHRISTMAS PIE

Bound to Please: The Remarkable Russet

There's something special about southern Idaho soil. Fertile with volcanic ash, it needed only nature's warm days and cool nights and man's addition of irrigation to produce the Russet Burbank potato. The famous Idaho spud is an "all-meat potato," its solids evenly distributed to ensure perfect baking and frying.

Stored in sophisticated, temperature-controlled environments, the Russets are available almost year-round. And how to fix them? Every Idahoan has a favorite recipe for baking, stuffing, frying, dressing up or gulping down the potato – as long as it's a Russet.

Potatoes

Basque Potatoes 8
Bavarian Potatoes 9
Breakfast Potato Pancakes . 16
Dilled New Potatoes 7
Hot Potato Casserole 14
Idaho Potatoes Anna 6
Pea and Potato Sauté 7
Poppy Seed Potatoes 7
Potato Cakes 17
Potato Top Hat 17
Potatoes Rosemary 6
Sheepherder Potatoes 8

Scalloped or
au Gratin

Hash Brown au Gratin 11
New Potato Gratin 12
Potatoes Parmesan 9
Potatoes Romanoff 14
Swiss Scalloped Potatoes . . 12
Welsh Casserole au Gratin . . 10

Stuffed

Caviar Potatoes 3
Cheese Soufflé à la Potato . . 13
Crab Stuffed Potatoes 2
Greek Stuffed Potatoes 4
Princely Potatoes 2
Shrimp Curry Potatoes 3

Potato Skins

Potato Skin Boats 5
Potato Skin Chips 5
Potato Skins 4

Mashed

Glazed Mashed Potato Ring . 15
Heavenly Sour
    Cream Potatoes 13
Orange Potato Rosettes 16
Potato Puffs 15

Salads

Hot German
    Potato Salad 20
Mussel and Potato Salad . . . 19
Posh Potato Salad 20
Prime Potato Salad 18

"A Guide to Idaho® Potatoes"

Buying and Storing

When buying Idaho® potatoes, look for the "Grown in Idaho" seal and these qualities: oval shape, few and shallow eyes, net-textured skin and russet brown color.

Store potatoes in a cool, dry and well-ventilated place. At 45°F. to 50°F. potatoes will keep for several weeks; at room temperature for about a week.

Don't refrigerate. It causes a sweet taste as the potato starch turns to sugar.

Store away from strong light or potatoes will turn green and develop a bitter flavor.

Keep away from heat or skin will shrink.

Nutritional Value

Idaho® potatoes are low in sodium and almost fat-free. They're also low in calories. For instance, a five-ounce potato has only 100 calories.

Potatoes offer protein, iron, thiamine, niacin, potassium and a significant amount of vitamin C.

Carbohydrates and Fiber

An ideal source of the energy burned in the body is the complex carbohydrates contained in the potato — about 24 grams in a five-ounce baker.

And because the American diet is relatively low in fiber, the Idaho® potato makes another healthful contribution to your diet with its vital fiber content.

How to Prepare Idaho® Potatoes

BOILING
— *Keep potatoes white by adding a teaspoon of vinegar or lemon juice to the soaking water.*
— *Add a little milk to the cooking water to improve the flavor.*
— *Add a dash of sugar to the boiling liquid to add flavor and retain the vitamin C.*

BAKING
— *A high oven temperature means a shorter cooking time and a crustier skin. Use medium-sized potatoes.*
— *Rub the potato with butter or olive oil for a soft skin.*
— *Line the oven bottom with foil, preheat 250° or 350°, place the potatoes on the foil and bake slowly.*
— *Always pierce the skin to allow steam to escape.*

1

Crab-Stuffed Potatoes

8 servings

4 large Idaho® potatoes, baked
½ cup butter, melted
½ cup heavy cream
1 teaspoon salt
⅛ teaspoon cayenne
4 teaspoons grated onion
1 cup grated sharp Cheddar cheese
1½ teaspoons paprika
1 6½-ounce can crab meat, drained

Grease potatoes and bake at 400° for 1 hour. Remove from oven and cut in half. Scoop out skins, leaving a thin shell.

Whip potatoes with butter, cream, salt, cayenne, onion, cheese and **½ teaspoon** of the paprika. Gently fold in crab. Refill shells and sprinkle with remaining paprika. Bake at 450° for 15 minutes.

Princely Potatoes

6 servings

6 large Idaho® potatoes, baked
½ cup butter, melted
½ cup milk
1½ cups sour cream
¾ cup diced celery
1½ cups grated Swiss cheese
¼ cup chopped green onions
½ teaspoon salt
¼ teaspoon pepper
Dash paprika

Bake potatoes at 450° for 1 hour. Remove from oven and cut a long oval slit in the top of each. Scoop out potato, leaving a thin shell of skin. Mash potato meat.

Combine remaining ingredients, **except** paprika, and add mashed potatoes.

Stuff potato skins. Sprinkle with paprika. Bake at 450° for 10 minutes.

Use hot milk when mashing potatoes to keep them from becoming heavy or soggy.

Caviar Potatoes

2 servings

2 Idaho® potatoes, baked
¾ cup sour cream
1 hard boiled egg,
  chopped
¼ cup chopped onion
2 ounces red caviar
Watercress

Cut a thin slice from the top of each potato. Remove pulp, leaving a thin shell.

Combine pulp and sour cream and mash well. Add egg and onion. Spoon mixture into shells. Top with caviar. Garnish with watercress. Serve either hot or cold.

NOTE: Good with watercress salad and fruit marinated in Grand Marnier.

For fluffier mashed potatoes, add a pinch of baking soda as well as milk and butter.

Shrimp-Curry Potatoes

2 servings

2 Idaho® potatoes, baked
⅛ cup chopped onion
1 tablespoon butter
1 teaspoon curry powder
9 ounces canned shrimp,
  drained
½ cup milk
4 tablespoons capers,
  drained
Cayenne

Cut a thin slice from the top of each potato. Remove pulp, leaving a thin shell. Mash pulp and set aside.

Sauté onion in butter until tender. Add curry powder and shrimp. Sauté lightly.

Add milk to potato pulp and mix well. Add potato mixture to shrimp and onions. Heat through. Stir in capers. Spoon mixture into potato shells and garnish with cayenne.

Greek-Stuffed Potatoes

2 servings

2 Idaho® potatoes, baked
1 onion, chopped
1 garlic clove, minced
1 tablespoon olive oil
2 tablespoons chopped
  parsley
¾ cup tomato sauce
¼ cup dry red wine
½ teaspoon oregano
1 tablespoon butter
1 tablespoon flour
½ cup milk
Dash salt
½ cup chopped cooked
  lamb
½ cup grated Monterey
  Jack cheese
¼ cup grated Parmesan
  cheese

Cut a thin slice from the top of each potato. Remove pulp, leaving a thin shell. Mash pulp and set aside.

Sauté onion and garlic in oil. Add parsley, tomato sauce, wine and oregano. Simmer for 30 minutes. Remove from heat.

In a saucepan, heat butter and flour. Gradually add milk, stirring constantly, until thickened. Salt to taste.

Add potatoes and white sauce to tomato/onion mixture. Add lamb and **half** of both cheeses. Mix well over low heat.

Spoon mixture into potato shells. Top each with remaining cheese. Bake at 350° until cheese melts.

Potato Skins

8 servings

Specialty of Red Robin Restaurant, Boise.

4 Idaho® potatoes
Oil for deep frying
1 pound Cheddar cheese,
  grated
8 slices bacon, fried and
  crumbled
4 green onions, sliced
1 cup sour cream

Boil or fry potatoes until tender. Halve lengthwise. Scoop out pulp.

Deep fry "skins" and drain on paper towels.

Place skins on a baking sheet. Sprinkle with cheese and bacon. Broil until cheese melts. Garnish with green onions and a dollop of sour cream.

Potato Skin Boats
8 servings

4 large Idaho® potatoes, baked
3 tablespoons oil
1 tablespoon grated Parmesan cheese
½ teaspoon salt
¼ teaspoon garlic powder
¼ teaspoon paprika
⅛ teaspoon pepper

Prick potatoes and bake at 425° for 45 minutes, or until tender. Cool.

Cut in half lengthwise and scoop out potato so that shells are ¼-inch thick.

In a small bowl, combine remaining ingredients and mix well. Brush shells with mixture.

Set on oiled cookie sheets, hollow side up, and bake at 475° for 7 minutes. Turn over and bake until crisp, about 7 more minutes.

Great as is or with a dip or filling.

Potato Skin Chips
8 servings

4 large Idaho® potatoes, baked
3 tablespoons oil
1 tablespoon grated Parmesan cheese
½ teaspoon salt
¼ teaspoon garlic powder
¼ teaspoon paprika
⅛ teaspoon pepper

Prick potatoes and bake at 425° for 45 minutes, or until tender. Cool.

Cut in half lengthwise and scoop out potato so that shells are ¼-inch thick. Cut each shell into sixths.

In a mixing bowl, combine remaining ingredients. Add chips and toss to coat well.

Spread single layer on oiled cookie sheets. Bake 8 to 10 minutes at 475° until crisp, turning once.

Potatoes Rosemary

6 servings

2 pounds Idaho® potatoes,
  peeled and thinly sliced
Salt and pepper to taste
½ cup grated Parmesan
  or Swiss cheese
1 teaspoon crushed
  rosemary
⅓ cup butter, melted
Parmesan or Swiss
  cheese, grated, for
  topping

In a greased 8x8-inch pan, layer ⅓ of the potatoes, salt and pepper, cheese and rosemary. Drizzle with melted butter and repeat layers twice. Sprinkle with more grated cheese.

Place on lowest rack in oven. Bake covered at 425° for 35 minutes; uncover and continue baking another 35 minutes.

Idaho Potatoes Anna

6-8 servings

2 tablespoons oil
5 to 6 tablespoons butter
5 to 6 medium-sized
  Idaho® potatoes
Beau Monde, to taste
Pepper, to taste
Parsley

Melt oil and **2 tablespoons** of the butter in an au gratin pan or a large omelet pan with sloping sides.

Peel potatoes and slice into rounds or ovals (do not cut in half lengthwise before slicing) using a sharp knife or medium-thick slicing blade of a food processor.

In the au gratin pan, arrange a layer of potatoes in a circular pattern overlapping the slices. Sprinkle with Beau Monde and pepper. Continue to layer potatoes, dotting with remaining butter and sprinkling with seasonings between each layer.

Bake uncovered on bottom shelf of a preheated 400° oven for 15 to 20 minutes. Cover loosely with foil, move to middle shelf and bake for 25 to 30 minutes.

To serve, separate from edge of pan and invert onto a large serving platter. Garnish with parsley.

Poppy Seed Potatoes
8 servings

6 large Idaho® potatoes
1 cup grated sharp
  Cheddar cheese
1 pint sour cream
½ cup light cream
⅛ cup poppy seeds
4 green onions, chopped
Salt and pepper to taste
Butter

Boil or steam potatoes until barely tender. Refrigerate until cold, then peel and grate coarsely. Combine with remaining ingredients and place in a lightly buttered 2-quart casserole. Bake at 350° for 20 to 25 minutes, covered. Uncover and bake 10 minutes longer.

Dilled New Potatoes
4-6 servings

24 small red-skinned or
  Idaho® potatoes
½ cup butter
12 medium-sized
  mushrooms, sliced
Salt and pepper
4 tablespoons chopped
  fresh dill

Boil potatoes until barely tender. Drain.

In a saucepan, melt butter, add mushrooms, salt, pepper and dill. Toss with hot potatoes. Serve immediately.

Pea and Potato Sauté
4 servings

4 Idaho® potatoes, peeled
½ pound mushrooms,
  thinly sliced
4 tablespoons butter
¼ cup olive oil
½ teaspoon salt
⅛ teaspoon white
  pepper
¾ cup frozen peas,
  cooked
2 tablespoons chopped
  parsley
1 garlic clove, minced

Cut potatoes into 1-inch cubes. Boil uncovered for 4 minutes. Drain.

Sauté mushrooms in **2 tablespoons** of the butter.

Sauté potato cubes in oil in a heavy skillet until tender and brown. Season with salt and pepper. Add mushrooms, peas and remaining butter. Simmer 4 minutes. Stir in parsley and garlic. Serve immediately.

7

Basque Potatoes

6 servings

½ pound bacon slices,
  diced
4 Idaho® baking potatoes
  peeled and sliced ¼
  inch thick
6 tomatoes, peeled,
  quartered and seeded
3 garlic cloves, crushed
2 teaspoons minced fresh
  thyme or ¾ teaspoon
  dried, crumbled
¼ pound sliced
  mushrooms
1½ cups pitted black
  olives, quartered
  Salt and freshly ground
  pepper
½ cup medium-dry Sherry
½ cup (1 stick) butter,
  melted
3 garlic cloves, minced

Preheat oven to 350°F. Cook bacon in heavy medium skillet over medium-high heat until almost crisp, 2 to 3 minutes. Drain on paper towels. Arrange potatoes and tomatoes in 10x15-inch glass baking dish. Sprinkle with bacon, crushed garlic and thyme. Add mushrooms and olives. Season with salt and pepper. Pour Sherry over. Cover with foil and bake 30 minutes.

Combine butter and minced garlic. Pour over potatoes. Bake uncovered until potatoes are tender, 40 to 45 minutes. Serve immediately.

Sheepherder Potatoes

4 servings

8 bacon slices, minced
2 onions, chopped
4 Idaho® potatoes, peeled
  and sliced ½-inch thick
Salt and pepper to taste

Fry bacon until not quite crisp. Add onion and sauté until limp. Pour off all but **2 tablespoons** of the drippings.

Center potatoes on a piece of heavy-duty foil and pour bacon and onion mixture over them. Season with salt and pepper. Seal the foil so that there is space between the potatoes and the foil. Slide the foil packet onto a cookie sheet and bake at 300° for 1½ hours.

Potatoes Parmesan
4-6 servings

3 tablespoons butter
3 tablespoons oil
2 pounds Idaho® potatoes, peeled and diced
6 tablespoons grated Parmesan cheese
1 tablespoon beef bouillon
Dash paprika

In a large skillet over medium heat, melt butter and oil. Add potatoes and stir until coated. Cover and cook until tender, about 15 minutes, stirring often. Add **3 tablespoons** of the Parmesan and the bouillon.

Pour into a greased 2-quart casserole and sprinkle top with rest of cheese and the paprika. Bake uncovered at 350° for 30 minutes.

Bavarian Potatoes
6-8 servings

Good with cold sliced meats.

5 to 6 medium-sized red-skinned or Idaho® potatoes
½ pound bacon, cut in 1-inch pieces
1 medium onion, chopped
½ cup sugar
½ cup vinegar
2 tablespoons cornstarch
1 cup water
½ teaspoon salt

In a large saucepan, boil potatoes with skins on. Chill, peel and slice in ¼-inch slices. Place potatoes in a 2½-quart casserole.

In a large skillet, fry bacon until browned. Drain on paper towels. Remove most of the drippings from the skillet.

Sauté onion in remaining drippings over medium heat. Add sugar, vinegar, cornstarch dissolved in water and salt. Cook and stir over medium heat until thickened. Pour over potatoes, add bacon and toss gently. Bake covered at 350° until hot, about 30 minutes.

Half a potato, pierced with a knitting needle in several places and placed flat side down in a vase of water, makes a holder for flower stems.

Welsh Casserole au Gratin   14-16 servings

2½ pounds Idaho®
   potatoes
1 egg
1 egg yolk
3 tablespoons heavy
   cream **or** sour cream
2 pounds leeks, about
   1½ inches in diameter
½ cup butter
2 cups chicken stock
Salt to taste

Peel potatoes and cut into fourths. In a large pan of boiling, salted water, boil potatoes until fork tender. Mash potatoes and combine with egg, egg yolk and cream.

Cut off tops of leeks, leaving ½ to 2½ inches of the green part. Pry apart the leaves and rinse carefully. Cut into 3-inch lengths.

In a pan large enough to hold all leeks in one layer, melt butter. When butter foams, add leeks. Add chicken stock and braise 15 to 20 minutes or until leeks are fork tender. Salt to taste. Set aside.

Butter a large, shallow casserole. Pour ¼ of the mornay sauce in the bottom of the casserole. Spread ½ of the potatoes over the sauce, then layer ¼ of the sauce over the potatoes. Arrange the braised leeks over potatoes and sauce, pour leek braising liquid over all. Layer another ¼ of the mornay sauce and the remaining potatoes. Pour the remaining sauce over the potatoes. Bake covered at 350° for 20 minutes.

Spread topping over casserole and continue baking uncovered at 375° for 20 minutes longer.

Welsh Casserole au Gratin *(Continued)*

MORNAY SAUCE

3 tablespoons butter
3 tablespoons flour
2 cups milk
2 teaspoons salt
1 teaspoon nutmeg
1 garlic clove, crushed
1½ cups grated Gruyère
   or Swiss cheese

In a small saucepan melt butter. Add flour and stir in the milk, a little at a time, cooking and stirring until thick and smooth. Add salt, nutmeg and garlic. Remove from heat and stir in cheese, a little at a time.

TOPPING

2 cups dry bread crumbs
¾ cup grated Parmesan
   cheese
3 tablespoons butter,
   melted

Combine bread crumbs, Parmesan cheese and melted butter in a small bowl.

Hash Brown au Gratin   6-8 servings

2 pound bag frozen
   Idaho® hash brown
   potatoes
½ cup chopped green
   onions
1 cup heavy cream
2 cups grated Swiss
   cheese
½ cup butter, melted

Put potatoes in a greased 9x13-inch shallow baking dish. Add onions, cream and cheese and stir gently. Pour butter evenly over top. Bake at 350° for 1 hour.

Plain yogurt with fresh mint makes a delicious topping for baked potatoes.

11

New Potato Gratin

4-6 servings

2 pounds red-skinned
   potatoes or Idaho®
   new potatoes, unpeeled
1 tablespoon salt
1 cup ricotta cheese
½ cup chopped fresh
   parsley
Salt and pepper
Dash nutmeg
1 egg
1 cup heavy cream
1 cup grated Jarlsberg
   Swiss cheese

Thinly slice potatoes and boil in water with salt for 1 minute. Drain and rinse. Drain again and pat dry.

Combine ricotta, parsley, salt, pepper and nutmeg.

In a bowl, beat egg lightly and add cream.

Arrange 1 layer of potatoes in a buttered 9x13-inch pan. Dot with ricotta mixture. Sprinkle with Jarlsberg cheese. Repeat layers, ending with a potato layer. Pour egg and cream mixture over all.

Bake at 350° for 35 to 45 minutes until potatoes are tender and cheese is bubbly. Let stand 10 minutes before serving.

Swiss Scalloped Potatoes

8 servings

4 Idaho® potatoes,
   peeled and thinly sliced
2 garlic cloves, minced
2 cups milk
1½ cups heavy cream
¾ teaspoon salt
½ teaspoon white
   pepper
1 cup grated Swiss
   cheese

In a heavy saucepan, combine potatoes, garlic, milk, cream, salt and pepper and cook, stirring constantly, until mixture thickens.

Place potato mixture in a buttered 10x14-inch casserole. Top with grated cheese. Bake uncovered at 400° for 40 minutes.

Clean wood and silver with a slice of raw potato.

Cheese Soufflé à la Potato
2 servings

2 Idaho® potatoes, baked
2 tablespoons butter
1 tablespoon flour
½ cup hot milk
1 egg yolk
½ cup grated Cheddar
    cheese
¼ teaspoon salt
¼ teaspoon
    Worcestershire sauce
3 egg whites
⅛ teaspoon cream of
    tartar

Cut a thin slice from the top of each potato. Remove pulp, leaving a thin shell. Mash pulp, reserve ¾ cup and set aside. Place shells in an ovenproof dish.

Melt butter in a saucepan and stir in flour. Whisk in milk. Stir constantly until mixture boils and thickens. Remove from heat and stir in egg yolk. Add cheese, salt, Worcestershire sauce and reserved potato pulp. Mix well.

Beat egg whites and cream of tartar until stiff but not dry. Add ¼ of the egg whites to the potato/cheese mixture. Fold in remaining egg whites, being careful not to overmix.

Spoon mixture into shells. Place in a preheated 400° oven. Turn oven to 375° and bake 15 to 20 minutes. Serve immediately.

Heavenly Sour Cream Potatoes
6 servings

2 cups mashed Idaho®
    potatoes
1½ cups creamed
    cottage cheese
½ cup sour cream
¾ tablespoon grated
    onion
1¼ teaspoons salt
Pepper to taste
2 tablespoons butter,
    melted
¼ cup chopped almonds

Mix potatoes and cottage cheese. Add sour cream, onion, salt and pepper. Spoon into a buttered 1-quart casserole. Brush surface with melted butter.

Bake at 350° for 30 minutes. Sprinkle with almonds. Place under broiler to brown lightly.

13

Potatoes Romanoff

4-6 servings

5 cups Idaho® potatoes,
  sliced ¼-inch thick
¾ cup water
¾ teaspoon salt
2 chicken bouillon cubes,
  crumbled
½ cup chopped green
  onions
1 tablespoon butter
1 tablespoon flour
¼ teaspoon dill weed
Dash white pepper
½ cup milk
1 cup sour cream
½ teaspoon prepared
  mustard
1 cup pitted ripe olives,
  drained and quartered
½ cup grated Cheddar
  cheese
Paprika

In a large saucepan, cook potatoes in water, **½ teaspoon** of the salt and the bouillon cubes until just tender. DO NOT DRAIN.

In a skillet, cook green onions in butter until soft. Stir in flour, remaining salt, dill weed and pepper. Stir in milk and cook until thickened. Add sour cream, mustard and olives. Pour mixture over undrained potatoes and mix lightly.

Pour into a casserole. Top with grated cheese and paprika. Bake at 350° for 20 minutes until heated through and cheese is melted.

NOTE: May be made ahead and refrigerated. Remove from refrigerator 15 minutes before baking and bake for 5 minutes longer.

Hot Potato Casserole

4-6 servings

8 boiled Idaho® potatoes,
  peeled and diced
1 onion, chopped
2 celery stalks, diced
½ pound Cheddar
  cheese, grated
1 teaspoon salt
¼ teaspoon pepper
1 cup mayonnaise
1 tablespoon prepared
  mustard
6 bacon slices, diced

In a buttered casserole, combine potatoes, onion, celery and cheese. Season with salt and pepper.

Combine mayonnaise and mustard. Fold into potato mixture. Top with bacon.

Bake uncovered at 350° for 30 minutes, then place under broiler to crisp bacon.

Glazed Mashed Potato Ring
8 servings

Perfect for holiday dinners.

6 cups mashed Idaho®
  potatoes
1 cup grated sharp
  Cheddar cheese
2 tablespoons melted
  butter
Watercress **or** parsley

In a mixing bowl, combine mashed potatoes and cheese. Pour into well-greased 2-quart ring mold. Brush top with **1 tablespoon** of the melted butter.

Bake at 400° for 25 minutes or until top is golden. Unmold ring onto an ovenproof serving platter. Brush top with remaining butter and place under broiler for 3 to 5 minutes, until browned. Garnish with watercress or parsley.

Potato Puffs
10 servings

4 cups mashed Idaho®
  potatoes
8 ounces cream cheese,
  softened
1 small onion, grated
2 eggs, beaten
2 tablespoons flour
Salt and pepper to taste
1 3½-ounce can French
  fried onions

In a large mixer bowl, place hot mashed potatoes. Add cream cheese, onion, eggs and flour. Mix at medium speed until blended. Mix at high speed until fluffy. Season with salt and pepper.

Spoon mixture into a greased 9-inch square pan or round casserole. Bake uncovered at 300° for 1 hour. Sprinkle onions over top the last 10 to 15 minutes of baking.

NOTE: This dish may be prepared a day ahead and baked just before serving.

To keep boiling oil from splattering in a fondue pot, place a large slice of raw potato in the oil.

Orange Potato Rosettes

4 servings

2 pounds Idaho® potatoes
Salt
Grated rind of 1 orange
1 egg
White pepper
2 tablespoons butter
2 tablespoons hot milk

Peel potatoes and cut in half. Place in a saucepan and cover with cold water. Add salt and heat to boiling. Simmer until potatoes are soft. Drain and return to pan to dry.

Beat potatoes with an electric mixer until smooth. Add orange rind, egg (unbeaten), pepper, butter and milk. Beat thoroughly.

Place potato mixture into a pastry bag fitted with a #8 or #9 star tube. Pipe out rosettes onto a buttered baking sheet and bake at 350° for 15 minutes or until golden. Arrange rosettes around an entrée as a garnish or separately as a side dish.

Breakfast Potato Pancakes

4 servings

Great for breakfast with bacon and applesauce.

4 eggs
⅔ cup flour
1½ teaspoons salt
2 tablespoons bacon
    drippings **or** oil
½ cup milk
½ small onion, diced
2 cups diced, peeled raw
    Idaho® potatoes
1 teaspoon ascorbic acid
Butter
Sour cream
Chives

In a blender, beat eggs until fluffy. Add remaining ingredients, in order, and blend about 5 seconds until potatoes are shredded. Shape into four patties and bake on a hot grill for 2 minutes per side. Turn only once.

Top with butter and sour cream with chives.

DO NOT STACK.

Potato Cakes

4 servings

3 large Idaho® potatoes,
  grated
½ bunch green onions,
  chopped
1 garlic clove, minced
1 egg, beaten
¼ cup heavy cream
½ cup (or more) flour
Salt and pepper to taste
1 tablespoon grated
  Parmesan cheese
Oil

Squeeze potatoes dry in a ricer or dish towel. In a large bowl combine potatoes, onion, garlic, egg and cream. Blend well.

Add flour, salt, pepper and cheese. Mix well. Fry in hot oil until golden brown. Drain on paper towels.

NOTE: Zucchini may be added in place of one of the potatoes.

Potato Top Hat

4-6 servings

5 Idaho® potatoes, peeled
2 cups flour
1 teaspoon salt
⅔ cup margarine
2 tablespoons butter
4 tablespoons cold water
¼ cup chopped fresh
  parsley
2 tablespoons minced
  shallots
Salt and freshly ground
  pepper to taste
1 egg, beaten
1 cup sour cream
2 tablespoons milk
Fresh chives, chopped

Cover potatoes with salted water and let stand 1 hour.

Mix flour and salt. Cut in margarine and butter until mixture resembles cornmeal. Sprinkle with water, a little at a time, and mix until dough cleans sides of bowl. Divide dough in half. Roll out half the dough on a lightly floured surface. Trim to a 10-inch circle. Place on a baking sheet.

Drain and rinse potatoes. Pat dry. Slice potatoes and combine them with parsley, shallots, salt and pepper. Arrange mixture on pastry, leaving a 1-inch border. Brush border of pastry with egg.

Roll remaining dough to a 13-inch circle. Place over potatoes. Flute edge. Brush top with egg. Make a lid by making ½-inch cuts around a 4-inch circle in center. Bake at 375° about 55 minutes.

Combine sour cream and milk. While pie is still hot, cut out lid and remove. Spoon sour cream mixture over potatoes; replace lid. Garnish with chives. Serve at room temperature.

17

Prime Potato Salad

6 servings

1 16-ounce package frozen green beans
2 pounds Idaho® new potatoes
¼ cup minced shallots
3 tablespoons beef broth
2 Bermuda onions, sliced and separated into rings
2 pounds leftover roast beef, cut into 2-inch cubes
2 tablespoons chopped chives
2 tablespoons chopped parsley

In a saucepan, cook beans in boiling salted water for about 8 minutes. Drain and rinse in cold water. Dry on paper towels. Toss beans with ½ cup of the dressing and set aside.

In a medium saucepan, boil potatoes until tender. Drain, peel and slice thinly. Add shallots and toss gently. Pour broth over potatoes. Add remaining dressing and toss until well coated.

In a large salad bowl, layer in the following order: onion rings, green beans, potatoes and roast beef. Sprinkle with chives and parsley. Serve at room temperature.

MUSTARD FRENCH DRESSING

1 cup

¼ cup cider vinegar or lemon juice
2 tablespoons Dijon mustard
1 teaspoon salt
Pepper to taste
1 cup olive oil

In a bowl, blend vinegar, mustard, salt and pepper. Gradually blend in olive oil. Adjust seasonings if necessary.

For the best French fries, first let cut potatoes stand in cold water for an hour before frying. Dry thoroughly before cooking. The trick then is to fry them twice. The first time just fry them for a few minutes and blot off the grease. The second time fry until golden brown. There's no better way.

Mussel and Potato Salad

4 servings

2 quarts mussels
1 teaspoon dry mustard
1 cup water
5 peppercorns
1 onion, sliced
1 carrot, sliced
2 celery stalks
4 Idaho® potatoes
½ cup dry white wine
2 dill pickles, thinly sliced

Scrub the mussels with the mustard in cold water. In a saucepan, cover mussels with the **1 cup** water and add peppercorns, onion, carrot and celery. Cover and heat to boiling. Shake the pan over the heat 5 to 6 minutes until the shells open. Discard shells and set mixture aside.

Boil potatoes in their skins until tender. Remove skins while still hot. Cut into thick slices. Sprinkle with wine.

Arrange alternate layers of potatoes, mussels (reserve a few for garnish) and mayonnaise dressing in a salad bowl, ending with a layer of dressing. Garnish with sliced pickles and reserved mussels.

MAYONNAISE DRESSING

2 egg yolks
½ teaspoon salt
Cayenne
½ teaspoon Dijon
   mustard
¾ cup oil
1 teaspoon lemon juice
1 teaspoon chopped
   tarragon
1 teaspoon chopped
   parsley
1 dill pickle, finely
   chopped

Place egg yolks, salt, cayenne and mustard in a mixing bowl and mix well. Add oil and lemon juice, drop by drop, beating constantly. Stir in tarragon, parsley and pickle.

Soak raw potatoes in cold water at least 30 minutes before frying to improve crispness.

19

Posh Potato Salad

12 servings

6 cups sliced, cold
   cooked Idaho®
   potatoes (2½ pounds)
1 cup minced yellow
   onion
1 cup chopped celery
½ cup finely chopped
   parsley
1½ teaspoons prepared
   mustard
1½ teaspoons salt
¼ teaspoon pepper
¼ pound salami, slivered
4 hard boiled eggs, sliced
1½ cups mayonnaise
Lettuce
Chives, chopped
Cherry tomatoes, halved

In a large bowl, combine potatoes, onion, celery, parsley, mustard, salt and pepper and mix well.

Add salami, eggs and mayonnaise. Toss well and refrigerate.

To serve, spoon into lettuce-lined bowl. Garnish with chives and tomatoes.

Hot German Potato Salad

4 servings

2 pounds Idaho® new
   potatoes
¾ cup chopped onion
1 teaspoon minced garlic
2 tablespoons chopped
   parsley
1 tablespoon celery leaf
1 tablespoon chervil
1½ teaspoons salt
1 teaspoon freshly
   ground pepper
3 tablespoons olive oil,
   warmed
½ cup vegetable oil,
   warmed

Cook potatoes in their skins in boiling, salted water until tender. Drain.

Warm a large wooden salad bowl in the oven with the door open. Add onion, garlic, herbs, salt and pepper to the warmed bowl.

Remove the skins from the potatoes and slice them into the bowl. Pour the warmed oils over potatoes and toss well. Serve at once.

Bound to Please: A Wealth of Waters

"... the water runs with great violence from one rock to another on each Side foaming & roreing ..." So wrote an early explorer who saw the Salmon River for the first time, not realizing that water – for irrigation, recreation, transportation, fishing, mining, electricity, and human consumption – is the lifeblood of Idaho.

And water gives pleasure, too, whether to children on inner tubes floating a peaceful afternoon away, to campers at one of Idaho's more than 2,000 lakes, to fishermen at streams and man-made reservoirs, to rafters shooting the rapids of fast-moving rivers. There for all to enjoy, water is one of Idaho's most important resources.

Hot Appetizers

Cold Appetizers

Dips & Spreads

Continental Paté
1 quart

3 tablespoons unsalted butter
2 small white onions, chopped
1 tablespoon dried rosemary, crumbled
1½ teaspoons salt
1½ teaspoons white pepper, freshly ground
1½ teaspoons ground thyme
½ teaspoon dried basil, crumbled
½ teaspoon nutmeg
1 pound, 3 ounces chicken livers, washed, trimmed and patted dry
1¾ cups unsalted butter, softened
1½ hard boiled eggs
2 tablespoons cognac
2 tablespoons dry sherry
1 tablespoon chopped fresh parsley

In a large ovenproof skillet, melt the **3 tablespoons** butter. Add onion, rosemary, salt, pepper, thyme, basil and nutmeg. Sauté over medium heat until onion is soft.

Add chicken livers to skillet and sauté until browned, about 5 minutes. Transfer skillet to oven and bake at 400° until livers are cooked through. Remove from oven and let cool completely.

In a food processor, mix the **1¾ cups** butter until light and fluffy. Add liver mixture, eggs, cognac, sherry and the **1 tablespoon chopped** parsley. Puree until smooth.

Transfer to serving dish or crock. Chill until firm or overnight. Garnish with fresh parsley, dipped in water, then in paprika. To serve, accompany with crackers.

GARNISHES

Parsley
Paprika

Smoked Salmon Paté

2 cups

1 15½ or 16-ounce can of salmon, drained **or** 1 pound fresh/frozen cooked salmon
1 8-ounce package cream cheese, softened
2 tablespoons finely chopped onion
¼ teaspoon salt
1 tablespoon lemon juice
1 teaspoon Tabasco sauce
Liquid smoke to taste
Prepared horseradish to taste

Remove skin and bones from salmon and flake.

In a medium bowl, combine salmon with remaining ingredients, **except** garnishes, mixing well. Pour into fish-shaped mold and freeze several hours.

To serve, invert mold onto platter. It will thaw in 15 minutes. Garnish with olives for eyes, pimiento for mouth, thin lemon slices for scales and tops of green onions for tail. Serve with crackers.

NOTE: This may be made ahead and frozen for later use.

GARNISHES

Olives
Pimiento slices
Lemon slices
Green onion tops

Shrimp Paté

2⅓ cups

1 pound cooked shrimp
⅓ cup crumbled Bleu cheese
1 cup mayonnaise
1 tablespoon prepared horseradish
Juice of ½ lemon
1 teaspoon Worcestershire sauce
2 drops Tabasco sauce

Using the fine blade of a food processor, process shrimp and Bleu cheese together. Add remaining ingredients and mix thoroughly. Chill until ready to use.

Serve on crisp crackers, party-size rye bread or use as a dip for fresh vegetables.

Shrimp Chafing Dish

6-8 servings

1 pound medium-sized raw shrimp
1 6-ounce jar marinated artichoke hearts
½ pound small whole mushrooms
2 garlic cloves, minced
¼ teaspoon salt
¼ teaspoon pepper
½ teaspoon oregano
2 tablespoons lemon juice
2 tablespoons chopped parsley

Peel and devein shrimp.

Drain oil from artichokes into skillet, add shrimp and mushrooms and cook until shrimp is pink, about 3 minutes. Add artichoke hearts, garlic, salt, pepper, oregano and lemon juice; heat through.

Serve in a chafing dish; garnish with chopped parsley when ready to serve. Provide toothpicks.

To get people to circulate – everyone will gather in the kitchen if they can find it – serve different courses of a buffet or a variety of appetizers in various rooms.

Curried Olive Appetizers

2 dozen

Great accompaniment to soup.

1 4-ounce can chopped ripe olives
¼ cup minced green onions
¾ cup grated Cheddar cheese
½ cup mayonnaise
¼ teaspoon salt
¼ teaspoon curry powder
Bread slices
2 tablespoons minced parsley

In a medium bowl, combine olives, onions, cheese, mayonnaise, salt and curry powder. Mix well.

Using a cookie or biscuit cutter, cut bread into rounds or desired shapes. Spread with mixture and broil 8 to 10 minutes or until hot and bubbly.

To serve, garnish with minced parsley.

Avocado Appetizer   4 servings

2 just-ripe avocados
4 tablespoons butter
4 tablespoons chili sauce
2 teaspoons sugar
½ teaspoon salt
2 tablespoons water
2 tablespoons vinegar
2 teaspoons
   Worcestershire sauce
4 bacon slices, cooked
   and crumbled

Halve avocados and remove seeds, DO NOT PEEL.

In a medium saucepan, combine remaining ingredients, **except** bacon, and heat until bubbly. Add bacon and pour sauce into center and on top of each avocado.

Serve on individual plates as an appetizer or salad.

You can never plan ahead too much – the more you plan and work from checklists the more time you have to enjoy the preparation and your guests.

Marinated Mushrooms   1 quart

1 pound fresh
   mushrooms, small to
   medium-size
½ cup olive oil
⅓ cup red wine vinegar
2 garlic cloves, minced
1 teaspoon salt
1 teaspoon oregano
½ teaspoon crushed,
   dried hot red chilis

Wash and trim mushrooms. Place in a saucepan of boiling water. Turn off heat and let stand 15 minutes. Drain and place in cold water.

In a medium bowl, combine remaining ingredients. Drain mushrooms; cut into bite-sized pieces, if desired, and add to marinade. Let stand at least 1 hour before serving. Best if made the day before.

NOTE: Will keep in the refrigerator for several weeks.

Ham/Chutney Mushrooms   20 mushrooms

⅓ to ½ cup sour cream
1 cup finely chopped ham
2 small green onions,
    chopped
1 tablespoon chutney
1 teaspoon vinegar
Salt and pepper
20 medium mushrooms,
    cleaned, stems
    removed

In a medium bowl, combine all ingredients, **except** mushrooms. Mix until spreading consistency. Fill mushrooms and serve.

Spinach-Stuffed Mushrooms   30 mushrooms

Larger mushrooms make a nice accompaniment to either broiled or roast beef.

1 10-ounce package
    frozen chopped spinach
½ cup sour cream
¼ cup tomato sauce
Dash red wine vinegar
1 cup grated Parmesan
    cheese
30 medium fresh
    mushrooms, cleaned,
    stems removed

In a saucepan, cook spinach. Drain well.

In a mixing bowl, combine spinach, sour cream, tomato sauce, vinegar and cheese. Mix until well blended. Fill mushroom caps with spinach mixture and place in a buttered baking dish. Bake at 350° for 15 minutes.

Decorate your home with fresh flowers. Proper lighting and your choice of music will set the mood for your party theme. Be sure that everyone is properly introduced.

Sausage-Stuffed Mushrooms
25 mushrooms

1 12-ounce package hot
   sausage
1 8-ounce package cream
   cheese, softened
2 tablespoons chives
25 large fresh
   mushrooms, cleaned,
   stems removed

In a medium bowl, combine sausage, cream cheese and chives. Mix well. Stuff mushrooms and place on broiler pan. Broil on middle rack 10 minutes or until browned and sausage is fully cooked. Serve hot.

Molded Roquefort Creme
8-10 servings

¼ cup water
1 envelope unflavored
   gelatin
¼ pound Roquefort or
   Bleu cheese, softened
2 3-ounce packages
   cream cheese,
   softened
2 tablespoons white
   vinegar
2 tablespoons dried
   parsley flakes
2 teaspoons onion salt
2 tablespoons chopped
   pimiento
1 cup well-drained,
   grated unpeeled
   cucumber
1 cup heavy cream,
   whipped

In a double boiler, combine water and gelatin; blend together. Place over simmering water and heat until gelatin is dissolved.

In a medium bowl, combine cheeses and beat together until blended. Stir in dissolved gelatin. Add vinegar, parsley and onion salt and mix well. Fold in pimiento and cucumber. Add whipped cream. Pour into an oiled 3 to 4 cup mold and chill until set.

Unmold and serve surrounded by Melba toast rounds or crackers. Or serve as a salad on a bed of lettuce, surrounded by cucumber and tomato slices and cold meats.

Lemon perks up the flavor of sour cream dips.

Seafood Mousse
4 cups

1 envelope unflavored gelatin
¼ cup cold water
1 cup undiluted cream of mushroom **or** shrimp soup
1 8-ounce package cream cheese, softened
1 cup mayonnaise
¾ cup finely chopped celery
1½ to 2 cups shrimp **or** crabmeat
½ cup chopped green onions
1¼ teaspoons Worcestershire sauce

In a small bowl, soften gelatin in cold water.

In a medium saucepan, heat soup and add gelatin, stirring well. Add cream cheese, beating until smooth. Add remaining ingredients and pour into a 4-cup mold that has been sprayed with a vegetable spray. Refrigerate overnight.

Unmold on a platter and serve as a salad or as an hors d'oeuvre with crackers.

NOTE: If fish-shaped mold is used, garnish with olive for eye, pimiento and lemon slices for body.

GARNISHES

Green olives
Pimiento
Lemon slices

Artichoke/Chile Bake
8 servings

2 8-ounce cans artichoke hearts in water, drained and cut into quarters
2 4-ounce cans chopped green chiles
½ cup chopped green onions
1 cup mayonnaise
1 cup grated Parmesan cheese

In a medium bowl, combine all ingredients and mix well. Place in a 1-quart casserole. Bake, uncovered, at 350° for 20 minutes. Serve with tortilla chips.

Artichoke Frittata
60 servings

2 6-ounce jars marinated
   artichoke hearts
1 small onion, finely
   chopped
1 garlic clove, minced
4 eggs
¼ cup fine bread **or**
   cracker crumbs
¼ teaspoon salt
2 tablespoons minced
   parsley
⅛ teaspoon pepper
⅛ teaspoon oregano
⅛ teaspoon Tabasco
   sauce
2 cups grated sharp
   Cheddar cheese

Drain marinade from **1 jar** of artichokes into medium skillet. Drain second jar and discard marinade. Add onion and garlic to skillet and sauté until onion is limp. Chop all artichokes and set aside.

In a bowl, beat eggs with a fork and add remaining ingredients, Stir in onion mixture and artichokes. Pour into a greased 7x11-inch baking dish. Bake uncovered at 325° for 30 minutes.

Cool and cut into 1-inch squares. Use toothpicks if desired.

NOTE: Freezes beautifully.

Hot Appetizer Pie
12 servings

1 8-ounce package cream
   cheese, softened
2 tablespoons milk
1 2½-ounce jar dried
   beef, rinsed in boiling
   water, drained and
   sliced
2 tablespoons finely
   chopped green pepper
2 tablespoons finely
   chopped onion
½ teaspoon pepper
½ cup sour cream
1½ teaspoons curry
   powder, optional
¼ cup or more chopped
   walnuts

In a medium bowl, beat cream cheese with milk. Add remaining ingredients, **except** nuts, and mix well. Pat into an 8-inch pie pan.

Spread nuts over top. Bake at 350° for 15 minutes. Serve hot with crackers or Melba toast.

Cocktail Quiches

24 servings

PASTRY

⅓ cup butter, softened
1 3-ounce package
   cream cheese,
   softened
1 cup flour

In a medium bowl, cream butter and cheese. Mix in flour and **chill overnight.** Form dough into 24 small balls and press into mini-muffin tins.

FILLING

1 cup milk
1 egg, slightly beaten
¼ teaspoon salt
¼ teaspoon pepper
½ to 1 tablespoon
   chopped chives
1 cup grated sharp
   Cheddar cheese

In a medium bowl, mix together milk, egg, salt, pepper and chives. Evenly distribute cheese in muffin tins. Pour milk and egg mixture gently over grated cheese. Bake at 350° for 30 minutes. Serve warm.

Clam/Cheese Spread

2 cups

2 5-ounce jars sharp
   cheese
2 green onions, finely
   chopped
2 tablespoons finely
   chopped green pepper
1 7½-ounce can minced
   clams, with ½ the
   liquid drained
½ tablespoon
   Worcestershire sauce
3 dashes Tabasco sauce
½ teaspoon paprika
¼ teaspoon garlic salt

In a medium bowl, combine all ingredients. Mix well. Pour into ramekins or ovenproof serving dish and bake, uncovered, at 350° for 20 minutes or until cheese is melted.

Serve warm with wafers or crackers.

NOTE: May also be served cold.

Divine Crab

20 servings

2 8-ounce packages
cream cheese, softened
2 6-ounce cans crab
meat, drain **one** can
only
1 green onion, chopped,
including top
1 teaspoon
Worcestershire sauce
½ teaspoon salt
Catsup

In a medium bowl, combine cream cheese, crab, onion, Worcestershire sauce and salt. Mix well. Add enough catsup to give a pleasing color.

Serve warm in chafing dish, accompanied by basket of crackers.

NOTE: This is also wonderful served cold or spread on English muffins and toasted.

Think about what your guests will be doing – if they will be standing up most of the time, serve finger food – not drippy, awkward or soggy hors d'oeuvres.

Shrimp Canapés

12 canapés

1½ cups consommé
2 tablespoons sherry
Lemon juice to taste
1 envelope unflavored
gelatin
½ pound cocktail shrimp
Mayonnaise
Parsley

In a medium saucepan, combine consommé, sherry, lemon juice and gelatin. Heat until gelatin dissolves.

Place a few shrimp in the bottoms of 12 individually oiled muffin tins and pour the consommé mixture over the top until not quite full. Chill well and serve on toast rounds or wheat thins, garnished with a bit of mayonnaise and parsley.

30

Crab Canapés

32 canapés

1 6½-ounce can crab
meat, drained
1 cup grated Swiss
cheese
½ cup mayonnaise
1 tablespoon chopped
green onion
1 teaspoon lemon juice
½ teaspoon curry
powder
1 package butterflake
rolls
½ cup sliced water
chestnuts

In a medium bowl, combine crab, cheese, mayonnaise, onion, lemon juice and curry powder. Mix thoroughly. Separate each roll into 3 to 4 pieces, spread each with crab mixture and place a slice of water chestnut on top. Place on a cookie sheet and bake at 400° for 12 minutes.

Serve warm.

Seafood Dip à la Bread Basket

8 servings

A fun traveler for picnics.

1 pint sour cream
1 tablespoon prepared
horseradish, drained
1 tablespoon lemon juice
½ teaspoon salt
¼ teaspoon curry
powder
¼ teaspoon dry mustard
½ package dry onion
soup mix
1 7-ounce can shrimp,
drained
1 7-ounce can crab
meat, drained
1 round loaf French
bread, whole

In a bowl, combine sour cream and seasonings, mixing well. Fold in seafood and chill. Cut off the top of the loaf of bread and hollow out the loaf. Bake at 250° for 20 minutes or until lightly toasted. Place chilled seafood mixture in hollow loaf and add top for a lid.

Serve with fresh vegetables for dipping and later eat the bread container itself!

31

Shrimp Dip

2 cups

½ pint sour cream
1 8-ounce package
  cream cheese,
  softened
1 6½-ounce can shrimp,
  drained
2 tablespoons chili sauce
2 teaspoons
  Worcestershire sauce
1 teaspoon grated onion

In a medium bowl, blend all ingredients. If too thick, add a little milk or cream. Serve with chips or raw vegetables.

Snow Crab Dip

2 cups

1 8-ounce package cream
  cheese, softened
2 teaspoons chopped
  dried chives
¼ teaspoon garlic
  powder
¼ teaspoon salt
6 ounces snow crab
  meat, shredded
½ cup or more chopped
  pecans

In a medium bowl, combine cream cheese, chives, garlic powder and salt. Fold in crab.

To serve, top with chopped pecans and accompany with crackers or fresh vegetables.

Easy Caviar Dip

1½ cups

1 8-ounce package cream
  cheese, softened
½ pint sour cream
1 teaspoon
  Worcestershire sauce
3 drops Tabasco sauce
½ .12-ounce jar dried
  chives
1 2 to 4-ounce jar red
  caviar

In a blender, combine cream cheese, sour cream, Worcestershire sauce and Tabasco sauce. Pour mixture into a small bowl and stir in chives. Just before serving, stir in caviar so its color won't "run".

Serve with vegetables or crackers.

Spinach Dunk

3-4 cups

1 10-ounce package
   frozen chopped
   spinach, thawed and
   well drained
2 cups mayonnaise
1 cup chopped parsley
1½ cups chopped green
   onions
1 teaspoon salt
1 teaspoon pepper
⅛ teaspoon oregano
⅛ teaspoon marjoram
1 tablespoon Beau
   Monde **or** Bon Appetit

In a medium bowl, mix all ingredients
and refrigerate 12 hours for flavors to
blend. Serve with an assortment of
fresh vegetables.

NOTE: May be made in a food
processor.

Spinach in a Loaf

6 servings

1 cup mayonnaise
1 cup sour cream
1 10-ounce package
   frozen chopped
   spinach, drained and
   squeezed dry
1 package dry vegetable
   soup mix
1 8-ounce can water
   chestnuts, drained and
   chopped
2 to 4 green onions,
   chopped
1 round loaf bread,
   unsliced
1 loaf French bread,
   cubed for dipping

In a medium bowl, combine
mayonnaise and sour cream, mixing
until smooth. Add spinach, soup mix,
water chestnuts and onions, blending
thoroughly. Refrigerate overnight,
covered.

Cut off the top of the loaf of bread and
hollow out the loaf. Bake at 250° for
20 minutes or until lightly toasted. Pour
chilled spinach mixture into loaf and
add top for a lid.

Serve with lid removed, accompanied
by cubed bread or fresh vegetables
for dipping.

Broccoli at Its Best

12 servings

½ cup butter
1 large onion, chopped
12 ounces processed American cheese
1 10-ounce can cream of mushroom soup, undiluted
2 10-ounce packages frozen chopped broccoli, cooked and drained
½ package dry onion soup mix
1 4-ounce can chopped green chiles
1 tablespoon prepared horseradish
1 8-ounce can sliced mushrooms, drained
½ teaspoon garlic powder

In a large saucepan, melt butter. Sauté onion until tender. Add remaining ingredients and heat until bubbly, stirring frequently.

Serve hot in chafing dish with raw vegetables.

Beer/Cheese Fondue

4 servings

The skiers will love this one on cold winter nights.

1 cup beer
2 tablespoons flour
½ pound sharp Cheddar cheese, grated
½ pound Swiss cheese, grated
8 to 10 drops Tabasco sauce
1 garlic clove, minced, optional

In a medium saucepan or fondue pot, combine beer and flour. Using medium to low heat, add cheeses, ½ cup at a time, blending until melted. Add Tabasco sauce and garlic, stirring well.

Serve in a fondue pot with baskets of cubed French bread and bite-sized raw vegetables.

Elegant and Easy Escargot

½ cup butter, softened
2 small garlic cloves, minced
2 teaspoons chopped green onions, including tops
1 tablespoon minced parsley
18 extra-large canned snails, washed and drained thoroughly
18 snail shells, real **or** ceramic
½ cup grated Parmesan cheese
18 slices French bread (small loaf) **or** 2 French bread rolls, sliced ¼-inch thick, lightly toasted

In a small bowl, combine butter, garlic, onion and parsley. Mix until well blended. Place a small portion of butter mixture in each snail shell, then put in snail. Add another small amount of butter mixture and sprinkle with cheese.

Place each shell, opening up, on snail pans or shallow baking dish. Bake uncovered at 500° for 5 minutes or until browned and bubbly.

To serve, remove snail from shell, place on toast and pour remaining butter mixture over. May also be served on a snail platter with toast and small forks alongside.

Having something prepared in advance is a wonderful way to entertain but have something for your guests to smell when they arrive even if it's only herbs simmering in water.

Hot Clam Dip in a Shell   12-15 servings

Here's one you can eat, container and all.

3 7-ounce cans minced clams, drained, reserve liquid
½ cup clam liquid
½ teaspoon salt
2 8-ounce packages cream cheese, softened
2 teaspoons Worcestershire sauce
6 drops Tabasco sauce
2 tablespoons chopped parsley
2 teaspoons lemon juice
½ cup white wine
1 large round loaf French bread
Additional bread for dipping, if desired
Paprika

In a medium bowl, combine all ingredients **except** French bread and paprika.

Slice top off loaf of bread and scoop out the inside, reserving for later use. Be careful not to cut through sides or bottom of the loaf.

Pour clam mixture into loaf, replace lid and wrap in foil. Place on a cookie sheet and bake at 250° for 2 to 3 hours. Remove foil, place on a platter surrounded by the additional cubes of "dipping bread." Remove lid and sprinkle with paprika.

Serve with wooden skewers or toothpicks.

Don't forget bamboo skewers when planning your hors d'oeuvres – the many things too messy for fingers like meatballs or marinated shrimp can be speared and served attractively.

Baked Clam Appetizers

Fresh clams in the shell
Favorite barbecue sauce
Butter
Cheddar cheese, grated

Discard any clams that do not close when touched. Place clams in a sink or large container. Fill with cold water and let soak 3 to 6 hours to remove sand. (Cornmeal may be added to water.)

Place clams on a cookie sheet. Bake at 300° until they open, inserting knife in side and opening all the way. Discard any that do not open.

On each open shell, place barbecue sauce, dot of butter and cheese. Barbecue over hot coals until mixture boils. Serve immediately.

NOTE: Oysters or mussels may be substituted for clams.

The cocktail hour should be just that – any more than that and your guests won't enjoy your fabulous meal.

Chinese Chicken Wings   10-12 servings

3 pounds chicken wings
  (discard tips and cut
  each wing into
  2 pieces)
Salt and pepper to taste
2 tablespoons oil
1 cup honey
½ cup soy sauce
1 garlic clove, minced
2 tablespoons catsup

Arrange chicken wings in a 10x15-inch shallow baking dish. Sprinkle with salt, pepper and oil.

In a small bowl, combine remaining ingredients. Pour over wings. Bake uncovered at 375° for 1 hour, basting frequently.

Chicken Wings as Hors d'Oeuvres

6-8 servings

¼ cup Worcestershire sauce
2 tablespoons steak sauce
½ teaspoon curry powder
½ teaspoon garlic powder
¼ cup bourbon
1 tablespoon sugar
2 tablespoons catsup
¼ teaspoon salt
1 to 2 pounds chicken wings

In a bowl, combine all ingredients, **except** chicken wings.

Using a knife, pierce the wings on the fatty side, cut off and discard the tips and cut at the joint, making 2 pieces per wing. Marinate in the sauce overnight or for several hours.

Preheat broiler 15 minutes. Place wings on broiler pan; broil for ½ hour, 4 to 6 inches from heat, basting with sauce several times, until dark brown. WATCH CLOSELY.

Chicken Livers Sautéed with Rosemary

4-6 servings

3 tablespoons flour
1 teaspoon rosemary
1 teaspoon thyme
Lemon herb to taste
Salt and pepper to taste
1 pound chicken livers
¼ cup butter
1 4-ounce can button mushrooms, drained
1 cup heavy cream
2 to 3 drops Tabasco sauce
1 teaspoon garlic powder
¼ cup white wine

In a small bowl, combine flour, rosemary, thyme, lemon herb, salt and pepper. Mix thoroughly. Roll livers in flour mixture until well coated.

In a skillet, melt butter and sauté livers until browned and well done. Add any leftover flour mixture to skillet. Add remaining ingredients and stir until thickened.

Serve warm with toothpicks or cocktail forks.

NOTE: May also be served as an entrée over rice.

Homemade Salami   6 rolls

5 pounds ground chuck
3 teaspoons garlic salt
4½ teaspoons mustard
  seed
5 heaping teaspoons
  meat tenderizer
4½ teaspoons coarsely
  ground pepper
2 teaspoons liquid smoke

In a large roaster or pan, combine all ingredients and mix well. Divide into 4 equal parts and put into double plastic bags. Refrigerate for 3 days, kneading thoroughly each day in bags **without opening.** On third day, make into rolls and place on broiler pan (one with a pan under rack to allow for dripping). Bake at 150° for 8 hours.

OPTIONAL SPICES

2 garlic cloves, minced
1 teaspoon crushed red
  pepper
1 teaspoon dill seed

Beef Jerky   ¾ pound

Delicious snack for hunters to take in the field.

1½ pounds flank steak,
  partially frozen (may
  be elk or deer meat)
¼ cup soy sauce
¼ cup Worcestershire
  sauce
1 teaspoon salt
1 teaspoon liquid smoke
⅓ teaspoon garlic
  powder
⅓ teaspoon pepper
⅓ teaspoon MSG
1 teaspoon onion powder

Slice steak in thick strips diagonally across grain.

In a small bowl, combine remaining ingredients. Brush seasoning mixture on both sides of meat slices and arrange slices on 2 10x15-inch jelly-roll pans. Bake at 200° for 8 to 12 hours, turning meat several times to dry evenly. Or hang meat outside on a string, away from animals, in a cool, airy place to dry.

Store in plastic bags in refrigerator or freezer.

39

Steak Tartare

12-16 servings

2 pounds very lean sirloin, finely ground
2 egg yolks
⅓ cup minced onion
½ teaspoon minced garlic
1 tablespoon Worcestershire sauce
⅛ teaspoon Tabasco sauce
1 tablespoon chopped parsley
2 tablespoons capers, optional
1 teaspoon lemon juice
1½ teaspoons salt
1½ teaspoons pepper

In a bowl, combine all ingredients **except** garnishes. Place in a 1-quart ring mold and chill at least 3 hours. Invert onto a serving platter and decorate with garnishes. Serve with small slices of sourdough toast or crackers.

GARNISHES

Parsley
Black olives
Capers
Chopped red onion

Making your guests feel welcome is a sign of a successful hostess. In planning your food, an attractive and delectable presentation is best. Serve finger foods only if your guests will be standing. Heavier appetizers are usually more elaborate and require a small plate and fork.

40

Cocktail Meatballs

12 servings

1 pound ground round
1 envelope dry onion soup
  mix
Oil
1 18-ounce bottle garlic
  barbecue sauce
1 6 to 8-ounce jar apple
  or currant jelly
Water chestnuts,
  optional
1 cup cubed pineapple,
  optional

In a medium bowl, mix ground round and onion soup. Form into 1-inch balls. In a skillet, brown meatballs in oil. Drain on paper towels.

In a saucepan, mix barbecue sauce and jelly. Heat to boiling. Add meatballs and gently stir. Remove from heat.

Options: Place a water chestnut in center of each meatball. Add 1 cup cubed pineapple to sauce.

Serve hot in a chafing dish and provide toothpicks.

Barbecued Sausage Balls

12 servings

1 pound pork sausage
1 egg, lightly beaten
⅓ cup fine dry bread
  crumbs
½ teaspoon ground sage

In a bowl, mix sausage, egg, bread crumbs and sage. Shape into bite-sized meatballs.

In a skillet, brown slowly on all sides; drain off excess grease. Pour sauce over meatballs. Cover and simmer 30 minutes, stirring occasionally to coat evenly.

Serve warm in a chafing dish. Provide toothpicks.

SAUCE

½ cup catsup
2 tablespoons brown
  sugar
1 tablespoon vinegar
1 tablespoon soy sauce

In a small bowl, combine ingredients and mix well.

41

Stuffed Grape Leaves

4-5 dozen

¼ cup olive oil
1 medium onion, finely chopped
1 pound lean ground lamb
½ cup short-grained rice
1 tablespoon dried dill weed
⅓ cup shelled pine nuts
¼ cup water
3 tablespoons tomato paste
Freshly ground pepper
2 8-ounce jars grape leaves in brine, rinsed well, blanched in boiling water 2 to 3 minutes until pliable
¾ cup chicken broth
3 tablespoons fresh lemon juice
1 lemon, thinly sliced

In a large skillet, heat oil and sauté onion until translucent. Crumble meat and add to onion, stirring until lightly browned. Add rice, dill, pine nuts, water and tomato paste. Season to taste with pepper. Cook over medium heat until water is absorbed, about 10 minutes.

Cover bottom of Dutch oven with layer of grape leaves. Stuff remaining leaves by placing leaf shiny side down on palm of hand, with base of leaf toward wrist and tip toward fingers. Place a spoonful of meat mixture in center. Fold leaf over stuffing like an envelope, tucking edges in snugly. Roll up and tuck tip of leaf under to prevent unrolling. Arrange, tip side down, in pan.

Add broth to within 1 inch of top layer in Dutch oven. Use any leftover leaves to cover top layer. Place a plate upside down over top layer and press. Cover and cook on medium heat until rice is tender, about 30 minutes. Sprinkle with lemon juice.

Garnish with lemon slices and serve hot or cold.

Shrimp-Cheese Stack
12 servings

2 8-ounce packages cream cheese, softened
2 tablespoons Worcestershire sauce
¼ teaspoon grated lemon peel
1 tablespoon lemon juice
½ cup thinly sliced green onions
⅛ teaspoon Tabasco sauce
1 12-ounce bottle chili sauce
1 tablespoon horseradish sauce
¾ pound small cooked shrimp

In a mixing bowl, beat together cream cheese, Worcestershire sauce, lemon peel, lemon juice, green onions and Tabasco sauce.

Spread on a rimmed serving platter. Cover and chill if made ahead.

To serve, bring to room temperature. Combine chili sauce and horseradish sauce, spread over cheese mixture. Top with shrimp, serve with assorted crackers.

Un-Mexican Stack-Up
20 servings

2 8-ounce packages cream cheese, softened
2 to 3 tablespoons mayonnaise **or** cream
8 green onions, chopped
1 green pepper, chopped
1 tablespoon Worcestershire sauce
1 teaspoon garlic powder
Dash Tabasco sauce
Salt and pepper to taste
2 cups cooked and shredded ham
12 medium-sized flour tortillas
½ cup chopped walnuts
Fresh parsley

In a large mixing bowl or food processor, combine cheese, mayonnaise, onions, green pepper, Worcestershire sauce, garlic powder, Tabasco sauce, salt and pepper. Mix well. Stir in ham, blending thoroughly.

Place a tortilla on a large round plate. Spread a thin layer of ham mixture over tortilla. Repeat layers, ending with ham mixture on top of entire stack. Sprinkle with nuts. Chill 6 to 8 hours or overnight. Garnish with fresh parsley. Cut in small cubes and serve with toothpicks.

Juarez Chile con Queso

6-8 servings

1 small onion, minced
2 tablespoons butter
1 cup solid pack
  tomatoes, chopped
1 4-ounce can chopped
  green chiles
Salt and pepper to taste
1 8-ounce package cream
  cheese, cubed
1 cup heavy cream

In a medium saucepan, sauté onion in butter. Add tomatoes, chiles, salt and pepper. Simmer 15 minutes and add cream cheese. When cheese begins to melt, add cream.

Serve warm in a chafing dish, accompanied with tortilla chips.

The most important part of entertaining is to be yourself and bring together people you care about to have a good time.

Chile con Queso

12-15 servings

4 bacon slices, diced
1 small onion, chopped
1 small ripe tomato, finely
  chopped
1 4-ounce can chopped
  green chiles
½ pound American
  cheese, grated
½ pound sharp Cheddar
  cheese, grated

Fry bacon in skillet until crisp; drain on paper towels and set aside.

Sauté onion in drippings until limp and slightly golden. Add tomato and stir well. Add green chiles. Stir and continue to cook on medium heat for a few minutes. Add cheeses, a handful at a time, continuing to stir until all is melted. Be careful not to burn cheese. Stir in bacon.

Serve in chafing dish with tortilla chips.

Super Nachos

1 pound ground beef
1 large onion, chopped
Salt to taste
Tabasco sauce to taste
2 17-ounce cans refried
   beans
1 4-ounce can chopped
   green chiles
2 to 3 cups grated
   Monterey Jack **or**
   Cheddar cheese
¾ cup taco sauce
¼ cup chopped green
   onions
1 cup whole pitted ripe
   olives
1 cup thawed avocado
   dip **or** 1 medium
   avocado, mashed
1 cup sour cream
8 cups tortilla chips

In a skillet, fry beef. Add onion, stir until lightly browned. Drain. Season with salt and Tabasco sauce; set aside.

Using a 10x15-inch shallow pan, spread refried beans evenly over bottom. Top with meat mixture, green chiles, cheese and taco sauce. Bake uncovered at 400° for 20 to 25 minutes. Garnish with green onions and olives. In center, mound avocado dip and top with sour cream.

Tuck wing of tortilla chips around edge and serve.

Schedule enough time to relax before the party begins – giving you a moment to catch your breath and be refreshed. Greet your guests with a smile and above all, enjoy your own party.

Mexican Haystack

10-12 servings

2 10½-ounce cans
 jalapeño bean dip
2 avocados, mashed with
 1 tablespoon lemon
 juice
Salt to taste
¾ cup sour cream
½ cup mayonnaise
½ package taco
 seasoning mix
2 bunches green onions,
 chopped, including
 tops
1 4½-ounce can
 chopped ripe olives,
 drained
2 medium tomatoes,
 peeled, seeded,
 chopped and squeezed
 to remove juice
1½ to 2 cups grated
 Cheddar cheese
Alfalfa sprouts, optional

Using a large round platter or pizza pan, spread bean dip into a circle, covering the pan. Spread mashed avocado over dip and salt lightly.

In a small bowl, combine sour cream, mayonnaise and taco seasoning mix. Blend well. Spread over avocado and layer remaining ingredients carefully.

Tuck round taco chips around edge and serve with extra chips.

Taos Salsa

1 pint

1 tomato, diced
4 to 5 yellow hot chili
 peppers, chopped
1 8-ounce can tomato
 sauce
3 to 4 green onions, sliced

In a small bowl, combine all ingredients. Refrigerate for 1 hour. Serve with tortilla chips or use in any recipe calling for salsa.

All Strong Men Go Crazy Some Time

8 servings

Here's one for cooks with poor memories at the grocery store — the name supplies clues to the ingredients.

2 large **A**vocados, mashed
½ cup **S**alsa
1½ cups **M**onterey Jack cheese, grated
6 **G**reen onions, sliced
1½ cups **C**heddar cheese, grated
1½ cups **S**our cream
1 or 2 **T**omatoes, chopped

Using an 8x10-inch serving dish, layer ingredients in order given. Serve with tortilla chips.

Chorizo-Filled Won Tons

50-60 won tons

3 Basque chorizo sausages
½ pound ground beef
6 green onions, thinly sliced
3 jalapeño chiles, diced
¼ pound Monterey Jack cheese, grated
1 package won ton skins (50-60 count)
2 tablespoons water, mixed with 2 tablespoons cornstarch

Using a food processor, finely chop chorizos.

In a medium skillet, sauté chorizos and ground beef about 5 minutes or until meat is done. Add green onions and chiles. Stir in cheese gradually and cook until melted. Cool.

Fill each won ton skin with meat filling and fold as for a deep-fried won ton. Seal with water and cornstarch mixture. Fry won tons in deep fryer at 360° for 1 to 2 minutes. Drain on paper towels and serve warm.

NOTE: May be made ahead and even frozen. Reheat at 200°, or bake at 350° for 15 minutes if frozen.

Garden Salsa
3 cups

4 ripe tomatoes, peeled, seeded and coarsely chopped
1 large red onion, minced
1 medium green pepper, minced
½ small hot red chili pepper, seeded and minced **or** 1 4-ounce can chopped green chiles, drained
1 garlic clove, minced
1 tablespoon red wine vinegar
1 tablespoon olive oil
1 teaspoon salt
¼ teaspoon coriander **or** 1 teaspoon minced fresh coriander leaves
Pinch of ground cloves

In a medium bowl, combine all ingredients and chill well. Taste for salt and adjust as needed.

Serve cold with tortilla chips for an appetizer or with any Mexican food or steak.

Kneadery Guacamole
2 cups

Recipe of Chef Linda Spearing, The Kneadery, Ketchum.

3 large avocados
2 green onions, finely minced
1 tomato, diced
¼ cup diced green chiles
1 teaspoon lemon juice
¼ teaspoon garlic powder
1 teaspoon parsley flakes

Mash avocados with a potato masher. Add remaining ingredients and mix thoroughly. Let stand for 1 hour and serve.

Gourmet Guacamole

1½ cups

Great with tortilla chips or as a topping for hamburgers or omelets.

3 medium-sized avocados, peeled and mashed with a fork
1 tablespoon lemon juice
1 8-ounce package cream cheese, softened
1 teaspoon garlic salt
¼ teaspoon Tabasco sauce
½ teaspoon Worcestershire sauce
½ teaspoon seasoned salt
½ teaspoon onion salt
1 medium onion, finely chopped
1 tomato, finely chopped
3 bacon slices, cooked and crumbled, optional

In a medium bowl, combine avocado, lemon juice and cream cheese; mix well. Add seasonings and mix well. Add onions and tomatoes, being careful not to mash tomatoes.

To serve, garnish with crumbled bacon.

Brie en Croûte

10-12 servings

¼ to ⅓ of a 1-pound package phyllo leaves
1 pound Brie cheese
1 egg yolk, beaten

Unfold phyllo leaves. Place Brie on top, fold up sides and pinch phyllo to seal. Place on baking sheet and brush with egg yolk. (May be frozen at this point for later use.) Bake at 450° for 10 minutes, then reduce heat to 350° for 20 minutes or until crust is lightly browned.

To serve, cut into wedges and accompany with crackers and fresh fruit.

Camembert/Caviar Quickie

6-10 servings

1 8-ounce wheel
  Camembert **or** Brie
  cheese
1 2½-ounce jar caviar
1 medium onion, minced,
  soaked in milk if
  strong, then drained

Arrange cheese in center of serving plate, top with caviar and surround with onion. Serve immediately with crackers.

Cranberry Chutney

2 quarts

This may be served as a tasty alternative to cranberry sauce and the color is wonderful for the holidays.

3½ cups sugar
1 cup cider vinegar
1 10½-ounce package
  frozen chopped onions
1 cup currants **or** raisins
  or ½ cup of each
1 teaspoon allspice
3 tablespoons finely
  grated fresh ginger
2 12-ounce packages
  cranberries
1 cup walnuts, pecans **or**
  almonds

In a large saucepan, combine sugar, vinegar, onions, currants, allspice and ginger. Cook, uncovered, on medium-high until sugar dissolves. Add cranberries and cook on medium for 10 minutes or until all of them have popped. Add nuts, stir and remove from heat. Pour into 1-cup jars, seal with paraffin or freeze.

To serve, spoon over block of cream cheese and accompany with crackers.

Jalapeño Jelly for Cream Cheese

6 cups

1½ cups finely chopped
   green **or** red bell
   peppers
½ cup seeded and finely
   chopped jalapeño
   chiles
1½ cups cider vinegar
1 large onion, finely
   chopped
6⅓ cups sugar
Few drops green **or** red
   food coloring
2 foil packages Certo
Paraffin

In a large kettle, combine green peppers, chiles, vinegar, onion and sugar. Heat to boiling and cook 10 minutes, stirring constantly. Add food coloring and Certo, continue boiling 5 minutes longer. Strain through cheesecloth, pour into sterilized jars and seal with paraffin.

Serve over a block of cream cheese with crackers.

Try serving a sauce for crudités or a tray of sliced meats in a hollowed purple cabbage leaving the outside leaves whole to fold back.

Oyster/Cream Cheese Roll

2 cups

1 8-ounce package cream
   cheese, softened
1 teaspoon Beau Monde
   seasoning
½ teaspoon
   Worcestershire sauce
1 3¾-ounce can smoked
   oysters, drained and
   chopped
Minced parsley

In a mixing bowl, beat cream cheese, Beau Monde and Worcestershire sauce until soft and fluffy. On waxed paper, spread into a 6x8-inch rectangle. Place oysters in center lengthwise and fold over sides of the cheese to form a roll. Refrigerate or freeze until ready to serve.

Place on serving plate, sprinkle with parsley and accompany with crackers.

Easy Cheese Ball
8 servings

1 8-ounce package cream cheese, softened
1 3-ounce package pimiento cream cheese, softened
1 2-ounce package Bleu cheese, softened
2 garlic cloves, minced
1 tablespoon minced onion
1 tablespoon mayonnaise
½ cup chopped walnuts or sliced almonds

Using a mixer, blend all ingredients, **except** nuts. Form into a ball and roll in nuts. Refrigerate until ready to use. Serve with crackers.

East Indian Cheese Ball
12 servings

1 8-ounce and 1 3-ounce package cream cheese, softened
½ cup cottage cheese
½ cup finely chopped green onion, including tops
½ cup peanuts (do not chop)
½ cup raisins
¼ to ½ cup shredded coconut
¼ to ½ teaspoon curry powder
Chutney, optional

In a medium bowl, combine all ingredients, **except** chutney, and mix well. Form into a ball and wrap in waxed paper. Chill. To serve, place on a platter, cover with chutney if desired and surround with crackers.

Sherry/Cheese Log

8-10 servings

2 cups grated Cheddar
cheese
1 3-ounce package cream
cheese, softened
2 tablespoons dry sherry
or orange juice
½ teaspoon
Worcestershire sauce
½ teaspoon garlic **or**
onion salt
½ cup chopped ripe
olives
2 tablespoons minced
parsley
½ cup chopped pecans

In a medium bowl, combine cheeses, sherry, Worcestershire sauce and onion salt. Mix well. Add chopped olives and parsley, mixing well. Form into a log and roll in chopped pecans. Refrigerate several hours or overnight.

Serve with pumpernickel or crackers.

Fantastic Cheese Ball

8 servings

This is best if made the day before.

1 ounce Roquefort **or**
Bleu cheese, softened
4 ounces Cheddar
cheese, grated
1 8-ounce package
cream cheese,
softened
1 garlic clove, minced
¼ medium onion, minced
Dash Tabasco **or**
Worcestershire sauce
½ cup chopped pecans
Paprika

In a medium bowl, combine cheeses, garlic, onion and Tabasco; mix well. Form into a ball, roll in pecans and sprinkle with paprika. Serve with crackers.

NOTE: May be frozen.

Elegant Stuffed Easter Eggs

16 halves

8 hard boiled eggs
1 cup flaked cooked crab meat
½ cup minced celery
½ cup chopped walnuts
2 tablespoons minced green pepper
1 teaspoon prepared mustard
¼ teaspoon salt
Mayonnaise
Watercress or chicory

Shell eggs and cut in half lengthwise. Remove yolks and mash. Add remaining ingredients except watercress, mixing in enough mayonnaise to moisten.

Stuff whites with mixture and arrange on a bed of watercress.

Harlequin Eggs

8 halves

1 cooked carrot
1 cooked beet
½ cup minced green beans
¼ cup mayonnaise
¼ teaspoon salt
⅛ teaspoon pepper
4 hard boiled eggs
Paprika

Shred carrot and beet. Mix with beans, and blend with mayonnaise and seasoning. Cut eggs in half lengthwise. Remove yolks and fill with vegetable mixture. Sprinkle with sieved egg yolks. Dust with paprika.

Mushroom-Deviled Eggs

12 halves

6 hard boiled eggs
3 tablespoons Green Goddess salad dressing
1 teaspoon Dijon-style mustard
1 2-ounce can mushrooms, drained and finely chopped **or** ¼ cup fresh mushrooms, finely chopped

Halve eggs lengthwise. Remove yolks and mash them. Add dressing and mustard. Stir in mushrooms. Add salt and pepper to taste. Spoon mixture into whites.

Bound to Please: The Wonders of Winter

Horses on snowshoes, skis 8 to 10 feet long, washbasins used as
eds – early Idahoans enjoyed their winter sports and often turned
o sleighs for transportation through the snow-covered hills and
neadows.

Today the traditions continue at Idaho's ski areas, on miles of
ails for cross-country skiers and snowmobilers, on frozen lakes
vaiting for ice skaters and ice fishermen. Lightweight fabrics have
eplaced the bulky coverings and long, voluminous skirts worn by
esterday's snow lovers, but deep powder and mountains
Ilanketed in white make Idaho a year-round recreational state.

Potage Paysanne

4 servings

2 medium potatoes,
    peeled and sliced
2 medium onions, sliced
¾ cup water
½ pound fresh spinach
1 chicken bouillon cube
    or 1 teaspoon stock
    base
1 teaspoon salt
⅛ teaspoon freshly
    ground pepper
⅛ teaspoon nutmeg
1 cup heavy cream
Sour cream

In a large saucepan, combine all ingredients, **except** cream and sour cream, and heat to boiling. Simmer 15 minutes. Place the vegetables and ½ cup of the liquid in a blender. Cover and purée on high. Remove cover while blender is still on and gradually add remaining cooking liquid. Add cream.

Serve soup hot or chilled with a dollop of sour cream.

Vichyssoise

6 servings

4 potatoes, peeled and
    sliced
4 leeks, rinsed and sliced
2 celery stalks, sliced
1 Bermuda onion, sliced
1 cup water
1 teaspoon salt
4 cups chicken stock
1¼ cups light cream
½ cup heavy cream
White pepper
Fresh chives, chopped

In a heavy pan, combine potatoes, leeks, celery and onion with water and salt. Heat to boiling, cover and simmer until vegetables are tender. Stir in chicken stock. Purée mixture in a food processor. Correct the seasoning. Chill overnight.

To serve, stir in creams and white pepper. Top with chives.

Chilling will mute the seasoning of soup, particularly salt. Taste the soup just before serving to test for extra seasoning needed.

55

German Potato Soup

6 servings

4 slices lean bacon,diced
6 leeks, thinly sliced
½ cup chopped onion
2 tablespoons flour
4 cups chicken bouillon
3 large potatoes, thinly
    sliced
2 egg yolks, beaten
1 cup sour cream
1 tablespoon minced
    parsley
1 tablespoon minced
    chervil

In a large soup pot, sauté bacon for 5 minutes. Add leeks and onion; continue to sauté 5 more minutes. Stir in flour. Slowly add bouillon, stirring constantly. Add potatoes and simmer for 1 hour or longer.

Combine egg yolks and sour cream. Stir into soup. Simmer 10 minutes, stirring constantly. Add parsley and chervil.

Crab Chowder

6 servings

½ cup chopped onion
½ cup chopped celery
3 tablespoons butter **or**
    margarine
3 cups frozen potato
    soup (if unavailable,
    use canned, undiluted)
3 cups milk
7 ounces fresh **or** canned
    crab meat
1 8-ounce can creamed
    corn
2 tablespoons chopped
    pimiento
¼ teaspoon salt
½ teaspoon thyme
1 bay leaf
White pepper to taste
¼ cup dry sherry
Fresh parsley

In a Dutch oven, sauté onion and celery in butter. Add remaining ingredients, **except** sherry and parsley. Cook gently for 15 minutes. Stir in sherry and remove from heat. Garnish with fresh parsley.

Fish Chowder

12 servings

2 medium potatoes, diced
2 carrots, diced
1 onion, diced
4 celery stalks, diced
1 bay leaf
2 teaspoons parsley
1 teaspoon salt
½ teaspoon pepper
4 bacon slices, diced
1 to 2 teaspoons dried,
  minced onion
2 large potatoes, diced
1 5-pound block frozen
  cod
1 14-ounce can chicken
  broth
1 7-ounce bottle clam
  juice
1 13-ounce can
  evaporated milk

In a Dutch oven, place the first 8 ingredients. Cover with water and simmer until tender, about 8 to 10 minutes. Remove bay leaf and purée in blender. Return to Dutch oven.

In a skillet, cook bacon and minced onion until browned. Add the **2 large** diced potatoes, cover with water and simmer until tender. Add to Dutch oven.

In another pot, simmer cod in a little water until it flakes easily. Check for bones and add to Dutch oven mixture. Add any remaining seafood you choose. Stir well.

Add chicken broth, clam juice and milk. Stir and bring to a simmer.

To serve, float a large pat of butter on each serving. May be diluted with additional milk or water to desired consistency.

OPTIONAL INGREDIENTS

Crab meat, fresh or
  canned
Minced clams
Lobster meat
Shrimp, peeled and
  deveined

Chilled Corn Chowder   6 servings

½ pound lean bacon
2 medium potatoes,
  diced
1 onion, chopped
2 cups water
2 10-ounce packages
  frozen corn
1 13-ounce can
  evaporated milk
1 cup milk
Salt and pepper

Fry bacon in a Dutch oven. Remove bacon and reserve drippings. Add potatoes and onions to drippings and stir well. Add water and heat to boiling. Cook until potatoes are tender, about 10 to 15 minutes. Add corn and both milks, heat through, but do not boil.

Add crumbled bacon and season with salt and pepper.

Chill and serve.

Clam Chowder   6-8 servings

¾ pound fresh clams or
  2 7-ounce cans
  minced clams
1 cup chopped onion
1 cup chopped celery
2 cups diced potatoes
¾ cup butter
¾ cup flour
1½ teaspoons salt
Pepper
½ teaspoon sugar
1 quart light cream
6 bacon slices, cooked
  and crumbled
Parsley

Wash and steam fresh clams or drain juice from canned clams, reserving ½ cup nectar.

In a medium saucepan, combine clam juice and vegetables. Add enough water to cover. Heat to boiling and simmer 20 minutes or until vegetables are tender.

In a large pan, melt butter and add flour, salt, pepper and sugar. Slowly stir in cream. Cook until smooth.

Add vegetable mixture and clams. Stir and cook until desired consistency. May be thinned with more cream or milk.

Garnish with bacon and minced parsley.

Sherried Clam Chowder
6 servings

8 bacon slices, cut into
  small pieces
2 medium onions,
  chopped
2 cups chopped celery
2 10-ounce cans potato
  soup, undiluted
1 8-ounce bottle clam
  juice
1 soup can milk
2 7-ounce cans minced
  clams, undrained **or**
  1 cup chopped
  steamed clams and
  ½ cup nectar
3 tablespoons sherry
6 large dollops sour
  cream

In a large kettle, cook bacon until transparent but not crisp. Add onions and celery and cook until vegetables are tender. Add potato soup, clam juice and milk. Heat just to boiling. Add minced clams with nectar and heat through. Remove from heat and add sherry.

Ladle into soup bowls. Top each with a dollop of sour cream.

Oyster and Brie
Champagne Soup
8 servings

1 cup unsalted butter
½ cup flour
2 quarts oyster liquid,
  bottled clam juice **or**
  seafood stock
5 cups heavy cream
1½ teaspoons cayenne
1½ pounds Brie cheese,
  rind removed and cut
  into small pieces
2 cups dry champagne
3 dozen fresh oysters
1 cup green onion stems,
  finely minced
Salt to taste

In a saucepan, melt butter over low heat. Add flour and cook 3 minutes, whisking constantly. Add stock and continue to cook and whisk until flour is absorbed, about 3 to 4 minutes.

Heat to boiling, simmer for 10 minutes, stirring occasionally. Add cream, simmer 5 minutes, stirring constantly. Add cayenne and cheese, stirring until cheese is melted completely. Stir in champagne, oysters and green onions.

Remove from heat, cover and let stand 10 minutes. Taste for seasoning, stir and serve.

Clam Broth

8 servings

This broth is also good without the clams.

1 medium onion, chopped
1 garlic clove, minced
6 sprigs fresh parsley,
  chopped
1 bay leaf
½ cup olive oil
Salt and pepper to taste
5 medium tomatoes,
  peeled and chopped
2 cups tomato juice
1 10-ounce can beef
  consommé, undiluted
1 10-ounce can beef
  broth, undiluted
1 10-ounce can chicken
  broth, undiluted
Tabasco sauce, optional
3 7-ounce cans baby
  clams, undrained
Lemon slices
Parmesan cheese, grated

In a soup pot, sauté onion, garlic, parsley and bay leaf in olive oil, stirring frequently until onion is tender. Add salt and pepper to taste. Add tomatoes and simmer gently. Put mixture through a fine sieve or blender and return to pot.

Add tomato juice, consommé, beef broth and chicken broth. Season with salt, pepper and Tabasco sauce. Bring to a slow boil and add clams.

To serve, place a slice of lemon and/or a sprinkle of Parmesan on each serving.

A rich, homemade stock is an excellent contribution to any soup. Take advantage of some free time to prepare stocks ahead of time. Freeze them in ice cube trays or individual plastic containers for convenient use at a later time.

Bouillabaisse

12 servings

½ cup butter
1 cup coarsely chopped
onion
1 garlic clove, minced
3 tablespoons flour
1 cup coarsely chopped
fresh tomato
3 cups fish stock **or**
water
1½ cups tomato juice
1 lemon, sliced
6 potatoes, coarsely
chopped
12 carrots, coarsely
chopped
2 teaspoons salt
⅛ teaspoon cayenne
⅛ teaspoon thyme
3 whole allspice
1 small bay leaf
Pinch of saffron
4 pounds red snapper,
skin removed and cut
in slices or large
chunks
2 pounds fresh shrimp,
peeled and deveined
2 pounds fresh scallops
or clams **or** 1 pint
oysters

In a Dutch oven, melt butter. Add onion and garlic and sauté until tender. Blend in flour. Add tomato, fish stock and tomato juice. Mix well. Add lemon, potatoes and carrots. Season with salt, cayenne, thyme, allspice, bay leaf and saffron. Simmer for 30 minutes until flavors are well blended.

Add snapper, shrimp and scallops to the tomato mixture. Simmer 15 to 20 minutes or until fish flakes easily when tested with a fork and shrimp are tender.

Keep a container in your freezer and add all leftover vegetables. When you have a sufficient amount, thaw, blend and freeze in ice cube trays. Good for adding additional flavor to soups, etc.

Seafood Gumbo

6 servings

3 tablespoons shortening
3 tablespoons flour
2 onions, chopped
1 16-ounce can tomatoes
1 16-ounce can okra and
   tomatoes
½ cup water
Salt and pepper to taste
¼ cup chopped parsley
5 drops Tabasco sauce
1 small package shrimp
   seasoning
1 pound fresh crab meat
2 pounds fresh shrimp,
   peeled and deveined
1 pint fresh oysters
2 cups cooked rice

In a medium saucepan, make a roux by combining shortening and flour. Stir constantly until dark brown, being careful not to burn. Add onions and stir a few minutes.

Add tomatoes and okra and tomatoes. Stir in water and simmer a few minutes.

Meanwhile, put 2½ to 3 quarts water into a large soup pot or Dutch oven. Heat to boiling. Stir roux mixture into boiling water, reduce heat to simmer. Add salt and pepper, parsley and Tabasco sauce.

Drop in the package of shrimp seasoning, being careful not to tear the bag. Add seafood and simmer until shrimp are done. Serve in soup bowls with a scoop of rice.

Turkey Gumbo

10-12 servings

1 turkey carcass
½ cup butter **or** margarine
1 cup chopped onion
1 cup chopped celery
⅓ cup flour
1 28-ounce can tomatoes
3 cups sliced okra
4 to 5 bay leaves
⅛ teaspoon thyme
⅛ teaspoon marjoram
2 tablespoons chopped parsley
2 teaspoons gumbo filet (found with gourmet spices)
Salt and pepper
Steamed rice

Boil turkey carcass in 8 cups water until meat falls away from the bones, about 2 to 3 hours. Remove meat from bones and set aside. Reserve broth.

In a large soup kettle, melt butter or margarine and sauté onion and celery. Add flour and stir mixture over medium heat until golden, the color of caramel. Stir in reserved broth, add tomatoes, okra, bay leaves, thyme, marjoram, parsley, gumbo filet and reserved turkey meat. Heat to boiling and simmer 30 minutes. Add salt and pepper to taste.

To serve, put ½ cup rice in each bowl. Ladle gumbo over rice.

Beer-Cheese Soup

6 servings

Goes well with French or garlic bread, tossed salad and white wine.

¾ cup butter
½ cup diced celery
½ cup diced carrots
½ cup diced onions
½ cup flour
2 tablespoons Parmesan cheese
6 ounces grated Cheddar cheese
1 12-ounce bottle of beer
5 cups chicken stock
½ teaspoon dry mustard
Salt and pepper to taste

In a large saucepan, sauté vegetables in butter until tender, but not brown. Blend in flour then cheeses and beer. Add stock and seasonings and simmer 10 minutes.

Cheesy Chowder

4-6 servings

*This favorite from The Sandpiper, Boise, is easy to
prepare and always a hit.*

1 cup chopped onion
½ cup chopped carrot
½ cup chopped celery
2 tablespoons butter
1½ teaspoons paprika
3 cups chicken broth
1½ cups grated Cheddar
    cheese
3 ounces Swiss cheese,
    grated
½ cup light cream
⅓ cup flour
1 cup milk
½ teaspoon
    Worcestershire sauce
⅛ teaspoon pepper
Grated Parmesan cheese

In a heavy saucepan, sauté onion,
carrot and celery in butter for
5 minutes. Blend in paprika. Add
chicken broth. Heat to boiling, reduce
heat and simmer, covered, for
10 minutes. Add cheeses, stir until
melted. Add cream. Blend flour with
milk and add to chowder. Cook and
stir until slightly thickened. Add
Worcestershire sauce and pepper.
Ladle into soup bowls. Sprinkle with
Parmesan cheese.

Cheese Soup

8 servings

½ cup butter **or**
  margarine
⅓ cup finely chopped
  carrots
⅓ cup finely chopped
  onion
⅓ cup finely chopped
  celery
⅓ cup flour
4 cups chicken broth
2 cups milk
3 cups grated Cheddar
  cheese
½ teaspoon Dijon-style
  mustard
1 teaspoon
  Worcestershire sauce
5 bacon slices, cooked
  and crumbled

In a large saucepan, melt butter. Sauté carrots, onion and celery until soft but not brown, about 10 minutes. Add flour. Cook and stir 2 minutes or until blended.

Slowly add **3 cups** of the chicken broth, stirring with a whisk until mixture comes to a boil and thickens. Place mixture in a blender or food processor. Blend until smooth.

Return mixture to a clean saucepan. Stir in remaining broth and the milk. Stir in cheese, mustard and Worcestershire sauce. Simmer over low heat until soup is hot and cheese is melted. Garnish with crumbled bacon.

Tortilla Soup

4 servings

2 cups chicken broth
2 tablespoons chopped
  parsley
6 corn tortillas, cut in
  strips 1 x ½ inch
3 tablespoons oil
1 medium onion,
  chopped
1 garlic clove, minced
¼ cup tomato sauce
1 teaspoon mild chili
  powder
Salt to taste
¼ cup grated Parmesan
  cheese

In a medium saucepan, heat broth with **1 tablespoon** of the parsley.

In a skillet, fry tortillas in hot oil and drain on paper towels. In the same skillet, sauté onion and garlic until tender. Add tomato sauce, remaining parsley and the chili powder.

Strain broth into the mixture and salt lightly. Stir in tortillas and allow to simmer 1 hour.

Sprinkle with cheese just before serving.

Curried Fresh Mushroom Soup

6 servings

4 tablespoons butter
1 onion, finely minced
1 pound fresh
   mushrooms, diced
1 teaspoon curry powder
½ cup flour
2 quarts whole milk
10 chicken bouillon
   cubes
½ teaspoon MSG
⅛ teaspoon ground
   coriander
½ teaspoon grated lemon
   peel
5 tablespoons lemon
   juice
2 tablespoons sherry
1 tablespoon plum **or**
   currant jelly
1 lemon, thinly sliced

In a large skillet over medium heat, sauté onion and mushrooms in butter for 3 minutes. Add curry powder and flour. Blend well. Gradually add milk, stirring until smooth. Add bouillon cubes, MSG and coriander. Continue cooking, stirring occasionally for about 20 minutes until cubes are dissolved and soup has thickened.

Add lemon peel, lemon juice, sherry and jelly. Reduce heat. Stir and keep warm for another 30 minutes to allow flavors to blend. Serve garnished with a slice of lemon.

Salt and pepper should be added at the end of any long cooking process.

Soups can be the most versatile item on the menu – served hot they can banish the cold winter evening but served chilled they can be totally refreshing on a summer day.

Lentil Soup with Lemon
6 servings

1½ cups lentils, rinsed
7 to 8 cups water
4 beef bouillon cubes
1 potato, peeled and
  cubed
2 carrots, sliced
1 onion, finely chopped
3 tablespoons oil
3 garlic cloves, minced
2 tablespoons chopped
  fresh parsley
¾ teaspoon salt
¼ teaspoon freshly
  ground pepper
½ teaspoon cumin
3 tablespoons lemon
  juice

GARNISHES

Parsley
Lemon slices

In a large soup kettle, combine lentils, water and bouillon cubes. Cover, heat to boiling and reduce to simmer. Add potatoes and carrots. Simmer 40 minutes.

In a skillet, sauté onion in oil slowly for 15 to 20 minutes. Add garlic and parsley and sauté 5 minutes longer. Add to lentils. Stir in salt, pepper, cumin and lemon juice. Cook 5 minutes longer. Garnish with chopped parsley or lemon slices.

Black Bean Soup

10-12 servings

1 pound black beans **or**
  pinto beans
3 quarts soup stock **or**
  3 quarts water + ham
  bone + 1 pound ham
1 onion, chopped
2 bay leaves
1 celery stalk, chopped
½ hot red chili pepper
1 tablespoon
  Worcestershire sauce
½ teaspoon ground
  cloves
½ cup catsup
½ cup sherry
1 hard boiled egg, sliced
1 lemon, sliced

Soak beans in water overnight. Drain. Place beans, stock, onion, bay leaves, celery and chili pepper in a large soup pot. Simmer for 6 hours.

Stir in Worcestershire sauce, cloves, catsup and sherry.

Serve with a slice of egg and lemon.

Minestrina di Spinaci

5-6 servings

A favorite from the Café Rose, Boise.

2 10-ounce packages
  frozen spinach **or**
  2 pounds fresh spinach
4 tablespoons butter
1 cup chicken broth
2 cups milk
¼ teaspoon nutmeg
5 tablespoons grated
  Parmesan cheese
Salt
Croutons

Cook spinach in a covered saucepan for about 5 minutes. Drain, cool and coarsely chop.

Place spinach and butter in a Dutch oven or large saucepan and sauté over medium heat for 2 to 3 minutes. Add chicken broth, milk and nutmeg. Heat to boiling, simmer briefly, stirring frequently. Add Parmesan and cook 1 to 2 minutes stirring 2 or 3 times. Season with salt if desired.

Serve immediately with croutons.

Italian Minestrone

*Finely chopped fresh basil elevates this country soup
into the "gourmet class."*

1 cup dried kidney **or**
haricot beans **or**
canned red kidney
beans, drained
¼ pound salt pork **or**
bacon, diced
2 garlic cloves, minced
1 large onion, cut in
fourths or eighths
2 quarts beef stock
2 carrots, finely sliced
4 stalks celery, finely
sliced
½ small head cabbage,
sliced or shredded
4 sprigs chicory, sliced,
optional
4 to 6 tomatoes, thickly
sliced
½ pound green beans,
sliced in large pieces
¾ cup frozen peas
2 cups macaroni
Salt and freshly ground
pepper to taste
4 tablespoons chopped
fresh parsley
2 teaspoons chopped
basil
2 tablespoons olive oil
6 tablespoons freshly
grated Parmesan
cheese

Soak dried beans overnight, drain.
Simmer beans in 1 quart salted water
for 2 hours, drain.

In a thick-bottomed casserole dish or
soup pot, sauté salt pork until brown.
Add garlic and onion and sauté with
pork until golden in color. Add beef
stock, carrots and celery and simmer
gently. Add all remaining vegetables,
except peas, to the stock, heat to
boiling, cover and reduce heat until the
soup barely simmers. Continue
simmering for 1½ hours or longer. The
taste of the vegetables is enhanced in
the cooking.

Twenty minutes before serving, add
peas and macaroni and heat to boiling.
Simmer until macaroni is tender. If
soup is too thick, thin with water. Add
salt and pepper to taste.

Just before serving, stir in fresh
parsley, basil and olive oil. Serve hot,
sprinkled with Parmesan cheese.

*If flour is added to a soup to thicken it should cook for
at least 40 minutes.*

Minestrone Soup in a Dutch Oven

8-10 servings

This is best when made ahead. Serve with Swiss cheese fondue and French bread.

½ cup chopped onion
½ cup chopped celery
1 garlic clove, minced
2 tablespoons olive oil
1 10-ounce can beef
   bouillon, undiluted
1 cup chopped cabbage
1 1-pound can kidney
   beans, drained
2 8-ounce cans tomato
   sauce
2½ quarts water
1½ teaspoons crushed
   rosemary
¾ cup salad macaroni
1 10-ounce package
   frozen peas and
   carrots

In a Dutch oven, brown onion, celery and garlic in oil. Add bouillon, cabbage, kidney beans, tomato sauce, water and rosemary. Stir well and simmer for 1 hour. Add macaroni and peas and carrots. Cook for 10 minutes longer.

Oktoberfest Soup

4-6 servings

2 pounds bratwurst
1 24-ounce can whole
   tomatoes, undrained
4 medium potatoes,
   peeled and diced
2 cups sliced carrots
1½ cups chopped celery
8 cups beef stock
2 garlic cloves, minced
2 teaspoons brown sugar
4 cups shredded cabbage
Salt and pepper
Parmesan cheese, grated

In a saucepan, gently parboil bratwurst about 7 minutes. Drain and cut into ¼-inch slices. Brown in skillet. Drain.

In a soup pot, combine tomatoes, potatoes, carrots, celery, beef stock, garlic and brown sugar. Add bratwurst. Heat to boiling, cover and reduce heat to a gentle simmer for 1 hour. Stir occasionally. Add cabbage and simmer 10 minutes longer. Salt and pepper to taste.

Serve topped with Parmesan cheese.

Hearty Ham and
Broccoli Soup

6-8 servings

1¾ cup minced onion
1 garlic clove, minced
2 tablespoons olive **or**
vegetable oil
2 tablespoons butter
½ pound cooked ham,
minced
2 quarts beef stock **or**
2 10-ounce cans broth
+ water to equal
2 quarts
2 pounds broccoli,
flowerets and stems
separated and chopped
6 ounces spaghetti,
broken into 2-inch
pieces
Salt and pepper
French bread, sliced
Parmesan cheese, grated

In a heavy kettle, sauté onions and garlic in oil and butter until soft and light brown, about 15 minutes. Add ham and cook covered another 5 to 10 minutes. Stir in beef stock, heat to boiling, reduce heat and simmer, covered, 25 minutes.

Add broccoli stems and simmer covered 5 minutes. Add broccoli flowerets and spaghetti, season with salt and pepper and simmer uncovered 15 minutes, until spaghetti is tender.

Pour soup into individual bowls and float a piece of French bread which has been buttered and fried or broiled. Sprinkle with Parmesan cheese.

Stir in a chunk of butter just before serving to add a glossy finish to a hot puréed soup.

If puréeing is needed, remove the soup from the stove and allow it to cool slightly before you purée. Any herbs or spices should be added just before puréeing to assure fresh flavor.

Soup Unlimited

8-10 servings

This is an easy, convenient recipe that keeps well. Most of the ingredients are already in your cupboard.

1 pound ground beef
1 package dry onion soup
  mix
1 16-ounce can stewed
  tomatoes
1 6-ounce can tomato
  paste
1 8-ounce can tomato
  sauce
1 teaspoon sugar
1 10-ounce package
  frozen mixed
  vegetables
2½ to 3 cups water
1 bay leaf
3 tablespoons chopped
  parsley
½ teaspoon oregano
Seasoned salt and
  ground pepper to taste

In a Dutch oven, brown ground beef and drain. Add remaining ingredients and simmer 20 minutes, until ready to serve.

Peasant-Style Beef Soup 　　10-12 servings

2¼ pounds beef chuck
　cross rib pot roast
8 cups water
1 tablespoon lemon juice
2 teaspoons salt
½ teaspoon pepper
1 teaspoon crumbled bay
　leaf
½ teaspoon ground
　allspice
2 beef bouillon cubes
⅔ cup chopped onion
6 medium potatoes,
　peeled and cubed
　(approximately 4 cups)
2 cups celery, including
　leaves, cut in ½-inch
　slices
2 cups carrots, cut in
　¼-inch slices
⅔ cup cut-up cauliflower
1　16-ounce can stewed
　tomatoes
1　16-ounce can whole
　tomatoes
½ cup sliced fresh
　mushrooms **or**
　1 4-ounce can
　mushrooms
1 cup frozen peas **or** 1
　cup chopped fresh
　spinach

Trim all fat from roast. Cut into 1½-inch cubes. Discard bone.

In a large Dutch oven, brown meat. Stir in water, lemon juice, salt, pepper, bay leaf, allspice, bouillon cubes and onion. Heat to boiling, reduce heat. Cover and simmer 2 hours. Stir in remaining ingredients. Cover and cook until meat is tender, 1 to 1½ hours. Serve in heated bowls.

Add two or three eggshells to your soup stock, simmer for 10 minutes. The shells will help clarify the broth.

73

Mulligatawny Soup

10-12 servings

1 medium onion, sliced
¼ cup butter
⅓ cup flour
3 carrots, diced
2 celery stalks, diced
1 green pepper, diced
1 apple, peeled, cored
  and diced
2 cups diced cooked
  chicken **or** turkey
1 teaspoon curry powder
⅛ teaspoon mace,
  optional
2 whole cloves
1 sprig parsley, minced
2 10-ounce cans chicken
  consommé, undiluted
1 cup cooked **or** fresh
  tomatoes, diced
Salt and pepper to taste

In a soup kettle, sauté onions in butter;
stir in flour and allow to thicken. Add
carrots, celery, green pepper, apple
and chicken. Gradually stir in
remaining ingredients. Simmer,
covered, 45 minutes to 1 hour.

Oo Soup

8 servings

10 cups canned chicken
  broth, undiluted
½ cup julienned raw pork
1 10-ounce package
  frozen peas
½ cup julienned country
  ham
½ cup julienned bamboo
  shoots
12 ounces tofu **or** bean
  curd, julienned

In a large soup kettle, heat broth, add
pork and peas and cook over low
simmering heat until peas are tender,
about 10 minutes. Add ham, bamboo
shoots, tofu, black mushrooms, button
mushrooms, both soy sauces and
pepper. Simmer for 2 minutes.

Mix cornstarch with 1 tablespoon
water and a little hot broth. Add slowly
to soup and heat to boiling. Remove
from heat.

Oo Soup *(Continued)*

4 dried black oriental
    mushrooms, soaked in
    warm water for
    25 minutes, drained
    and diced
12 button mushrooms,
    cut in half
1 teaspoon dark soy
    sauce (available at
    oriental markets)
2 teaspoons light soy
    sauce (regular type)
¼ teaspoon pepper
1 tablespoon cornstarch
2 large eggs
2 tablespoons milk

When ready to serve, reheat. Beat eggs and milk together. Remove soup from heat and slowly pour in egg mixture, stirring constantly to form tiny "threads" as the egg cooks. Serve at once.

NOTE: Julienne slices should be approximately the size of matchsticks.

Garden Salad Soup   4-6 servings

2 tablespoons butter
1 cup thinly sliced
    unpeeled potatoes
1 cup chopped green
    onions
2 13-ounce cans chicken
    broth, undiluted
1 large cucumber, diced
2 cups shredded lettuce
    or fresh spinach,
    washed and well
    drained
1 teaspoon dill weed
1 teaspoon salt
Dash of pepper
1 8-ounce carton plain
    yogurt
Thinly sliced radishes for
    garnish

In a large pot, sauté potatoes and onions in butter for 5 minutes. Add remaining ingredients, **except** yogurt, and simmer for 15 minutes. Remove from heat and add yogurt.

Place ⅓ to ½ of the mixture in a blender and blend well. Repeat until all is blended. Serve hot or cold, garnished with radishes.

Tomato Bisque

8-10 servings

¼ pound bacon
4 large garlic cloves, minced
1½ onions, finely chopped
6 celery stalks, finely chopped
1 bay leaf
1 teaspoon thyme
1 28-ounce can tomatoes, diced (do not drain)
1 6-ounce can tomato paste
2 tablespoons butter
3 tablespoons flour
2 cups heavy cream
2 cups light cream
½ onion, finely chopped
1 bay leaf
2 whole cloves
Salt and freshly ground pepper

In a Dutch oven, cook bacon until fat is rendered. Remove meat and reserve for another use. Add garlic to fat and sauté until lightly browned. Add the **1½ onions,** celery, bay leaf, and thyme and sauté until onion is transparent.

Add tomatoes with liquid and tomato paste. Heat to boiling, stirring occasionally. Reduce heat, cover and simmer for 30 minutes.

Make a white sauce by heating butter in a large saucepan. Stir in flour and heat to boiling, stirring constantly. Remove from heat and slowly add heavy and light creams.

Add the **½ onion,** bay leaf and cloves. Place over medium heat and cook uncovered for 45 minutes, stirring occasionally.

Strain mixture through a fine strainer into the tomato mixture. Add salt and pepper to taste. Cover and simmer, stirring occasionally, about 15 minutes.

A chilled purée should be enriched or diluted with cream or sour cream.

Winter squash shells make a very pretty and interesting soup tureen or bowl.

Bell Pepper Soup   6 servings

2 medium onions, cut into
  chunks
6 tablespoons butter
6 cups fresh bell pepper,
  cut into chunks
3 tablespoons flour
2 cups chicken broth
2 cups light cream
1 teaspoon white pepper
1½ teaspoons salt
½ teaspoon thyme
Dill weed

In a large saucepan, sauté onion in butter until soft. Do not brown. Add peppers and sauté until soft. Sprinkle with flour and stir constantly for 1 minute. Add broth. Cover and simmer until vegetables are just tender.

Place ½ of the mixture in a blender and blend until smooth. Repeat with the other half. Return to the saucepan and add cream and seasonings. Heat and stir. Consistency should be that of a thin white sauce. Ladle into bowls and garnish with dill weed.

Cream of Broccoli and Leek Soup   6-8 servings

1½ pounds fresh or
  3 10-ounce packages
  frozen broccoli
¾ pound leeks
½ cup butter
8 cups chicken broth
1 large potato, peeled
  and cubed
Salt and white pepper to
  taste
1 cup heavy cream

Trim and coarsely chop broccoli, separating stems and flowerets. Wash leeks well and trim off green tops. Chop.

In a large soup pot, sauté broccoli stems and leeks in butter for 3 minutes. Add broccoli flowerets and sauté 3 minutes longer. Add chicken broth and potato. Season with salt and pepper. Heat to boiling and simmer 20 minutes or until vegetables are tender. Purée mixture in a blender or food processor.

Add cream and heat just to boiling, but DO NOT BOIL.

77

Leek Soup

8 servings

3 tablespoons unsalted
  butter
5 cups sliced leeks
  (2 large bunches)
1 onion, chopped
2 celery stalks, sliced
6 cups chicken stock
1 bay leaf
1 tablespoon chopped
  fresh parsley
2 teaspoons salt
2 teaspoons thyme
½ teaspoon pepper
2 pounds fresh spinach
1 cup heavy cream
Brie cheese, optional

In a large Dutch oven, melt butter over medium heat. Add leeks, onion and celery and cook about 10 minutes or until vegetables are soft. Add remaining ingredients, **except** cream and cheese. Heat to boiling, reduce heat, cover and simmer 20 minutes. Remove bay leaf.

Pour soup, about 3 cups at a time, into a blender and blend at high speed until puréed. Return soup to Dutch oven. Add cream and heat through. Adjust seasonings. Top with slices of Brie cheese, if desired.

Authentic French Onion Soup

6 servings

⅓ cup butter
5 onions, thinly sliced
2 tablespoons flour
7 cups beef stock **or**
  3 10-ounce cans beef
  consommé and 2 cans
  water
½ teaspoon pepper
6 slices toasted French
  bread
6 thin slices Gruyère
  cheese
4 tablespoons grated
  Gruyère cheese

In a heavy saucepan, melt butter. Add onions and sauté over very low heat until tender. Add flour and mix until smooth. Add stock gradually, stirring constantly. Add pepper, cover and cook over low heat 30 minutes. (Cool and freeze at this point if desired.)

To serve, place cheese **slices** on bread on bottoms of individual soup bowls. Pour hot soup into bowls. Place under broiler 1 minute. Sprinkle with **grated** cheese and serve.

Chilled Green Bean Bisque   4-6 servings

Good served hot or cold.

2 tablespoons butter
1 garlic clove, minced
1 medium onion, chopped
1 pound (4 heaping cups) fresh green beans, cut in 1-inch pieces
2 14-ounce cans chicken broth
¼ teaspoon savory leaves
¼ teaspoon dried dillweed
Salt and pepper
Sour cream
⅓ cup slivered almonds, toasted

In a Dutch oven, melt butter over medium heat. Add garlic and onion and sauté until limp. Stir in beans and broth. Cover and simmer 10 minutes until beans are just tender.

Turn mixture into a blender or food processor and purée. Season with savory, dill, salt and pepper. Cover and chill well.

To serve, pour into chilled mugs or bowls. Top each with a dollop of sour cream and a sprinkle of almonds.

Cream of Zucchini Soup   4 servings

Good served hot or cold.

1 carrot, thinly sliced
1 celery stalk, thinly sliced
1 medium onion, thinly sliced
1 14-ounce can chicken stock, undiluted
3 medium zucchini, unpeeled and thinly sliced
Salt and pepper to taste
½ pint heavy cream
Garlic croutons or sour cream

In a large pot, place carrot, celery, onion and chicken stock. Cover and simmer for 15 minutes.

Add zucchini and continue cooking for 20 minutes or until vegetables are tender. Place in a blender and purée. Season with salt and pepper. Soup may be frozen at this point.

To serve HOT, add cream to the heated soup and continue to heat until hot, but DO NOT BOIL. Top with garlic croutons.

To serve COLD, add cream to cooled soup and mix well. Top with a dollop of sour cream.

79

Creamy Celery-Spinach Soup   6 servings

2 cups chopped celery
1 cup chopped onion
1 10-ounce package
   frozen spinach
1 10-ounce can chicken
   broth, undiluted
1 cup cottage cheese
2 cups milk
½ teaspoon salt
¼ teaspoon pepper
½ teaspoon Beau Monde
   seasoning
⅛ teaspoon nutmeg
Sour cream

In a 3-quart saucepan, combine celery, onion, spinach and chicken broth. Heat to boiling, cover, reduce heat and simmer 10 minutes until vegetables are tender. In blender or food processor, place soup mixture and cottage cheese. Cover and blend until smooth.

Return mixture to saucepan. Stir in milk and seasonings. Simmer over low heat for 15 minutes, stirring occasionally. Cover and chill at least 4 hours.

To serve, pour into chilled mugs or bowls. Top each with a dollop of sour cream.

Cold Cucumber and Spinach Soup   6 servings

14 large green onions,
   chopped
3 tablespoons butter
4 cups diced cucumbers
3 cups canned chicken
   broth, undiluted
1⅓ cups frozen chopped
   spinach (thawed) or
   fresh
¾ cup sliced peeled
   potatoes
½ teaspoon salt
½ teaspoon pepper
½ teaspoon lemon juice
1 cup light cream

In a large pot, sauté green onions in butter until soft. Add cucumbers, broth, spinach, potatoes, seasonings and lemon juice. Cook over medium heat until potatoes are tender.

Purée entire mixture in a blender. Stir in cream until well mixed and chill for several hours.

Herb-Zucchini Soup

4-6 servings

This recipe lends itself to many variations. In the summertime it may be served cold, with a slice of lemon or a dollop of sour cream. In the wintertime pieces of cooked sausage may be added.

6 zucchini, cut into 1-inch cubes
Salt
2 tablespoons olive oil
2 tablespoons sweet butter
2 onions, minced
1 garlic clove, minced
5 cups chicken broth
1 teaspoon oregano
1 teaspoon chopped fresh parsley
2 teaspoons basil
2 teaspoons chives
1 to 2 teaspoons lemon juice
Ground pepper

Place zucchini on paper towels. Sprinkle with salt and let drain.

In a large pot, heat oil and butter. Add onion and garlic, cook over low heat for 5 minutes. DO NOT BROWN.

Pat zucchini dry with paper towels. Add to onion mixture and cook 7 minutes or until tender. Add chicken broth and simmer 15 minutes or until soft. Turn off heat and allow to cool.

Place mixture in a blender and purée. Add herbs, lemon juice and pepper. Let stand. Reheat when ready to serve.

Fish-Potato Stew

4-6 servings

2 1-pound cans stewed
   tomatoes
1 bay leaf
1 garlic clove, minced
1 teaspoon basil
1 teaspoon thyme
2 tablespoons chopped
   fresh parsley
½ teaspoon crushed red
   pepper flakes
Peel from 1 orange, cut
   in 1 long strip
4 medium potatoes, cut
   in chunks
4 carrots, thinly sliced
1 pound fresh fish filets
   (cod, snapper, halibut),
   cut in 2-inch chunks
1 10-inch package
   frozen peas
1 cup freshly grated
   Parmesan cheese

In a kettle, combine tomatoes, bay leaf, garlic, basil, thyme, parsley, red pepper flakes and orange peel. Add potatoes and carrots, cover and bring to boil over medium heat. Reduce heat and simmer slowly 40 to 45 minutes, stirring occasionally until potatoes and carrots are fork tender.

Add fish and peas. Stir gently and cover. Simmer 5 to 10 minutes. Remove bay leaf and orange peel.

Ladle into shallow soup bowls. Pass Parmesan separately.

Beef Stew Idaho Style

6 servings

2½ pounds stew meat
6 large carrots
3 celery stalks
3 medium onions
3 large tomatoes
4 large potatoes
1 15-ounce can tomato
   sauce
1 10-ounce can beef
   consommé, undiluted
1½ teaspoons salt
1½ teaspoons sugar
3 tablespoons tapioca
Beef stew seasoning

Cut up meat, carrots, celery, onions, tomatoes and potatoes into stew size. Place all ingredients, **except** beef stew seasoning, into a large soup pot with a tight lid. Stir well and season to taste with beef stew seasoning. Bake at 250° for 5 hours.

Basque Stew

10 large servings

3 cups dried **or**
  3 16-ounce cans
  garbanzo beans
1 large onion
4 celery stalks
4 carrots
5 medium potatoes
4 chicken bouillon cubes
2 4-ounce jars
  pimientoes
8 chorizos, cut up
Salt and pepper to taste

In a large soup pot, cover dried garbanzo beans with water and cook until tender, about ½ hour. Add more water if needed.

Cut all vegetables into chunky pieces. Add vegetables to beans and add remaining ingredients. Add additional water if needed. Cook until vegetables are tender.

Kneadery Chili

8-10 servings

Recipe of Chefs Chris Hudgens and Linda Spearing, The Kneadery, Ketchum.

2 pounds ground beef
1 small onion, minced
1 green pepper, minced
3 16-ounce cans kidney
  beans, drained
1 24-ounce can whole
  tomatoes
1 16-ounce can tomato
  sauce
2 teaspoons parsley
  flakes
½ teaspoon granulated
  garlic
⅓ cup chili powder
2 tablespoons ground
  cumin
¼ cup chopped green
  chiles
¼ cup Salsa Victoria
Grated cheese
Tortilla chips

Brown ground beef. Add onion and green pepper. Sauté slightly. Add remaining ingredients and mix well. Season to taste. Simmer for 30 minutes. Top with grated cheese and tortilla chips.

World Famous
Chili con Carne

12-16 servings

8 tablespoons bacon
  drippings
4 pounds ground round
2 pounds ground pork
4 garlic cloves, minced
2 large onions, finely
  diced
6 tablespoons chili
  powder
2 tablespoons flour
2 28-ounce cans
  tomatoes
3 bay leaves
2 teaspoons oregano
2 teaspoons salt
4 teaspoons cumin seed
1 teaspoon coriander
½ ounce bittersweet **or**
  semisweet chocolate

In a large skillet over low heat, brown ground round, ground pork, garlic and onions in bacon drippings. When meat is browned and onions are soft, add chili powder which has been blended with the flour.

Press tomatoes through a fine sieve and add to meat mixture. Add remaining ingredients and mix well. For a thinner chili, add water or tomato juice. Simmer.

Serve garnished with chopped ripe olives.

NOTE: A separate pot of pinto beans may be served on the side so each person has a choice, with or without beans.

Sandwiches are fun served in a variety of ways . . . on large breadboards, shallow baskets lined with gingham or napkins coordinating your party theme, heavy pottery platters, or make a giant loaf of bread (preferably round), scoop out the inside and place the sandwiches inside.

Pantry Chili

6-8 servings

Children especially love this chili!

1 pound ground beef
1 teaspoon salt
Dash pepper
½ medium onion, diced
½ green pepper, diced
1 10-ounce can tomato
   soup, undiluted
1 16-ounce can red
   kidney beans
1 16-ounce can pinto
   beans
1 16-ounce can chili
   beans
1 quart tomatoes
1 tablespoon cumin
1 tablespoon chili
   powder **or** to taste

In a Dutch oven, brown ground beef. Season with salt and pepper. Add onion and green pepper and sauté a few minutes.

Add remaining ingredients, bring to a moderate heat, then simmer on low for 30 minutes or longer to combine flavors.

Hot Crab Sandwiches

2 servings

Men love these sandwiches.

4 ounces fresh crab meat
2 tablespoons chopped
   green pepper
1½ teaspoons prepared
   mustard
1½ teaspoons grated
   onion
¼ teaspoon
   Worcestershire sauce
¼ cup mayonnaise
1 hamburger bun, split
2 thin tomato slices
¼ cup finely grated
   American cheese

Combine crab, green pepper, mustard, onion, Worcestershire sauce and **half** of the mayonnaise. Mix well.

Pile mixture onto bun halves. Top each with a tomato slice.

Blend cheese with the remaining mayonnaise. Spread on tomato slices. Broil 4 inches from heat until topping puffs and browns.

85

Ham Sandwiches in Foil   18 servings

*These sandwiches are great for backyard parties, buffets
or tailgate parties before a football game.*

½ cup butter **or**
   margarine, softened
1 tablespoon prepared
   mustard
1 tablespoon dill seed
1 tablespoon chopped
   onion
18 Parkerhouse-style
   rolls
Ham, thinly sliced
Swiss cheese, thinly
   sliced

Combine butter, mustard, dill seed and
onion in a small bowl. Mix well.

Slice rolls in half and spread mixture on
bottom half. Top with slices of ham and
Swiss cheese and top half of roll.

Wrap sandwiches in aluminum foil.
Bake at 300° for 20 minutes.

Mini-Pizza Sandwiches   8 servings

½ pound sliced
   pepperoni
1 cup sliced mushrooms
1 cup sliced zucchini
¼ cup chopped onion
1 medium garlic clove,
   minced
¼ teaspoon oregano
   leaves, crushed
1 tablespoon olive oil
1 12-ounce can
   vegetable cocktail juice
1 tablespoon cornstarch
¼ cup sliced pitted ripe
   olives
2 tablespoons grated
   Parmesan cheese
4 English muffins, split
   and toasted
Grated Mozzarella
   cheese

In a large skillet, brown pepperoni and
mushrooms. Cook zucchini and onion
with garlic and oregano in olive oil until
tender. Add to pepperoni and
mushrooms.

In a small bowl, mix juice and
cornstarch. Gradually stir into
pepperoni mixture. Cook, stirring until
thickened. Add olives and Parmesan.

Arrange English muffins on a baking
sheet. Spoon about ⅓ cup pepperoni
mixture onto each muffin. Sprinkle with
Mozzarella. Broil 5 inches from heat
until cheese melts.

Deluxe Chicken Salad Sandwich

6 servings

Excellent as an hors d'oeuvre on toast rounds.

4 hard boiled eggs, chopped
1 6-ounce can chunk chicken **or** 1½ cups chopped cooked chicken
½ cup chopped cucumber
½ cup mayonnaise
⅓ cup diced Cheddar cheese
⅓ cup chopped fresh spinach
¼ cup chopped green onions
3 tablespoons chopped pimiento-stuffed olives
¼ teaspoon dill weed, crushed
¼ teaspoon seasoned salt
6 slices whole wheat bread, toasted

In a bowl, combine all ingredients **except** toast. Chill. Spread about ½ cup of the mixture on each slice of toast.

NOTE: Also good served in pocket bread.

Sandwiches look and taste marvelous – reviving the appetite while making it easy on the cook. Accompany with chilled beverages, a variety of salads and a finger type dessert and you can rest assured the party will take care of itself.

87

Stuffed Hard Rolls

24 rolls

2 green peppers
4 to 5 green onions
1 pint stuffed green olives
1 pound sharp Cheddar
cheese
½ cup olive oil
1 8-ounce can hot taco
sauce
24 hard rolls

Grind green peppers, green onions, olives and cheese. Combine all ingredients, **except** rolls, and mix well.

Cut off tops of rolls and scoop out center. Fill with mixture. Replace tops. Place rolls on a baking sheet. Bake at 350° for 30 minutes. Serve hot.

French Bread Topping

6-8 servings

½ cup mayonnaise
½ cup grated Parmesan
cheese
½ teaspoon chopped
parsley
¼ cup chopped green
onions
1 tablespoon horseradish
Sourdough French bread,
sliced
Paprika

In a medium bowl, combine mayonnaise, Parmesan cheese, parsley, green onions and horseradish. Spread generously on bread slices and sprinkle with paprika. Place under broiler until cheese bubbles and is lightly browned.

Good bread is the foundation for a great sandwich. Fresh, homemade bread is ideal but not always available. When choosing a bread, make sure it complements the filling.

Bound to Please: The Basque Tradition

They came to Idaho from Spain and France, leaving their
homelands along the Pyrenees Mountains. The Basques brought
with them their own language, Eskuara, and a vigorous commit-
ment to their new country.

Today Idaho boasts the largest Basque population outside of
Spain. Successful in business, public service, education, and the arts,
the Basques – from the famous Oinkari Basque Dancers to dark-
eyed children watching the yearly St. Ignatius Feast Day procession
– have added rich threads to the state's cultural fabric.

Yeast Breads

Rolls

Quick Breads

Muffins

Pancakes & Crêpes

Special

Italian Breadsticks

15-20 breadsticks

3 to 3½ cups flour
1 tablespoon sugar
1 teaspoon salt
2 packages dry yeast
¼ cup olive oil **or** salad oil
1¼ cups hot water
1 egg white, beaten with
   1 tablespoon water
Sesame or poppy seeds

Using a food processor, place **1 cup** of the flour, the sugar, salt and yeast in the bowl. Process on high for 2 seconds to mix. Add oil and mix 2 seconds more. Gradually add water, blending constantly. Add the remaining flour, ½ cup at a time, blending well. Use the last ½ cup flour only if the dough seems too soft.

Turn dough out onto a well-floured board and work into a smooth ball. Cut into 15 to 20 equal pieces. Roll each piece into a rope that will fit on the width of a cookie sheet. Arrange about 1 inch apart on greased cookie sheets. Cover and set in a warm place to rise until puffy, about 15 minutes.

With a pastry brush, paint each stick with egg white mixture. Sprinkle lightly with sesame seeds, if desired.

Bake at 300° for 25 to 30 minutes or until lightly browned. Serve warm or cool.

Store in airtight bags or freeze for longer storage.

Wheat flour is most often used in bread baking. It contains a substance called gluten, which is an elastic protein that helps achieve the desired light texture.

Gourmet Parisian Bread   4 baguettes

2 tablespoons sugar
1 tablespoon salt
2½ cups warm water
1 package dry yeast **or**
  1 yeast cake
7-8 cups flour
1 egg white
Shortening

In a large bowl, combine sugar, salt, warm water (100°-120° for dry yeast, 80°-85° for yeast cake), and yeast (crumble yeast cake). Stir until dissolved.

Add **5 cups** of the flour and stir until mixed. Add **1 cup** of the flour. Mix until dough is sticky.

On a well-floured board, knead dough, adding flour as needed to prevent stickiness, about 1 more cup. Knead for about 10 minutes.

Grease the sides of a large container in which the dough can double. Place in container and turn to coat dough with shortening. Put in a warm place and allow to rise until doubled, about 1½ hours. Punch down 5 or 6 times.

Rub 4 standard baguette pans well with shortening, being sure to cover all indentations. Divide dough into 4 equal parts. Roll each piece into a rope of uniform size and about 1 inch shorter than pan at each end (about 17 inches). Place in greased pan.

With a sharp knife, slash each loaf 4 to 5 times diagonally, about ⅜-inch deep. Beat egg white with a fork until foamy. Using a pastry brush, brush tops of loaves with egg white. Return loaves to a warm place and let rise until they fill the pans and the center stands well above the edge.

Place pans in a preheated 450° oven and bake for 15 minutes. Reduce oven to 350° and continue baking for 15 to

Gourmet Parisian Bread *(Continued)*

20 minutes. If bread appears to be browning too fast, rotate loaves, putting underside on top.

Remove from pans immediately. Cool on racks or across pans so air can circulate around loaves.

NOTE: Good French bread goes stale within 2 to 3 hours. If bread will not be eaten within this time, it should be wrapped and frozen.

Pain de Ménage
2 loaves

Thick but tasty!

1 package dry yeast
2 cups warm water
1 tablespoon sugar
2 teaspoons salt
5 cups flour
Cornmeal
Butter **or** egg white

In a large bowl, dissolve yeast in warm water. Add sugar and salt. Stir until dissolved. Add flour until dough will absorb no more. Knead about 4 minutes on a floured board, until elastic and smooth.

Place in a large greased bowl, cover with a damp cloth and let rise until doubled, about 1 hour. Divide dough in half. Shape into 2 long, thin loaves. Place far apart on a buttered cookie sheet which has been generously dusted with cornmeal. Allow loaves to rise in a warm place until double.

Brush tops of loaves with melted butter and place in a preheated 450° oven for 5 minutes. Reduce oven temperature to 375° and bake for an additional 35 minutes.

To make a **crusty** crust, put a large, shallow pan of water in bottom of oven during the baking period.

Food Processor French Bread   1 loaf

A very good and very easy French bread.

Cornmeal
1 package dry yeast
1 cup warm water
(105°-115°)
2½ cups flour
½ cup CAKE flour
1½ teaspoons salt
1 egg

Oil a cookie sheet and sprinkle with cornmeal.

Dissolve yeast in warm water and let stand until foamy, about 10 minutes.

Put flours and **1 teaspoon** of the salt in the food processor work bowl fitted with the steel knife. With the machine running, add yeast mixture in a thin stream through the feed tube. Mix about 40 to 50 seconds or until dough is smooth and elastic.

Remove from work bowl and place in a greased mixing bowl. Turn dough in bowl to coat entire surface. Cover with a damp towel and let rise in a warm place until doubled, about 1 hour. Punch down.

Turn out onto a heavily floured board, work in enough flour to make dough easy to handle and not sticky. Roll dough into a rectangle and beginning with the long side, roll dough into a tight loaf. Pinch edge well to seal and place seam side down on prepared cookie sheet. Cover again with a damp towel and let rise until doubled, about 45 minutes.

Slash on the diagonal with a sharp knife. Beat egg lightly with remaining salt. Brush over top of loaf. Bake at 425° for 30 to 35 minutes. Tapping on the bottom of loaf should make a hollow sound.

Gougère (Swiss Cheese Bread)

6-8 servings

½ cup butter
1 cup water
½ teaspoon salt
1 cup flour
4 eggs
1 cup grated Swiss
cheese

In a saucepan, heat butter and water until boiling. Lower heat and add salt and flour.

Cook, stirring constantly, until mixture leaves the sides of pan and forms a ball. Remove from heat. Beat in eggs, 1 at a time, with an electric mixer. Stir in cheese.

On a greased baking sheet, form a ring of dough 9 inches in diameter and 2 inches wide, shaping with a spatula.

Bake at 375° for 45 minutes or until puffed and brown, with no beads of moisture showing on the surface.

Swedish Rye Bread

4 loaves

2 packages dry yeast
1 tablespoon sugar
¾ cup warm water
¼ teaspoon baking soda
4 cups scalded milk
⅓ cup butter **or**
margarine
1 cup molasses
½ cup brown sugar
1 tablespoon salt
3 cups rye flour
9 cups white flour

Dissolve yeast and sugar in **½ cup** warm water. Dissolve baking soda in remaining warm water.

In a large bowl, combine yeast mixture and baking soda mixture with remaining ingredients in order given. Mix well. Cover and let rise until doubled. Punch down, knead and let rise again. Punch down and knead well.

Shape into 4 loaves and place into 9x5-inch greased pans. Let rise until doubled. Bake at 350° for 30 minutes. Reduce temperature to 225° and continue baking for 30 minutes. Remove from oven and brush tops with melted butter.

Talamee (Syrian Bread) — 15 flat rounds

This bread takes a long time to prepare, but it is very good and unusual.

1 package dry yeast
About 5 cups lukewarm
　　water
¼ cup butter
1 teaspoon salt
1 tablespoon oil
1 tablespoon sugar
5 pounds flour
½ cup butter, softened

Dissolve yeast in **1 cup** of the lukewarm water. Add butter to soften.

In a VERY LARGE BOWL (or plastic dishpan), add salt, oil and sugar to flour, by making a small indentation in center of flour. Add yeast mixture. Add **2 cups** of the water to flour mixture. Add more water if needed.

Knead dough from edge to center, moving bowl around as you knead. Knead dough 20 to 30 minutes until it is smooth to the touch, adding water if needed.

Flip dough over in bowl, cover with a towel or large piece of plastic. On top of plastic, place a heavy blanket. Set in a warm place for 1½ to 2 hours until dough rises.

Cut off pieces of dough the size of grapefruit and roll between cupped hands until smooth. Place on floured bed sheets. Cover with another bed sheet, the plastic and the heavy blanket. Leave for 1 hour until dough is about doubled in size. Uncover and flatten slightly with fingertips to ¼-inch thick. Cover again and let rise another 45 minutes to 1 hour. Preheat oven to 450°.

Uncover and flatten dough again with fingertips. Pierce dough with fork several times to prevent pockets from forming. Place loaves on greased

Talamee (Syrian Bread) *(Continued)*

cookie sheets (only 2 will fit on a standard sized sheet). Bake until brown, about 15 minutes. Check frequently.

Brush tops with butter, turn and brush again. Cover with a towel to cool.

Oatmeal-Beer Bread
1 loaf

2 cups flour
1 cup rolled oats
3 tablespoons baking powder
1 tablespoon salt
½ cup sugar
½ cup water
1 12-ounce can regular beer
Melted butter for top

Combine all ingredients and place batter in a well-greased and well-floured 9x5-inch loaf pan. Bake at 350° for 30 minutes. Brush top of loaf generously with melted butter and bake for an additional 10 minutes. Brush top with butter again, return bread to oven and bake another 20 to 30 minutes or until done. Remove from oven and brush with butter once more.

Beer Bread
1 loaf

3 cups self-rising flour
2 tablespoons sugar
1 12-ounce can beer, at room temperature
7 tablespoons unsalted butter, melted

In a large bowl, combine flour, sugar and beer. Mix thoroughly.

Pour into a 9x5-inch loaf pan or a 1½ to 2 quart casserole. Spoon **4 tablespoons** of the melted butter evenly over the top. Bake at 350° for 20 minutes.

Brush top with remaining butter. Continue baking until top is golden and tester inserted in center comes out clean, about 25 minutes.

Cracked Wheat Bread
4 loaves

2 cups milk, scalded
1½ to 2 tablespoons salt
1 tablespoon sugar
4 tablespoons corn oil
½ cup molasses
1 cup cracked wheat
3 cups lukewarm water
2 packages dry yeast
12 to 14 cups unsifted
flour

In a very large bowl, combine scalded milk with salt, sugar, oil, molasses and cracked wheat. Set aside to cool.

Combine yeast and **1 cup** of the lukewarm water. Dissolve and set aside.

To the milk mixture, add remaining warm water. Add **4 cups** flour and stir until a good paste is produced. Stir vigorously with a heavy spoon. Add yeast mixture and continue adding flour as needed to make a stiff dough (about 8 to 10 cups).

Knead until smooth and elastic on a floured board. Place in a greased bowl. Cover with a towel that has been rinsed in hot water and wrung out. Set in a warm place to rise until doubled, about 2 hours. Punch down, form into 4 loaves.

Grease 4 9x5x3-inch bread pans with solid shortening. Place dough in pans, allow to rise again until doubled, about 1 hour. Bake at 375° for 40 minutes. Remove from pans immediately, cool on rack.

Water added to bread dough makes crusty breads with good flavor.

Whole Wheat-Potato Bread   2 loaves

3½ cups bread flour
1½ cups mashed potato
  flakes
2½ teaspoons salt
2 packages dry yeast
1½ cups water
1¼ cups milk
¼ cup margarine **or**
  butter
¼ cup honey
2 eggs
2½ to 3½ cups whole
  wheat flour

In a large bowl, combine **1½ cups** of the bread flour, the potato flakes, salt and yeast. Blend well.

In a medium saucepan, heat water, milk, margarine, and honey until very warm (120° to 130°). Add warm liquid and eggs to flour mixture. Blend at low speed until moistened.

Beat 4 minutes at medium speed. By hand, stir in remaining bread flour and **1½** to **2 cups** of the whole wheat flour until dough pulls cleanly away from sides of bowl.

On a floured surface, knead in remaining whole wheat flour until dough is smooth and elastic, about 10 minutes.

Place dough in a greased bowl and cover loosely with plastic wrap and cloth towel. Let rise in a warm place (80° to 85°) until double in size, about 1 hour.

Punch dough down. Divide into 2 parts and shape into balls. Allow to rest on counter, covered with inverted bowl, for 15 minutes. Shape dough into 2 loaves and place in 2 8x4-inch or 9x5-inch loaf pans.

Cover and let rise in a warm place until doubled in size, 30 to 45 minutes. Bake at 375° for 35 to 40 minutes or until deep golden brown and loaves sound hollow when tapped lightly. Immediately remove from pans. If desired, brush with margarine or butter.

Bran Bread
2 loaves

1 package dry yeast
3 cups lukewarm water
½ cup (scant) sugar
1 tablespoon salt
1 cup All Bran
7 to 8 cups flour
1 to 2 tablespoons
    butter, melted

Dissolve yeast in water. Add sugar, salt and cereal. Stir until bran is moistened. Add flour, 1 cup at a time, until a stiff dough is formed. Place dough in a large greased bowl and let rise until doubled.

Knead well and divide into 2 equal pieces. Shape into loaves and put into 2 greased 9x5x3-inch pans. Let rise again until doubled. Bake in a preheated 350° oven for 1 hour. Remove from oven and brush tops with melted butter.

Mexican Cornbread
1 12x12-inch pan or
2 loaves

1 cup butter
1 cup sugar
4 eggs
1 16-ounce can creamed
    corn
1 4-ounce can chopped
    green chiles
½ cup grated Monterey
    Jack cheese
½ cup grated Cheddar
    cheese
1 cup flour
1 cup cornmeal
4 teaspoons baking
    powder
¼ teaspoon salt

In a large bowl, cream butter and sugar. Add eggs, 1 at a time, beating well after each addition. Mix in remaining ingredients and blend well.

Grease and flour 2 standard-size loaf pans or 1 12x12-inch pan. Pour batter into prepared pans and bake at 350° for 1 hour for loaf pans, or at 400° for 30 minutes for square pan. Reduce temperature to 300° and continue baking for 10 to 15 minutes.

Grandmother's Everlasting Dough

6 dozen dough cakes

This dough will keep in the refrigerator for up to 2 weeks.

2 cups milk, scalded
1 cup water
½ cup oil
2 packages dry yeast
2 eggs
1 cup potato flakes **or** leftover mashed potatoes
½ cup sugar
1 teaspoon baking powder
½ teaspoon baking soda
2 teaspoons salt
6 cups flour

In a large bowl, combine milk, water and oil. When mixture has cooled to warm, add yeast and stir until dissolved.

Add eggs and stir until mixture is smooth. Mix in potatoes, sugar, baking powder, soda, salt and flour. Cover and refrigerate for 24 hours.

To make DOUGH CAKES, heat a small amount of oil in a large skillet. Pinch off a 2-inch piece of dough and pull into a circular shape. Fry in hot oil and serve with butter and warm maple syrup.

NOTE: Dough may also be made into clover leaf rolls by filling greased muffin tins about ⅓ full with 3 small balls of dough. Bake at 400° for 12 minutes.

With increasing amounts of sugar and fat, the action of yeast is retarded; more yeast is often needed for rolls than for loaves.

Most rolls require only thorough mixing, with little or no kneading.

Refrigerator Crescent Rolls   3 dozen rolls

1 package dry yeast
½ teaspoon sugar
2 tablespoons warm
  water
1 cup scalded milk **or**
  boiling potato water
½ cup sugar
½ cup butter **or**
  margarine
½ teaspoon salt
2 eggs, beaten
4 cups flour, measured,
  then sifted

Dissolve yeast and **½ teaspoon** sugar in **warm** water. Let stand until soft.

In a large mixing bowl, combine scalded milk or **boiling** potato water, the **½ cup** sugar, butter and salt. Cool. Add yeast mixture. Mix well. Add eggs and mix well.

Stir in **2 cups** flour. Add remaining flour but do not knead. Mixture will be quite thick. Place in a greased bowl and cover with greased waxed paper and a towel. Refrigerate at least 2 hours or overnight.

Divide dough into thirds. Roll each piece into a thin circle. Cut like a pie into 12 triangles. Roll out each triangle slightly and roll up, beginning with wide end. Put on greased cookie sheet and let rise until doubled, about 1 hour. Bake at 400° for about 10 minutes. WATCH CAREFULLY.

Rolls will be crusty if they are placed 1 inch apart when baking.

Dough for rolls is softer than for plain bread, as soft as can be handled without sticking to hands or board. Softer dough makes lighter and more tender rolls.

Dinner Rolls

1-2 dozen rolls

1 cup milk, scalded
2 tablespoons sugar
1 teaspoon salt
2 tablespoons melted
  shortening
3 to 4 cups sifted flour
1 yeast cake **or**
  1 package dry yeast,
  dissolved in ¼ cup
  warm water
2 eggs, beaten

To scalded milk, add sugar, salt and shortening. Cool to lukewarm. Add 1½ to **2 cups** of the flour. Add dissolved yeast and beat until smooth. Add eggs and remaining flour, a small amount at a time until dough is moderately firm. Knead lightly, using as little flour as possible.

Place dough in a well-greased bowl. Cover and place in a warm spot and allow to rise until doubled, about 1 to 2 hours.

Shape into rolls. Place in well-greased muffin tins. Cover again and allow to rise until double, about 40 minutes. Brush tops with melted butter. Bake at 450° for 10 minutes or until brown.

Refrigerator Potato Rolls

3 dozen rolls

1 package dry yeast
1 cup lukewarm water
⅞ cup shortening
1 heaping tablespoon
  sugar
1 cup hot mashed
  potatoes
1 cup cold water
1 heaping teaspoon salt
6 cups flour
Melted butter

Dissolve yeast in water. Add shortening, sugar and potatoes to yeast mixture; stir until mixed and let stand 2 hours.

Add cold water, salt and flour. Mix well. Cover and refrigerate until ready to use. Take out amount wanted, knead for 1 minute.

Fill each greased muffin tin about ⅓ full with 3 small balls of dough. Let rise 2½ to 3 hours until rolls are of desired size. Brush with melted butter. (Sprinkle with poppy seeds or sesame seeds if desired.) Bake at 400° for 18 minutes, or until golden.

101

Whole Wheat Sesame Crescents

32-40 rolls

1 package dry yeast
1 cup warm water
¾ cup evaporated milk
1½ teaspoons salt
½ cup honey
1 egg
4 cups whole wheat flour
¼ cup butter, melted and cooled
2 cups flour
1 cup cold butter
1 egg white
1 tablespoon water
¼ to ½ cup sesame seeds

In a large mixing bowl, dissolve yeast in warm water. Add milk, salt, honey, egg and **2 cups** of the whole wheat flour. Mix on medium speed until mixture is smooth. Stir in **melted butter**.

In another large bowl, stir together the remaining whole wheat flour and the all-purpose flour. With a pastry blender, cut in **cold** butter until particles are the size of peas. Pour the yeast batter into the butter/flour mixture and gently stir until all the flour is just moistened. Cover well and refrigerate for 4 hours (may be refrigerated up to 4 days).

At least 3 hours before serving time, turn the dough out onto a floured board and knead for about 5 minutes. Divide dough into 4 parts. Working with 1 part at a time (refrigerate remaining portions), roll into a circle about 17 inches. Dough will be stiff. Using a sharp knife, cut the circle into 8 to 10 wedges. Shape into crescents by rolling each wedge from its base to the point.

Place crescents 1½ inches apart on an ungreased baking sheet, curving slightly, and placing the point on the underside. Cover with plastic wrap and let rise at room temperature until almost double in size, about 2 hours.

Uncover and brush tops of rolls with egg white mixed with water. Sprinkle with sesame seeds. Bake at 325° for 20 to 25 minutes until lightly brown.

Double-Quick Parkerhouse Rolls

18-24 rolls

1 cup boiling water
1 cup evaporated milk
½ (scant) cup sugar
2 eggs
2 packages dry yeast
1 teaspoon salt
4 cups flour
Butter **or** margarine,
    softened

In a large bowl, pour boiling water over evaporated milk and sugar. Cool and add eggs, yeast, salt and flour. Mix well. This will be a thin dough.

Place dough on well-floured waxed paper. Pat until flat. Spread dough with butter as you would butter a slice of bread. Fold dough in half and pat the dough out to double size. Spread dough with butter again. Fold in half. Pat or roll again. Repeat this procedure (spread, fold and roll) 3 more times, ending with fold and roll to double the size. Cut in rounds with a biscuit cutter and put into well-greased muffin tins. Brush tops of rolls with melted butter. Let rise until doubled. Bake at 375° for 10 to 15 minutes.

NOTE: Cinnamon rolls may be made by covering the rolled out dough with ½ pint heavy cream, sprinkled with brown sugar, nuts and cinnamon. Roll up dough, jelly-roll style and slice in 1-inch slices, putting a cut side down in well-greased muffin tins. Let rise until doubled and bake at 375° for 12 to 15 minutes.

Rolls brushed with salad oil or melted fat before baking will have tender crusts. Those brushed with milk or 1 beaten egg diluted with 1 tablespoon milk will have crisp crusts.

Potato-Onion Rolls

24 rolls

4½ to 5½ cups bread flour
1 cup mashed potato flakes
3 tablespoons sugar
2 teaspoons salt
2 packages dry yeast
2 cups milk
½ cup margarine or butter
½ cup sliced green onions
2 eggs

In a large bowl, combine **1½ cups** of the flour, the potato flakes, sugar, salt and yeast and blend well.

In a medium saucepan, heat milk, margarine and onions until very warm (120° to 130°).

Add warm liquid and eggs to flour mixture. Blend at low speed until moistened. Beat 3 minutes at medium speed. By hand, stir in enough flour to make a soft dough.

On a floured surface, knead in remaining flour until dough is smooth and elastic, about 10 minutes.

Place in a greased bowl and cover loosely with plastic wrap and a cloth towel. Let rise in a warm place (80° to 85°) until double in size, 45 to 60 minutes.

Punch down dough. Rest it on counter, covered with inverted bowl, for 15 minutes. Divide dough in 24 pieces and shape into balls. If desired, dip tops of balls in additional potato flakes.

Place in 1 greased 9x13-inch or 2 9-inch round cake pans. Cover and let rise in a warm place until double in size, about 30 to 45 minutes. Bake at 375° for 25 to 35 minutes until golden brown. Remove from pans immediately.

Aluminum foil under the napkin in a bread basket will keep rolls warm longer.

Yorkshire Pudding

1 dozen

⅞ cup flour
½ teaspoon salt
½ cup milk
2 eggs
½ cup water
½ cup unsalted butter

In large mixing bowl, combine flour and salt. Gradually add milk, beating with electric mixer until smooth.

In another bowl, beat eggs until fluffy. Add eggs to flour and milk mixture. Beat until well mixed. Add water and beat until mixture bubbles. Let mixture stand for ½ hour.

Melt butter. Pour ¼ inch of the butter into each muffin cup. Place muffin tin in oven until hot.

Pour batter into muffin cups, dividing evenly among 12 cups. Bake at 400° for 20 minutes. Reduce oven temperature to 350° and bake for 15 minutes longer. Serve immediately.

Wheat Germ Muffins

1 dozen

1 cup flour
1 cup whole wheat flour
3 teaspoons baking
  powder
½ teaspoon salt
2 tablespoons honey
1 cup milk
⅓ cup oil
1 egg
½ cup wheat germ

Combine flours, baking powder and salt.

In another bowl, combine honey, milk, oil and egg. Stir into dry ingredients. Blend in wheat germ. Spoon into greased muffin tins. Bake at 350° for 20 minutes.

English Muffins

1 cup milk
2 tablespoons sugar
1 teaspoon salt
3 tablespoons butter
1 cup warm water
1 package dry yeast
5 to 6 cups unsifted flour
Cornmeal

In a saucepan, scald milk. Stir in sugar, salt and butter. Cool.

Measure warm water into a large bowl. Stir in yeast until dissolved. Add lukewarm milk mixture and **3 cups** of the flour. Beat until smooth. Add enough additional flour to make a stiff dough. Turn out onto a floured board; knead 2 minutes or until dough is manageable. (Dough may be a little sticky.)

Place dough in a greased bowl, turning to coat. Let rise in a warm place for 1 hour. Punch down. Divide dough into 2 pieces.

On a board heavily sprinkled with cornmeal, pat each piece to ½-inch thickness. Cut into circles with a 3-inch cookie or biscuit cutter. Place on an ungreased baking sheet about 2 inches apart. Cover and let rise in a warm place for ½ hour.

Place in a lightly greased medium hot (300°) skillet with cornmeal side down. Bake until brown (about 10 minutes each side). Cool on wire racks. Split in half when cool.

Melba Toast

1 loaf unsliced bread,
    white or whole wheat
Melted butter, optional

Slice bread as thin as possible. Place on a buttered cookie sheet (or brush melted butter on top of each slice).

Bake at 300° for 20 to 25 minutes.

NOTE: Chilled bread slices more easily.

Buttermilk Muffins

30 muffins

1 cup quick cooking rolled
  oats
1 cup buttermilk
1 egg, lightly beaten
½ cup oil
½ cup brown sugar
  (loosely packed)
1 cup flour
½ teaspoon salt
1 teaspoon baking soda

In a medium bowl, soak oats in buttermilk at least 1 hour. Add egg, oil, brown sugar and dry ingredients.

Fill greased muffin cups at least ½ full. Bake at 400° for 15 to 20 minutes.

Banana-Carrot Bread

1 loaf

2 cups unbleached flour
1 teaspoon baking
  powder
1 teaspoon baking soda
½ teaspoon cinnamon
½ teaspoon salt
⅛ teaspoon ground
  cloves
¼ cup butter or
  margarine, softened
¾ cup brown sugar
2 eggs
2 large bananas, very
  ripe, peeled and
  mashed
1¼ teaspoons vanilla
2 large carrots, finely
  grated
1 cup chopped walnuts

Preheat oven to 350°.

In a large bowl, combine flour, baking powder, baking soda, cinnamon, salt and cloves.

In a separate bowl, cream butter with sugar. Beat in eggs, bananas and vanilla. Add banana mixture to dry ingredients and stir in carrots and walnuts. Pour into a greased and floured 9x5-inch loaf pan and bake for 1 hour or until knife inserted in center of loaf comes out clean.

Mash overripe bananas, add a little lemon juice and freeze for use in cake or bread recipes.

107

Braided Squash Bread

2 loaves

This may be made easily in a food processor.

2 packages dry yeast
¼ cup warm water
  (105°-115°)
1 12-ounce package
  frozen cooked yellow
  squash, thawed
  (1¼ cups)
1 cup milk
⅓ cup brown sugar
⅓ cup butter **or**
  margarine, softened
1 egg, lightly beaten
1½ teaspoons salt
5½ to 6 cups flour

In a small bowl, dissolve yeast in warm water. Let stand until bubbly, about 10 minutes.

In a large bowl, combine squash, milk, brown sugar, butter, egg and salt. Stir in yeast mixture. Mix in enough flour to make dough easy to handle. (It will be sticky.)

Turn dough out onto a lightly floured surface. Knead until smooth and elastic, about 10 minutes. Place in a buttered bowl, turning a few times to butter all sides.

Cover and let rise in a warm place until doubled, about 1 hour. Dough is ready if a finger impression remains when poked.

Butter 2 9x5x3-inch loaf pans. Punch down dough, divide into 6 parts. Shape each part into a 14-inch rope. Place 3 ropes side-by-side, and beginning in the middle, braid to the ends. Tuck under to form smooth ends. Repeat procedure with remaining ropes.

Place braids in prepared pans. Cover and let rise in a warm place until doubled, about 1 hour.

Preheat oven to 375°. Bake until golden, about 30 to 35 minutes. Let cool about 15 minutes before removing from pans. Cool bread on wire racks.

Braided Sweet Loaves

2 large loaves

3½ cups unsifted flour
Grated rind of 1 lemon
1½ teaspoons salt
¼ cup sugar
¼ cup butter **or**
  margarine
¼ cup shortening
1½ packages dry yeast
¼ cup warm milk
2 tablespoons sugar
2 eggs
1 cup light cream
Melted butter

Combine flour, lemon rind, salt and sugar. Add butter and shortening and blend well until the consistency of pastry dough.

Dissolve yeast in milk, add sugar, and mix well. Add eggs and cream and mix well.

Combine the 2 mixtures and beat well with a spoon. Cover and refrigerate for at least 5 hours or overnight. Dough should be sticky.

Separate dough in half and then each half into thirds. Roll into ropes about 1 inch in diameter. Brush with melted butter and braid into 2 long braids on ungreased cookie sheets. Let rise 1½ to 2 hours. Bake at 375° for about 15 minutes. Watch carefully. While still warm, brush with topping.

TOPPING

½ cup powdered sugar
2 tablespoons butter,
  optional
1 drop vanilla
Lemon juice
Milk

Combine ingredients using lemon juice to taste and milk to make a thin paste.

Yeast doughs are doubled in bulk when an indentation made with your finger remains in the dough.

Holiday Pumpkin Bread

1 10-inch tube bread
or 2 loaves

⅓ cup dry sherry
⅔ cup golden raisins
⅔ cup shortening
2 cups brown sugar
⅔ cup molasses
4 eggs, lightly beaten
2 cups mashed pumpkin
3⅓ cups unsifted flour
1 teaspoon cinnamon
½ teaspoon ground
  cloves
½ teaspoon allspice
1 teaspoon baking soda
½ teaspoon salt
½ teaspoon baking
  powder
1 cup chopped almonds
  or walnuts

In a saucepan, heat sherry and add raisins to plump. Set aside to cool.

In a large bowl, with an electric mixer, beat shortening, sugar and molasses until light and fluffy. At lower mixer speed beat in eggs and pumpkin.

Sift together remaining dry ingredients and mix with nuts. Add raisins and sherry and combine with pumpkin mixture, stirring until well moistened.

Grease and flour a large tube pan or 2 9x5x3-inch loaf pans. Pour batter into prepared pans and bake at 350° for 50 to 60 minutes or until pick inserted comes out dry. Allow to cool for 10 minutes in the pans. Remove from pans and let cool completely before slicing.

Refrigerate flour for long-term storage.

Milk has a higher food value and when added to bread dough will produce a softer and browner crust.

Chocolate Chip Pumpkin Surprise

2 loaves

⅔ cup shortening **or**
   1 cup oil
2⅔ cups sugar
4 eggs
2 cups pumpkin
⅔ cup water
3⅓ cups flour
½ teaspoon baking
   powder
2 teaspoons baking soda
1½ teaspoons salt
1 teaspoon nutmeg
1 cup nuts
1½ cups chocolate chips

Cream shortening and sugar. Add eggs, pumpkin, and water. Sift flour, baking powder, baking soda, salt and nutmeg. Add to pumpkin. Stir in nuts and chocolate chips.

Pour into 2 greased 9x5-inch loaf pans. Bake at 350° for 1 hour.

Cool, then frost.

NOTE: Bake the day before. Freezes well.

FROSTING

1 cup powdered sugar
2 tablespoons butter
1 tablespoon milk

Blend together.

Lemon Tea Bread

1 large or 2 small loaves

½ cup shortening
1 cup sugar
2 eggs, beaten
1⅔ cups flour
½ teaspoon salt
1 tablespoon baking
   powder
½ cup milk
½ cup chopped nuts,
   optional
Grated rind of 1 lemon

Combine ingredients in order given and mix well. Bake in 1 greased 9x5x3-inch loaf pan or 2 small loaf pans at 350° for 1 hour. Remove from oven. While still hot, pierce bread several times with a toothpick and pour topping over loaves. When cool, remove from pans.

NOTE: Best if allowed to stand (wrapped) for 24 hours before cutting.

TOPPING

¼ cup sugar
Juice of 1 lemon

Combine ingredients and mix well.

Orange Rolls

3 dozen

2 packages dry yeast
¼ cup warm water
½ cup sugar
½ cup shortening
2 teaspoons salt
1 cup hot water
3 eggs, well beaten
4 (or less) cups flour

In a small bowl, sprinkle yeast over warm water and set aside.

In a large bowl, combine sugar, shortening and salt with hot water and stir until shortening is melted. Add eggs and **1 cup** of the flour. Stir in yeast mixture. Add the remaining flour and mix well. Cover and refrigerate overnight (be sure the container allows for expanding dough).

Three or four hours before serving, turn dough out onto a floured board. Divide in half and roll each piece into a rectangle about ¼-inch thick.

Spread with filling. Roll dough lengthwise; cut into 1-inch slices.

Place on a greased baking sheet. Let rise 3 to 4 hours. Bake at 375° for 10 to 12 minutes. Drizzle glaze over top while rolls are still warm and before removing from the pan.

NOTE: These rolls may also be made into crescents.

FILLING

⅓ cup butter
⅓ cup sugar
Grated rind of 1 orange

Combine all ingredients and cream until smooth.

GLAZE

Juice of 1 orange
¼ cup butter
1 pound powdered sugar
½ cup sour cream

In a saucepan, combine orange juice, butter and powdered sugar. Boil 3 minutes over medium heat. Remove from heat and stir in sour cream. Mix well.

Fruit Rolls

3 dozen

⅔ cup butter
1 cup sugar
2 teaspoons salt
2 cups milk, scalded
7 cups flour
3 eggs
2 packages dry yeast
¼ cup warm water
Melted butter
3 cups cooked fruit
  (prunes, apricots **or**
  raisins)
Cinnamon
Sugar

Combine butter, sugar, salt and hot milk. When lukewarm, add part of the flour. Add eggs, 1 at a time, beating well. Add yeast, dissolved in warm water, and remaining flour, enough to make a soft dough. Cover and let rise until doubled. Divide dough in half.

Roll each piece into a rectangle, about 12x9 inches. Brush liberally with melted butter.

Sprinkle **half** of the fruit on each piece. Sprinkle generously with cinnamon and sugar.

Roll dough lengthwise, cut into slices about ¾-inch thick and place on a greased baking sheet. Let rise until doubled. Bake at 350° for 15 to 20 minutes.

While rolls are still hot, brush with topping.

TOPPING

¼ cup water
¼ cup butter
1 cup sugar
2 tablespoons heavy
  cream

Combine all ingredients in a saucepan and cook until slightly thick.

Salt brings out the flavor and is important in controlling the action of the yeast.

Special Cinnamon Rolls

2 dozen

2 packages dry yeast
½ cup lukewarm water
½ cup + 1 tablespoon
sugar
Pinch ginger
2 cups warm water
2 teaspoons salt
3 eggs, beaten
8 cups flour
2 cups raisins, plumped
in hot water
1 cup butter, melted and
cooled slightly
1 cup brown sugar
4 teaspoons cinnamon

In a very large bowl, place yeast, **lukewarm** water, **1 tablespoon** of the sugar and ginger. When yeast is dissolved, stir in **warm** water, remaining sugar, salt, eggs and **3 cups** of the flour. Mix well. Add raisins, **½ cup** of the butter and the remaining flour. Knead until smooth, place in a greased bowl, cover with a cloth and let rise until doubled.

Roll out dough into a rectangle. Brush with remaining melted butter, sprinkle with brown sugar and cinnamon. Roll up lengthwise and cut ½-inch thick. Place cut side down on a greased baking sheet. Let rise until almost doubled.

Spread topping over raised rolls. Bake at 375° for 20 to 25 minutes.

TOPPING

1 cup heavy cream,
whipped
1 teaspoon cinnamon
½ cup brown sugar
½ to ¾ cup chopped nuts

Combine all ingredients and mix well.

Slice rolled dough with heavy-duty thread instead of a knife, place the thread crosswise under the roll, pull the ends up and cross them over the roll.

Caramel Pull-Aparts

1 large ring

Simple and delicious for a morning meeting or coffee.

½ package frozen roll
dough (18 rolls)
½ cup butter **or**
margarine
½ cup brown sugar
1 3-ounce package
butterscotch **or** vanilla
pudding and pie filling
½ cup chopped walnuts

Arrange frozen rolls in a fluted tube pan. Pour melted butter over rolls and sprinkle with brown sugar and dry pudding mix. Top with nuts.

Cover and let rise at room temperature for 10 to 12 hours or overnight. Bake at 350° for 30 minutes.

To serve, slice or pull apart.

Sweet Jammies

12 muffins

Children love these, especially when made in mini-muffin tins.

2 cups flour
¼ cup sugar
1 tablespoon baking
powder
½ teaspoon baking soda
½ teaspoon salt
¼ cup butter
1 cup plain yogurt
¼ cup milk
1 egg
½ teaspoon vanilla
¼ cup (approximately)
jam or preserves
Powdered sugar, optional

In a bowl, blend dry ingredients.

Melt butter in a medium saucepan. Remove from heat, stir in yogurt and milk and when smooth, beat in egg and vanilla. Add butter mixture to dry ingredients and stir to moisten.

Spoon half the batter into buttered muffin cups. Place about a teaspoonful of jam over batter in each cup and top with remaining batter.

Bake at 425° for 15 to 20 minutes until golden. Let stand 5 minutes before removing from cups. Sift a little powdered sugar over muffins just before serving, if desired.

115

Lemon Muffins

1 dozen

Good as a meal accompaniment or as shortcake with fresh strawberries.

2 cups flour
½ cup + 2 tablespoons sugar
1 tablespoon baking powder
1 teaspoon salt
½ cup butter
½ cup fresh lemon juice
2 eggs
Finely grated peel of 1 lemon

In a large bowl, combine flour, ½ cup of the sugar, baking powder and salt. Blend well.

In a saucepan, melt butter. Remove from heat and stir in lemon juice, eggs and lemon peel. Stir egg mixture into dry ingredients and blend until just moistened.

Spoon into buttered muffin cups and sprinkle top of batter with remaining sugar. Bake at 400° for 15 to 20 minutes until lightly brown.

Pineapple-Bran Muffins

1 dozen

1 cup all-bran cereal
½ cup milk
1 cup crushed pineapple
¼ cup raisins
¼ cup shortening
1 egg
1 cup flour
2 teaspoons baking powder
½ teaspoon salt
¼ teaspoon baking soda
½ cup brown sugar

In a large bowl, combine cereal, milk, pineapple and raisins. Mix well. Add shortening and egg, blending well.

Combine dry ingredients, add to the first mixture and stir until moistened. Divide dough evenly among 12 paper-lined muffin cups. Bake at 400° for 25 to 30 minutes.

Spudnuts

Fry the centers, too. Kids love them.

7 packages dry yeast
1 cup warm water
1 tablespoon sugar
8 tablespoons shortening
1 cup sugar
3 tablespoons salt
2 cups mashed potatoes
4 to 6 eggs, slightly
   beaten
1 quart scalded milk,
   cooled to lukewarm
12 to 14 cups sifted flour

Dissolve yeast in warm water with the **1 tablespoon** sugar.

Cream shortening, the **1 cup** sugar, salt and potatoes. Add eggs, milk, yeast and flour. Beat together until smooth and elastic. Knead well. Dough will be soft.

Let rise to double, about 45 minutes. Roll out and cut with doughnut cutter. Let rise until double. Fry in deep hot oil, cooking about 1½ minutes on each side. Drain on paper towels and glaze while still warm.

Dip in glaze and drain on rack with pan to catch drippings. May be dipped in sugar intead of glaze, if desired.

GLAZE

1 teaspoon unflavored
   gelatin
1 tablespoon cold water
2 pounds powdered sugar
1 cup boiling water
1 teaspoon vanilla

Dissolve gelatin in cold water. Add to sugar, water and vanilla. Beat until smooth.

Dissolve yeast in warm water in a warm bowl. Yeast needs a warm, even temperature to work.

French Breakfast Puffs

1 dozen

⅓ cup butter, softened
½ cup sugar
1 egg
1½ cups flour
1½ teaspoons baking
   powder
½ teaspoon salt
¼ teaspoon nutmeg
½ cup milk
6 tablespoons (or more)
   butter, melted
½ cup sugar
1 teaspoon cinnamon

In a large bowl, combine butter, sugar and egg.

Sift together flour, baking powder, salt and nutmeg. Stir into first mixture alternately with milk, being careful not to overmix. Fill greased miniature muffin tins ⅔ full with batter. Bake at 350° for 20 minutes or until golden.

While still warm, roll in melted butter and then in sugar mixed with cinnamon. Serve warm. May be reheated.

NOTE: These freeze well.

Kuchen

6-8 servings

½ cup butter, softened
½ cup sugar
3 eggs
½ teaspoon vanilla
1 cup flour
Fruit (such as peaches or
   berries)

Cream butter and sugar in small mixer bowl until fluffy. Add eggs, 1 at a time, beating after each addition. Mix in vanilla and flour.

Butter and flour an 8x10-inch pan and spread with batter. Place sliced or halved fruit or whole berries in rows, covering the batter.

Sprinkle topping over fruit and bake at 350° for 1 hour.

TOPPING

1 cup sugar
1 tablespoon butter
1 tablespoon flour

Mix all ingredients with fingers until the consistency of cornmeal.

Chocolate Chip Coffee Cake   12 servings

¼ cup butter, at room
  temperature
1 8-ounce package
  cream cheese,
  softened
1¼ cups sugar
2 eggs
1¾ cups flour
1 teaspoon vanilla
1 teaspoon baking
  powder
½ teaspoon baking soda
¼ teaspoon salt
¼ cup cold milk
1 6-ounce package
  semisweet chocolate
  chips
¼ cup chopped walnuts

In a large bowl, cream together butter, cream cheese and sugar. Add eggs, 1 at a time, beating well after each addition. Add flour, vanilla, baking powder, baking soda and salt. Mix well.

Stir in milk, chocolate chips and walnuts. Mixture will be thick.

Pour into a greased 9x3-inch springform cake pan. Sprinkle with topping. Bake at 350° for 50 minutes. Let cool 15 minutes and remove ring to cool completely.

NOTE: This recipe requires a springform pan with an angelfood divider for hole in center.

TOPPING

¼ cup sugar
1 teaspoon cinnamon
¼ cup chopped walnuts

Combine all ingredients and mix well.

Oil your hands a little if the dough is hard to knead.

Crêpes I

12 crêpes

1 cup flour
1½ cups milk
2 eggs
1 tablespoon oil
¼ teaspoon salt

In a medium bowl, combine all ingredients. Beat until well blended.

Heat a lightly greased skillet or omelet pan to medium-high. Place 2 tablespoons batter in the pan and tilt on all sides to evenly distribute batter. Cook until crêpe loses its shine and is slightly browned around edges. Brown on one side only. Invert pan over paper towels to remove crêpe. Repeat with remaining batter.

Herb Crêpes

10-12 crêpes

These crêpes are wonderful stuffed with a chicken or crab filling.

½ cup cold water
½ cup cold milk
2 eggs
1 cup sifted flour
2 tablespoons oil
⅓ cup mixed, finely
  chopped dill, chives
  and parsley
Oil for frying

In a bowl, mix the first 5 ingredients in order given. Place in a blender and blend until smooth. Stir in herbs. Refrigerate covered for 3 hours.

Lightly brush a crêpe pan or skillet with oil and place over high heat. Remove from heat and place about ¼ cup batter in pan. Tilt pan to coat bottom evenly. Cook until just set, about 1 minute. Turn and cook until golden, about 30 seconds. Stack with waxed paper between layers.

NOTE: These may be stacked and wrapped and refrigerated for up to 2 days, or wrapped in foil and frozen for up to 3 weeks. To reheat, place in foil in 325° oven for 5 to 10 minutes.

Overnight Waffles

1 package dry yeast
5 cups unsifted flour
⅓ cup sugar
¾ teaspoon salt
2 teaspoons soda
1 quart buttermilk
¾ cup melted butter **or** margarine
4 eggs
¾ cup finely chopped blanched almonds, optional

In a large bowl, sift together first 5 ingredients. Stir in buttermilk and melted butter. Add eggs and stir until batter is blended, but still lumpy. Stir in nuts, if desired.

Cover bowl and let rise in a warm place until bubbly, about 30 minutes, or refrigerate overnight.

Bake in a preheated waffle baker, using a little less batter than usual, as these expand more than regular waffles.

After waffles are baked, place in a single layer, directly on racks in 300° oven for at least 5 minutes or until serving time.

NOTE: You may also cool waffles completely on racks, wrap in foil and freeze up to 1 month. Reheat (without thawing) in a toaster.

Whole Grain Pancakes

1½ cups rolled oats
½ cup yellow cornmeal
2½ cups buttermilk
½ cup whole wheat flour
2 tablespoons sugar
1 teaspoon baking soda
2 teaspoons baking powder
1 teaspoon salt
2 eggs, beaten
5 tablespoons melted butter
Milk, if necessary

In a large bowl, combine oats, cornmeal and buttermilk. Cover and refrigerate overnight.

In the morning, sift together **twice** the flour, sugar, baking soda, baking powder and salt, and add to the oat mixture. Stir in eggs and butter. If thinner pancakes are desired, add milk to desired consistency.

Spoon batter onto a hot griddle, turn when bubbles appear on top and remove to a warm platter until ready to serve.

121

Pfannkuchen (German Pancakes)

2 pancakes

3 eggs, lightly beaten
½ cup flour
4 tablespoons melted butter
½ cup milk
¼ teaspoon salt
Powdered sugar
Fresh lime wedges

In a medium bowl, slowly beat flour into eggs. Add **2 tablespoons** of the butter, the milk and salt. Pour batter into a well-greased heavy baking pan or ovenproof glass pie plate.

Bake at 450° for 20 minutes. Remove from pan with 2 spatulas. The pfannkuchen will have risen high above the sides of the pan, but will settle as it cools.

Pour the remaining butter over the pancake, sprinkle with powdered sugar and serve with lime to squeeze over the top.

Cottage Cheese Pancakes

4 generous servings

6 eggs
2 cups cottage cheese
4 tablespoons melted butter
4 tablespoons flour **or** cornmeal
2 tablespoons sugar
½ teaspoon salt
¼ teaspoon cinnamon

Using a mixer, blender or food processor, beat eggs. Add cottage cheese and mix until fairly smooth. Add remaining ingredients and mix well.

Drop by large spoonfuls onto an oiled griddle, skillet or a non-stick pan. Fry the pancakes as usual and serve.

Homemade Syrup

2 cups

½ cup light corn syrup
½ cup brown sugar
½ cup sugar
½ cup water
Dash salt
Vanilla **or** maple extract

In a saucepan, heat all ingredients, **except** salt and vanilla, to boiling. Turn off heat. Continue to boil with heat turned off for 2 minutes. Add salt and vanilla to taste.

Bound to Please: The Diversity of Wildlife

Meriwether Lewis and William Clark reached the Lemhi Pass in
05, the first explorers to enter what would become Idaho. Fur-
ppers searching for beaver pelts began to arrive three years
er.

Today Idaho's hunting and fishing opportunities are unsurpassed.
the Snake River Birds of Prey Natural Area, raptors are both pro-
cted and studied. Deer that bound across the highways, foxes
at explore campgrounds, herds of elk that graze in the meadows,
gles soaring through the skies, Rocky Mountain big-horn sheep
king down from mountain cliffs – all are still a part of Idaho.

Omelets

Eggs

Soufflés

Quiches

Cheese

Sauces

Not-So-Spanish Omelet   2 servings

6 eggs
½ cup chopped fresh
  spinach
Dash salt and pepper

In a small bowl, slightly mix **3 eggs**, **¼ cup** of the spinach, salt and pepper. Cook quickly in omelet pan over medium-high heat. Transfer to warm plate. Use **¼** of the sauce on **half** the omelet, fold, use another **¼** of the sauce remembering to save half the sauce for the second omelet. Repeat for second omelet.

SAUCE

1 tablespoon chopped
  green pepper
3 tablespoons chopped
  onion
2 teaspoons butter
1 8-ounce can tomato
  sauce
1 4-ounce can sliced
  mushrooms, drained
1 teaspoon chopped
  capers
1 teaspoon chopped
  pimiento
2 teaspoons sugar
1 teaspoon
  Worcestershire sauce
Dash cayenne
Generous dashes of:
  oregano, garlic salt,
  celery salt, crushed bay
  leaves
3 bacon slices, cooked
  and crumbled

Sauté green pepper and onion slowly in butter until soft. Add remaining ingredients, **except** bacon, and simmer until thickened. Add bacon and stir in quickly.

Warm the knife when cutting cheese, and you will find the cheese cuts as easily as butter.

Avocado-Tortilla Omelet 4-6 servings

¾ cup diced avocado
¼ cup sour cream
2 tablespoons diced
green chiles
1 teaspoon lemon juice
Dash salt
Dash Tabasco sauce
2 tablespoons butter
1 corn tortilla, broken
into small pieces
6 eggs
¼ cup milk
1 cup grated Monterey
Jack cheese

In a medium bowl, combine avocado, sour cream, green chiles, lemon juice, salt and Tabasco sauce. Mix until smooth and set aside.

In a 10-inch ovenproof skillet, melt butter over medium heat. Add tortilla and cook until soft. Pour in eggs beaten with milk. Cook 3 to 5 minutes, lifting eggs to let uncooked mixture flow underneath. Remove from heat and sprinkle with cheese. Bake at 325° until cheese melts.

Spread avocado mixture over **half** the omelet and return to oven for 5 to 7 minutes. Fold and serve immediately.

¼ teaspoon cream of tartar added to egg whites will ensure that a soufflé stays light and fluffy.

Here's how to give the soufflé a high crown. For a top hat (it puffs in the oven), use tip of spoon to trace circle in mixture 1 inch from edge and about 1 inch deep. To help the soufflé "climb," use ungreased casserole.

Shrimp Omelet

4 eggs, separated
Dash white pepper
¼ cup water
¼ teaspoon salt
¼ teaspoon cream of
tartar
2 teaspoons butter
Tomato slices
Diced artichoke hearts,
optional

In a small bowl, beat egg yolks and pepper until thick and lemon-colored. In a small mixing bowl, beat egg whites, water, salt and cream of tartar until stiff but not dry. Fold yolks into whites.

In a 10-inch ovenproof skillet, melt butter and heat until just hot enough to sizzle a drop of water. Turn egg mixture into skillet and cook over low heat until puffy and browned on the bottom; approximately 5 minutes. Transfer to oven and bake at 325° for 12 to 15 minutes or until a knife inserted near the center comes out clean.

To serve, place omelet on heated platter. Score down the center with spatula. Place tomato slices and/or artichoke hearts on one side and pour **half** the shrimp sauce on that half. Fold the omelet and top with remaining sauce.

SHRIMP SAUCE I

1 tablespoon butter
1 tablespoon flour
1 teaspoon dry mustard
1 cup milk
1 cup grated Cheddar or
Monterey Jack cheese
¼ teaspoon basil
1 cup diced cooked
shrimp

In a 1-quart saucepan, melt butter. Blend in flour and mustard. Cook over low heat until mixture is smooth. Remove from heat. Stir in milk. Over medium heat, heat to boiling, stirring constantly. Boil and stir one minute. Blend in cheese just until melted. Stir in basil and shrimp. Keep warm until ready to serve. Makes 2 cups.

Baked Omelet Layers

6 servings

8 eggs, separated
¼ cup water
¾ teaspoon salt
Dash pepper
¼ cup flour
1 cup soft bread crumbs
Chopped fresh parsley
and/or green pepper
rings for garnish

In a medium bowl, beat egg whites until frothy. Add water and salt and beat until stiff, but not dry.

In a small bowl, add pepper and flour to yolks. Beat until thick and lemon-colored.

Fold yolks and bread crumbs into the egg whites. Spoon into 2 greased 8-inch cake pans.

Bake at 350° for 15 minutes or until firm and light brown.

To serve, layer omelets with sauce in between and on top. Garnish with chopped fresh parsley and/or green pepper rings. Cut into wedges and serve immediately.

SAUCE

1 10-ounce can cream of
mushroom soup,
undiluted
½ cup milk
Dash pepper
1 cup grated Cheddar
cheese or ½ cup
Cheddar and ½ cup
processed cheese
1 teaspoon
Worcestershire sauce

In a medium saucepan, combine sauce ingredients and heat slowly until bubbly.

For a more tender omelet, add a small amount of water instead of milk or cream.

Spanakopita

8 servings

2 pounds fresh spinach
1 tablespoon salt
9 eggs, beaten
¾ pound Feta cheese,
    crumbled
1 onion, chopped
2 tablespoons olive oil
½ teaspoon freshly
    ground pepper
Salt, oregano, basil and
    parsley to taste
1 pound phyllo dough
1½ cups butter, melted

Wash spinach and remove stems. Rub salt into the spinach. This will reduce the spinach to ¼ its original volume. Rinse and drain well.

Combine eggs and cheese and add to spinach. Sauté onion in olive oil and add to the spinach and egg mixture. Mix in pepper and remaining spices.

With buttered fingers, pick up the phyllo dough sheets one at a time and butter each. Set aside 8 buttered sheets. Lay remaining sheets one on top of the other in a 9x13-inch pan fanning the corners of the dough around the pan in a circular pattern.

Pour the spinach filling on top of the dough and fold in the edges. Lay the remaining 8 sheets of dough on top and tuck in the edges. Brush dough with the remaining melted butter. Make steam pricks in the top. Bake at 375° for 50 minutes.

Cool 5-10 minutes, cut in pie-shaped wedges and serve.

To prevent mold, store cheese in a tightly covered container with some sugar cubes.

Cheese-Spinach Roll

8-10 servings

7 eggs, room temperature
5 tablespoons butter or
margarine
6 tablespoons unsifted
flour
1½ teaspoons salt
Dash cayenne
1¼ cups milk
½ cup Parmesan cheese
½ cup grated sharp
Cheddar cheese
¼ teaspoon cream of
tartar
Parmesan cheese
Parsley sprigs for garnish

Make the cheese roll 24 hours in advance. Separate eggs, placing the whites in one large bowl and the yolks in another large bowl.

Lightly grease the bottom of a 15x10x1-inch jelly-roll pan. Line the bottom with waxed paper and lightly grease the paper.

Preheat oven to 350°.

In a medium saucepan, melt butter and remove from heat. Using a wire whisk or wooden spoon, stir in flour, **1 teaspoon** of the salt and cayenne until smooth. Gradually stir in milk; bring to a boil stirring constantly. Reduce heat, stirring until mixture is set and leaves bottom and sides of pan. Remove from heat. Beat in the ½ **cup** Parmesan and the Cheddar cheeses.

With a wire whisk or wooden spoon, beat egg yolks. Gradually beat cheese mixture into the yolks.

At high speed, beat egg whites with remaining salt and cream of tartar until stiff peaks form. With a wire whisk, gently fold ⅓ of the whites into the warm cheese mixture. Carefully fold in remaining egg whites until just barely combined. Pour into prepared jelly-roll pan. Bake 15 to 20 minutes or until surface is puffy and feels firm when lightly pressed with fingertips.

Make the spinach filling while the roll is baking. The filling should be ready to spread when the roll is baked.

Cheese Spinach Roll *(Continued)*

Invert baked cheese roll on foil that has been sprinkled lightly with Parmesan cheese. Gently peel off waxed paper. Spread spinach filling evenly on top. Starting with the long side, roll up. Place seam side down on a wire rack to cool completely. Wrap in foil and refrigerate. Make cheese sauce and refrigerate.

To serve, preheat oven to 350°. Remove foil from roll and place on a greased, ovenproof serving dish. Bake 40 minutes or until heated through.

Meanwhile, heat cheese sauce slowly. If too thick, thin with milk. Serve roll at once with cheese sauce. Garnish with parsley sprigs, if desired.

SPINACH FILLING

2 10-ounce packages frozen chopped spinach
½ cup water
2 tablespoons butter **or** margarine
¼ cup finely chopped onion
½ teaspoon salt
¼ cup grated sharp Cheddar cheese
½ cup sour cream

In a medium saucepan, cook spinach gently in water until just thawed. Turn into a sieve and press to remove all water. In a medium skillet, sauté onion in butter until golden and tender. Remove from heat and add spinach, salt, cheese and sour cream. Mix well.

CHEESE SAUCE I

2 tablespoons butter **or** margarine
2 tablespoons flour
½ teaspoon dry mustard
¼ teaspoon salt
Dash pepper
1 cup milk
1 cup grated sharp Cheddar cheese

In a small pan, melt butter and remove from heat. Add dry ingredients and stir until smooth. Add milk slowly, stir. Return to medium heat and heat to boiling, stirring constantly. Reduce heat and simmer 3 minutes. Add cheese, stirring until just melted. Refrigerate until needed.

129

Seafood Frittata

2 servings

A delightful mix of shrimp and zucchini from the Café Rose in Boise.

6 eggs
½ cup milk
Butter
4 ounces cooked bay
shrimp
4 ounces fresh zucchini,
grated
½ ounce green onion,
finely chopped
Salt and pepper to taste
4 ounces Mozzarella
cheese, grated
Parsley

Beat eggs and milk together until combined but not frothy. Lightly butter 2 omelet pans and place over medium high heat. Add bay shrimp to each pan and sauté for approximately 1 minute. Add zucchini, green onions, salt and pepper to each pan and sauté until zucchini is tender.

Add Mozzarella to each pan and stir until cheese is partially melted.

Add egg mixture to each pan, stirring constantly, until ingredients are evenly distributed throughout the frittata.

When the eggs begin to firm up, flip each frittata. Cook approximately 1 minute longer.

Transfer to serving dishes, top with parsley and serve immediately.

Egg whites will have more volume if they are at room temperature before beating.

Brush a little oil on the grater before you start grating, and cheese will wash off easier.

Fancy Egg Scramble

10 servings

1 cup diced Canadian
  bacon (approximately
  4 ounces)
¼ cup chopped green
  onions
3 tablespoons butter **or**
  margarine
12 eggs, beaten
1 4-ounce can
  mushroom stems and
  pieces, drained
4 teaspoons butter **or**
  margarine, melted
2¼ cups soft bread
  crumbs (3 slices)
⅓ teaspoon paprika

In a large skillet, sauté Canadian bacon and onion in butter until onion is tender, but not brown. Add eggs and scramble until barely set.

Fold mushrooms and cheese sauce into cooked eggs. Pour into a 7x12-inch baking dish.

Combine melted butter, bread crumbs and paprika and sprinkle over eggs. Cover and refrigerate until ready to bake.

Bake uncovered at 350° for 30 minutes.

CHEESE SAUCE II

2 tablespoons butter **or**
  margarine
2 tablespoons flour
½ teaspoon salt
⅛ teaspoon pepper
2 cups milk
1 cup grated processed
  American **or** Cheddar
  cheese

In a medium saucepan, melt butter and stir in flour, salt and pepper. Add milk, stirring until smooth. Cook over medium heat until bubbly and slightly thickened. Remove from heat and stir in cheese until melted.

To keep natural cheese smooth in cooking, place sauce over hot water before adding crumbled or shredded cheese. (Use water bath with chafing dish, or a double boiler.)

131

Eggs Benedict

4-8 servings

4 English muffins
8 slices Canadian bacon
  or thinly sliced ham
8 slices tomato
8 eggs
1 teaspoon white vinegar
Hollandaise Sauce (see
  index)

Split and toast muffins. Cover each half with a slice of bacon or ham and 1 slice of tomato. Keep warm while poaching eggs.

In a large skillet filled about half full of boiling water, add vinegar and poach eggs 3 to 5 minutes, depending on taste. With a slotted spoon, carefully remove eggs and place 1 on each muffin half. Cover with warm hollandaise sauce. Serve 1 to 2 halves per person, depending on appetite.

Options: 2 cups sliced fresh mushrooms, sautéed in butter and/or one can artichoke bottoms, quartered and drained. Place on top of tomato before the egg and sauce.

Special Baked Breakfast

6 servings

1 medium onion, chopped
1 tablespoon butter
Kitchen Bouquet
6 4x3-inch slices dry
  French bread, ⅓-inch
  thick with crusts
  removed
6 thin slices cooked ham
6 tomato slices, broiled

In a skillet, sauté onion in butter until well done. Add a few drops Kitchen Bouquet for color.

In a large, flat buttered baking dish, place bread in an even layer. Spread with sautéed onions, then ham. Spoon topping evenly over casserole. Bake at 375° for 20 minutes or until golden brown. Serve with slices of broiled tomato on top.

Special Baked Breakfast *(Continued)*

TOPPING

¼ cup cold milk
2 tablespoons flour
¼ teaspoon baking
   powder
4 eggs
Salt
½ pound Swiss cheese,
   grated
¼ teaspoon paprika
Dash cayenne **or** Tabasco
   sauce
2 tablespoons cognac,
   kirsch **or** rum

In a cold mixing bowl, combine milk, flour and baking powder. Stir thoroughly to blend. Add remaining ingredients and mix well.

Three-Cheese Brunch   **15-18 servings**

Good with hot corn muffins and fresh fruit salad.

1½ teaspoons baking
   powder
¾ cup flour
9 eggs, beaten
1½ teaspoons salt
1½ teaspoons sugar
⅛ teaspoon cayenne
1½ pounds Monterey
   Jack cheese, cubed
18 ounces cream cheese,
   cubed
1½ cups small curd
   cottage cheese
1 tablespoon butter, cut
   in small pieces
1 4-ounce can chopped
   green chiles, drained,
   optional

The night before, sift baking powder and flour together in a small bowl. In a medium bowl, mix eggs, salt, sugar and cayenne and refrigerate. In a large bowl, mix Jack cheese, cream cheese, cottage cheese and butter and refrigerate.

In the morning, add dry ingredients and egg mixture to cheese mixture and mix well. Stir in green chiles, if used.

Bake in a greased 9x13-inch pan at 350° for 45 minutes. Let stand 5 to 10 minutes before serving.

Deviled Egg Brunch

6 servings

Great the Sunday after Easter.

12 hard boiled eggs
Mayonnaise
Prepared mustard
Salt and pepper
1 10-ounce can cream of
     shrimp soup, undiluted
1 10-ounce can cream of
     chicken soup, undiluted
1 soup can milk
1 7-ounce can shrimp,
     drained
1 cup sliced mushrooms
½ cup chopped green
     onion
1 cup grated Cheddar
     cheese

Peel eggs and carefully cut in half lengthwise. Devil yolks with mayonnaise, mustard, salt and pepper to taste. Place stuffed eggs in a greased 9x13-inch baking dish.

Mix together soups, milk, shrimp, mushrooms and green onion. Pour over eggs. Sprinkle cheese over top. Refrigerate up to one day.

Bake at 350° for 45 minutes. Let stand 5 minutes before serving.

Eggplant Soufflé

6 servings

1 medium eggplant
2 tablespoons butter
2 tablespoons flour
1 cup milk
1 cup grated cheese
¾ cup soft bread cubes
2 teaspoons onion juice
1 tablespoon catsup
1 teaspoon salt
2 eggs, separated

Peel eggplant and cut into small pieces. Steam until tender and mash well.

In a saucepan over medium heat, melt butter. Add flour and milk. Cook until thickened, stirring constantly. Remove from heat and add eggplant, cheese, bread cubes, onion juice, catsup, salt. Beat egg yolks, add and mix well.

Beat egg whites until stiff and fold into mixture. Pour into greased 2-quart casserole or soufflé dish. Bake at 325° for 40 to 60 minutes until evenly browned.

Hominy Soufflé

6 servings

¼ cup butter **or**
    margarine
¼ cup flour
1 teaspoon salt
¼ teaspoon paprika
2 drops Tabasco sauce
1 cup milk
2 cups grated sharp
    Cheddar cheese
1 20-ounce can hominy,
    drained
5 eggs, separated

In a medium saucepan, melt butter over low heat. Stir in flour, salt, paprika and Tabasco sauce. Cook for 30 seconds and remove from heat. Slowly stir in milk. Return to heat and heat to boiling, stirring constantly. Add cheese and hominy. Remove from heat and allow to cool slightly. Beat in egg yolks, 1 at a time.

In a large bowl, beat egg whites until very stiff. Gently fold into cheese mixture.

Attach a 3-inch collar of foil to a greased 1½ quart soufflé dish. Gently pour soufflé mixture into dish.

Place in oven on lowest rack and bake at 350° for 40 to 45 minutes. Serve immediately.

Zucchini Soufflé

8 servings

2 pounds zucchini, sliced
2 eggs, separated
2 tablespoons flour
1 teaspoon salt
1 pint sour cream
5 bacon slices, cooked
    and crumbled
½ cup dry bread crumbs
2 tablespoons butter,
    melted
½ cup grated Cheddar
    cheese

Cook zucchini in boiling salted water for 2 minutes. Drain.

Beat egg yolks and combine with flour, salt and sour cream. Beat egg whites until stiff and fold into sour cream mixture.

In a greased soufflé dish, place **half** the zucchini and sprinkle with bacon. Top with **half** the sour cream mixture. Add remaining zucchini and top with remaining sour cream mixture.

Combine bread crumbs, butter and cheese. Sprinkle over top. Bake uncovered at 350° for 35 minutes.

135

Cheese-Rice Soufflé

6 servings

¼ cup white rice, cooked
2 tablespoons butter
3 tablespoons flour
¾ cup milk
2 cups grated American
  cheese
4 eggs, separated
¼ teaspoon salt
Dash cayenne

Preheat oven to 325°.

In a double boiler, melt butter. Stir in flour, then milk. Cook over medium heat until thickened. Add cheese. Stir to melt. Beat yolks with salt. Stiffly beat egg whites and fold all ingredients together. Pour into greased 1½-quart casserole.

Bake for 40 minutes.

Quiche Lorraine

6-8 servings

4 eggs
2 cups heavy cream
¾ teaspoon salt
Pinch of each: sugar,
  nutmeg, cayenne,
  black pepper
1 9-inch deep-dish
  unbaked pie shell **or**
  10-inch unbaked pie
  shell
Soft butter
12 bacon strips, cooked
  and coarsely crumbled
½ cup grated Swiss
  cheese
½ cup grated Cheddar
  cheese

In a medium bowl, beat together the eggs, cream and seasonings.

Rub soft butter over the inside of the pie shell and sprinkle bacon over bottom. Cover with the cheeses and pour egg mixture over all.

Bake at 450° for 10 minutes. Reduce heat to 300° and bake until custard is set, about 30 minutes longer.

Be sure that egg whites are at room temperature when you beat them for soufflés.

Salmon Quiche

6 servings

A lovely use for salmon from the HasBrouck House, Nampa.

1 15½-ounce can
   salmon, drained
3 eggs, beaten
1 cup sour cream
¼ cup mayonnaise
½ cup grated sharp
   Cheddar cheese
½ teaspoon dill weed
3 drops Tabasco sauce
Salt to taste

Place flaked salmon in bottom of pie crust. Mix all other ingredients into beaten eggs and pour over salmon. Bake at 375° for 25 to 30 minutes, until quiche has puffed and browned, and a small knife inserted in center comes out clean.

CRUST

1 cup whole wheat flour
⅓ cup grated sharp
   Cheddar cheese
¼ cup chopped almonds
½ teaspoon salt
¼ teaspoon paprika
6 tablespoons oil

Mix dry ingredients, add oil and mix well. Press into pie pan.

To fold beaten egg whites into a very heavy or thick batter, first fold a small amount of the egg whites into the batter to lighten it, then fold in the remaining egg whites.

Crab-Mushroom Quiche 6-8 servings

1 10-inch baked pie shell
3 cups sliced fresh
mushrooms
3 tablespoons butter
1 fresh crab, picked of all
meat **or** 1 7-ounce can
crab
1⅓ cups finely diced
Gruyère **or** Swiss
cheese
¾ cup sour cream
¼ cup mayonnaise
½ teaspoon salt
1 teaspoon flour
Light cream
3 eggs
½ teaspoon Tabasco
sauce

Sauté mushrooms in butter. Drain liquid and reserve.

Scatter sautéed mushrooms in pie shell. Scatter crab and cheese over the mushrooms.

Mix sour cream and mayonnaise with reserved mushroom liquid, salt and flour. Add enough cream to make a total of 2 cups. Blend in eggs and Tabasco sauce and pour into baked pie shell.

Bake at 350° for 55 minutes or until set. Let stand 15 minutes before serving.

Crustless Crab Quiche 6 servings

½ pound fresh
mushrooms, sliced
2 tablespoons butter
4 eggs
1 cup sour cream
1 cup small curd cottage
cheese
½ cup grated Parmesan
cheese
¼ cup flour
1 teaspoon onion powder
¼ teaspoon salt
4 drops Tabasco sauce
2 cups grated Monterey
Jack cheese
6 ounces crab meat

Sauté mushrooms in butter until tender. Remove from heat and drain.

In a blender or food processor, combine eggs, sour cream, cottage cheese, Parmesan cheese, flour, onion powder, salt and Tabasco sauce. Blend until smooth.

Spray a 9-inch deep-dish pie plate or a 10-inch quiche dish with non-stick cooking spray. Pour mixture into pan. Fold in cheese, crab and mushrooms.

Bake at 350° for 45 minutes. Let stand about 5 minutes before serving.

Cottage Quiche

8 servings

CRUST

½ cup butter, softened
3-ounce package cream
   cheese
1 cup flour

Cut butter and cream cheese into flour, using a pastry cutter, until mixture becomes crumbly.

Press mixture into a 10-inch pie plate or 10-inch quiche pan, forming crust on the bottom and sides. Bake at 450° for 10 minutes.

FILLING

1 cup canned shrimp,
   drained
½ cup chopped green
   onion
½ cup grated Cheddar
   cheese
3 eggs
1 cup light cream
1 cup cottage cheese
1 tablespoon flour
½ teaspoon curry
   powder
¼ teaspoon salt
¼ teaspoon pepper
2 tablespoons Parmesan
   cheese
1 tablespoon chopped
   parsley

Spread shrimp, onion and Cheddar cheese over the bottom of the baked pastry shell.

In a medium bowl, combine eggs, cream, cottage cheese, flour, curry powder, salt and pepper and beat until well blended. Pour mixture over shrimp mixture. Sprinkle with Parmesan cheese and parsley.

Bake at 350° for 35 to 45 minutes or until a knife inserted in the center comes out clean. Serve immediately.

Substitutions: 1 cup diced sausage for shrimp. ½ teaspoon dry mustard for curry powder.

To hard boil eggs, put the eggs in a small saucepan and cover with water. Bring to a boil. Cover the pan, turn off the burner and let the eggs stand 15 to 20 minutes. Plunge immediately into cold water and a gray band will not form around the yolk.

Spicy Green Quiche

6-8 servings

1 10-ounce package
frozen chopped spinach
4 eggs, beaten
Salt and pepper
¼ cup chopped green
onions
1½ cups evaporated milk
1 cup grated Swiss
cheese
1 cup grated jalapeño
cheese
¼ cup grated Parmesan
cheese
½ pound hard salami,
finely diced, optional
Deep dish pie shell,
prebaked 10 minutes
at 400°, optional

Cook spinach according to package directions. Squeeze out excess water.

In a medium bowl, beat eggs with a whisk. Add salt, pepper, onions, spinach and evaporated milk. Stir lightly and add cheeses and salami. Stir until mixed.

Pour into a greased 7x11-inch oblong pan or a pie shell. Sprinkle Parmesan cheese over top. Bake at 350° for 30 minutes. Cool 5 to 10 minutes before cutting.

Pastrami Quiche

6-8 servings

1 7¾-ounce can spinach,
well drained
1½ cups diced pastrami
4 green onions, chopped
10 fresh mushrooms,
sliced
½ green pepper, chopped
2 tablespoons butter
6 eggs, well beaten
1 8-ounce package
cream cheese,
softened
1 cup grated Monterey
Jack cheese
1 cup grated Cheddar
cheese
1 8-inch unbaked pie shell

In a medium skillet, sauté spinach, pastrami, green onions, mushrooms and green pepper in butter until soft. Drain.

In a medium bowl, mix eggs with cooked mixture. Add cream cheese, Jack cheese and Cheddar cheese and stir until well mixed. Pour into pie shell. Bake at 350° for 30 minutes or until set.

140

Spinach Quiche

6-8 servings

1 9-inch baked pie shell
2 medium onions,
   chopped
2 tablespoons olive oil
1½ packages frozen
   chopped spinach,
   thawed and drained
¼ pound ham **or** bacon,
   cooked and diced
½ cup grated fresh
   Parmesan cheese
¾ cup ricotta cheese
3 eggs, lightly beaten
¼ teaspoon salt
⅛ teaspoon pepper

Sauté onions in oil until transparent.

In a medium bowl, combine remaining ingredients with onions. Spread into baked pie shell.

Bake at 350° for 45 minutes.

Southwestern Quiche

4-6 servings

1 9-inch unbaked pie
   shell, made with
   1 teaspoon chili powder
   added to flour
¾ cup grated Cheddar
   cheese
½ cup grated Monterey
   Jack cheese
3 eggs, beaten
1 teaspoon salt
¼ teaspoon white
   pepper
1½ cups light cream
1 4-ounce can diced
   green chiles (or more),
   drained
1 2½-ounce can sliced
   ripe olives, drained
2 tablespoons finely
   chopped green onions

Preheat oven to 400°. Prick bottom of pie shell and bake 8 to 10 minutes. Remove from oven and turn oven to 350°.

Mix cheeses together and spread over bottom of pie shell. Combine remaining ingredients and pour over cheese. Bake 40 to 45 minutes.

141

Chiles Rellenos con Queso   4 servings

½ pound Monterey Jack
  cheese
8 canned whole green
  chiles
4 eggs, separated
4 tablespoons flour
Oil for frying

Cut cheese into strips 1x2x½-inch.
Place a strip of cheese inside each
green chile, using wooden toothpicks
to hold chiles and cheese together, if
necessary.

Beat egg whites until stiff. Lightly beat
egg yolks and fold into whites with
flour.

Drop stuffed chiles into batter and
coat well. With a spoon, place each in
a skillet with 1½ inches of medium hot
oil and fry until golden on both sides.
Drain on paper towels and remove
toothpicks.

To serve, place chiles in boiling sauce
long enough to heat through, about
4 to 5 minutes.

NOTE: Chiles may be prepared a day
in advance and heated in the sauce
just before serving.

SAUCE

½ onion, minced
1 garlic clove, minced
1 tablespoon oil
2 cups solid pack
  tomatoes
2 cups chicken stock
½ teaspoon salt
¼ teaspoon pepper
1 teaspoon oregano,
  crushed

In a large skillet, sauté onion and
garlic in oil until tender. Strain
tomatoes into skillet, forcing purée
through a sieve. Add chicken stock.
Heat to boiling and add salt, pepper
and oregano.

*Yolks aren't as likely to break if you separate them from
the whites while still cold from refrigerator.*

Fiesta Chile Bake

6 servings

2 4-ounce cans whole
   green chiles
½ pound Monterey Jack
   cheese, grated
½ pound Cheddar
   cheese, grated
2 eggs
2 tablespoons flour
1 13-ounce can
   evaporated milk
1 4-ounce can tomato
   sauce **or** salsa
½ cup sour cream
1 4-ounce can sliced
   mushrooms, drained
Fresh parsley

Drain and split chiles. Remove seeds and rinse in cold water, keeping them in large pieces. Layer **half** the chiles on the bottom of a 7x12-inch glass baking dish. Layer Jack cheese, the remaining chiles and Cheddar cheese.

In a medium bowl, beat eggs, flour and milk and pour over all. Do not stir.

Bake at 350° for 30 minutes. Top with tomato sauce or salsa and sour cream. Add mushrooms and parsley. Turn oven off and return casserole to oven for 15 minutes. The residual heat will finish the cooking. Cut into squares to serve.

If beaten eggs are to be combined with a hot mixture, stir about ½ cup hot mixture into eggs before adding the eggs to the remaining mixture. This keeps the eggs from cooking into hard lumps.

"Thick and lemon-colored" is the word on beating egg yolks. Egg whites are beaten until stiff and glossy – never dry.

Hollandaise Sauce I
1 cup

4 egg yolks
½ cup butter **or** margarine
¼ cup boiling water
2 tablespoons lemon juice
¼ teaspoon salt

In a bowl which will fit a double boiler base, beat egg yolks until light in color and thick.

In top of double boiler, melt butter. With electric beater running, slowly add butter to egg yolks until the consistency of mayonnaise. Blend in boiling water.

Place bowl on double boiler over low heat and beat with whisk until thick.

Remove from heat and add lemon juice and salt. Return to double boiler which has been removed from heat until ready to serve.

Serve with Eggs Benedict, artichokes or broccoli.

Blender Hollandaise Sauce
1 cup

3 egg yolks
2 tablespoons lemon juice
Pinch of salt
Dash Tabasco sauce
½ cup butter, melted

In blender, combine egg yolks, lemon juice, salt and Tabasco sauce on low speed. Remove cover and pour butter into egg mixture in a slow stream.

NOTE: If not used immediately, place blender container in warm water.

Keep yolks centered in eggs by stirring the water while cooking hard boiled eggs. (Especially good for deviled eggs.)

Bound to Please: Mysteries of the Earth

In Idaho, the old still seems new. Until the turn of the century cool-
ng ice was cut from underground caves and today visitors still ex-
lore the dark caverns. Astronauts trained at Craters of the Moon,
n 80-square-mile area of desolation left by volcanic eruptions
,OOO years ago.

Idaho is a land of geological wonder. The Shoshone Falls on the
nake River are higher than Niagara, while the nearby Hagerman
'alley boasts its "Thousand Springs" as well as world-famous fossil
eds. Hot springs, sand dunes, archaeological sites, the Silent City
f Rocks with the granite carvings left by emigrants on the Califor-
ia Trail – with all of this and more, Idaho has much to offer its peo-
le and its visitors.

Main Dish

Vegetable

Molded

Fruit

Dressings

Bengal Salad

4 servings

1½ cups finely diced celery
2 ounces sliced water chestnuts
½ cup cubed pineapple
8 ounces small shrimp
8 ounces crab
1 ounce pine nuts
½ ounce shredded coconut

Toss celery, water chestnuts, pineapple and shrimp together lightly. Arrange in lettuce cup. Sprinkle crab meat over the top. Top with dressing. Sprinkle with pine nuts and coconut.

BENGAL DRESSING

1 cup whipping cream
1 cup mayonnaise
½ cup sour cream
⅛ teaspoon curry powder
Juice of one lemon
Dash of garlic powder
Dash of Worcestershire sauce
Pinch of salt

Whip cream until fluffy. Blend mayonnaise and sour cream. Fold into whipped cream. Gently fold remaining seasonings into mixture.

NOTE: Dressing becomes stronger as it sits.

Vermicelli-Seafood Salad

10-12 servings

1 12-ounce package vermicelli
6 hard boiled eggs, chopped
6 celery stalks, chopped
6 medium sweet pickles, chopped
¼ yellow onion, chopped
Salt to taste
1½ cups mayonnaise
2 4½-ounce cans shrimp or crab, drained
Paprika

Break vermicelli in half and cook according to package directions. Drain and rinse in cold water.

In a large bowl, combine vermicelli, eggs, celery, pickles, onion, salt and mayonnaise. Mix well and refrigerate.

To serve, add seafood and toss lightly. Garnish with paprika.

145

Shrimp-Walnut Salad

6-8 servings

2 tablespoons butter
½ teaspoon rosemary, crushed
1 cup walnut halves
2 pounds small shrimp, cooked
2 tablespoons chopped chives
1 tablespoon chopped parsley
6 radishes, sliced
12 stuffed green olives, sliced
3 ounces feta cheese, crumbled
½ cup small pickled onions, optional
Crisp salad greens
3 firm tomatoes, cut in wedges
1 large avocado, sliced

In a heavy skillet, melt butter over low heat. Stir in rosemary. Add walnuts and cook about 10 minutes or until walnuts are lightly toasted, stirring often. Remove from skillet and set aside.

In a medium bowl, pour dressing over shrimp. Add chives and parsley. Mix gently, cover and refrigerate at least 1 hour.

Add walnut mixture, radishes, olives, feta cheese and onions to shrimp and toss gently.

Line a serving plate with salad greens. Arrange salad on greens. Garnish with tomatoes and avocado.

DRESSING

¼ cup lemon juice
1 tablespoon seasoned salt
½ teaspoon oregano, crushed
½ teaspoon marjoram, crushed
¼ teaspoon pepper
⅛ teaspoon garlic powder
½ cup olive oil

In a blender, combine all ingredients and blend well.

146

Hot Prawn and
Grapefruit Cocktail Salad

8 servings

½ cup catsup
¼ cup chili sauce
¼ cup grapefruit juice
2 tablespoons lemon
  juice
1 tablespoon chopped
  green onions, including
  tops
¾ teaspoon salt
1 teaspoon prepared
  horseradish
1½ teaspoons
  Worcestershire sauce
2 to 3 drops Tabasco
  sauce
1 tablespoon butter
1½ pounds raw prawns,
  peeled and deveined
1½ cups grapefruit
  sections, membrane
  removed
Lettuce
1 green onion, chopped

In a saucepan, combine catsup, chili sauce, grapefruit juice, lemon juice, onions, salt, horseradish, Worcestershire sauce, Tabasco sauce and butter. Bring to simmer.

Add prawns and cook for 6 minutes or until pink. Add grapefruit and heat through.

To serve, spoon mixture over chilled lettuce and garnish with green onion.

Small, smooth-skinned lemons at room temperature make best juice.

147

Spicy Seafood Salad

4 servings

¼ cup dried cloud ears **or** wood ear mushrooms
½ pound medium raw shrimp
Pinch salt
½ pound scallops
1 small head romaine lettuce, rinsed and dried
Vegetable oil
12 won ton skins, cut into ¼-inch strips
½ cup slivered blanched almonds

Soak mushrooms in warm water to cover until soft, about 20 minutes.

In a large kettle, bring 1 quart of water to a boil. Add shrimp and salt. Reduce heat and simmer for about 3 to 4 minutes. Remove shrimp with slotted spoon to a colander, reserving liquid, and rinse under cold water. Drain and set aside.

Add scallops to simmering liquid and poach for about 5 minutes. Rinse under cold water and pat dry with paper towels. Cut scallops crosswise into ¼-inch pieces. Set aside.

Shell and devein shrimp. Cut crosswise into ¼-inch slices. Set aside.

Stack romaine leaves, a few at a time, and roll tightly into a cylinder. Cut crosswise at ¼-inch intervals. Put into salad bowl and refrigerate until needed.

In a wok heat 2 inches of oil to 350°. Fry won ton strips, a few at a time, until golden, about 20 seconds, pushing them gently into oil with slotted spoon after they rise to the surface. Drain on paper towels and set aside.

Add almonds to oil and cook until golden, about 15 seconds. Drain on paper towels and set aside.

Once mushrooms have softened, drain and rinse under cold water. Drain on paper towels and pat dry. Trim any tough spots and cut into bite-sized pieces. Set aside.

Spicy Seafood Salad *(Continued)*

To assemble, add shrimp, scallops and mushrooms to lettuce. Crush won tons into small pieces and add to salad. Add almonds and toss well.

To serve, pour desired amount of dressing over salad and toss well. Adjust seasoning with salt and chili oil if necessary and serve immediately.

DRESSING

2 small scallions, cut into
   1-inch lengths
1 garlic clove
1¼-inch slice fresh
   ginger, peeled
2 tablespoons red wine
   vinegar
1 scant tablespoon
   sesame oil
1 tablespoon vegetable
   oil
1 teaspoon chili oil
1 teaspoon sugar
½ teaspoon salt

Into a food processor, with machine running, drop scallions, garlic and ginger. Process until minced. Add vinegar, sesame oil, vegetable oil, chili oil, sugar and salt and process until well blended, about 10 seconds.

Oriental Luncheon Salad   4 servings

1 10-ounce package
   frozen Italian green
   beans
1 6½-ounce can tuna,
   drained
1 cup sliced celery
½ cup mayonnaise
1 tablespoon lemon juice
1½ teaspoons soy sauce
Dash garlic powder
1 cup chow mein noodles

Cook beans according to package directions. Drain and cool.

In a salad bowl, combine tuna, celery, mayonnaise, lemon juice, soy sauce and garlic powder. Chill.

Just before serving, add beans and chow mein noodles and toss gently.

149

Macaroni-Seafood Salad   10-12 **servings**

1 cup salad macaroni
½ cup mayonnaise
1 tablespoon
    Worcestershire sauce
1 tablespoon lemon juice
½ teaspoon salt
⅛ teaspoon pepper
1 cup cooked peas,
    drained
1 cup diced celery
½ cup diced onion
½ cup grated hot pepper
    cheese
1 2-ounce jar pimiento,
    chopped
1 tablespoon chopped
    parsley
½ cup diced green
    pepper
2 hard boiled eggs, diced,
    optional
1 7-ounce can shrimp **or**
    tuna, drained
½ cup sliced stuffed
    green olives
1 cup cherry tomatoes

Cook macaroni according to package directions and rinse in cold water. Drain well and place in salad bowl.

In a small bowl, combine mayonnaise, Worcestershire sauce, lemon juice, salt and pepper. Add to macaroni and mix well.

Add remaining ingredients, **except** olives and tomatoes, and toss gently. Chill 2 to 3 hours.

To serve, garnish with olives and tomatoes.

*Flowers make a lovely garnish but use them sparingly –
some may have too much scent and spoil the effect.*

150

Shrimp Aspic

2 tablespoons unflavored
  gelatin
½ cup cold water
1 cup tomato soup,
  undiluted
1 8-ounce package
  cream cheese,
  softened
1 cucumber, finely
  chopped
1 cup chopped celery
4 cups salad shrimp
1 teaspoon salt
3 teaspoons minced
  onion
1 cup mayonnaise
Juice of ½ lemon
Dash cayenne

In a large bowl, soften gelatin in cold water.

Heat soup to boiling, remove from heat and add to gelatin mixture.

Blend in cream cheese and allow to cool.

Stir in remaining ingredients, **except** garnishes. Pour into a 2-quart mold and chill overnight or for several hours.

To serve, unmold on a serving plate lined with salad greens. Garnish with artichoke hearts, deviled eggs or asparagus tips.

GARNISHES

Crisp salad greens
Artichoke hearts
Deviled eggs
Asparagus tips

Green Salad Herbs

2½ tablespoons minced, dried parsley
2 tablespoons chopped dried chives
1 tablespoon dried thyme
1 tablespoon dried basil
1 teaspoon dried dill weed
1 teaspoon dried tarragon
Mix all ingredients well and store in a tightly covered container.

Seafood and Pasta Salad Pescara

6 servings

1 pound small pasta
(penné, elbows, shells,
swirls)
3 cups diced cooked
fresh seafood (shrimp,
mussels, calamari,
lobster, crab or white
fish)
¾ cup diced, seeded
fresh plum tomatoes
¼ cup fresh parsley
3 tablespoons chopped
fresh basil
½ cup finely chopped
fresh dill
½ cup minced shallots
3 tablespoons small
capers
¼ cup chopped pimiento
¼ cup chopped ripe
olives
½ cup lemon juice
2 tablespoons oil
¼ cup Dijon mustard
1 tablespoon vinegar
½ cup halved ripe olives
¼ cup grated fresh
zucchini

Cook pasta according to package
directions. Drain.

In a large bowl, combine pasta,
seafood, **½ cup** of the tomatoes,
parsley, basil, dill, shallots, capers,
pimiento, **chopped** olives and lemon
juice. Add oil and toss.

In a small bowl, mix mustard and
vinegar together until smooth. Pour
over salad and toss well.

Garnish with remaining tomatoes, the
halved olives and zucchini.

West Coast Salad

6-8 servings

2 heads romaine lettuce
1 cup plain croutons
½ cup Parmesan cheese
¼ cup Bleu cheese,
crumbled
1 egg

Tear lettuce into bite-sized pieces.
Place in a large salad bowl, add
croutons and cheeses and toss gently.

To serve, add egg to dressing and
blend well. Pour desired amount of
dressing over salad and toss gently.

West Coast Salad *(Continued)*

DRESSING

½ cup oil
¼ cup red wine vinegar
1 large anchovy fillet,
   mashed, optional
1 large garlic clove,
   minced
2 teaspoons
   Worcestershire sauce
¼ teaspoon salt
Dash pepper

Blend together all ingredients and refrigerate.

Classic Caesar Salad   4 servings

1 large head romaine
   lettuce, washed and
   torn into bite-sized
   pieces
2 garlic cloves
6 tablespoons good
   quality olive oil
2 tablespoons lemon juice
¼ teaspoon
   Worcestershire sauce
½ teaspoon dry mustard
4 drops Tabasco sauce
½-1 inch anchovy paste
6 slices bacon, cut in
   ¼-inch pieces and fried
1½ cups garlic croutons
1 egg, coddled
Salt and pepper to taste
½ cup freshly grated
   Parmesan cheese

Chill romaine while preparing remaining ingredients.

Slice 1 garlic clove in half lengthwise and rub inside a large wooden salad bowl. Discard remainder of clove. In the bottom of the bowl, combine olive oil, lemon juice, Worcestershire sauce, dry mustard, Tabasco, anchovy paste, and remaining garlic clove (pressed). Whisk lightly.

Add romaine and top with bacon, croutons and egg; salt and pepper to taste. Toss well. Add Parmesan cheese and toss. Serve immediately on chilled plates.

Reef Street Special Salad · 4-6 servings

2 tablespoons olive oil
Salt
1 garlic clove
2 heads romaine, sliced
    into 1-inch strips
2 tomatoes, peeled and
    chopped
¼ cup chopped green
    onions
½ cup freshly grated
    Romano cheese
1 pound bacon, cooked
    and crumbled
1 cup croutons

In a large salad bowl, pour in olive oil. Sprinkle with salt and rub in garlic. Remove garlic and add romaine, tomatoes, green onions, cheese and bacon.

To serve, pour desired amount of dressing over salad. Add croutons and toss well.

DRESSING

3 ounces olive oil
Juice of 2 lemons
½ teaspoon freshly
    ground pepper
¼ teaspoon chopped
    fresh mint
¼ teaspoon oregano
1 egg, coddled

In a small bowl, combine all ingredients and whip vigorously.

Italian Seasoning

1 tablespoon dried basil
1 tablespoon dried oregano
1 tablespoon minced, dried parsley
1 teaspoon rosemary
1 teaspoon thyme
½ teaspoon paprika
½ teaspoon coarsely ground black pepper
Mix all ingredients well and store in a tightly covered container.

Korean Salad   8 servings

½ pound fresh spinach
1 small head romaine
  lettuce
1 15-ounce can bean
  sprouts, drained
1 8-ounce can water
  chestnuts, drained and
  sliced
½ cup slivered almonds
1 pound bacon, cooked
  and crumbled
3 hard boiled eggs, sliced

Tear spinach and romaine into bite-sized pieces. Place in a salad bowl. Add bean sprouts, water chestnuts and almonds. Toss gently.

To serve, pour desired amount of dressing over salad. Garnish with bacon and eggs.

DRESSING

1½ cups mayonnaise
1 teaspoon prepared
  mustard
½ teaspoon Tabasco
  sauce
1½ teaspoons chili
  powder
1 tablespoon grated
  onion
2 teaspoons lemon juice
¾ teaspoon thyme
¾ teaspoon garlic salt
¾ teaspoon marjoram

In a blender, combine all ingredients and blend until smooth.

Place salad dressing in the bottom of the bowl with layered ingredients on top – toss just before serving.

155

Sweet and Sour Spinach Salad

6-8 servings

3 bunches fresh spinach

1½ cups fresh bean sprouts **or** 1 15-ounce can, drained

½ cup chopped green onions

½ cup chopped celery, optional

8 bacon slices, cooked and crumbled

2 hard boiled eggs, chopped

Tear spinach into bite-sized pieces.

In a large bowl, combine spinach, bean sprouts, onion and celery.

To serve, pour desired amount of dressing over salad and toss gently. Garnish with bacon and eggs.

DRESSING

1 cup oil

¼ cup white vinegar

¾ cup sugar

½ cup catsup

1 tablespoon Worcestershire sauce

In a quart jar, combine all ingredients and shake well.

Mandarin Salad

4-6 servings

1 head lettuce

1 cup chopped celery

1 tablespoon chopped parsley

2 green onions, sliced, including tops

1 11-ounce can mandarin oranges, drained

¼ cup slivered almonds

Tear lettuce into bite-sized pieces.

In a salad bowl, combine all ingredients **except** almonds and toss gently.

To serve, pour desired amount of dressing over salad. Garnish with almonds.

Mandarin Salad *(Continued)*

DRESSING

½ teaspoon salt
¼ teaspoon Tabasco
   sauce
¼ cup olive oil
2 tablespoons sugar
2 tablespoons tarragon
   vinegar

In a blender, mix all ingredients until well blended.

Flaming Spinach Salad   6 servings

2 bunches fresh spinach
¼ cup white vinegar
8 bacon slices, cut into
   ½-inch pieces
4 tablespoons sugar
4 tablespoons red wine
   vinegar
1 tablespoon
   Worcestershire sauce
Juice of 1 lemon
1 jigger cognac

Rinse spinach in cold water and white vinegar. Dry carefully. Tear into bite-sized pieces and put into a large bowl.

In a skillet, sauté bacon. Add sugar, wine vinegar and Worcestershire sauce. Heat to boiling, then strain. Pour sauce over spinach, leaving bacon pieces in skillet.

Pour lemon juice over spinach and toss. Put spinach on individual salad plates. Add cognac to bacon pieces and ignite. Spoon over spinach and serve immediately.

Store garlic at room temperature. Fresh garlic has milder taste.

Apple-Spinach Salad

8 servings

2 bunches fresh spinach
6 green onions, chopped
1 red apple, diced
8 bacon slices, cooked
and crumbled

Tear spinach into bite-sized pieces.
Add green onion, apple and bacon.
Toss gently.

To serve, add desired amount of
dressing to salad and toss gently.

DRESSING

1 garlic clove, minced
Dash dry mustard
1 teaspoon salt
⅓ cup catsup
⅓ cup sugar
⅓ cup vinegar
1 cup oil
Dash ground cloves
Dash pepper

In a blender, combine all ingredients
and blend well.

Wilted Spinach Salad

4-6 servings

1 pound fresh spinach
3 slices bacon, cooked
and crumbled

Tear spinach into bite-sized pieces.
Place in a large salad bowl.

To serve, pour desired amount of hot
dressing over spinach. Garnish with
bacon and serve immediately.

DRESSING

1 tablespoon oil
4 tablespoons sesame
seeds
2 tablespoons sugar
4 tablespoons vinegar
1 tablespoon soy sauce

In a heavy skillet, gently heat oil.
Brown sesame seeds lightly over
medium heat. Remove from heat. Add
sugar, vinegar and soy sauce. Return
to heat and cook until almost boiling.

Chicken and Curried Rice Salad

6-8 servings

1⅓ cups cooked rice
3 tablespoons finely chopped onion
1 tablespoon vinegar
2 tablespoons corn oil
½ teaspoon curry powder
½ teaspoon salt
1 10-ounce package frozen peas, cooked and drained
1½ cups diced cooked chicken, turkey **or** seafood
1 cup chopped celery
¾ cup mayonnaise

While rice is still hot, stir in onion, vinegar, oil, curry powder and salt. Add peas and chicken and toss gently.

To serve, add celery and mayonnaise and toss gently.

Know your salad apples:

Crisp red-cheeked DELICIOUS, with 5 rounded points on the blossom end is mellow, sweet, and juicy with a fruity fragrance. GOLDEN DELICIOUS has a speckled bright yellow skin, a brisk flavor. And it doesn't darken when cut, making it ideal for salads. Crispy yellow GRIMES GOLDEN is noted for its distinctive tart flavor. Rosy-cheeked JONATHANS, McINTOSH, and STAYMANS are juicy, tart and crunchy. McIntosh and Stayman are best in fall, early winter. WINESAP is a winter-spring apple with glossy red skin, tart wine-like flavor. It "pops" with juice. YELLOW NEWTON has pale yellow-green skin, is juicy and fresh-flavored.

Chicken and Green Grape Salad

8-10 servings

6 chicken breasts, cooked and skinned
4 celery stalks, finely chopped
½ cup chopped green onions
Dash cayenne
2 cups whole Thompson seedless grapes
Bottled French dressing
½ cup mayonnaise
1 cup heavy cream, whipped
1 cup slivered almonds, toasted

Cut chicken into bite-sized pieces. Place in a large bowl.

Add celery, onion, cayenne and grapes. Mix well. Add enough French dressing to cover chicken. Refrigerate overnight.

Bring to room temperature and drain French dressing from chicken. Combine mayonnaise and whipped cream and add to salad. To serve, add almonds and toss well.

Chicken-Cantaloupe Salad

9 servings

4 chicken breasts, cooked
2 cups thinly sliced celery
1¼ cups slivered almonds
2 11-ounce cans mandarin oranges, drained
1 teaspoon salt
3 medium cantaloupes, well chilled

Cut chicken into bite-sized pieces.

In a large bowl, combine chicken, celery, almonds, oranges and salt.

Blend just enough dressing with chicken mixture to bind ingredients together. Cover and chill.

Just before serving, cut each cantaloupe into thirds and scoop out seeds. Spoon chicken salad over each wedge.

Pass remaining dressing in a small bowl.

Chicken-Cantaloupe Salad   *(Continued)*

DRESSING

¾ cup sour cream
¾ cup mayonnaise
3 tablespoons finely
   minced preserved
   ginger
2 tablespoons lemon
   juice
1 teaspoon grated
   orange peel
Dash nutmeg

In a small bowl, blend sour cream,
mayonnaise, ginger, lemon juice,
orange peel and nutmeg.

Chicken-Pineapple Salad   8 servings

4 cups cooked and diced
   chicken breasts
1½ cups thinly sliced
   celery
1 20-ounce can
   pineapple tidbits,
   drained
1½ cups halved
   Thompson seedless
   grapes
1 cup slivered almonds
1 8-ounce can water
   chestnuts, drained and
   chopped

In a large bowl, combine all
ingredients. Toss gently.

To serve, pour desired amount of
dressing over salad and toss gently.

DRESSING

1¼ cups mayonnaise
1 tablespoon soy sauce
½ teaspoon curry
   powder
Juice of 1 lemon

In a quart jar, combine all ingredients
and shake well.

161

Oriental Chicken Salad

6-8 servings

1 pound chicken breasts
½ cup sesame seeds
½ pound fresh bean
    sprouts
2 cups shredded cabbage
4 large green onions with
    tops, chopped

Cook chicken, skin and cut into small pieces.

Spread sesame seeds on a baking sheet and bake at 350° for 5 minutes, being careful not to burn.

Blanch bean sprouts by placing in boiling water for 30 seconds. Drain.

In a salad bowl, combine all ingredients and mix well.

Add dressing and refrigerate.

DRESSING

1 teaspoon ginger juice*
2 teaspoons dry mustard
½ cup soy sauce
3 tablespoons peanut oil
2 tablespoons rice wine
    vinegar
2 garlic cloves, minced
1 tablespoon sugar
2 teaspoons sesame oil
¼ cup chopped green
    onion tops

Combine all ingredients and mix well. Let stand for 5 minutes.

NOTE: Dressing may be made up to 2 days ahead or frozen.

*GINGER JUICE

3 tablespoons peeled,
    chopped fresh ginger
    root
5 tablespoons soy sauce
2 teaspoons white wine

Combine all ingredients in blender and blend until smooth.

Chinese Chicken Salad

6 servings

4 chicken breasts
4 slices fresh ginger root
1 head lettuce, shredded
½ package won ton skins
5 green onions, sliced
1 4-ounce package
   toasted almonds
¼ cup toasted sesame
   seeds

Cook chicken breasts in boiling water with ginger root for about 20 minutes or until tender. Let chicken stand in broth for 2 hours. Drain, skin and shred.

Deep fry won ton skins according to package directions. Drain on paper towels and allow to cool. Place won tons in a plastic bag and crush lightly.

In a large bowl, combine all ingredients and toss.

To serve, pour desired amount of dressing over salad and toss gently. Serve immediately.

NOTE: Salad should not stand for more than 20 minutes.

DRESSING

4 tablespoons sugar
2½ teaspoons salt
1 teaspoon MSG
½ teaspoon pepper
4 tablespoons vinegar
½ cup good quality oil

In a quart jar, combine all ingredients and shake well.

Grate citrus rinds and freeze for use when needed.

Avocado and Chicken Salad   8-10 **servings**

*A very popular item on the luncheon menu at the
HasBrouck House, Nampa.*

6 cups cooked chicken
**½ cup finely minced
onion**
1 cup finely diced celery
2 tablespoons capers
1 tablespoon lemon juice
**¼ cup minced fresh
parsley**
**3 hard boiled eggs,
chopped**
Salt and pepper to taste
1 to 1½ cups mayonnaise
**2 avocado halves per
person**
Shredded lettuce
Paprika

In a large bowl, toss chicken, onion,
celery, capers, lemon juice and
parsley. Add eggs, seasonings and
mayonnaise. Toss until well mixed.

To serve, place 2 avocado halves on a
bed of shredded lettuce, fill with
chicken salad, sprinkle with paprika
and garnish with tomato and parsley.

GARNISHES

Tomato
Parsley

*Cutting avocados – cut fruit in half lengthwise; then cup
it between palms of hands and gently twist halves apart.
Tap seed with sharp edge of knife. Lift or pry seed
gently out.*

164

No Fault Salad

12-16 servings

1 12-ounce package
vermicelli noodles
2 tablespoons sugar
1 8-ounce bottle
Bernstein's Italian
dressing
2 heads iceberg lettuce
1 green pepper, chopped
6 celery stalks, chopped
1 large red onion,
chopped
2 tomatoes, sliced
½ pound Provolone
cheese
½ pound hard salami
½ pound cooked turkey

Cook vermicelli according to package directions. Drain.

Add sugar to Italian dressing. Pour over vermicelli. Cool.

Tear lettuce into bite-sized pieces. Add green pepper, celery, onion, tomatoes and vermicelli, and toss gently.

Cut Provolone, salami and turkey into bite-sized pieces. Add to salad and mix well.

Salad Combo

4 servings

1 small head iceburg
lettuce
3 small tomatoes
½ cup olive oil
2 tablespoons white
wine vinegar
1 tablespoon soy sauce
¼ teaspoon sugar
Coarsely ground black
pepper
¾ pound round steak,
thinly sliced
1 tablespoon oil
½ cup chopped salted
peanuts

Tear lettuce into bite-sized pieces and place in a large salad bowl. Slice tomatoes ¼-inch thick and cut each slice in half. Toss with lettuce.

In a small bowl, combine olive oil, vinegar, soy sauce, sugar and pepper. Pour over lettuce and tomatoes. Toss gently.

Stir fry beef in oil over high heat for 2 to 3 minutes. Place on top of salad and garnish with peanuts. Serve immediately.

165

Artichoke and Wild Rice Salad

6-8 servings

1 5-ounce package wild
  and white rice mix
1 6-ounce jar artichoke
  hearts, drained
12 to 15 cherry
  tomatoes, halved
1 cup frozen peas,
  thawed
4 cups chopped green
  onions

Cook rice according to package directions. Cut artichoke hearts into bite-size pieces.

In a large bowl, combine rice, artichokes, tomatoes, peas and onions. Refrigerate overnight.

To serve, pour desired amount of dressing over salad and toss.

DRESSING

¼ cup wine vinegar
¾ cup oil
2 teaspoons minced
  parsley
1 teaspoon tarragon
  leaves

Combine all ingredients and mix well.

Marinated Vegetable Salad

6-8 servings

1 10-ounce package
  frozen mixed
  vegetables
4 celery stalks, chopped
½ green pepper, chopped
1 onion, chopped
1 2-ounce jar pimiento,
  chopped
1 15-ounce can kidney
  beans, rinsed and
  drained

In a medium saucepan, cook vegetables according to package directions and drain. Combine with remaining ingredients in a salad bowl.

Pour marinade over vegetables, cover and refrigerate 24 hours. Toss before serving.

166

Marinated Vegetable Salad *(Continued)*

MARINADE

¾ cup sugar
2 tablespoons flour
1 tablespoon dry
   mustard
½ cup vinegar

In a small saucepan, combine all
ingredients and cook, stirring
constantly, until clear.

Marinated Summer Salad   12-16 servings

1 head cauliflower,
   divided into flowerets
3 carrots, sliced
1 green pepper, sliced
1 cup chopped celery
1 onion, sliced
2 15-ounce cans Chinese
   vegetables, drained
1 15-ounce can sliced
   green beans, drained
1 8-ounce can sliced
   water chestnuts,
   drained
1 15-ounce can white
   whole kernel corn,
   drained
1 4-ounce can mushroom
   buttons, drained
1 4-ounce jar pimientos

In a large salad bowl, combine all
ingredients and toss well.

Pour marinade over vegetables, cover
and refrigerate 24 hours.

NOTE: Salad will keep 3 to 4 weeks.

MARINADE

2 cups vinegar
1½ cups sugar
½ cup brown sugar
1 cup oil
3 teaspoons salt
Pepper to taste

In a blender, combine all ingredients
and mix well.

167

Marinated Carrot Salad

8 servings

5 cups carrots, cut into
   1-inch pieces
1 large onion, cut in
   sections
1 large green pepper,
   sliced
1 16-ounce can garbanzo
   beans, drained
1 16-ounce can regular
   cut green beans,
   drained
2 cups fresh broccoli
   flowerets
2 cups fresh cauliflower
   flowerets

Blanch carrots in boiling water for
1 minute. In a large salad bowl,
combine all vegetables.

Pour dressing over vegetables and
refrigerate overnight.

DRESSING

1 10-ounce can tomato
   soup, undiluted
½ cup oil
⅔ cup vinegar
½ cup sugar
1 teaspoon prepared
   mustard
1 teaspoon celery seed
1 teaspoon salt
1 teaspoon pepper

In a large bowl, combine all ingredients
and whip with a wire whisk.

Beet Salad

1 3-ounce package lemon
   gelatin
1 cup boiling water
1 cup diced canned beets,
   drained (reserving
   liquid)
¾ cup reserved beet
   liquid
3 tablespoons white
   vinegar
½ teaspoon salt
2 teaspoons grated onion
1 tablespoon prepared
   horseradish
¾ cup diced celery
Lettuce **or** endive leaves
Mayonnaise

In a bowl, dissolve gelatin in water.
Add beet liquid, vinegar, salt, onion
and horseradish. Blend well and
refrigerate until partially set.

Fold in beets and celery. Pour into wet
ring mold and chill until firm.

To serve, unmold salad onto lettuce or
endive leaves and garnish with
mayonnaise.

Sour Cream Cole Slaw

1 garlic clove, minced
1 teaspoon salt
⅛ teaspoon pepper
½ teaspoon dry mustard
3 tablespoons tarragon
   wine vinegar
3 tablespoons chopped
   chives **or** green onions
⅓ cup minced parsley
1 cup mayonnaise
½ cup sour cream
Fresh dill to taste
1 small head cabbage,
   shredded

In a large bowl, combine all ingredients
and toss gently. Chill.

NOTE: Will keep in refrigerator for
1 week without cabbage.

Cucumber and Yogurt Salad   6 servings

4 medium cucumbers
1 teaspoon salt
1 cup yogurt **or** sour
  cream
1½ teaspoons cider
  vinegar
1 garlic clove, minced
¼ teaspoon dill seed
2 tablespoons minced
  fresh mint **or** chives

Peel cucumbers, cut lengthwise into quarters and slice. Sprinkle with salt, drain and chill.

In a bowl, blend yogurt, vinegar, garlic and dill.

To serve, add cucumbers to yogurt mixture. Put in glass bowl and garnish with mint or chives.

Bean and Bacon Slaw   8 servings

½ pound bacon, cooked
  and crumbled
1 small head cabbage,
  finely sliced or
  shredded
1 15-ounce can kidney
  beans, rinsed and
  drained
¾ cup chopped celery
⅓ cup finely chopped
  onion
2½ tablespoons chopped
  parsley
Salt and pepper to taste

Combine all ingredients in a salad bowl and toss well.

Add dressing, mix well, cover and chill.

DRESSING

½ cup mayonnaise
2 tablespoons vinegar

Combine mayonnaise and vinegar.

Broccoli-Cauliflower Salad   8 servings

1 medium head
  cauliflower
4 stalks fresh broccoli
1 bunch green onions,
  sliced
1 green pepper, diced

Divide cauliflower and broccoli into bite-sized pieces.

In a large salad bowl, combine all ingredients.

Pour dressing over salad, toss well, cover and refrigerate overnight.

DRESSING

1 cup mayonnaise
½ cup sour cream
1 package ranch salad
  dressing mix
Salt to taste
1 tablespoon
  Worcestershire sauce
Dash Tabasco sauce
1 tablespoon vinegar
1 tablespoon sugar

In a blender, combine all ingredients and blend well.

Blend Your Own Herbs

Now with so many home herb gardens, there is no reason why we can't make up our own herb and spice blends at home. This way you can be assured of the freshness of the combinations. Feel free to experiment with the amounts if you favor a special herb or like a hotter, spicier taste.

171

Butter Lettuce Salad
with Hearts of Palm

6-8 servings

4 heads butter lettuce
1 14-ounce can hearts of
  palm, drained and sliced
1 bunch radishes, sliced
1 avocado, chopped
½ cup raw cashews

Tear lettuce into bite-sized pieces.

In a large salad bowl, combine all ingredients.

To serve, add dressing to salad and toss gently.

DRESSING

¼ cup white wine
  tarragon vinegar
1 large egg yolk
1 tablespoon Dijon
  mustard
1 shallot, minced
1 teaspoon salt
¼ teaspoon freshly
  ground pepper
¾ cup olive oil

In a quart jar, combine all ingredients, **except** oil, and shake well.

Slowly add oil to vinegar mixture and mix well.

NOTE: Dressing may be prepared ahead and refrigerated.

Bermuda Salad

8-10 servings

1 medium head
  cauliflower, divided into
  flowerets
½ cup sliced green olives
½ large Bermuda onion,
  sliced
1 head iceburg lettuce
½ cup crumbled Bleu
  cheese

In a large salad bowl, combine cauliflower, olives and onion. Add dressing and refrigerate overnight.

To serve, tear lettuce into bite-sized pieces. Combine with Bleu cheese and marinated vegetables. Toss.

Bermuda Salad *(Continued)*

DRESSING

1 cup oil
½ cup catsup
1 teaspoon salt
Dash sugar
Dash onion juice
½ cup wine vinegar

Put all ingredients in blender and blend well.

Tomato-Dill Aspic   8-10 servings

3 envelopes unflavored
  gelatin
5½ cups + 2 tablespoons
  tomato juice
⅓ cup lemon juice
1 tablespoon grated
  onion
1 garlic clove, minced
2 teaspoons dried dill
  weed
2 teaspoons salt
1 teaspoon basil
1 teaspoon oregano
1 bay leaf, crushed
2 8-ounce cans
  artichoke hearts,
  drained

In a small bowl, soften gelatin in ½ cup of the tomato juice.

In a large saucepan, combine remaining tomato juice, lemon juice, onion, garlic, dill weed, salt, basil, oregano and bay leaf. Simmer for 10 minutes and strain.

Add gelatin and stir until dissolved. Cool.

Arrange artichokes on bottom of a 2-quart mold. Add a ¼-inch layer of tomato mixture. Chill until partially set. Add remainder of aspic and refrigerate until set.

Serve with caviar mayonnaise.

CAVIAR MAYONNAISE

1 cup mayonnaise
1 cup sour cream
1 tablespoon lemon juice
2 teaspoons prepared
  mustard
1 1-ounce jar black
  caviar, drained

In a bowl, blend mayonnaise, sour cream, lemon juice and mustard. Fold in caviar. Chill.

Chilled Asparagus Mousse   6 servings

3 10-ounce packages
   frozen asparagus
2 envelopes unflavored
   gelatin
½ cup cold water
1 cup hot consommé
1 5-ounce can sliced
   water chestnuts,
   drained
1 tablespoon lemon juice
1 teaspoon thyme
1 cup mayonnaise

Cook asparagus according to package directions. Drain and purée. Set aside.

Sprinkle gelatin over water and soak for 10 minutes. Pour in hot consommé and stir until dissolved. Fold in water chestnuts, lemon juice, thyme, mayonnaise and puréed asparagus.

Pour mixture into a wet 6-cup mold and refrigerate until set.

To serve, unmold mousse and spread with emerald dressing.

NOTE: Good with chicken or shrimp salad served in the center of the mousse.

EMERALD DRESSING

¼ cup chopped chives
4 parsley sprigs
½ teaspoon thyme
1 green onion, chopped
½ cup packed spinach,
   watercress **or** sorrel
½ teaspoon dry mustard
2 tablespoons tarragon
   vinegar
1½ cups mayonnaise

Process chives, parsley, thyme, green onion, spinach, mustard and vinegar in a blender or food processer. Whisk in mayonnaise.

Make your own dried grated orange or lemon peel by finely grating the peel onto waxed paper. Let it dry on the counter uncovered 3 or 4 hours.

Spiced Peach Mold

6 servings

1 3-ounce package lemon gelatin
1 17-ounce jar spiced peaches, drained and sliced (reserving 1 cup liquid)
½ cup orange juice
½ cup water
1 cup Tokay grapes **or** Queen Anne cherries, halved and seeded
1 cup chopped pecans

In a large bowl, dissolve gelatin in peach liquid. Add orange juice and water and mix well. Add peaches, grapes and pecans and pour into a ring mold. Refrigerate until set. Serve with dressing.

DRESSING

1 cup heavy cream, whipped
4 tablespoons mayonnaise
½ cup orange juice

In a small bowl, combine all ingredients and chill.

Molded Cranberry Salad

12-16 servings

1 3-ounce package lemon gelatin
1 3-ounce package raspberry gelatin
3½ cups boiling water
1 orange
½ cup crushed pineapple, drained (reserving liquid)
1 pound fresh cranberries
1½ cups sugar
½ cup pecans
¼ cup sour cream
¼ cup mayonnaise

In a large bowl, dissolve gelatins in water, **juice of the orange** and reserved liquid from pineapple. Refrigerate until partially set.

In a food processor, chop cranberries and rest of orange, including rind.

Add sugar to cranberry mixture and blend well. Fold pineapple, cranberry mixture and pecans into partially set gelatin. Pour into a 2-quart mold and refrigerate for 24 hours.

To serve, blend sour cream and mayonnaise together. Gently unmold salad onto serving dish and frost with dressing.

175

Jellied Avocado and Orange Salad

6 servings

1 3-ounce package lemon gelatin
½ teaspoon salt
1 cup hot water
1 3-ounce package cream cheese, softened
½ cup mayonnaise
1 7¾-ounce container frozen avocado dip **or** 2 avocados, mashed
2 tablespoons lemon juice
⅛ to ¼ teaspoon Tabasco sauce
¼ cup finely chopped green onions **or** celery
Lettuce greens
3 large oranges, peeled and sliced

In a large bowl, combine gelatin, salt and water; stir until thoroughly dissolved. Chill until syrupy.

In a medium bowl, combine cheese, mayonnaise, avocados, lemon juice, Tabasco sauce and onion. Mix well and stir into gelatin. Pour into a 3 or 4-cup mold. Chill until set.

To serve, unmold salad onto lettuce greens and garnish with orange slices.

Daiquiri Mold

8-10 servings

2 envelopes unflavored gelatin
½ cup lime juice
1 14-ounce can pineapple tidbits, undrained
Water
1½ teaspoons grated lime peel
½ cup sugar
¼ teaspoon salt
1 cup orange juice
½ cup light rum
1 avocado, cut into balls

In a small bowl, soften gelatin in lime juice, set aside. Drain syrup from pineapple and combine syrup with enough water to make 2 cups.

In a medium saucepan, stir grated lime peel, sugar and salt into syrup-water mixture. Heat, stirring to dissolve sugar. Add softened gelatin, continue cooking and stirring until dissolved. Cool. Stir in orange juice and rum. Chill until mixture begins to thicken. Fold in drained pineapple and avocado balls, turn into a 1½-quart mold. Chill until ready to serve.

176

Summer Fruit Salad
8 servings

½ cantaloupe, diced
½ honeydew melon, diced
2 apples, sliced
½ cup halved seedless grapes
1 10-ounce can pineapple tidbits, drained
2 bananas, sliced

In a bowl, combine fruit and toss. Pour sauce over fruit and let stand for a few minutes. Toss, chill and serve.

SAUCE

½ cup mayonnaise
1 banana
1 cup vanilla ice cream
2 ounces frozen orange juice concentrate
½ teaspoon cardamom
1 teaspoon cinnamon
¼ cup powdered sugar

In a blender, combine mayonnaise, banana, ice cream and orange juice. Add cardamom and cinnamon to sugar and blend with rest of ingredients.

Raspberry Ribbon Salad
10-12 servings

2 3-ounce packages raspberry gelatin
1 3-ounce package lemon gelatin
2 cups hot water
1 cup cold orange juice
1 20-ounce can crushed pineapple, undrained
2 bananas, mashed
2 10-ounce packages frozen raspberries
1 pint sour cream

In a large bowl, dissolve gelatins in hot water; add orange juice. Combine remaining ingredients, **except** sour cream. Pour **half** the mixture into a 10x14-inch glass dish. Chill.

When firm, spread with sour cream and add other half of the mixture. Cover and refrigerate.

Honey French Dressing

1 pint

1 teaspoon dry mustard
1 teaspoon paprika
1 teaspoon celery seed
¼ teaspoon salt
⅔ cup sugar
⅓ cup honey
5 tablespoons vinegar
1 tablespoon lemon juice
1 teaspoon grated onion
1 cup oil, chilled

Mix dry ingredients together and place in blender with remaining ingredients, **except** oil. Blend until smooth.

Slowly add oil in a thin stream with blender running. Blend until thick and smooth.

NOTE: Dressing will keep in refrigerator for weeks. Add more lemon juice and stir if it should separate.

Celery Seed Dressing

1 pint

½ cup sugar
3 tablespoons finely
   chopped onion
2 teaspoons celery seed
1 teaspoon salt
1 teaspoon dry mustard
½ cup vinegar
1 cup oil

In a blender, combine sugar, onion, celery seed, salt, mustard and vinegar. Blend on high for 1 minute. Reduce speed to low and slowly add oil in a thin stream. Chill.

Great on fruit salad or fresh spinach salad.

French Dressing

1 quart

1 garlic clove
½ cup sugar
1 cup catsup
1½ cups oil
1 teaspoon paprika
1 cup vinegar
1 small onion, grated
Juice of 1 lemon
1 teaspoon salt
1 teaspoon
   Worcestershire sauce
½ teaspoon celery salt

Place garlic in a quart jar.

In a blender, combine remaining ingredients and blend well. Pour into jar and chill.

178

Creamy Italian Dressing
1 quart

2 teaspoons salt
1 teaspoon white pepper
½ teaspoon cracked
  black pepper
¼ teaspoon sugar
½ teaspoon dry mustard
Juice of ½ lemon
1 garlic clove, minced
5 tablespoons tarragon
  red wine vinegar
½ cup oil
2 tablespoons olive oil
1 egg, lightly beaten
½ cup light cream

In a quart jar, combine all ingredients and shake well. Chill.

Oil and Vinegar Dressing
¾ cup

1 garlic clove
½ teaspoon salt
¼ teaspoon pepper
½ teaspoon prepared
  mustard
6 tablespoons olive oil
4 tablespoons red wine
  vinegar

In a small bowl, mash garlic. Rub salt into garlic. Rub in pepper and set aside.

In a blender or food processor, combine mustard, olive oil and wine vinegar. Blend well.

Add garlic mixture and blend. Chill.

NOTE: May be prepared ahead of time. Makes a good marinade for tomatoes and Bermuda onion.

Even good olive oil can turn rancid if not stored properly – after two weeks opened oil should be stored in the refrigerator – it may become cloudy but it will turn clear when it reaches room temperature.

179

Christiania's House Dressing   ¼ cup

*Chef Phillippe's own recipe from the Christiania
Restaurant in Ketchum.*

1 tablespoon red wine
   vinegar
1½ teaspoons lemon
   juice
1 teaspoon prepared
   mustard
Salt and pepper
2 tablespoons oil
1 tablespoon heavy
   cream

Combine vinegar, lemon juice,
mustard, salt and pepper. Mix well and
add remaining ingredients.

Roquefort (Bleu Cheese) French Dressing   1½ cups

1 cup oil
3 tablespoons vinegar
1½ teaspoons salt
¼ teaspoon pepper
¼ teaspoon paprika
½ teaspoon celery salt
1 tablespoon lemon juice
1 teaspoon steak sauce
Dash Tabasco sauce
½ cup crumbled
   Roquefort **or** Bleu
   cheese

In a blender, combine all ingredients
except cheese and blend until
smooth. Fold in cheese and chill.

Try lemon juice instead of vinegar in salad dressings.

180

Minted French Dressing
2 cups

1 cup olive oil
1 cup red wine vinegar
¼ teaspoon freshly
   ground pepper
¼ teaspoon salt
¼ teaspoon chopped
   fresh mint
1 garlic clove, minced
¼ teaspoon oregano

Place all ingredients in a quart jar and allow to stand 1 hour. Shake vigorously and serve.

Roquefort Salad Dressing
1½ quarts

1 quart mayonnaise
1 pint sour cream
¼ cup grated onion
¼ cup lemon juice
1 tablespoon prepared
   horseradish
2 tablespoons chopped
   parsley
1 teaspoon
   Worcestershire sauce
½ teaspoon garlic salt
6 ounces Roquefort
   cheese, crumbled

In a food processor, combine all ingredients and blend well. Chill.

The best salads stick to a single theme.

181

Chutney Dressing for Fruit Salad

1 quart

Especially good on avocado and grapefruit or fresh pears.

1 12½-ounce jar Major
  Grey Chutney
½ teaspoon salt
1 teaspoon sugar
1 teaspoon paprika
¼ cup rice wine vinegar
¼ cup cider vinegar
½ cup oil
½ cup olive oil

In a blender or food processor, blend chutney until smooth. Add remaining ingredients and blend well. Chill.

Fruit Juice Dressing

1½ cups

½ cup sugar
Juice of 1 lemon
Juice of 1 orange
1½ teaspoons pineapple
  juice
2 eggs, beaten
⅓ cup heavy cream,
  whipped

In a saucepan, combine sugar, juices and eggs and heat to boiling. Cool.

Fold in cream and refrigerate.

Remember to squeeze lemon over cut-up apples, avocados, mushrooms, bananas or pears so they won't turn brown.

Fresh Mint Sauce

1 cup

½ cup sugar
1½ teaspoons cornstarch
Dash salt
¾ cup water
12 fresh mint leaves
1 tablespoon butter
2 drops green food
   coloring

In a medium saucepan, combine sugar, cornstarch and salt. Blend in water. Stir in mint leaves and bruise by pressing them with the back of a spoon.

Stirring constantly, heat to a rapid boil. Cook until mixture is transparent and slightly thickened. Remove from heat. Cool slightly and strain out leaves, using colander if necessary. Mix in butter and add food coloring. Chill.

Pour over fresh fruit halves, slices or fruit salad.

Mustard Ring

8 servings

1 envelope unflavored
   gelatin
½ cup cold water
4 eggs, well beaten
3 tablespoons dry
   mustard
¾ cup sugar
¾ cup white vinegar
½ cup heavy cream,
   whipped

In a small bowl, soften gelatin in cold water and set aside.

In a medium saucepan, combine eggs, mustard, sugar and vinegar. Cook over low heat, stirring constantly, until mixture is the consistency of mayonnaise. Remove from heat, add gelatin and stir until well blended. Cool completely.

Fold whipped cream into cooled mixture. Pour into a lightly greased ring mold. Refrigerate until well set.

To serve, unmold and fill center with coleslaw or cherry tomatoes.

Pickled Peaches or Pears
8 pints

4 pounds sugar, white **or** brown
1 quart cider vinegar
8 pounds whole peaches or pears, peeled
4 whole cinnamon sticks
1½ tablespoons whole cloves

In a large kettle, combine sugar and vinegar.

Tie cinnamon sticks and cloves in a cheesecloth bag and drop into kettle. Heat to boiling and add fruit. Boil 3 to 5 minutes, using a fork to test for doneness. Discard spices. Pack fruit and juice into pint jars. Process according to canning directions.

Curried Fruit
8-10 servings

Excellent served with seafood or meat.

1 28-ounce can pear halves
1 28-ounce can sliced peaches
1 16-ounce can pineapple chunks
1 4-ounce jar maraschino cherries
1 16-ounce can green grapes
1 28-ounce can plums, optional

Drain fruit. In a large bowl combine all ingredients and pour into a 9x13-inch glass baking dish. Pour dressing over fruit and bake at 350° for 30 minutes.

DRESSING

½ cup butter **or** margarine
1 cup brown sugar
Juice of 1 lemon
1 teaspoon curry powder or ½ cup rum

In a saucepan, combine all ingredients and heat to boiling.

Bound to Please: The Fertile Land

In 1838, missionary Henry Harmon Spalding developed an irrigation system to add the gift of water to Idaho's natural assets: rich soils, sunshine, and a mild climate. Little did he realize what treasures would be produced in time: sugar beets, golden grains, dry peas and lentils, beans, sweet fruits, pungent mint, hops, onions, corn, and, of course, the Russet Burbank potato.

The pink locust, the Sugar Snap pea, the Spellbinder rose – all are Idaho products. Today Idaho is a leading agricultural state for both dry and irrigated crops, exporting its products throughout the world.

Vegetables

Asparagus Supreme
6 servings

4 cups fresh asparagus,
cut up, **or** 2 8-ounce
packages frozen
asparagus
1 10-ounce can cream of
shrimp soup, undiluted
½ cup sour cream
2 tablespoons shredded
carrots
1 teaspoon grated onion
⅛ teaspoon pepper
½ cup herb seasoned
stuffing mix
1 tablespoon butter,
melted

Cook fresh asparagus in boiling salted
water 5 to 6 minutes, or cook frozen
asparagus according to package
directions. Drain.

Combine soup, sour cream, carrots,
onion and pepper. Fold in asparagus.
Turn mixture into a greased 1-quart
baking dish.

Combine stuffing mix with butter and
sprinkle around the edge of the
casserole. Bake uncovered at 350°
for 40 minutes.

Gourmet Beans
6 servings

1 pound fresh green
beans, French-cut
1 teaspoon ground anise
1 cup butter
1 pound mushrooms,
sliced
3 ounces Grand Marnier

In a saucepan, blanch beans in a small
amount of boiling salted water until
barely tender. Drain.

In a skillet, combine ½ **teaspoon** of
the anise and ½ **cup** of the butter.
Add beans and sauté. Remove beans
from skillet, melt remaining butter and
sauté mushrooms. Return beans to the
skillet. Sprinkle remaining anise over
beans and mushrooms. Mix lightly.

Warm Grand Marnier, ignite and pour
over the vegetables. Serve
immediately.

185

Beets and Mushrooms Venetian Style

6 servings

1 pound fresh beets
½ cup butter
3 tablespoons minced shallots
1 pound mushrooms, sliced
2 tablespoons honey
2 tablespoons red wine vinegar
1 cup chicken stock
2 tablespoons green peppercorns, drained

In a medium saucepan, boil beets until tender. Drain. Peel and slice thinly.

In a medium skillet, sauté shallots in **6 tablespoons** of the butter. Add beets and mushrooms and sauté for 2 minutes longer.

Add honey, vinegar and stock. Simmer uncovered 2 minutes. Remove vegetables with a slotted spoon.

Boil the remaining sauce over high heat until it is reduced to about ½ cup. Swirl in remaining butter, add peppercorns and pour over the vegetables.

Broccoli Jarlsberg

4 servings

1 10-ounce package frozen broccoli spears
½ cup ham strips
3 tablespoons butter
3 tablespoons flour
2 cups milk
1 teaspoon dry mustard
¼ teaspoon salt
⅛ teaspoon pepper
1½ cups grated Jarlsberg cheese (or Swiss)

Prepare broccoli according to package directions. Drain and keep warm.

In a saucepan, sauté ham in butter. Add flour. Cook and stir until smooth. Remove from heat and gradually blend in milk. Add mustard, salt, pepper and cheese. Cook and stir until thick and smooth.

Pour cheese sauce over warm broccoli and serve immediately.

Cook a stalk or two of celery with broccoli, cabbage and sauerkraut to prevent strong odors.

Broccoli Hélène with Lime Sauce
8 servings

2 bunches fresh broccoli Italian salad dressing	Trim broccoli and cut into flowerets with 3-inch stems. Cook in a small amount of boiling salted water until crisp-tender. Cool in ice water. Drain. Refrigerate overnight. To serve, sprinkle broccoli with Italian dressing. Arrange on a large platter and serve with small bowls of lime sauce for dipping.

LIME SAUCE

1 cup mayonnaise 1 cup sour cream 8 teaspoons fresh lime juice ½ tablespoon finely grated lime peel 1 teaspoon prepared horseradish 1 teaspoon Dijon mustard ½ teaspoon salt	Combine all ingredients and refrigerate.

Corn-Baked Broccoli
6 servings

1 10-ounce package frozen chopped broccoli 1 17-ounce can creamed corn 2 eggs, beaten Bread crumbs ¼ cup grated Cheddar cheese	In a greased casserole, break up frozen broccoli. Add corn and eggs. Mix well. Top with bread crumbs and cheese. Bake covered at 350° for 30 minutes. Uncover and bake 10 minutes longer.

187

Bavarian Cabbage

4 servings

2 tablespoons butter, melted
2 pounds cabbage, shredded
1 apple, shredded
1 bay leaf
Salt and pepper to taste
5 juniper berries
1 cup water
1 tablespoon flour
½ cup white wine
⅔ cup sugar
½ cup vinegar

In a 2-quart saucepan, melt butter. Add cabbage and apple. Mix in bay leaf, salt, pepper and berries. Add water and cook over medium heat until tender, or until liquid has almost evaporated.

Sprinkle cabbage mixture with flour. Add wine, sugar and vinegar. Heat through and serve immediately.

To absorb cabbage odor while cooking, place a small cup of vinegar on the range or add a wedge of lemon to the pot.

Carrots Piquant

6 servings

1½ pounds carrots
¼ cup butter, melted
2 tablespoons brown sugar
2 drops Tabasco sauce
½ teaspoon salt
Dash pepper
1 tablespoon prepared mustard

Peel carrots and cut into ¼-inch slices.

Arrange carrots in a buttered 10x6-inch baking dish.

In a small bowl, combine butter, brown sugar, Tabasco sauce, salt and pepper. Pour over carrots.

Bake covered at 350° for 1 hour. Just before serving stir in mustard.

Festive Carrots

6 servings

4 cups sliced carrots
⅓ cup minced onion
¼ cup butter, melted
3 tablespoons powdered sugar
2 tablespoons minced parsley
¼ teaspoon salt
⅛ teaspoon grated fresh ginger

Cook carrots in boiling salted water for 10 minutes. Drain.

Combine onion, butter, sugar, parsley, salt and ginger. Pour over carrots and stir lightly until carrots are coated. Place mixture in a buttered 2-quart casserole. Bake uncovered at 350° for 25 minutes.

Baked Carrots with Horseradish

8 servings

1 pound carrots
½ cup mayonnaise
1 tablespoon chopped onion
1 tablespoon prepared horseradish
Salt and pepper to taste
¼ cup bread crumbs
Paprika
Parsley
2 tablespoons butter

Peel carrots and leave whole. In a saucepan, cover carrots with water and cook until tender. Drain, reserving ¼ cup of the liquid. Slice carrots lengthwise. Layer in a buttered baking dish.

Combine reserved liquid, mayonnaise, onion, horseradish, salt and pepper. Pour over carrots. Top with bread crumbs, paprika and parsley. Dot with butter. Bake uncovered at 375° for 15 minutes.

Remember, remove the tops of carrots before storing. Tops drain the carrots of moisture, making them limp and dry.

Carrots in Orange Sauce
4 servings

6 carrots, peeled
2 celery stalks
1 bunch green onions
3 tablespoons butter
¼ teaspoon salt
1 tablespoon water
4 teaspoons flour
⅔ cup milk
3 tablespoons orange
  juice
2 teaspoons grated
  orange peel
Chopped parsley

Cut celery and carrots into ¼-inch slices. Thinly slice green onions, including tops.

Melt butter in a skillet. Add carrots, celery and onions and sauté 3 minutes. Add salt and water; cover and steam until carrots are almost tender, about 7 minutes.

Sprinkle with flour and cook and stir until bubbly. Remove from heat and stir in milk, juice and orange peel. Cook, stirring constantly, until thickened. Sprinkle with parsley and serve.

Snip chives with scissors – chopping crushes out juice.

Celery Root in Mustard Mayonnaise
6 servings

4 tablespoons
  mayonnaise
4 tablespoons sour cream
1 tablespoon Dijon
  mustard
3 tablespoons lemon juice
1 tablespoon chopped
  chives
Salt and white pepper to
  taste
1 pound celery root,
  about 3 inches in
  diameter
Boiling water

In a glass bowl, combine mayonnaise, sour cream, mustard, **1 tablespoon** of the lemon juice, chives, salt and pepper. Mix well and refrigerate.

Peel the celery root with a very sharp knife. Place it in a saucepan with the remaining lemon juice and enough boiling water to cover. Blanch about 8 minutes. Cool.

Grate the cooked celery root in a food processor and add to the chilled mayonnaise mixture. Toss well. Refrigerate overnight.

190

Scalloped Corn with Oysters   6 servings

1½ cups whole kernel
  corn, undrained
Heavy cream
2 tablespoons flour
1 teaspoon salt
Dash pepper
2 tablespoons butter,
  melted
½ cup fresh **or** canned
  oysters, chopped and
  drained
2 eggs, beaten
½ cup buttered bread
  crumbs
Dash paprika

Drain liquid from corn into measuring cup. Add enough cream to make 1 cup. Reserve.

In a saucepan, add flour, salt and pepper to butter and stir until blended. Slowly add cream mixture and heat until thickened, stirring constantly. Remove from heat and add drained corn.

Fold in oysters. Stir in eggs. Pour into a greased casserole and top with bread crumbs and paprika. Place dish in a shallow pan of water. Bake uncovered at 350° for 45 to 50 minutes.

Mexican Corn   6 servings

2 eggs, beaten
1 cup cornmeal
1 17-ounce can cream-
  style corn
¼ cup milk
⅓ cup margarine, melted
½ teaspoon baking soda
½ teaspoon salt
⅓ pound Cheddar
  cheese, grated
1 4-ounce can diced
  green chiles

In a bowl, combine eggs, cornmeal, corn, milk, margarine, baking soda and salt. Place **half** the mixture in the bottom of a greased casserole. Top with **half** the cheese, then add the chiles. Repeat with remaining corn mixture and remaining cheese.

Bake uncovered at 350° for 45 minutes.

To remove cornsilk: dampen a toothbrush and brush downward on the cob of corn. Every strand should come off.

191

Dutch Cucumbers in Sour Cream

6 servings

2 cucumbers, thinly sliced
1 onion, sliced
1½ teaspoons salt
¾ cup water
¾ cup vinegar
1 teaspoon sugar
½ cup sour cream
1 teaspoon dill weed
2 drops Tabasco sauce
Dash pepper

In a large bowl, combine cucumbers and onions. Sprinkle with salt. Combine water, vinegar and sugar and pour over vegetables. Let stand at room temperature for 1 hour.

Combine sour cream, dill weed, Tabasco sauce and pepper. Toss with cucumbers. Cover and chill at least 1 hour.

Sautéed Cucumbers

6 servings

A good potato substitute with a summer menu.

4 cucumbers, peeled
4 tablespoons butter, melted
1 garlic clove, minced
1 tablespoon sesame **or** poppy seeds

Cut cucumbers lengthwise. Remove seeds with a teaspoon and slice crosswise.

In a skillet, sauté garlic in butter until golden. Add cucumbers and sauté until translucent. To serve, sprinkle with seeds.

Run fork prongs down unpared cucumber before slicing for fluted edges.

Artichokes and red vegetables will not discolor if vinegar is added to the cooking water.

Eggplant-Tomato Casserole 6 servings

1 large eggplant
½ onion, chopped
2½ tablespoons
    margarine, melted
1 1-pound can peeled
    tomatoes
2 chicken bouillon cubes
1 teaspoon
    Worcestershire sauce
1 teaspoon vinegar
1 teaspoon sugar
Dash garlic salt
Dash pepper
1 teaspoon flour
2 tablespoons grated
    Parmesan cheese

Peel eggplant and cut into ½-inch cubes. Boil in salted water for 1 minute. Drain.

Sauté onion in **2 tablespoons** of the margarine. Add tomatoes, bouillon cubes, Worcestershire sauce, vinegar, garlic salt, pepper, sugar and flour. Mix well.

Add remaining margarine to eggplant and stir gently to coat each cube.

Place **half** the eggplant in a casserole. Layer **half** the tomato sauce over eggplant. Repeat layers. Sprinkle with Parmesan cheese. Broil until cheese melts. Serve immediately.

Jicama 4 servings

Excellent as part of a Mexican dinner or as an hors d'oeuvre.

1 fresh jicama
2 limes
Salt

Peel jicama and slice thinly. Overlap slices on a plate and squeeze lime juice over them. Sprinkle with salt and serve.

Broccoli stems can be cooked in the same length of time as the flowerettes if you make "X" incisions from top to bottom through stems.

Marvelous Mushroom Pie   5-6 servings

1½ pounds mushrooms, sliced
1 cup thinly sliced onions
4 tablespoons butter
⅓ cup flour
8-ounce carton small curd cottage cheese
¼ cup chopped parsley
¼ cup dry sherry
1 teaspoon salt
⅛ teaspoon pepper
1 9-inch pie shell, unbaked
Pastry strips left over from pie crust

Preheat oven to 400°.

Sauté mushrooms and onions in butter until glossy. Add flour and mix well. Remove from heat and mix in cottage cheese, parsley, sherry, salt and pepper.

Pour filling into unbaked pie shell and arrange pastry strips in a lattice pattern on top of the filling. Tuck in the overhanging crust and flute the edge.

Bake on the bottom shelf of the oven for 30 to 40 minutes. If the pastry appears to be browning too fast, cover the edge with foil after about 15 to 20 minutes.

Let stand 15 to 20 minutes before serving.

Scalloped Mushrooms   8 servings

3 pounds fresh mushrooms, chopped
½ cup butter
1 cup heavy cream
1 teaspoon salt
½ teaspoon pepper
⅛ teaspoon cayenne
3 cups grated Monterey Jack cheese
Mushroom caps, cooked, optional

In a large skillet, sauté mushrooms in butter for 5 minutes. Gradually stir in cream. Season with salt, pepper and cayenne. Place mixture in a shallow casserole. Cover with cheese.

Bake at 400° for 10 minutes or until lightly browned. Garnish with drained mushroom caps if desired.

For prime mushrooms, buy only those with closed caps. The gills should not be showing.

Creamed Mushroom Crêpes   8-10 servings

2 tablespoons butter or margarine
2 tablespoons chopped onion
1 pound mushrooms, sliced
1 cup heavy cream
¼ teaspoon seasoned salt
⅛ teaspoon pepper
2 tablespoons flour
2 tablespoons water
⅓ cup Gruyère cheese
8 to 10 crêpes (see index)
⅓ cup grated Parmesan cheese
Chives

In a skillet, melt butter and add onion and mushrooms. Cook over moderate heat several minutes until tender. Stir in cream, salt and pepper. Remove mushrooms with a slotted spoon and set aside.

Mix flour with water; stir into cream mixture in skillet. Simmer, stirring constantly, until thickened. Add Gruyère cheese.

Meanwhile, fill crêpes with cooked mushrooms and fold. Place in a shallow baking pan and spoon cream sauce over all. Sprinkle with Parmesan.

Bake at 350° for 10 to 15 minutes. Top with chives and serve.

Idaho Curried Onions   8 servings

5 onions, thinly sliced
1 cup boiling water
3 tablespoons butter
2 tablespoons flour
1 teaspoon curry powder
2 teaspoons beef extract or beef flavor base
1 cup milk
½ cup grated Cheddar cheese

Simmer onions, covered, in boiling water until tender.

In a saucepan, melt butter. Blend in flour, curry powder and beef extract. Gradually stir in milk, cooking and stirring until mixture thickens. Add cheese, reserving **2 tablespoons.**

Place onions in a buttered casserole. Pour sauce over onions and top with reserved cheese. Bake uncovered at 325° for 30 minutes.

195

Burgundy Onions

6 servings

¼ cup unsalted butter
3 pounds Spanish onions,
thinly sliced
1 tablespoon sugar
2 cups burgundy wine
1 teaspoon salt
¼ teaspoon pepper
1 teaspoon cider vinegar

In a 4-quart non-aluminum saucepan, melt butter. Add onions, cover and cook over low heat 45 minutes. Remove cover and increase heat to medium-high. Continue cooking another 20 minutes, stirring frequently. Sprinkle with sugar and cook 2 minutes more, stirring frequently. Reduce heat to low and add wine. Cook, stirring frequently for 2½ hours. Stir in salt, pepper and vinegar.

Martini Onions

6 servings

4 to 6 Walla Walla sweet
onions
⅔ cup heavy cream
3 tablespoons dry
vermouth
½ teaspoon salt
Freshly ground pepper
2 tablespoons butter
Stuffed green olives

Peel and slice onions. In a saucepan, cover onions with water and boil 20 minutes. Drain and press out liquid with a spatula. Place in a buttered casserole.

Mix cream, vermouth, salt and pepper. Pour over onions. Dot with butter.

Bake covered at 325° for 3 hours. To serve, garnish with olives.

Outdoor Onions

4 servings

4 Walla Walla sweet
onions
½ cup butter
Salt and pepper to taste
8 fresh mushrooms,
sliced
Grated Parmesan cheese

Quarter each onion, but do not cut all the way through. Spread the quarters apart and dot each onion with **2 tablespoons** of the butter and salt and pepper. Place **2** sliced mushrooms in each onion. Sprinkle with Parmesan.

Wrap each onion in foil and place on the grill for 45 to 60 minutes, or bake at 350°.

Onion Pie
6 servings

½ cup butter
1 cup crushed saltine crackers
4 cups diced onions
1½ cups milk
4 eggs, lightly beaten
1½ teaspoons salt
Dash pepper
Dash thyme
½ cup grated Cheddar cheese

Melt ¼ **cup** of the butter and toss with saltines. Press these into a 10-inch pie pan.

Melt the remaining butter in a skillet and sauté onions. Pour onions over the crumb mixture.

Combine the remaining ingredients, **except** cheese, and pour over onions. Sprinkle cheese over the top. Bake at 350° for 25 minutes.

Spinach-Stuffed Onions
6 servings

3 yellow onions
1 10-ounce package frozen chopped spinach
3 tablespoons mayonnaise
1 tablespoon lemon juice
½ cup Parmesan cheese, freshly grated
½ teaspoon salt
Dash nutmeg
¼ teaspoon pepper
Pimiento strips

Peel and halve the onions. Parboil in boiling salted water 10 to 15 minutes. Drain. Remove centers leaving a ¾-inch shell. Chop centers yielding about ¾ cup.

Cook spinach according to package directions. Drain, then squeeze out excess moisture. Combine spinach, chopped onion, mayonnaise, lemon juice, Parmesan cheese, salt, nutmeg and pepper. Spoon into centers of onions.

Place in baking dish and bake uncovered at 350° for 20 minutes. Garnish with pimiento strips.

Use leftover mashed potatoes by making patties and coating with flour. "Flash-freeze" and store in freezer for frying potato cakes later.

Almond-Onion Casserole

6 servings

3 medium onions
2 tablespoons butter, melted
2 tablespoons flour
1 cup chicken broth
¼ cup heavy cream
½ teaspoon salt
¼ teaspoon pepper
¼ cup chopped celery
¼ cup sliced blanched almonds
½ cup grated Cheddar cheese
1 cup bread crumbs

Cut onions in ¾-inch wedges. Parboil until just tender and drain.

In a saucepan, blend butter, flour, salt and pepper. Slowly add broth and cream, heating and stirring until thickened. Add celery, almonds and onions.

Pour mixture into a buttered casserole. Place casserole in a shallow pan of water. Bake uncovered at 350° for 45 minutes. Just before serving, mix bread crumbs and cheese and sprinkle over casserole. Brown under broiler and serve.

Chilled onions cause fewer tears.

Pea Pods and Walnuts with Zucchini

6 servings

½ cup coarsely chopped walnuts
2 tablespoons butter
1 zucchini
2 teaspoons thyme
¾ teaspoon salt
2 cups pea pods

In a large skillet, sauté walnuts in butter for 5 minutes. Remove with a slotted spoon and reserve.

Cut zucchini lengthwise, then slice crosswise into ¼-inch slices. Sauté in same skillet in remaining butter for 5 minutes. Sprinkle with thyme and salt. Add pea pods and walnuts and cook for 2 minutes longer. Serve immediately.

Spinach Crêpes   12 servings

1 pound fresh spinach
1 cup ricotta cheese
½ cup grated Parmesan
  cheese
2 eggs, lightly beaten
½ teaspoon salt
Dash pepper
1 teaspoon lemon juice
2 tablespoons butter
Crêpes (see index)
Paprika

Remove stems from spinach and rinse in cold water. Place in a saucepan with only the water that clings to the leaves. Cover tightly and cook on medium heat for 5 minutes. Drain, press out all water and chop finely.

In a medium bowl, combine cheeses, eggs, salt, pepper and lemon juice. Place approximately 2 tablespoons of the spinach mixture on the edge of each crêpe and roll cigarette fashion. Place, seam side down, in a large buttered baking dish. Bake at 375° for 15 minutes.

Pour cheese sauce over crêpes and garnish with a sprinkle of paprika. Serve immediately.

CHEESE SAUCE III

4 tablespoons butter **or**
  margarine
2 tablespoons flour
1½ cups milk
½ cup heavy cream
1 teaspoon dry mustard
½ cup grated Cheddar
  cheese

In a saucepan, melt butter over medium heat. Add flour and mix thoroughly. Add milk, cream and mustard and stir until smooth. Cook, stirring constantly, until thick. Remove from heat and add cheese. Stir until cheese is melted.

Try adding some fresh dill, lemon juice and Dijon mustard to butter and add to your vegetables.

Spinach in Pastry

⅓ cup minced onion
3 tablespoons butter
1 tablespoon flour
1⅓ cups sour cream
½ cup dry white wine
¼ teaspoon salt
⅛ teaspoon white
pepper
1 10-ounce package
frozen chopped
spinach, thawed and
squeezed dry
½ pound mushrooms,
sliced
1¼ teaspoons basil
1 egg, beaten

In a medium saucepan, sauté onion in **2 tablespoons** of the butter. Whisk in flour and cook until bubbly. Remove from heat and stir in sour cream, wine, salt and pepper.

Sauté mushrooms in remaining butter and set aside.

Combine spinach, mushrooms and basil with **1 cup** of the sour cream mixture and add the mushrooms and basil.

Prepare sour cream pastry. Roll each ball into a 9-inch circle. Save any trimmings.

Place one pastry round on a baking sheet and spread spinach filling over it, leaving a ½-inch border. Moisten border with water. Place second pastry round on top and seal edges. Flute and decorate top with shapes cut from reserved trimmings. Make 3 cuts in top. Brush with egg.

Bake at 375° for 40 minutes. Cut into wedges and serve with remaining warm sour cream mixture.

SOUR CREAM PASTRY

1½ cups flour
¼ teaspoon salt
½ cup butter
⅔ cup sour cream

Combine flour and salt. Cut in butter until crumbly. Stir in sour cream. Form mixture into 2 balls.

Squeeze fresh lemon juice over steamed vegetables and toss with butter for a special touch.

Spinach Madeline

6-8 servings

Excellent served as a dip for fresh vegetables, as a stuffing for mushrooms or as a vegetable.

2 10-ounce packages
   frozen chopped spinach
4 tablespoons butter
2 tablespoons flour
2 tablespoons chopped
   onion
½ cup evaporated milk
¾ teaspoon celery salt
½ teaspoon salt
½ teaspoon pepper
1 teaspoon
   Worcestershire sauce
1 6-ounce roll jalapeño
   cheese **or** hot pepper
   cheese, cubed
1 tablespoon prepared
   horseradish
1 slice buttered bread,
   crumbled

In a medium saucepan, cook spinach as directed; drain, reserving ½ **cup** liquid for later use.

Melt butter in saucepan, add flour and stir until smooth. Add onion and cook until soft. Add milk and reserved spinach liquid, stirring constantly until smooth and thickened. Stir in seasonings, cheese and horseradish. Heat until cheese is melted. Add spinach and pour into a 1½-quart casserole. Top with bread crumbs and bake at 350° for 20 minutes.

Cheese-Stuffed Acorn Squash

4 servings

2 acorn squash
Salt and pepper
3 ounces Monterey Jack
   cheese, diced
2 slices bread, toasted
   and diced
2 teaspoons butter,
   melted
⅔ cup milk

Cut a slice from pointed ends of squash so they stand upright. Cut a 1½-inch slice from stem ends and reserve as caps. Scoop out seeds and sprinkle insides with salt and pepper.

In each squash, layer **half** the cheese, toast, butter and milk. Sprinkle with salt and pepper. Replace caps. Bake uncovered at 325° for 1½ hours.

To serve, halve each squash lengthwise.

Holiday Sweet Potatoes   8 servings

3 cups cooked sweet
 potatoes, mashed
¼ cup sugar
1 cup brown sugar
½ teaspoon salt
2 eggs, beaten
1 cup butter, melted
½ cup milk
½ teaspoon vanilla
1 cup chopped walnuts
⅓ cup flour

Combine potatoes, sugar, ¼ **cup** of
the brown sugar, salt, eggs, ½ **cup** of
the butter, milk and vanilla. Place in a
buttered 2-quart casserole.

Combine remaining brown sugar and
butter, and the walnuts and flour.
Spoon topping over potato mixture.
Bake uncovered at 350° for
30 minutes.

Roquefort-Stuffed Tomatoes   8 servings

8 firm, ripe tomatoes
1¼ pounds mushrooms,
 sliced
½ cup butter
1 tablespoon +
 1 teaspoon flour
1 cup sour cream
3 ounces Roquefort
 cheese, crumbled
1 teaspoon chopped
 parsley
2 tablespoons sherry
Salt and pepper
Sesame seeds

Cut a slice from top of tomatoes and
scoop out pulp. Drain upside down on
paper towels.

In a skillet, sauté mushrooms in butter
until moisture has evaporated.

Blend flour with sour cream. Add to
mushrooms and heat over low until
thick and bubbly. Stir in Roquefort until
smooth. Add parsley, sherry, salt and
pepper. Cool.

Stuff tomatoes loosely. Sprinkle with
sesame seeds. Bake at 375° for
15 minutes. Serve immediately.

Italian Tomato Pie

6 servings

1 9-inch baked pastry
   shell
6 to 8 Italian tomatoes,
   sliced and peeled
1 teaspoon salt
½ teaspoon pepper
1 teaspoon basil
1 cup mayonnaise
1 cup grated Cheddar
   cheese
2 tablespoons chopped
   chives
Grated Parmesan cheese

Place sliced tomatoes in baked pastry shell. Sprinkle with salt, pepper and basil.

In a bowl, mix mayonnaise, Cheddar cheese and chives. Spoon over top of tomatoes. Sprinkle with Parmesan cheese.

Bake at 375° for 20 minutes or until golden and puffy.

Jack Straw

4 servings

1 cup flour
½ teaspoon salt
1 egg, beaten
1 cup milk
1 tablespoon oil
3 medium zucchini **or**
   12 ounces mushrooms
   or 1 pound broccoli
   flowerets **or** 1 eggplant
Oil for deep frying
Freshly grated Parmesan
   cheese and salt to
   taste

Combine flour and salt. Mix together egg, milk and oil and add to dry ingredients.

Slice zucchini lengthwise into several long fingers, similar to large french fries; slice large mushrooms or leave small mushrooms whole; peel eggplant and cut like zucchini. Dip vegetables into fritter batter and deep fry until golden. Sprinkle with cheese and salt.

As a variation, cook a combination of the vegetables.

203

Zucchini Casserole

12 servings

2 cups cooked rice
1 7-ounce can whole
   green chiles
1 4-ounce can green chili
   salsa
3 zucchini, diced and
   blanched
1 tomato, sliced
2 tablespoons chopped
   onion
2 tablespoons chopped
   green pepper
1 teaspoon salt
1 teaspoon oregano
1 pound Monterey Jack
   cheese, grated
2 cups sour cream

In a greased 10-inch casserole, layer rice, chiles, salsa, zucchini, tomato, onion, green pepper, seasonings and cheese. Cover with sour cream.

Bake uncovered at 350° for 30 minutes; then at 325° for 40 minutes.

Zucchini Patties

36 small patties

1 cup flour
2 eggs
¼ cup grated Parmesan
   cheese
Salt and pepper to taste
4 small zucchini, thinly
   sliced
¼ cup chopped onion
2 garlic cloves, minced
½ cup chopped parsley
Beer or water as needed
Oil for frying

Mix flour, eggs, cheese, salt and pepper with a mixer until well blended. Add zucchini, onion, garlic and parsley. Add beer or water until mixture is thin enough to be poured.

Heat oil in an electric skillet. Drop small spoonfuls of batter into hot oil and fry until patties are light brown, turning once.

Drain on paper towels and salt again if needed.

204

Lo Mein
8 servings

6 eggs, beaten
2 tablespoons sesame oil
1 10-ounce package thin
   Chinese noodles
1 head cabbage, chopped
   in ¾-inch squares
2 bunches scallions **or**
   green onions, chopped
2 8-ounce cans sliced
   mushrooms, drained
½ pound bacon, cooked
   and crumbled
Sesame oil
Soy sauce

In a skillet, cook eggs in **1 tablespoon** of the sesame oil. When cool, cut into bite-sized pieces.

Cook noodles in boiling water for 3 minutes. Drain.

While water for noodles is heating, heat the wok. When ready, use remaining sesame oil and stir fry cabbage, scallions, mushrooms, eggs and bacon for about 3 minutes. Season to taste with more sesame oil and with soy sauce. Mix in noodles and stir fry briefly until mixed. Serve immediately.

Hot Vegetable Casserole
6-8 servings

2 cups fresh chopped
   tomatoes
1½ cups chopped onion
1 8-ounce can sliced
   water chestnuts,
   drained
1½ cups sliced carrots
¾ cup chopped green
   pepper
1 7-ounce package
   frozen pea pods
1 10-ounce package
   frozen French-sliced
   green beans
3 tablespoons instant
   tapioca
2½ teaspoons salt
1 tablespoon sugar
Dash pepper
4 tablespoons butter,
   melted

Combine all ingredients, **except** melted butter, in a large casserole. Pour butter over top. Bake covered at 350° for 1½ hours.

205

Vegetables and Brown Rice
4-6 servings

3 tablespoons oil
1 cup thinly sliced carrots
3 green onions, sliced, including tops
1 medium garlic clove, minced
1 green pepper, thinly sliced
1 cup thinly sliced zucchini
1 cup sliced fresh mushrooms
½ cup slivered almonds
3 cups cooked brown rice (1 cup uncooked)
4-6 tablespoons soy sauce

In a large skillet or wok, heat about **1 tablespoon** of the oil over high heat. Add carrots and stir fry 1 minute or until almost tender. Add onions, garlic and green pepper and stir fry 1 minute, adding more oil to prevent sticking. Add zucchini, mushrooms and almonds. Stir fry 2 minutes or until barely crisp-tender. Mix in rice and heat through. Season to taste with soy sauce.

Ratatouille
4 servings

½ onion, sliced
1 cup sliced fresh mushrooms
1½ cups diced peeled eggplant
1½ cups diced unpeeled zucchini
1 green pepper, chopped
1 tomato, diced
½ cup chicken stock
1½ cups tomato juice
Basil to taste
1 teaspoon salt
½ teaspoon pepper
1 teaspoon parsley

In a saucepan, combine all ingredients. Simmer covered for 30 minutes, then uncover and simmer for 15 minutes.

206

Greek Vegetables
12 servings

1 cup olive oil
1 tablespoon salt
1 teaspoon Tabasco sauce
1 teaspoon pepper
1 eggplant, peeled
1 potato, peeled
1 zucchini, unpeeled
1 Bermuda onion
2 green peppers
2 carrots
2 tablespoons chopped
  parsley
4 tomatoes
⅔ cup uncooked rice
2 tablespoons red wine
  vinegar
½ cup water
2 cups grated Monterey
  Jack cheese

In a large bowl, combine ½ **cup** of the olive oil, salt, Tabasco sauce and pepper.

Dice eggplant, potato, zucchini, onion, peppers and carrots. Add with parsley to olive oil mixture.

Grease a 4-quart casserole. Dice **2** of the tomatoes and spread over the bottom of the casserole. Layer **half** the vegetable mixture over the diced tomatoes. Layer rice over the vegetables. Add the remaining vegetables. Peel the remaining tomatoes and slice them. Lay over the vegetables.

Mix the remaining olive oil, vinegar and water and pour over the casserole. Bake uncovered at 350° for 1½ hours. Sprinkle cheese over the top and continue baking uncovered for ½ hour.

Vegetable Bake
8 servings

4 10-ounce packages
  frozen spinach **or**
  broccoli
8 ounces marinated
  artichoke hearts,
  drained
8 ounces cream cheese,
  softened
⅓ cup grated Parmesan
  cheese
6 tablespoons milk

Prepare spinach or broccoli according to package directions. Drain well. Chop artichoke hearts.

Beat cream cheese, Parmesan and milk.

Place spinach and artichoke hearts in a buttered casserole. Spoon cheese mixture over top.

Bake uncovered at 350° for 45 minutes.

207

Cauliflower-Black Olive Garnish

10 servings

1 head cauliflower
6 tablespoons olive oil
3 tablespoons white wine
   vinegar
1 tablespoon chopped
   capers
1 tablespoon minced
   parsley
1 tablespoon chopped
   pimiento
1 green onion, chopped
½ teaspoon salt
⅛ teaspon dry mustard
⅛ teaspoon pepper
½ cup sliced olives

Separate cauliflower into flowerets and blanch in boiling salted water 4 to 5 minutes, or until just tender. Drain. Rinse under cold running water until cool.

Combine remaining ingredients, **except** olives. Arrange cauliflower, heads down, in a bowl. Cover with oil and vinegar mixture. Cover and refrigerate overnight.

At serving time, drain, reserving marinade. Invert cauliflower into serving bowl. Add olives to marinade and spoon over cauliflower.

To keep cauliflower a bright white, add a little milk during boiling.

Pickled Asparagus

4 quarts

2 quarts vinegar
2 quarts water
1 tablespoon pickling
   spice
10 tablespoons pickling
   salt
2 garlic cloves, halved
2 tablespoons dill weed
Fresh asparagus

In a large saucepan, combine vinegar, water, pickling spice and salt. Boil for 15 minutes.

Blanch asparagus for 1½ minutes. Drain and immerse in ice water. Drain again. Pack into jars and add ½ garlic clove and ½ **tablespoon** dill weed to each jar. Cover with hot brine and process for 5 minutes once water is boiling.

Hot Dill Pickles

1½ quarts

The longer they sit, the hotter they become!

1½ quarts dill pickles
  (Kosher are best)
2 cups sugar
1 cup water
½ cup cider vinegar
1 tablespoon mustard
1 teaspoon celery seed
10 whole dried red chili
  peppers

Drain pickles, discarding juice, and slice into quarters lengthwise. Return to jar.

In a medium saucepan, combine remaining ingredients and boil for 10 minutes. Pour hot liquid over pickles. Let stand for 24 hours. Chill and serve.

Koski Dills

1½ quarts

1 46-ounce jar kosher dill
  pickles
3½ cups sugar
¾ cup white vinegar

Drain pickles, rinse well and slice into 1-inch lengths. Return to jar.

In a small saucepan, bring sugar and vinegar to a boil. Pour hot syrup over pickles and refrigerate.

Flip jar once daily for eight days. Serve as an hors d'oeuvre with toothpicks.

When serving artichokes and a dipping sauce, don't forget that the artichoke can be the bowl too. Just remove the choke after cooking and spoon your favorite filling into the cavity.

Beer Batter for Fresh Vegetables

8 servings

Try this for fish also!

2 eggs, separated
12 ounces beer
1 tablespoon butter, melted
1 teaspoon dry mustard
2 teaspoons salt
Dash pepper
1½ cups flour
Fresh vegetables
Flour
Oil for deep frying

Beat **egg yolks,** beer and butter. Add mustard, salt and pepper. Add the **1½ cups** flour and mix until smooth.

Beat **egg whites** until stiff. Fold into batter.

Dredge vegetables with a small amount of flour, coat with batter and fry in hot oil until golden.

Chow Chow

12 quarts

6 heads cabbage
1 gallon green tomatoes
4 cups chopped onions
25 green peppers
¾ cup salt
3 pints white vinegar
3 tablespoons mustard seed
1 tablespoon celery seed
1 tablespoon turmeric seed
4 cups sugar

Using a food grinder, coarsely grind cabbage, tomatoes, onions and peppers.

In a large bowl or crock, combine ground mixture with salt, stirring until well mixed. Let stand for 2 hours.

Using a colander, drain off liquid.

In a large kettle, combine ground mixture with remaining ingredients. Mix well and simmer uncovered for 1 hour. Place in quart jars and process 20 minutes.

If fresh vegetables are wilted or blemished, pick off the brown edges and soak vegetables for an hour in cold water to which the juice of a lemon or a few tablespoons of vinegar have been added.

Bound to Please: Towering Timber

Idaho's forest lands cover almost half the state. Until 1892, timber harvesting on Idaho's federal lands was restricted by law. But the growth of population in the northwest, the cutover of land around the Great Lakes, and construction of a transcontinental railroad spawned a lumber industry that eventually surpassed Idaho's mining ventures.

Idaho has chosen the Western White Pine, straight-grained and even-textured, as its state tree, but others – ponderosa and lodgepole pines, Douglas fir, western red cedar, the Englemann spruce – are among more than 20 species found throughout the state. Today seedling nurseries and reforestation projects assure continued growth to meet ecological, industrial, and recreational demands.

Classic Pasta Dishes

Baked Pasta Dishes

Pasta Doughs & Pasta Sauces

Rice & Grains

Beans

Seafood Fettuccine

4 servings

8 ounces fettuccine
2 tablespoons butter
1 large shallot, chopped
1 tablespoon
  Worcestershire sauce
1 teaspoon basil
Salt and pepper
12 ounces scallops
1 pound raw shrimp,
  peeled and deveined
1 pint sour cream
Fresh parsley, chopped
Grated Parmesan cheese

In a large pot, cook fettuccine according to package directions. Drain and set aside.

In a large skillet, sauté shallot in butter until limp. Add Worcestershire sauce, basil, salt and pepper. Add scallops and shrimp and stir until shrimp is pink.

Stir in sour cream and heat thoroughly. (If sauce appears too thin, a small amount of flour dissolved in milk may be added.)

To serve, place fettuccine on a large platter, pour sauce over top, garnish with parsley and Parmesan.

Fettuccine with Shrimp and Walnut Sauce

4 servings

Great with lemon fettuccine.

6 tablespoons butter
3 garlic cloves, minced
⅔ cup coarsely chopped
  walnuts
1½ cups light cream
¼ teaspoon nutmeg
8 ounces small shrimp,
  cooked and peeled
1 pound fresh fettuccine,
  cooked and drained
⅔ cup freshly grated
  Parmesan cheese
2 tablespoons minced
  fresh parsley

In a large skillet, melt butter over medium heat and sauté garlic and nuts until golden. Add cream and nutmeg and simmer until reduced slightly.

Add shrimp and cooked pasta, lower heat and toss lightly, gradually adding the cheese. Toss until noodles are heated through and well coated with sauce.

Garnish with parsley and serve immediately.

Spinach Fettuccine with Salmon

4-6 servings

Colors are as pleasing as the taste.

2 cups heavy cream
3 tablespoons butter
2 teaspoons salt
Pinch nutmeg
1 tablespoon oil
1 pound fresh spinach
  fettuccine
2 cups poached flaked
  salmon, skin and bones
  carefully removed
1 tablespoon freshly
  grated Parmesan
  cheese
⅓ cup chopped fresh dill

In a small saucepan, simmer cream, **2 tablespoons** of the butter, **1 teaspoon** of the salt and the nutmeg. Simmer gently until reduced by about ⅓.

In a large kettle, bring 4 quarts of water to boiling and add remaining salt and the oil. Add fettuccine and cook al dente.

Meanwhile, gently add salmon, cheese and dill to the cream. Stir 2 minutes and remove from heat.

When pasta is cooked, drain and return to hot kettle. Toss with remaining butter. Remove to a heated platter or shallow bowl and spoon sauce over. Serve immediately.

Fettuccine with Garlic Sausage

4-6 servings

3 tablespoons olive oil
1 pound garlic sausage
3 large garlic cloves,
  minced
¼ cup chopped fresh
  parsley
1 28-ounce can Italian
  plum tomatoes,
  undrained
Salt and pepper
1½ pounds fresh
  fettuccine
Freshly grated Parmesan
  cheese

In a large skillet, heat olive oil over medium heat and gently fry sausage, breaking it up with a spatula. Add garlic and **half** the parsley. Sauté until sausage is almost cooked. Add tomatoes with liquid and simmer for 10 minutes. Season with salt and pepper.

Cook pasta al dente in 5 quarts water. Drain and place in a large, heated shallow bowl. Pour sauce over top and garnish with remaining parsley and Parmesan.

Fettuccine Alfredo

4 servings

A popular menu item from Café Rose.

4 ounces garlic butter*
6 ounces fresh
  mushrooms, sliced
Salt and white pepper
4 cups heavy cream
Dash nutmeg
2 ounces freshly grated
  Parmesan cheese
1 tablespoon salt
2 tablespoons olive oil
1 pound fresh egg **or**
  spinach fettuccine
Parsley

In a large skillet, melt garlic butter over medium-high heat. Add mushrooms, salt and pepper, sauté until mushrooms are tender. Add cream and nutmeg and increase heat to high. Stir constantly until the cream begins to reduce and bubble.

When the cream is bubbling across the entire pan, add Parmesan and stir constantly until the cheese has melted. Reduce heat to medium-high and continue to cook for 1 to 2 more minutes until the sauce has thickened. Be careful not to let the cheese drop to the bottom of the pan and stick.

Heat 4 quarts of water, salt and olive oil to boiling. Add pasta, stirring frequently to keep the noodles from sticking together. If the noodles are very fresh, they should cook in 30 to 45 seconds.

Drain the noodles and put in a large serving bowl with the sauce. Toss lightly until noodles are coated with sauce. Garnish with parsley and serve immediately.

*GARLIC BUTTER

½ cup softened butter
2-3 cloves garlic, pressed
Salt and pepper to taste

Cream together.

Goat Cheese Sauce
with Fettuccine

4 servings

A French variation of a classic Alfredo sauce. Fabulous with fresh basil pasta.

2 garlic cloves, crushed
¼ cup + 2 tablespoons
   unsalted butter
2 cups heavy cream
6 ounces goat cheese
Salt and pepper
Nutmeg
Tabasco sauce
1 red bell pepper
1 pound fresh fettuccine
   or linguine

In a large skillet, simmer garlic, **¼ cup** of the butter and the cream until reduced slightly to approximately 1¾ cups. Strain and discard the garlic.

In a food processor fitted with metal blade, purée goat cheese. With machine running, slowly pour hot cream mixture through feed tube. Scrape down sides and process 5 more seconds. Season to taste with salt, pepper and nutmeg and add a dash of Tabasco sauce. Use immediately or set aside until ready to reheat covered with plastic wrap placed on top of the sauce to prevent skin from forming.

Broil pepper and remove skin. Slice into 24 julienne strips and set aside.

Cook pasta al dente and drain well. In a large skillet, melt remaining butter over low heat. Add pasta, tossing gently. When butter is absorbed, turn heat to very low.

To serve, ladle about ¼ cup of the reheated sauce onto a warmed, rimmed dinner plate or shallow bowl. Tilt to cover with sauce. Place generous mound of noodles over center of sauce leaving a 1-inch border of sauce around noodles. Garnish each with 6 slices of red pepper arranged like spokes of a wheel.

Alsatian Noodles

4-6 servings

1 cup cooked sandwich
ham, cut in ¼x1-inch
strips
½ cup butter, softened
⅓ cup Dijon mustard
¼ cup chopped parsley
2 tablespoons chopped
chives
2 garlic cloves, minced
1 pound fettuccine

In a small saucepan over low heat, warm ham.

In a bowl, cream butter. Add mustard, parsley, chives and garlic and mix well.

Cook fettuccine in 4 quarts boiling, salted water al dente. Drain and return to hot kettle. Add **half** the butter mixture and all of the ham and toss well. Add the remaining butter mixture, toss, and serve immediately.

Fettuccine with Bleu Cheese Sauce

4 servings

¼ cup butter
½ cup sliced mushrooms
1 tablespoon minced
green onion
1 cup heavy cream
1 cup crumbled Danish
Bleu cheese (3 to
4 ounces)
2 tablespoons chopped
parsley
8 ounces fresh fettuccine

In a medium skillet, heat butter until it begins to turn golden. Over medium-high heat, sauté mushrooms for 1 to 2 minutes, add green onion, and stir until coated. Add cream and cook until lightly browned around the edge of pan. Stir in **half** the Bleu cheese and the parsley and blend until smooth. Remove from heat.

Cook pasta in boiling, salted water al dente. Drain well and turn onto a heated serving dish.

Reheat the sauce, if necessary, and pour over the pasta; toss with 2 forks until evenly coated. Sprinkle with remaining Bleu cheese and serve immediately.

215

Spinach Pasta with Gorgonzola Sauce

4-6 servings – main dish
6-8 servings – side dish

¼ pound Gorgonzola
  cheese, crumbled
½ cup whole milk
3 tablespoons butter
⅓ cup heavy cream
1 pound spinach pasta,
  cooked
½ cup freshly grated
  Parmesan cheese

In a large non-aluminum skillet, combine cheese, milk and butter. Stir over low heat until smooth. Add cream and continue stirring until sauce is hot and well blended. Add cooked pasta and Parmesan cheese. Toss gently until noodles are evenly coated. Serve immediately.

Fettuccine with Lemon

6-8 servings

5 tablespoons oil
3 garlic cloves, minced
1 cup heavy cream
Grated rind of 1 lemon
1 cup beef consommé,
  undiluted
6 to 8 ounces cooked
  ham, cut into small
  cubes
1 cup freshly grated
  Parmesan cheese
1 pound fresh fettuccine

In a skillet over medium heat, cook garlic in oil until golden, about 20 seconds. Add cream, lemon rind and consommé. Simmer gently for 10 minutes, stirring occasionally. Add ham and ½ cup of the Parmesan to thicken and flavor the sauce.

In a large kettle, cook pasta in 4 quarts boiling, salted water until just tender, or for about 1 minute after water returns to a boil. Drain, return to kettle and toss with sauce. Serve immediately in shallow bowls topped with remaining cheese.

The water should be boiling furiously before adding 1½ tablespoons salt and 1 tablespoon oil. After adding pasta, maintain a steady boil, uncovered, stirring occasionally with wooden spoon or fork.

Linguine with
Red Clam Sauce

6-8 servings

¾ cup olive oil
½ cup butter
4 to 6 garlic cloves, minced
2 shallots, chopped
1 bunch fresh parsley, chopped (approximately 1 cup)
6 to 8 large fresh tomatoes, chopped
3 6½-ounce cans chopped clams
2 dashes Tabasco sauce
Salt and pepper to taste
Italian-style herbs to taste (oregano, thyme, basil, bay leaves, rosemary, etc.)
8 to 10 ounces linguine

In a deep skillet or Dutch oven, heat oil and butter over low heat. Add garlic and shallots and cook slowly for 1 to 2 minutes, stirring constantly to prevent burning. Add parsley and cook until limp. Add chopped tomatoes, undrained clams, Tabasco sauce, herbs, salt and pepper. Simmer 1 to 2 hours, stirring occasionally, until tomatoes are cooked and sauce has thickened.

Cook linguine according to package directions. Drain.

Taste the sauce and adjust seasonings, if necessary, adding more Tabasco sauce, salt and pepper.

To serve, arrange linguine on a large platter. Pour sauce evenly over the linguine and serve immediately.

As with other dehydrated foods, the yield of the finished product is greater than fresh. One pound of dry pasta will yield about 2.2 pounds of cooked pasta.

Pasta should be tender but firm to the bite – al dente.

217

Pasta Greek Style with Shrimp and Feta Cheese

4-6 servings (main dish)
8-10 servings (side dish)

1 pound Feta cheese
4 tomatoes
¾ pound medium cooked shrimp, shelled and deveined
6 green onions, finely chopped
4 teaspoons minced fresh oregano or
  1½ teaspoons dried oregano
Salt and freshly ground pepper
1 pound fresh spaghetti or linguine

Rinse and pat dry the feta cheese. Crumble into a large bowl.

Peel, core, seed and coarsely chop the tomatoes and add to bowl. Mix in the shrimp, green onions and oregano and let stand at room temperature for at least 1 hour. Season with salt and pepper before serving.

Cook pasta al dente. While hot, add pasta to sauce and toss to coat well. Serve immediately.

Pesto Linguine

8 servings

4 garlic cloves, minced
8 tablespoons olive oil
4 tablespoons butter
1 cup freshly grated Parmesan cheese
4 tablespoons basil
1 pound linguine
1 teaspoon salt
½ teaspoon white pepper

In a medium skillet, sauté garlic in oil and butter. Stir in Parmesan cheese until a pasty consistency. Stir in basil and remove from heat.

Cook linguine according to package directions. Drain well and immediately toss with basil mixture, salt and pepper. Serve on a heated platter.

One pound of pasta will serve 4 people as a main course.

218

Pasta Primavera

4-6 servings

⅓ cup butter
1 medium onion, minced
1 garlic clove, minced
1 pound thin fresh
 asparagus, tough ends
 trimmed, cut
 diagonally into 1-inch
 pieces
½ pound mushrooms,
 thinly sliced
6 ounces broccoli,
 broken into small
 flowerets
1 medium zucchini, cut
 into small slices
1 small carrot, halved
 lengthwise, cut
 diagonally into thin
 slices
4 ounces pea pods, cut
 into 1-inch pieces
1 cup heavy cream
½ cup chicken stock
2 teaspoons dried basil
 or 2 tablespoons fresh
 basil
1 cup frozen peas,
 thawed, **or** fresh peas
2 ounces prosciutto **or**
 ham, chopped, optional
4 green onions, chopped
Salt and pepper
1 pound fettuccine **or**
 linguine, cooked and
 drained
¾ cup grated Parmesan
 cheese

In a large skillet, sauté onion and garlic in butter. Add asparagus, mushrooms, broccoli, zucchini, carrots and pea pods and stir fry 2 minutes. Add cream, stock and basil. Heat to boiling and cook until liquid is slightly reduced, about 3 minutes. Stir in peas, prosciutto and green onions. Cook 1 minute longer. Season with salt and pepper.

Add pasta and cheese, tossing until well combined and until pasta is heated through. Serve immediately.

Noha Chau Fan

6-8 servings

An unusual use of lemon pasta, contributed by Aloha White, La Mia Cucina.

1½ pounds boneless
country-style pork
ribs, sliced thin
¼ cup vegetable oil
2 garlic cloves, minced
1 large onion, sliced
2 tablespoons bagoong
(fermented fish sauce,
available at oriental
food stores)
2 teaspoons black
pepper
Dash MSG
5 large mushrooms,
sliced
1 large carrot, sliced in
sticks about 2 inches
long
1 celery stalk, sliced in
sticks 2 inches long
1 8-ounce can bamboo
shoots, sliced
½ pound fresh bean
sprouts
3 green onions, chopped
1 10-ounce package
frozen sugar peas
1 pound fresh lemon
linguine (see Index for
Lemon Pasta)
Salt to taste

In a wok or large frying pan, stir fry pork in hot oil with garlic for 10 minutes. Lower temperature, add onion, bagoong, pepper and MSG, stir well. Simmer for 20 minutes.

Add mushrooms, carrot, celery, bamboo shoots and stir fry 2 minutes. Cover and continue cooking about 5 minutes.

Add bean sprouts, green onions, sugar peas and salt to taste. Stir well, cover and cook on low for 5 minutes.

Prepare lemon linguine and serve pork/vegetable mixture over pasta.

220

Spaghetti with Buitoni Sauce   6 servings

Tossed green salad, a dry white wine and hot sourdough bread can make this a quick and easy dinner.

1 cup butter
⅛ teaspoon salt
¼ teaspoon pepper
4 teaspoons oregano
4 teaspoons sweet basil
¼ teaspoon garlic powder
2 tablespoons chopped parsley
2 6½-ounce cans minced clams, drained (reserving liquid)
2 tablespoons Parmesan cheese
½ pound spaghetti
Fresh parsley sprigs

In a medium saucepan, simmer butter, salt, pepper, oregano, basil and garlic powder over low heat for about 10 minutes.

Begin cooking the spaghetti, according to package directions, timing the cooking so the spaghetti and sauce are done at the same time.

Add parsley and clam juice to the sauce and simmer another 5 minutes. Add clams, turn heat off and allow to stand about 5 minutes.

To serve, drain spaghetti and arrange evenly on a large platter. Add Parmesan cheese to the sauce and mix well. Pour evenly over spaghetti. Garnish with fresh parsley sprigs, if desired.

One pound of fresh pasta will yield about 1.6 to 1.8 pounds of cooked pasta, depending on the amount of moisture used in making the fresh pasta.

You cannot cook pasta in too much water. A pound of pasta must be cooked in a deep pot containing 5-6 quarts water.

Spaghetti Santa Margarita   12 servings

Colorful and attractive.

1 large onion, chopped
3 tablespoons light olive
   oil
2 garlic cloves, minced
¼ cup dry white wine
1½ teaspoons dried basil
   or 1½ tablespoons
   fresh basil
1 teaspoon dried
   marjoram **or**
   1 tablespoon fresh
   marjoram
2 cups canned plum
   tomatoes, well drained
1½ pounds mussels,
   scrubbed and
   debearded, **or**
   2 pounds small clams,
   scrubbed
1 pound sea scallops,
   halved
1 pound large shrimp,
   peeled, deveined and
   butterflied
Salt and freshly ground
   pepper
1 pound spaghetti,
   cooked al dente

In a large saucepan over medium-high heat, sauté onion in olive oil until lightly golden. Add garlic and sauté an additional 30 seconds. Stir in wine, basil and marjoram and cook 1 minute.

Add tomatoes, increase heat, and boil 5 minutes.

Reduce heat to medium, add mussels or clams, cover and cook until shells open about ½ inch (about 5 minutes).

Add scallops and shrimp, cover and cook an additional 2 to 3 minutes, until scallops and shrimp are barely firm. Season to taste with salt and pepper.

Add spaghetti and toss gently to mix. Serve immediately.

If you __must__ hold cooked pasta, toss with butter after draining, return to pot with lid. Keep in 175° oven no more than 30 minutes.

Spaghetti alla Gasparé

4 servings

Very volatile flavors!

2 tablespoons olive oil
2 dried whole red chili
  peppers
¾ pound small cooked
  shrimp
Salt and pepper
3 garlic cloves, minced
3 tablespoons minced
  fresh parsley
1 cup chopped green
  pepper
⅔ cup peas, cooked
1 pound fresh spaghetti

In a medium skillet, heat olive oil until quite hot. Add chili peppers and cook until brown. Remove with a slotted spoon and discard. Add shrimp and sauté 1 minute. Season with salt and pepper to taste. Reduce heat. Add garlic, parsley, green pepper and peas. Toss together and cook 1 to 2 minutes, being careful not to brown the garlic. Add tomato sauce and heat through.

Cook pasta al dente. Drain and return to hot kettle. Pour sauce over pasta and toss. Serve immediately.

TOMATO SAUCE

3 tablespoons olive oil
3 tablespoons minced
  shallots
3 tablespoons minced
  fresh parsley
1 teaspoon minced garlic
1 teaspoon tomato paste
3 cups canned Italian
  plum tomatoes, drained
  and coarsely chopped
1 teaspoon dried basil
1 teaspoon dried oregano
1 bay leaf
Salt and pepper

In a heavy skillet, heat olive oil over low heat and sauté shallots, parsley and garlic gently for 2 minutes. Add tomato paste, tomatoes, basil, oregano and bay leaf. Heat to boiling, reduce heat and simmer, partially covered, for 25 minutes. Season with salt and pepper to taste.

Set aside or refrigerate until ready to use.

One tablespoon butter in water will keep noodles from boiling over.

223

Zesty Italian Spaghetti and Meatballs

6 servings

1 to 2 tablespoons olive oil
1 large onion, chopped
1 garlic clove, minced
⅓ cup chopped celery
1 6-ounce can tomato paste
1 quart canned tomatoes, drained (reserving liquid)
1 cup water, including tomato liquid
1 tablespoon salt
1 tablespoon sugar
¼ teaspoon pepper
⅛ teaspoon allspice
⅛ teaspoon chili powder
¼ teaspoon thyme
⅓ cup chopped fresh parsley
1 bay leaf
1 garlic clove, on a toothpick
8 to 10 ounces spaghetti, cooked
Chopped fresh parsley and/or Parmesan cheese to garnish

In a deep kettle, gently sauté onion, garlic and celery in olive oil, stirring occasionally to prevent burning. When onions are translucent, add remaining ingredients, **except** spaghetti and parsley, and mix well. Add meatballs and simmer on low for 45 minutes.

To serve, arrange cooked spaghetti on a large platter. Remove bay leaf and garlic from the sauce and pour sauce and meatballs evenly over spaghetti. Garnish with a sprinkle of chopped parsley and/or grated Parmesan cheese.

MEATBALLS

1 pound ground beef
⅛ teaspoon minced garlic
2 eggs, beaten
1 teaspoon salt
⅛ teaspoon pepper
¼ cup Parmesan cheese
½ cup flour
1 to 2 teaspoons olive oil

Combine all ingredients, **except** flour and olive oil, and form into golfball-sized meatballs. Roll in flour and sauté in olive oil until almost done. Remove from skillet with a slotted spoon, draining well.

224

Italian Sausage and Peppers   4-6 servings

8 Italian link sausages **or**
  1 pound Italian bulk
  sausage
2 tablespoons olive oil
1 garlic clove, minced
2 green peppers, cut in
  1-inch chunks
2 red bell peppers, cut in
  1-inch chunks
2 onions, sliced
4 tomatoes, peeled,
  seeded and chopped
1 8-ounce can tomato
  sauce
½ teaspoon oregano
½ teaspoon basil
1 teaspoon parsley,
  minced
Dash of cinnamon
¼ cup burgundy wine
Salt and pepper to taste
1 pound spaghetti
Grated Parmesan **or**
  Romano cheese

Cut sausage links in half. Heat oil in a large skillet over medium-high heat. Add sausage and brown well. Remove and drain on paper towel. Remove excess grease from skillet and add garlic, peppers and onion. Sauté 5 minutes or until lightly browned. Return sausage and add tomatoes, tomato sauce, oregano, basil, parsley, cinnamon, wine, salt and pepper. Cover and simmer over low heat about 30 minutes. The sauce should be thick. If not, cook a bit longer, uncovered.

At serving time, cook spaghetti al dente. Drain and serve with sauce poured over noodles and topped with cheese.

Fresh pasta will keep for a week to 10 days if securely wrapped and refrigerated, 6 months if frozen. But of course, as with any other fresh food, the sooner eaten, the better.

Crab Spaghetti

6-8 servings

1 8-ounce package
    vermicelli **or** spaghetti
1 cup butter
3 medium onions,
    chopped
2 garlic cloves, minced
½ pound mushrooms,
    sliced
1 28-ounce can
    tomatoes, drained
½ pound Cheddar
    cheese, grated
½ pint sour cream
1½ to 2 pounds crab meat
1 2-ounce jar stuffed
    green olives, chopped

Cook vermicelli according to package directions. Drain.

In a large skillet, sauté onion, garlic and mushrooms in butter.

In a large casserole, combine all ingredients. Cover and bake at 350° for 30 minutes.

Fancy Spaghetti Casserole

6-8 servings

1 7-ounce package
    spaghettini **or**
    vermicelli
1 tablespoon butter
1½ pounds ground beef
2 8-ounce cans tomato
    sauce
Salt and pepper to taste
½ pound cottage cheese
8 ounces cream cheese,
    softened and diced
⅓ cup chopped green
    onions
1 tablespoon chopped
    green pepper
2 tablespoons butter,
    melted
Parmesan cheese,
    optional

Cook spaghettini according to package directions and drain.

In a skillet, sauté beef in butter until brown. Add tomato sauce, salt and pepper and remove from heat.

In a mixing bowl, combine cottage cheese, cream cheese, onions and green pepper.

In a square 2-quart casserole, spread half the spaghettini and cover with all of the cheese mixture. Top with the remaining spaghettini and pour melted butter over all. Spread meat sauce over the top.

Bake at 350° for 45 minutes. Sprinkle with Parmesan cheese, if desired.

Turkey-Spaghetti Bake

6-8 servings

¾ cup mayonnaise
⅓ cup flour
2 tablespoons minced onion
1 teaspoon garlic salt
2¼ cups milk
1 cup grated Swiss cheese
⅓ cup white wine
7 ounces spaghetti, cooked
2 cups cubed cooked turkey
1 10-ounce package frozen chopped broccoli, thawed
1¼ cups sliced almonds
1 4-ounce can sliced mushrooms, drained
¼ cup pimiento
2 to 3 drops Tabasco sauce
Grated Parmesan cheese

In a medium saucepan, combine mayonnaise, flour and seasonings. Gradually add milk. Cook over low heat, stirring until thick. Add cheese and wine. Stir until cheese melts.

In a large bowl, combine cheese mixture, spaghetti, turkey, broccoli, **¾ cup** of the almonds, the mushrooms, pimiento and Tabasco. Toss lightly and pour into a buttered 3-quart casserole. Top with remaining almonds.

Bake at 350° for 40 to 45 minutes. Sprinkle with Parmesan cheese.

Three-Cheese Noodle Casserole

6-8 servings

8 ounces cream cheese, softened
2 cups large curd cottage cheese
2 eggs, beaten
2 cups grated Cheddar cheese
1 green onion, chopped
¼ teaspoon salt
¼ teaspoon pepper
¼ teaspoon garlic salt
4 to 6 ounces flat noodles, cooked and drained

Blend cream cheese and cottage cheese thoroughly. Add eggs, stir and add remaining ingredients, mixing well. Toss with noodles and pour into a greased 3-quart casserole. Bake at 350° for 20 minutes.

227

Seafood Lasagne

12 servings

12 lasagne noodles
1 cup chopped onion
2 tablespoons margarine
1 8-ounce package cream cheese, softened
1½ cups cream-style cottage cheese
1 egg, beaten
2 teaspoons basil, crushed
Salt and pepper to taste
1 10-ounce can cream of mushroom soup, undiluted
⅓ cup milk
⅓ cup dry white wine
1 pound frozen cocktail-size shrimp, thawed
1 6½-ounce can crab, drained and flaked
¼ cup grated Parmesan cheese
½ cup grated sharp American **or** Cheddar cheese

Cook lasagne noodles according to package directions. Drain.

Cover bottom of a greased 9x13-inch baking dish with 4 noodles.

Sauté onion in margarine until tender. Blend in cream cheese. Stir in cottage cheese, egg, basil, salt and pepper. Spread approximately ⅓ of the mixture over the noodle layer.

Combine soup, milk and wine. Stir in shrimp and crab. Spread approximately ⅓ of the mixture over cream cheese/cottage cheese layer.

Repeat layers **twice** more, for a total of three layers.

Sprinkle with Parmesan cheese. Bake uncovered at 350° for 45 minutes. Top with grated cheese. Bake 2 minutes, until bubbly. Let stand about 10 minutes before cutting.

The higher proportion of eggs to flour, the richer will be the dough.

Vegetarian Lasagne   8 servings

1 8-ounce package
   lasagne noodles
2 10-ounce packages
   frozen chopped spinach
2 cups sliced fresh
   mushrooms
1 cup grated carrots
½ cup chopped onion
1 tablespoon oil
2 8-ounce cans tomato
   sauce
1 6-ounce can tomato
   paste
½ cup sliced ripe olives
1½ teaspoons oregano
2 cups cottage cheese,
   drained
1 pound Monterey Jack
   cheese, grated
½ cup freshly grated
   Parmesan cheese

Cook noodles in boiling unsalted water for 8 to 10 minutes or until tender. Drain and set aside.

Cook spinach and drain very well.

In a medium saucepan, cook mushrooms, carrot and onion in oil until tender. Stir in tomato sauce, tomato paste, olives and oregano.

In a greased 9x13-inch baking dish, layer **half** the noodles, cottage cheese, spinach, Jack cheese, and sauce mixture. Repeat layers, reserving about **½ cup** of the Jack cheese for the top. Sprinkle with Jack cheese and Parmesan cheese. Bake uncovered at 375° for 30 minutes. Let stand for 10 minutes before cutting.

When preparing noodles for a casserole, reduce their cooking time by one-third. They will finish cooking in the oven.

Lasagne with Mushroom Sauce

8 servings

Making pasta by hand requires extra time and effort but is certainly worth it.

2 eggplants, sliced ½ to ¾-inch thick lengthwise
Salt
2 cups olive oil
1½ pounds mushrooms, sliced
3 tablespoons butter
¾ cup grated Parmesan cheese

Generously salt eggplant slices and arrange vertically in a colander and drain for at least 30 minutes. Sauté in oil, drain (reserving oil) and set aside. Sauté mushrooms in oil until just tender, drain and set aside.

Butter a 9x13-inch baking dish with **1 tablespoon** of the butter and spoon in a small amount of béchamel sauce, just to cover the bottom. Add a layer of spinach pasta, layer of eggplant slices, several mushrooms, a thin layer of tomato sauce, approximately 4 tablespoons béchamel sauce and a thin sprinkling of Parmesan cheese. Repeat the layers until all ingredients are used. It is important to plan ahead so the ingredients will be evenly distributed. Dot the top of the lasagne with thin slices of remaining butter.

Bake in a preheated 450° oven for 10 to 15 minutes on an upper rack until a light, golden crust forms on top. Allow lasagne to settle 5 to 10 minutes before cutting. Serve directly from the pan.

NOTE: This may be refrigerated for 24 hours. In that case, cooking time must be extended. **Or,** lasagne may be baked and frozen for future use.

BECHAMEL SAUCE II

3 cups milk
6 tablespoons butter
4½ tablespoons flour
Scant ½ teaspoon salt

In a small saucepan, heat milk almost to boiling. While milk is heating, melt butter in a 1½-quart heavy saucepan. When butter is melted, add all the

Lasagna with Mushroom Sauce *(Continued)*

flour, stirring constantly with a wooden spoon. Let the flour and butter bubble for 2 minutes, stirring, constantly. Do not allow the mixture to become colored. Turn off heat and add hot milk, 2 tablespoons at a time, stirring constantly. When the first 2 tablespoons have been incorporated into the mixture, add another 2 tablespoons, stirring constantly. When ½ cup milk has been added, add remaining milk ¼ cup at a time until all is used. Never add more than ¼ cup at a time.

Return mixture to low heat and add salt, stirring constantly until the sauce is the consistency of thick cream. The sauce will be thicker if made in advance. Since it is easy to prepare, it is best to make and use immediately.

SPINACH PASTA

½ 10-ounce package frozen chopped spinach, thawed
1½ cups (approximately) flour
¼ teaspoon salt
2 eggs, beaten
Water
2 tablespoons oil

Cook spinach with salt in covered saucepan for 5 minutes over medium heat. Drain and let cool. Squeeze as much moisture from the spinach as possible and chop fine.

Pour flour and salt in a mound on a clean work surface and make a well in the center. Put eggs and spinach in the well and slightly beat together, using a fork or your fingers. Gradually incorporate the flour from the sides of the well. It is difficult to estimate exactly how much flour can be absorbed by the egg mixture, so proceed with as much flour as possible without allowing the pasta

Lasagna with
Mushroom Sauce   *(Continued)*

mixture to become stiff and dry. Knead dough for about 5 minutes with the heel of your palm until dough is smooth and easily forms a ball. Divide into 3 sections and place 2 sections under a damp cloth while rolling out the third.

Flour a clean work surface and roll with a rolling pin until dough is the thickness of a dime. Cut into workable sections (approximately 4x6-inches). Cover with a damp towel until ready to cook.

To cook pasta, fill a large kettle ⅔ full with water and add 2 tablespoons oil. Bring to a full boil and add pasta. Stir with a wooden spoon to avoid sticking. Fresh pasta will be done 5 to 10 seconds after water returns to a rapid boil. Remove carefully and drain on flattened towel. Top with another towel until ready to assemble.

TOMATO SAUCE

15 parsley sprigs, chopped
1 garlic clove, minced
1 teaspoon rosemary
6 tablespoons unsalted butter
3 tablespoons olive oil
1 28-ounce can Italian plum tomatoes, chopped

Sauté parsley, garlic and rosemary in butter and olive oil for 5 minutes. Add tomatoes and cook 5 minutes longer. Set aside.

Clam-Stuffed Manicotti   8-10 servings

1 cup sliced fresh
   mushrooms **or** 4
   ounces canned sliced
   mushrooms, drained
2 garlic cloves, minced
2 tablespoons butter **or**
   margarine
3 cups fresh bread
   crumbs, preferably
   French
3 6½-ounce cans minced
   clams, undrained
4 cups (1 pound) grated
   Mozzarella cheese
2½ cups grated
   Parmesan cheese
½ cup ricotta **or** cottage
   cheese
½ cup chopped fresh
   parsley
2 teaspoons basil
½ teaspoon salt
¼ teaspoon pepper
16 large manicotti shells
3 15-ounce cans
   Marinara sauce

In a large skillet, sauté mushrooms and garlic in butter. Remove from heat and stir in bread crumbs, clams with liquid, **half** the Mozzarella cheese, **half** the Parmesan cheese, **all** of the ricotta cheese, parsley, basil, salt and pepper.

Cook manicotti until limp but not fully cooked; about 5 to 6 minutes. Drain and cover with cold water until ready to fill.

Using both a 9x13-inch and an 8x8-inch baking dish, divide **1 can** of Marinara sauce evenly over the bottoms of both dishes. Fill manicotti loosely with clam mixture. Place filled manicotti on sauce in an even layer. Pour remaining **2 cans** of Marinara sauce over manicotti. Sprinkle with remaining cheeses. Bake uncovered at 375° for 30 minutes.

Crab or Smoked Salmon Canneloni

6-8 servings

This dish, contributed by JoAnn Stout, La Mia Cucina, is especially nice when crab and salmon canneloni are alternated.

**4-5 9x12-inch sheets
    fresh spinach pasta
    (often called sfoglia)
1 pound ricotta cheese
4-6 ounces fresh
    crabmeat or
    2-3 ounces smoked
    salmon
2 tablespoons finely
    chopped fresh dill (for
    salmon only)
Juice of one lemon
1 cup freshly grated
    Parmesan cheese**

Cut pasta into 4x9-inch pieces. Combine cheese, crab or salmon, dill (if necessary) and lemon juice. With large-tipped pastry bag or a spoon, lay a thick line of cheese mixture vertically down the edge of pasta pieces to within ½ inch of each end. Roll just to cover filling. Moisten bare edges and continue rolling, pressing edges and ends tgether. Repeat until all pasta and filling is used.

Ladle a ¼-inch base of balsamella into a 9x13-inch baking dish. Place canneloni in a single layer and top with remaining sauce.

Sprinkle with Parmesan cheese and bake at 325° about 20 minutes until hot and bubbly. Serve immediately.

BALSAMELLA

**5 cups milk
10 tablespoons butter
7½ tablespoons
    all-purpose flour
¾ teaspoon salt
½ teaspoon white
    pepper**

In a medium saucepan, heat the milk until almost boiling.

Meanwhile melt butter over low heat in a 6-cup capacity heavy enameled iron saucepan. When butter is melted, add flour, stirring constantly with a wooden

Crab or Smoked Salmon Canneloni *(Continued)*

spoon. Allow mixture to bubble gently for 2 minutes, stirring constantly. Do NOT allow flour to brown. Remove from burner and add hot milk **4 tablespoons** at a time, stirring constantly. Continue adding milk, ¼ cup at a time, stirring constantly.

Return to low heat, add salt and pepper; cook and stir until sauce is desired consistency.

Artichoke-Chicken Manicotti 4-6 servings

2 cups chicken, skinned, cubed and cooked
2 cups grated Mozzarella cheese
1 6-ounce jar marinated artichoke hearts, drained and sliced (reserving liquid)
½ cup oil from artichoke hearts
1 4-ounce can mushrooms, drained
½ cup undiluted cream of mushroom soup
¼ cup grated Romano cheese
1 teaspoon garlic salt
2 15-ounce cans spaghetti sauce
½ cup white wine
8 manicotti shells

In a medium bowl, combine all ingredients, **except** spaghetti sauce, white wine and manicotti.

Cover bottom of a 2-quart baking dish with **1 cup** of the spaghetti sauce.

Fill manicotti shells with chicken mixture and place in baking dish.

Add white wine and any remaining chicken filling to the remaining spaghetti sauce and mix well. Pour over manicotti. Bake covered at 375° for 1 hour.

Pasta Puttanesca
con Vongole

4-6 servings

"Puttanesca" means "streetwalker style." The spicy aroma of this dish was allegedly used to lure sailors in the dock areas of southern Italy.

¼ cup olive oil
1 tablespoon minced garlic
4 cups chopped tomatoes
½ cup chopped fresh parsley
2 tablespoons chopped fresh basil **or**
  1 tablespoon dried basil
1 teaspoon dried oregano
½ teaspoon red pepper flakes
2 tablespoons capers, drained
18 pitted ripe olives
2 ounces canned anchovies, optional
2 dozen littleneck clams
Salt and pepper to taste
½ cup golden raisins
¼ cup pine nuts
1 pound rotelle noodles

In a large skillet, heat oil and add garlic. Cook briefly until limp. Add tomatoes, **half** the parsley, the basil, oregano, pepper flakes, capers and olives. Cook over medium heat for 25 minutes.

Meanwhile drain and chop anchovies and wash clams until clean. Add both to sauce with remaining parsley, raisins, pine nuts, salt and pepper. Cover and cook 5 minutes or until clams open. Set aside.

Cook rotelle in rapidly boiling, salted water until al dente. Drain and cover with sauce.

Good hot or at room temperature accompanied by a green salad and garlic bread.

Drain but do not rinse pasta except for salad use.

Rotelle Salad

Great as a main dish on a hot summer night.

1 cup part skim milk
  ricotta cheese
3 tablespoons Dijon
  mustard
1 teaspoon salt
½ teaspoon pepper
16 ounces plain lowfat
  yogurt
2 pounds rotelle pasta
  noodles
2 tablespoons oil
1 cup grated Parmesan
  cheese
3 small zucchini, diced
4 large ripe tomatoes,
  diced
½ cup finely chopped
  green onions
½ cup mixture of:
  Fresh parsley
  Fresh marjoram
  Fresh basil
  Fresh thyme
1½ cups shelled
  pistachio nuts

Blend ricotta in food processor until smooth. Add mustard, salt, pepper and yogurt and process briefly. Pour into a bowl, cover and refrigerate until needed.

Cook pasta according to package directions and drain well. In a large bowl, toss pasta with oil and Parmesan cheese. Add zucchini, tomatoes, onions and herbs.

To serve, toss salad with dressing and garnish with nuts.

Shrimp Lo Mein

4-6 servings

8 ounces thin Chinese noodles **or** vermicelli
2 cups broccoli flowerets
2½ tablespoons cornstarch
3 tablespoons dry sherry
½ teaspoon salt
½ pound medium shrimp, shelled, cleaned and cut into thirds
⅔ cup chicken broth
¼ cup + 2 tablespoons soy sauce
¼ teaspoon Tabasco sauce
¼ teaspoon dried ginger
1 teaspoon sugar
4 tablespoons oil
2½ cups Chinese Bok Choy cabbage, cut into ½-inch slices
4 green onions, cut into ½-inch pieces
2 garlic cloves, minced
8 water chestnuts, sliced into thirds

In a large pot, cook noodles according to package directions. Drain and set aside.

In a large saucepan, cover broccoli with water and cook in boiling water for 3 minutes. Drain, place in cold water and set aside.

In a medium bowl, combine **½ tablespoon** cornstarch, **1 tablespoon** sherry and salt. Toss shrimp in mixture and set aside.

In a small bowl, combine broth, soy sauce, Tabasco sauce and ginger. Set aside.

In a small bowl, combine remaining cornstarch, sherry and sugar. Set aside.

In a wok or large skillet, heat **2 tablespoons** of the oil over high heat. Add drained noodles and stir fry 3 minutes. Remove from pan.

Add **1 tablespoon** of the oil to wok. When hot, add shrimp mixture and stir fry 3 minutes. Remove from pan.

Add remaining oil. When hot, add cabbage and stir fry 1 minute. Add onions and garlic and stir fry 30 seconds.

Add soy sauce mixture and shrimp and stir well. Add sherry mixture, broccoli and water chestnuts and continue to stir fry until mixture thickens. Add noodles and toss until well mixed and hot. Serve immediately.

Lemon Cream Pasta
with Strawberries
4 servings

A wonderful breakfast dish or yummy dessert following a light meal contributed by JoAnn Stout, owner of La Mia Cucina in Boise.

1 cup heavy cream
2 tablespoons sugar
Zest and juice of one
lemon
½ pound fresh vermicelli
1 pint fresh strawberries,
sliced and sprinkled
lightly with sugar

In a medium saucepan, combine cream, sugar, lemon zest and juice. Bring just to a boil over medium heat.

Meanwhile bring 3-4 quarts water to rapid boil and cook pasta al dente – about 30 seconds. Drain well and gently stir into cream mixture.

Serve immediately in warmed bowls topped with strawberries.

Easy Egg Pasta
(Food Processor Method)
1 pound

Very easy, quick and foolproof with a food processor and a pasta machine.

1½ cups unbleached
flour
½ teaspoon salt
2 large eggs, at room
temperature
1 tablespoon water

Place the flour and salt in the work bowl of a food processor fitted with a steel blade. Turn on and off once.

Beat eggs lightly in a small bowl. Turn on the machine, pour eggs through the tube and process for about 12 seconds or until the mixture resembles coarse meal. Add water and continue processing until the dough forms a ball. Remove the dough, divide it into 3 pieces, and lightly flour each piece. While working with 1 piece, cover others with a damp towel so they will not dry out.

239

Easy Egg Pasta *(Continued)*

For machine rolling: Run 1 piece of dough through the widest opening of the rollers 4 to 5 times or until it loses its wrinkles, flouring and folding the pasta in half after each run through.

Then proceed to run the pasta through subsequent, narrowing openings until you have a thin, smooth length of pasta. If during the rolling, the pasta becomes awkwardly long, just cut it in half. If the pasta seems moist or sticky during the rolling, flour it from time to time. Roll the other 2 pieces of dough and spread the rolled pasta out on towels, waxed paper or a floured surface to dry for 10 or 15 minutes. (For more even drying, turn dough over after 7 minutes.)

Change the handle of the pasta machine from roller to the cutting position desired: the wide (approximately ¼ inch) cut for fettuccine or noodles, the narrow (approximately ⅛ inch) cut for spaghetti. Send each length of pasta through the cutter and spread the cut pasta out to dry further while you prepare a sauce.

Pasta can be made ahead of cooking time since it keeps indefinitely, but the drier it is, the longer it takes to cook.

Easy Egg Pasta *(Continued)*

To cook: Bring 4 quarts of water to a rapid boil, add 1 tablespoon salt and pasta and stir with a wooden fork. When water returns to a boil, cook approximately 30 seconds to 1 minute, depending on thickness and dryness. Do not overcook, pasta should be tender, but firm to the bite – al dente. Drain and toss immediately.

Basil or Spinach Pasta
1 pound

Fantastic with Goat Cheese Sauce or Mushroom Sauce with Marsala Wine.

8 ounces fresh basil leaves, cleaned, dried and stems removed
1 large egg, at room temperature
1 teaspoon salt
1½ cups flour
1 tablespoon water

In a food processor fitted with the steel blade, place basil and process until finely chopped. Remove to a small bowl, add egg, and mix well with a fork.

Clean the work bowl, replace steel knife and add the salt and flour. Turn machine on and off to mix. Turn machine on and pour basil mixture through feed tube and process about 15 seconds or until the ingredients are the texture of coarse meal. Add water and continue processing until a ball of dough forms and begins to beat around the bowl. Remove from bowl and process as in Egg Pasta (see index).

To cook, heat 4 quarts salted water to boiling and cook for 1 to 2 minutes.

NOTE: For spinach pasta, use 3 ounces cooked fresh or frozen spinach, squeezed dry before weighing.

Lemon Pasta

1 pound

Good with any seafood or vegetable sauce.

3 cups flour
4 teaspoons salt
3 eggs
½ cup lemon juice at
  room temperature
Grated peel of 1 lemon
3 teaspoons oil
Warm water

Combine all ingredients (using **1 teaspoon** of the salt), **except** water in a food processor fitted with the steel blade. Process, adding a little water if needed. Dough should form a ball while processor is running.

Proceed as for Food Processor Pasta, machine or hand method.

Bring 4 quarts of water to a rapid boil. Add remaining salt and the pasta and stir with a wooden fork.

When water returns to a boil, cook approximately 30 seconds to 1 minute, depending on thickness. Do not overcook. Pasta should be tender but firm to the bite – al dente. Drain and toss with sauce immediately.

Creamy Zucchini Sauce

4-6 servings

Good with any pasta.

5 tablespoons light olive
  oil
5 small zucchini, cut in
  julienne strips
2 large onions, minced
1 garlic clove, minced
⅔ cup heavy cream
1 pound fresh pasta,
  cooked and hot
¾ cup freshly grated
  Parmesan cheese
Salt and pepper

In a large non-aluminum skillet, heat olive oil over medium-high heat. Add zucchini and sauté until golden. Remove with a slotted spoon and set aside on paper towels to drain.

Add onions and garlic to skillet and sauté until limp and lightly browned. Stir in cream, increase heat, and boil until reduced by ⅓. Add pasta, zucchini, ½ **cup** of the Parmesan, salt and pepper. Toss until heated through.

Serve immediately topped with remaining cheese.

242

Fresh Basil Pesto

1⅔ cups

Use in soups or, when mixed with melted butter, over hot, fresh pasta or vegetables.

2 cups packed fresh basil leaves, cleaned, and stems removed
2 large garlic cloves
½ cup pine nuts
¾ cup freshly grated Parmesan **or** Romano cheese
⅔ cup olive oil
Warm water

In the work bowl of a food processor, combine basil and garlic and process to a fine paste, scraping down sides of the bowl as necessary. Add pine nuts and cheese and process until smooth.

With machine running, pour olive oil through the feed tube in a slow steady stream and mix until smooth and creamy. If pesto is too thick, gradually pour up to ¼ cup warm water through feed tube with machine running.

Transfer pesto to jar. Cover surface of pesto with film of olive oil about ⅛-inch thick. Refrigerate up to 3 months.

Sugo di Funghi (Mushroom Sauce with Marsala Wine)

4 servings

1 medium onion, shredded
4 tablespoons unsalted butter
8 ounces fresh mushrooms, thinly sliced
¼ cup Marsala wine
Salt
Freshly ground pepper
1 pound fresh egg **or** spinach fettuccine, cooked and drained
¼ cup light cream
⅛ cup chopped parsley
Freshly grated Parmesan cheese

In a large saucepan over medium heat, sauté onion in butter until limp. Add mushrooms and continue cooking until natural juices appear. Add Marsala and cook 2 to 3 minutes longer. Add salt and pepper to taste, lower heat and stir in cream slowly, cooking 30 seconds.

Carefully pour into a warmed serving bowl (a wide shallow bowl is best). Place freshly cooked fettuccine over sauce. Top with parsley and cheese. Toss gently and serve with additional cheese.

243

Spaghetti Sauce

10-12 servings

3 pounds ground beef
3 large onions, chopped
1 teaspoon garlic salt
2 tablespoons Italian
  seasoning, tied in
  cheesecloth
2 tablespoons oregano
1 tablespoon minced
  garlic
3 tablespoons chili
  powder
3 12-ounce cans tomato
   paste
4 29-ounce cans tomato
   sauce
Chopped celery, optional

In a deep kettle, brown meat. Add onions and cook slightly. Add remaining ingredients and simmer at least 4 hours. Remove cheesecloth bag.

Serve over cooked spaghetti or freeze in plastic containers in 1-meal quantities. This will keep in the freezer for several months.

Afghan Rice

8-10 servings

2 cups oil (not olive oil)
6 large white onions,
  sliced
⅛ teaspoon red pepper
⅛ teaspoon ground
  ginger
½ teaspoon ground
  cardamom
½ teaspoon ground
  cumin
¼ teaspoon nutmeg
1 heaping tablespoon
  turmeric
Salt and pepper to taste
4 cups long grain white
  rice, uncooked
4 cups (approximately)
  chicken broth

In a deep kettle, sauté onions in oil until onions are BLACK (onions should be charcoalized). Remove onions from oil and discard or use as a snack.

Add spices to the oil in pan. Add rice and enough chicken broth to cover. Cover pan and cook until rice is tender, but not mushy. Serve as a rice ring filled with curry.

Good hot or cold.

NOTE: The slow part of this recipe is charring the onions. This can be done ahead of time if necessary, just refrigerate the spiced oil until time to cook the rice.

244

Armenian Rice

7-10 servings

A nice complement for beef roast or steak.

3 to 4 bacon slices, chopped
1 medium onion, chopped
4 tablespoons butter
3 cups long grain white rice, uncooked
3 tablespoons soy sauce
Dash garlic salt
1 4-ounce can mushrooms, drained
1 8-ounce package slivered almonds
2 cups beef consommé, undiluted
2 cups beef bouillon, undiluted

In a medium skillet, sauté bacon and onion. Add butter and heat just to melt butter.

In a 3 to 4-quart casserole, mix bacon/onion mixture with remaining ingredients. Bake covered at 300° for 2 hours or until rice is tender.

NOTE: Freezes well.

For special rice, add a little white wine or sherry to uncooked rice and butter in pan. Add liquid and cook as usual.

Polynesian Rice

6 servings

4 cups cooked rice
¼ tablespoon margarine
1 cup thinly sliced green pepper
1 13-ounce can pineapple chunks, drained
1 4-ounce can thinly sliced water chestnuts, drained
¼ cup soy sauce

TO BARBECUE: Combine all ingredients and place in doubled foil package. Seal tightly. Place on the barbecue and cook 10 minutes per side.

TO BAKE: Combine all ingredients and place in a 2-quart casserole dish. Bake covered at 350° for 25 minutes.

245

Rice Pilaf

6-8 servings

1 10-ounce can chicken
or beef consommé,
undiluted
1 can water
1 cup uncooked rice
(minute or regular)
3 green onions, chopped,
including tops
1 teaspoon minced
parsley
1 teaspoon celery salt
1 teaspoon
Worcestershire sauce
3 tablespoons butter or
margarine

In a 2-quart baking dish, combine
consommé and water and beat well.
Add remaining ingredients and mix.

Cover and bake at 325° for
45 minutes for minute rice or
60 minutes for regular rice. If there is
liquid left when the rice is tender, drain
before serving.

*Rice will be fluffier and drier if a slice of dry bread is
put on top after cooking and draining.*

Wild Rice
and Chicken Livers

6-8 servings

1½ cups wild rice
3 cups chicken bouillon
1 cup water
½ cup butter, softened
½ cup chopped onion
¼ cup chopped green
pepper
3 to 4 cups chopped
chicken livers
1 cup chopped
mushrooms
1 cup light cream

Soak wild rice for 6 hours in enough
water to cover. Drain well. Boil rice in
bouillon and water until moisture is
absorbed. Sauté onion, green pepper,
chicken livers and mushrooms in all but
1 tablespoon of the butter.

In a 2-quart casserole, mix rice,
sautéed ingredients, cream and
remaining butter. Refrigerate for at
least 2 hours. Cover and bake at 325°
for 30 minutes or until thoroughly
heated.

246

Wild Rice Casserole

6-8 servings

½ cup butter
1 cup sliced fresh
  mushrooms
2 tablespoons chopped
  green pepper
1 tablespoon chopped
  green onion **or** chives
2 tablespoons slivered
  almonds
1 cup wild rice
3 cups chicken broth

In a deep skillet, sauté mushrooms in butter until tender. Add green pepper, onions, almonds and rice.

In a saucepan, heat chicken broth to boiling and pour over mushroom/rice mixture. Simmer on top of stove for 5 minutes.

Pour into a 1½-quart casserole and bake covered at 325° for 1½ hours.

Good with wild game.

Basque Rice

12-15 servings

3 cups uncooked rice
1 large onion, chopped
1 large green pepper,
  chopped
2 cups canned pimiento,
  coarsely chopped
¼ cup butter
⅓ cup oil
4 to 5 chorizos, thinly
  sliced
2 thick ham slices, diced
2 8-ounce cans tomato
  sauce
1 cup beef bouillon
Salt and pepper to taste

Cook rice according to package directions. Set aside.

In a large skillet, sauté onion, green pepper and pimiento in butter and oil. Add meats and sauté.

In a very large mixing bowl, mix meat mixture with rice. Add tomato sauce and bouillon. If mixture seems too dry, add some water.

Place in 2 medium casseroles and bake covered at 350° for 1 hour.

To hold cooked rice and keep it warm, put it in a colander over simmering water and cover with paper towels.

247

Barley Bake

12 servings

1½ cups shelled pine
nuts
½ cup butter
1½ cups pearl barley
1 cup chopped onion
½ cup chopped chives
3 10-ounce cans beef
bouillon, undiluted
1 cup water
Salt and pepper

In a skillet, sauté pine nuts in ⅓ of the butter and place in a large casserole, reserving ½ cup of the nuts. In the same skillet, sauté barley in ⅓ of the butter and place in casserole. Sauté onion in remaining ⅓ of the butter and add to casserole. Add remaining ingredients and mix well.

Bake uncovered at 350° for 1½ hours. Stir after the first hour. Sprinkle reserved nuts over top and continue baking last ½ hour.

Old-Fashioned Hominy Grits

4 servings

1¼ cups water
1 teaspoon salt
½ cup hominy grits
1¼ cups milk
¼ cup butter
1 tablespoon sugar
2 eggs
2 tablespoons light
cream
Paprika

Heat water and salt to boiling and slowly add hominy grits, stirring constantly until thickened. Gradually add milk, reduce heat and cook 15 minutes, stirring occasionally until thickened again. Add butter and sugar and stir until butter is melted. Remove from heat.

Beat eggs with cream and fold into grits. Pour into a small buttered casserole and sprinkle with paprika. Bake, uncovered, at 350° for 40 minutes. Serve with pats of butter.

Brown rice has more food value, roughage and taste than white. It takes longer to cook, but is worth the trouble.

Basque Garbanzo Beans

4 servings

2 chorizo sausages
½ cup chopped onion
2 garlic cloves, minced
1 tablespoon oil
2 cups canned garbanzo
    beans, undrained
1 to 2 8-ounce cans
    tomato sauce

In a large saucepan, sauté sausages, onions and garlic in oil. Add beans, including liquid, and tomato sauce. Simmer gently for 1 hour.

Idaho Cassoulet

8-10 servings

1 pound small Twin Falls
    white beans
Water
5 carrots, sliced
2 large onions, cut in
    chunks
3 green peppers, cut in
    chunks
4 tablespoons butter
1 pound chorizos
2 16-ounce cans whole
    tomatoes, undrained
1 teaspoon cumin
1 teaspoon Mexican
    oregano
3 to 4 dried hot red
    peppers, crumbled, or
    ½ to 1 tablespoon
    crushed red pepper
½ teaspoon cinnamon
1 bay leaf
12 garlic cloves,
    6 minced, 6 pressed
Parsley to garnish

In a large pot, soak beans overnight in enough water to cover, plus 1 inch. In the morning, drain and add fresh water 1 inch above the beans. Heat to boiling, reduce heat to simmer and cook 1½ hours until beans are almost done.

In another large pot, sauté carrots, onions and green peppers in butter for 5 to 10 minutes. Drain excess water from beans and add vegetables, whole chorizos, tomatoes and seasonings. Be cautious with the red peppers — they are powerful. Simmer 1 hour to blend, lightly covered, adding more water if necessary.

To serve, remove bay leaf and discard. Remove chorizos, slice in ½-inch pieces and return to beans. Garnish with parsley.

249

Idaho Buckaroo Beans

8-10 servings

1 pound (2 cups) pink, red
  or pinto beans, soaked
  overnight in 6 cups
  water
½ pound smoked ham,
  salt pork or slab bacon,
  cut up
1 large onion, coarsely
  chopped
2 garlic cloves, sliced
1 small bay leaf
2 cups solid pack or fresh
  peeled tomatoes
½ cup chopped green
  pepper
2 teaspoons chili powder
2 tablespoons brown
  sugar
½ teaspoon dry mustard
¼ teaspoon crushed
  oregano leaves
Salt

Drain beans and add fresh water to
2 inches above beans. Add meat,
onion, garlic and bay leaf. Heat to
boiling and cover tightly. Cook over low
heat for 1½ hours or until beans are
almost tender.

Add all remaining ingredients, except
salt, and more water if necessary.
Simmer, uncovered, for 2 hours stirring
once or twice. Taste and add salt if
necessary. There should be enough
liquid left on the beans to resemble a
medium-thick gravy.

If desired, the beans may be baked,
covered, at 325° after the first step is
completed.

NOTE: Long, slow cooking helps to
give a rich, full flavor. May be made
ahead and refrigerated, then reheated,
even on a barbecue grill.

Bean Supreme

8 servings

1 pound dry small white
  beans
5 cups water
½ pound bulk pork
  sausage
2 cups sliced apples
½ cup brown sugar
2 large onions, chopped
3 garlic cloves, minced
2 cups diced tomatoes,
  fresh or canned
1 tablespoon salt
¼ teaspoon pepper
½ teaspoon chili powder

Cook beans in water until tender.
Drain.

In a large casserole or Dutch oven,
combine all ingredients.

Bake, covered, at 325° for 3 hours.
Remove cover and bake another
½ hour. Add more water if necessary.

250

Pineapple Baked Beans
10-12 servings

8 bacon slices, diced
5 tablespoons bacon
   drippings
1 cup chopped onion
1 green pepper, chopped
⅛ teaspoon garlic powder
1 15-ounce can of each:
   baked beans, kidney
   beans, butter beans
   and chili beans
½ cup catsup
½ cup red wine
½ cup dark molasses
1 teaspoon salt
1 teaspoon ginger
1 teaspoon dry mustard
½ teaspoon chili powder
2 tablespoons vinegar
2 tablespoons brown
   sugar
1 teaspoon liquid smoke
½ teaspoon pepper
1 15-ounce can pineapple
   chunks, drained

In a medium skillet, fry bacon. Drain on paper towels. Discard all but 5 tablespoons of the drippings and sauté onion and green pepper with garlic powder until tender.

Pour off excess liquid from kidney beans and butter beans, but do not drain completely.

Blend together catsup, wine, molasses, salt, ginger, dry mustard, chili powder, vinegar, brown sugar, liquid smoke and pepper.

In a large baking dish or crockpot, combine all mixtures, including pineapple and bacon. Bake at 350° until heated through, about 1 hour. Some pineapple juice may be added if beans appear too dry.

Mexican Hot Beans
10-12 servings

1 pound dry pinto beans
Water
½ pound bacon ends, cut
   in chunks
4 garlic cloves, minced
2 teaspoons oregano
2 canned hot jalapeño
   peppers
1 to 2 tablespoons salt

Rinse pinto beans. Fill a 5-quart kettle half full of water and heat to boiling. Add beans, stir and simmer uncovered for 1 hour with water barely covering the beans. Add more boiling water if needed.

Add bacon ends and cook 1 hour longer. Add garlic and continue cooking 1 hour. Add oregano and jalapeño peppers and continue cooking 1 hour longer. Add **1 tablespoon** salt and cook another hour.

Best in the West
Barbecue Bean Bake

20-24 servings

1 pound ground beef
1 pound bacon, chopped
1 onion, chopped
½ cup catsup
½ cup barbecue sauce
1 teaspoon salt
4 tablespoons prepared
  mustard
4 tablespoons molasses
1 teaspoon chili powder
¾ teaspoon pepper
2 16-ounce cans red
  kidney beans, drained
2 16-ounce cans pork
  and beans
2 16-ounce cans butter
  beans, drained
	In a Dutch oven or large casserole,
	brown ground beef, bacon and onion.
	Drain off excess fat. Add remaining
	ingredients, **except** beans, and stir
	well. Add beans and stir thoroughly.
	Bake uncovered at 350° for 1 hour.

Refried Beans Especial

4-6 servings

*Serve either as a side dish or as a hot dip with plain
tortilla chips.*

1 17-ounce can refried
  beans
1 4-ounce can diced
  green chiles
1 cup grated Cheddar
  cheese
½ cup sliced green
  onions
¼ teaspoon ground
  cumin
Sliced ripe olives
	In a 1½-quart casserole, combine all
	ingredients and mix well. Bake
	uncovered at 350° for 20 minutes or
	until heated through.
	
	If desired, sprinkle extra cheese on
	top the last 5 minutes of baking. Top
	with olives before serving.

Bound to Please: The Outdoor Invitation

They played polo, relaxed in geothermal hot springs, picnicked in the deserts and mountains, and went swimming, hiking, and fishing. Early Idahoans both worked the land and enjoyed it.

And nothing has changed – except, perhaps, the variety of outdoor sports. Idahoans sail on lakes and reservoirs, explore great forests, bicycle for fun and competition, raft through Hell's Canyon (the deepest gorge in North America), and camp in remote areas as well as federal and state parks. Idaho is made for enjoyment, and Idahoans do just that.

Fish

Sauces & Fillings

Seafood

Seafood-Stuffed Rainbow Trout

10 servings

5½ pounds whole, boned
   rainbow trout
¼ teaspoon salt
2 pounds fresh shrimp **or**
   seafood pieces, cooked
¼ cup sauterne
4 ounces stale bread
   cubes
2 tablespoons capers
Clarified butter
Salt
Paprika
Watercress
Lemon wedges

Rinse fish and pat dry. Sprinkle cavity with the **¼ teaspoon** salt.

In a large saucepan, combine white sauce, seafood and wine. Cool. Fold in bread cubes and capers.

Fill each trout with **½ cup** stuffing mixture and secure with toothpicks. Brush skin with butter, place on greased pan in a shallow pan of water. Cover and bake at 350° for 15 minutes. Uncover and continue to bake for about 5 minutes.

Brush again with butter. Sprinkle with salt and paprika. Place under broiler until skin is browned and glazed. Garnish with watercress and lemon wedges and serve immediately.

WHITE SAUCE

6 tablespoons butter
6 tablespoons flour
3 cups milk
Salt and pepper

In a medium saucepan, melt butter. Stir in flour. Slowly stir in milk and continue stirring until sauce thickens. Salt and pepper to taste. Makes 3 cups.

When pan-frying fish, cook it last, when the rest of the dinner is almost ready and serve it immediately.

Broiled Idaho Trout Minceur   4 servings

4 whole rainbow trout,
   deboned, fresh **or**
   frozen
1 8-ounce bottle clam
   juice **or** chicken broth
2 tablespoons minced
   onion
1 tablespoon oil
1 teaspoon
   Worcestershire sauce
¼ teaspoon salt
⅛ teaspoon oregano
⅛ teaspoon thyme
⅛ teaspoon pepper
3 cups steamed julienne
   cut carrots, green
   beans, celery, turnips
   and/or zucchini
Parsley
Lemon wedges

Place trout, skin side down, on a well-oiled broiler rack.

In a saucepan, combine clam juice, onion, oil, Worcestershire sauce and seasonings. Boil liquid rapidly for about 5 minutes, reducing to ½ cup.

Brush trout with sauce. Broil 3 inches from heat for about 5 minutes, brushing twice during broiling. Carefully lift trout from broiler and center on a warm platter. Surround with vegetables and garnish with parsley and lemon.

Idaho Trout Italiano   10 servings

1 whole rainbow trout,
   boned, approximately
   5½ pounds
Salt and freshly ground
   pepper to taste
¼ cup lemon juice
Flour
Olive oil
1½ cups bread crumbs
¾ cup chopped scallions
1¼ cups unsalted butter
Fresh spinach
1¼ pounds fresh
   mushrooms, sliced
Ripe olives

Rub trout inside and out with salt, pepper and lemon juice. Flour lightly.

Sauté in hot oil for 3 to 4 minutes per side and place in baking pan.

In a skillet, sauté bread crumbs and scallions in butter for 1 minute. Spread mixture over one side of trout. Bake at 350° for 10 minutes or until fish flakes easily when tested with a fork.

In the same skillet, sauté mushrooms in butter until soft.

Serve trout on a bed of fresh spinach surrounded by mushrooms. Garnish with ripe olives.

Idaho Rainbow Trout Oriental

6 servings

½ pound pasta
Chicken stock
4 tablespoons butter
1 pound fresh
  mushrooms, sliced
3 bunches green onions,
  diced
Garlic salt and pepper to
  taste
6 rainbow trout, boned,
  approximately
  10 ounces each
Teriyaki sauce
3 ounces sake
Salad greens
Celery curls
Carrot curls
1 small can spiced crab
  apples, drained

In a large pan, cook pasta in chicken stock. Drain well.

In a heavy skillet, sauté mushrooms in butter. Combine pasta, mushrooms, onions, garlic salt and pepper. Keep warm.

Brush trout cavities with teriyaki sauce. Place **½ cup** of the pasta filling in each trout. Brush with a generous amount of melted butter and broil until fish flakes easily when tested with a fork. When fish is cooked, pour **½ ounce** of sake over each.

Place trout on a large platter covered with greens. Garnish with celery curls, carrot curls and crab apples.

To store fish, wrap in waxed paper, plastic wrap or foil and refrigerate in coldest section of the refrigerator. Plan to use the same day if possible.

Baking fish on a bed of chopped onion, celery and parsley not only makes fish taste better, but also keeps it from sticking to the pan.

Truite en Papillote (Trout in Paper Case)

4 servings

2 to 3 tablespoons butter
4 trout, heads and tails
  intact
Salt and pepper to taste
Lemon wedges

Rinse and dry fish thoroughly. Cut 4 ovals of baking parchment or brown wrapping paper large enough to enclose each fish. Spread center of each oval generously with butter. Place fish on top and sprinkle with salt and pepper, including cavity. Spread the duxelles over top. Fold paper over fish, folding edges over twice. Moisten edges with beaten egg if regular brown paper is used. Place packages on a baking sheet and bake at 350° for 15 to 18 minutes. Garnish with lemon wedges.

NOTE: To prepare in advance, cool the duxelles before spreading on fish. Prepare packages and refrigerate until ready to bake. May be made 3 to 4 hours in advance.

DUXELLES

1 shallot
¼ pound mushrooms
2 tablespoons butter
3 parsley sprigs
Salt and pepper to taste

In a food processor, chop shallot very fine. Add mushrooms and process until finely chopped.

In a heavy saucepan, melt butter and add mushroom mixture. Cook over medium-high heat for 3 to 5 minutes, stirring until all moisture has evaporated. Remove from heat.

In a food processor, chop parsley. Add to mushroom mixture and season with salt and pepper.

256

Stuffed Boneless Brook Trout

2 servings

This recipe from the Sandpiper Restaurants features famous Idaho trout.

½ cup chopped fresh
  mushrooms
1 teaspoon chopped
  shallots
1 teaspoon chopped
  chives
½ cup chopped tomatoes
2 tablespoons butter
1 tablespoon flour
¼ cup milk
⅛ teaspoon salt
Dash pepper
3 tablespoons dry white
  wine
1 cup crab meat
½ teaspoon lemon juice
2 10-ounce rainbow
  trout, cleaned and
  boned

In a saucepan, sauté the mushrooms, shallots, chives and tomatoes in butter until tender. Blend in flour. Add milk, salt and pepper. Cook and stir until thickened and bubbly. Stir in wine. Add crab meat and lemon juice.

Stuff each trout with half the mixture. Wrap in foil and broil 5 minutes per side.

Marinated Salmon Steaks

8 servings

¼ cup oil
¼ cup olive oil
½ cup soy sauce
2 garlic cloves, minced
1 teaspoon finely minced
  ginger
Juice of 1 lemon
3 tablespoons seafood
  seasoning
8 salmon steaks

In a blender, combine oils, soy sauce, garlic, ginger, lemon juice and seafood seasoning. Blend well. Pour marinade into a 9x13-inch glass dish. Place steaks in marinade, cover and refrigerate for about 12 hours, turning occasionally.

Broil steaks 8 minutes per side.

257

Poached Salmon with Sherried Caper Sauce

10 servings

1 whole salmon,
   approximately 5 pounds
8 cups chicken bouillon
2 quarts cold water
2 carrots, sliced
2 celery stalks, sliced
1 large onion, sliced
Bouquet garni (2 sprigs
   parsley, 1 bay leaf,
   1 teaspoon thyme)
6 peppercorns
2 tablespoons vinegar **or**
   lemon juice
1 teaspoon salt
Lemon slices

Rinse fish and pat dry.

In a deep roasting pan, combine all ingredients, **except** salmon. Cover and heat to boiling. Simmer for 15 to 20 minutes. Strain and cool.

Lower fish, wrapped in cheesecloth, (with enough cloth at each end to act as handles) into strained poaching liquid. Liquid should just cover salmon. Bring broth almost to boiling, reduce heat and simmer 30 minutes or until fish flakes easily when tested with a fork. Drain well. Remove skin. Transfer to platter and chill. Serve with sliced lemons and sherried caper sauce.

SHERRIED CAPER SAUCE

1 tablespoon red wine
   vinegar
1 tablespoon white
   vinegar
2 teaspoons anchovy
   paste
1 teaspoon dry mustard
2 tablespoons sherry
¼ cup chopped parsley
1 tablespoon minced
   onion
⅓ cup capers
¼ teaspoon garlic
   powder
1 cup mayonnaise

Combine all ingredients and mix well. Cover and refrigerate overnight.

NOTE: Must be prepared in advance.

Baked Salmon

1 whole salmon,
approximately 6 pounds
2 lemons, sliced
1 large onion, sliced
2 tablespoons tarragon,
crushed
3 bay leaves, crushed
½ cup butter

Clean and pat dry cavity of salmon. Remove excess scales. Line cavity with lemon and onion slices. Sprinkle with tarragon and bay leaves.

Slit skin and insert pieces of butter in approximately 6 places on each side of salmon. Wrap in heavy foil and seal well. Bake at 325° for 15 minutes per pound. Garnish with lemon wedges. May be served hot or cold.

Salmon Crêpes

3 tablespoons butter
3 tablespoons flour
½ teaspoon salt
Dash white pepper
¼ teaspoon tarragon
1½ cups light cream
2 egg yolks, lightly
beaten
1 7-ounce can salmon,
drained and flaked
1 tablespoon chopped
chives
1 tablespoon lemon juice
12 large **or** 18 small
crêpes (see index)
3 tablespoons Parmesan
cheese

In a large skillet, melt butter. Stir in flour. Cook, stirring constantly, until bubbly. Stir in salt, pepper, tarragon and cream. Continue cooking and stirring until thickened. Boil 1 minute.

In a small bowl, combine egg yolks with **half** the sauce. Pour into remaining sauce and stir. Cook 1 minute longer. Remove from heat.

In a bowl, blend ¾ **cup** of the sauce with salmon and chives.

Stir lemon juice into remaining sauce.

Place a heaping tablespoon of the salmon mixture on each crêpe and roll. Place seam side down in a buttered 9x13-inch baking dish. Pour remaining sauce over crêpes. Sprinkle with cheese and bake at 400° for 10 minutes.

259

Sole with Mushroom Stuffing   8 servings

4 tablespoons butter
½ pound mushrooms,
    chopped coarsely
Salt and pepper to taste
Dash sugar
Butter
½ cup dry white wine
8 sole fillets
2 tablespoons flour
½ cup light cream
Dash nutmeg

In a small saucepan, melt
2 tablespoons of the butter. Add
mushrooms and sauté 2 minutes.
Season with salt, pepper and sugar.

Butter a large oval skillet. Pour in wine.
Lay **4** fillets in wine, cover with
mushrooms and top with remaining
fillets. Cut waxed paper to fit pan,
butter one side and fit buttered side
down over fillets. Heat to boiling.
Lower heat to medium and cook for
5 minutes.

In a medium saucepan, melt remaining
butter. Add flour and cook on low for
3 minutes. Slowly add cream and
nutmeg, stirring constantly until
thickened.

Place cooked fillets on ovenproof
platter. Strain poaching liquid into
sauce. Stir and cook 3 minutes longer.
Spoon over fillets and brown under
broiler.

To serve, cut each fillet in half.

When poaching, cover fish with a circle of waxed paper
with a small hole cut in the center. You can cook the
fillets without drowning them in liquid.

Stuffed Fillet of Sole with Mushroom Sherry Sauce
6 servings

3 tablespoons butter
4 ounces fresh
  mushrooms, chopped
1 small onion, chopped
2 celery stalks, finely
  chopped
½ pound fresh salad
  shrimp
6 large sole fillets
2 tablespoons lemon
  juice
½ pound fresh
  mushrooms, sliced
1 tablespoon flour
1½ cups heavy cream
1½ tablespoons sherry
Parmesan cheese, grated
Paprika

In a large skillet, sauté **chopped** mushrooms, onion and celery in **1 tablespoon** of the butter. Cool slightly. Add shrimp and stuff fillets. Roll and secure with toothpicks. Place in 8x8-inch baking pan.

In the same skillet, melt remaining butter with lemon juice. Add **sliced** mushrooms and sauté for 10 minutes, stirring occasionally. Blend in flour. Slowly add cream and stir until thickened. Simmer 10 minutes. Add sherry and stir well. Pour sauce over fillets and sprinkle with cheese and paprika. Bake at 350° for 20 minutes.

Fillet of Sole
4 servings

6 sole fillets
1 green onion, chopped,
  including top
Salt and pepper to taste
1 teaspoon curry powder
¾ cup dry sauterne **or**
  sherry
2 tablespoons butter
2 tablespoons flour
½ cup milk
2 tomatoes, quartered
¼ pound fresh
  mushrooms, quartered
Butter

Put fillets and green onion in a buttered skillet. Season with salt, pepper and curry powder. Add **½ cup** of the wine and cook slowly for about 10 minutes. Remove fillets and place in an ovenproof dish.

In the same skillet, melt butter and blend in flour. Slowly stir in milk and remaining wine. Cook until thickened, stirring constantly. Pour over fillets and garnish with tomatoes and mushrooms. Dot with butter. Bake uncovered at 350° for 20 minutes.

Establishment Sole

2-4 servings

4 sole fillets
1½ pounds fresh spinach
1 teaspoon salt
¼ teaspoon pepper
1 egg yolk, beaten
¼ cup heavy cream
½ cup grated Gruyère or
  Parmesan cheese
1 cup sliced fresh
  mushrooms
2 tablespoons butter
¼ cup sliced and toasted
  almonds

Broil sole just until meat is opaque. Set aside.

In a large covered saucepan, steam spinach until tender. Press out excess water. Season with salt and pepper.

Blend egg yolk and cream and add to béchamel sauce. Add cheese and stir until melted. DO NOT BOIL.

Sauté sliced mushrooms in butter until tender.

Place steamed spinach in an 8x8-inch baking dish. Layer fillets over spinach, spoon mushrooms over sole. Cover all with béchamel sauce and sprinkle with toasted almonds.

Bake uncovered at 350° for 10 minutes until top is golden brown.

BECHAMEL SAUCE III

4 tablespoons butter
4 tablespoons flour
1½ cups milk
½ cup heavy cream
1 teaspoon salt
¼ teaspoon white
  pepper

In a saucepan melt butter. Remove from heat and stir in flour. Cook over low heat for 1 minute. Slowly add milk, stirring constantly. When sauce boils, add cream, salt and pepper. Simmer 30 seconds or until thickened.

Freeze fish in milk cartons full of water or wrap each fish in plastic wrap then securely in heavy duty foil. Date package and use within 6 months.

Sole Sussannah

6 servings

6 3-ounce sole fillets
Salt
3 4x7-inch slices Swiss cheese, halved
1 7-ounce can crab meat
½ teaspoon basil
6 mushroom caps
2 tablespoons chopped mushrooms
½ teaspoon chopped shallots
1½ teaspoons lemon juice
4 tablespoons butter
3 tablespoons dry white wine **or** vermouth
3 tablespoons flour
1 cup fish stock
⅓ cup light cream
Salt to taste

Place sole on waxed paper and sprinkle with salt. On each fillet place an equal amount of cheese, crab, and basil and a mushroom cap. Roll up and place seam side down in a 12x8-inch baking dish. Set aside.

In a saucepan, sauté mushrooms and shallots in **1 teaspoon** of the lemon juice and **2 tablespoons** of the butter. Add wine and cook until liquid is almost evaporated. Stir in remaining butter and flour. Mix well. Stir in fish stock and cook until thick and bubbly. Add cream, remaining lemon juice and salt; stir well. Strain. Pour sauce over fish. Cover and bake at 400° for 30 minutes.

Fish continues to cook while it waits for you to complete the sauce.

Whole fish are more perishable so they are usually fresher than fillets.

Broccoli-Rice Fillets

6-8 servings

⅓ cup butter
⅓ cup lemon juice
2 teaspoons chicken
  bouillon granules
1 teaspoon Tabasco
  sauce
1 cup cooked rice
1 10-ounce package
  frozen chopped
  broccoli, thawed **or**
  1 cup cooked and
  chopped fresh broccoli
1 cup grated sharp
  Cheddar cheese
8 fresh fish fillets (red
  snapper, sole,
  flounder)
Paprika

In a small saucepan, melt butter. Add lemon juice, bouillon and Tabasco sauce. Heat slowly until bouillon dissolves. Set aside.

In a medium bowl, combine rice, broccoli, cheese and ¼ **cup** of the lemon butter sauce. Mix well.

Divide broccoli mixture evenly among fillets. Roll up each fillet and place seam side down in a shallow baking dish. Pour remaining sauce over fillets. Bake uncovered in a preheated 375° oven for 25 minutes or until fish flakes easily when tested with a fork. Spoon sauce over individual servings and garnish with paprika.

Super Seafood

4 servings

4 sole fillets, cut in half
  crosswise
12 scallops
½ cup Dungeness crab
½ cup small salad shrimp
½ cup grated Mozzarella
  or Monterey Jack
  cheese
Paprika
Parsley

Lightly butter four individual ramekins. Place a fillet half on the bottom and layer with scallops, crab, shrimp and cheese. Top with the second fillet half and cover with hollandaise sauce. Bake at 450° for 10 to 15 minutes. Garnish with paprika and parsley.

HOLLANDAISE SAUCE II

2 egg yolks
1 tablespoon fresh lemon
  juice
½ cup butter

In a double boiler over hot (not boiling) water, combine egg yolks and lemon juice. Add butter, 1 tablespoon at a time, stirring until melted. Continue stirring until thickened.

264

Flounder Fiesta

4 servings

4 flounder fillets
Salt and pepper to taste
2 tablespoons fresh lemon juice
2 tablespoons butter
¼ cup chopped onion
¾ cup dry white wine
2 cups peeled and chopped tomatoes
3 tablespoons chopped parsley
½ teaspoon salt
¼ teaspoon pepper
⅛ teaspoon sugar
2 cups (4 ounces) egg noodles
2 teaspoons flour
2 teaspoons water

Sprinkle fillets with salt, pepper and lemon juice. Roll up. Secure with toothpicks.

In a large skillet, sauté onion in butter until transparent.

Add rolled fillets, wine, tomatoes, parsley, salt, pepper and sugar. Heat to boiling, then simmer gently for 8 to 10 minutes or until fish flakes easily when tested with a fork.

Cook egg noodles according to package directions. Drain and spoon onto heated platter. Place fillets on noodles and cover to keep warm.

In a small bowl, stir flour and water into a smooth paste. Stir into poaching liquid and cook over medium heat, stirring constantly, until thickened. Continue cooking 5 minutes longer, stirring occasionally.

Pour sauce over fillets and noodles and serve immediately.

If you have the choice, buy where reputable restaurants get their fish.

Fillets should be firm with no fishy odor.

Fillets Farcis

4 servings

½ pound trout fillets **or** halibut
1 shallot, cut in half
¼ garlic clove
¾ teaspoon salt
¼ teaspoon white pepper
2 egg whites
⅓ cup light cream
4 medium flounder fillets
Salt to taste
½ cup dry white wine
½ cup water
1 bay leaf
3 peppercorns

Dry trout with paper towels (remove skin if necessary). Cut fillets into 2 to 3-inch pieces. Put in food processor with shallot, garlic, salt and pepper. Process until fish is puréed. Continue processing and add egg whites **1** at a time. With processor running, add cream, **1 tablespoon** at a time, until mixture easily falls from a spoon.

Lay flounder on waxed paper, remove skin, sprinkle both sides with salt. Spread each fillet with mousse and role up jelly-roll fashion. Secure with toothpicks. Place rolls in a lightly greased baking dish. Add wine, water, bay leaf and peppercorns. Cover with buttered waxed paper and bake at 350° for 15 to 20 minutes or until fish flakes easily. Remove from oven, transfer to an ovenproof serving dish and remove toothpicks. Reserve poaching liquid for shrimp sauce.

Spoon shrimp sauce over fillets and bake at 325° for 10 minutes.

SHRIMP SAUCE II

2 tablespoons butter
1 shallot, finely chopped
2 tablespoons flour
¾ cup poaching liquid
1 tablespoon tomato paste
½ cup light cream
¼ to ½ pound small cooked shrimp

In a saucepan, sauté shallot in butter for 5 minutes. Stir in flour. Gradually add poaching liquid, stirring constantly. Add tomato paste and continue stirring until thickened. Stir in cream and shrimp. Heat thoroughly.

Seafood Crêpes Délices   4 servings

5 tablespoons butter
1 shallot, minced, **or**
   2 tablespoons minced
   green onions
4 mushrooms, diced
6 tablespoons flour
1 cup milk
½ cup fish stock
1 cup heavy cream
¼ teaspoon dry mustard
1 teaspoon salt
½ teaspoon white
   pepper
1 tablespoon cognac
2 cups seafood (lobster,
   crab, shrimp)
8 to 10 crêpes (see
   index)
2 egg yolks
2 tablespoons grated
   Parmesan cheese
2 tablespoons dry sherry

In a saucepan, melt **2 tablespoons** of the butter. Sauté shallots and mushrooms for 2 minutes. Add remaining butter. Blend in flour and stir well.

Remove from heat and slowly stir in milk, stock and **½ cup** of the heavy cream, a little at a time.

Add mustard, salt, pepper and cognac. Stir well. Return to heat and allow sauce to thicken. Cook for 2 to 3 minutes stirring occasionally. Remove from heat and allow mixture to cool slightly.

Blend seafood with **1½ cups** of the sauce. Adjust seasoning if necessary. Place **2 to 3 tablespoons** of the mixture on each crêpe and roll up.

Place crêpes in a buttered glass baking dish. Bake at 400° for 10 minutes.

In a small bowl, beat egg yolks. Slowly add remaining sauce and stir well. Whip remaining heavy cream, fold in with cheese and sherry. Pour over crêpes and place under broiler until sauce bubbles (about 1 minute).

Skewer your shrimp in "shrimp-kin" style. Pair them – turn the second upside down and reverse its direction.

Seafood Sauté and Herb Butter

1 serving

A favorite at Jake's, Boise.

1½ ounces Herb Butter*
5 ounces scallops (halve
  if very large)
2 large shrimp, sliced in
  half lengthwise
1½ ounces Dungeness
  crab
1 tablespoon white wine
  (chablis)

Melt herb butter in sauté pan. Add scallops and sauté on medium-high heat abut 3 minutes or until scallops are half done and are turning white. Add remaining ingredients and continue cooking 4 to 5 minutes or until shrimp is very pink.

*HERB BUTTER

1 cup butter
⅛ teaspoon white
  pepper
¼ teaspoon tarragon
¼ tablespoon chervil
¼ tablespoon chopped
  parsley
¼ cup chopped green
  onions

Mix all ingredients together.

NOTE: You will not use all the herb butter for one serving, but save remaining butter. It keeps well and can be used for other recipes such as sautéed mushrooms.

Super Seafood Casserole

8-10 servings

6 ounces egg noodles
¾ cup butter
½ cup heavy cream
½ cup light cream
1 10-ounce jar pimiento
  cheese spread
1 10-ounce can cream of
  celery soup, undiluted
2 4½-ounce cans
  medium deveined
  shrimp, drained
1 6½-ounce can crab,
  drained and rinsed
½ cup buttered bread crumbs

Cook noodles according to package directions. Drain.

In a large saucepan, melt butter. Add creams, cheese spread and soup. Heat until cheese is melted. Add shrimp and crab. Stir in noodles. Mixture should be creamy.

Pour into a 2-quart baking dish and sprinkle with bread crumbs. Bake uncovered at 350° for 1 hour.

268

Camarones à la Veracruzana 8-10 servings

½ cup olive oil
2 large onions, sliced
2 large green peppers,
  sliced
3 large celery stalks,
  chopped
3 garlic cloves, minced
5 cups fresh or canned
  tomatoes
1½ jalapeño **or** serrano
  chiles, seeded and
  chopped
Salt and freshly ground
  pepper to taste
1 cup sliced fresh
  mushrooms
4 pounds large shrimp,
  deveined and
  butterflied
Cooked rice
1 avocado, sliced

In a large skillet, sauté onions, green pepper, celery and garlic in olive oil until onion is transparent. Add tomatoes, squeezing into skillet to release juices. Stir in chiles, add salt and pepper. Simmer covered for about 10 minutes.

Add mushrooms and simmer for 10 to 15 minutes. Add shrimp and cook until pink.

Serve with rice and garnish with avocado slices.

Fantastic Shrimp 6-8 servings

3 pounds raw shrimp,
  shelled and deveined
¾ cup butter
3 teaspoons
  Worcestershire sauce
1 garlic clove, minced
¼ cup chopped parsley
¼ cup chopped chives
Salt and pepper to taste
6 ounces dry vermouth
Juice of 1 small lemon
Bread crumbs
Drawn butter
Lemon slices

In a large skillet, sauté shrimp in the ¾ cup butter with Worcestershire sauce, garlic, parsley, chives, salt and pepper for 5 minutes. Remove from heat. Stir in vermouth and lemon juice.

Remove **half** the shrimp from butter mixture and put in a large casserole. Coat well with bread crumbs and repeat with remaining shrimp and bread crumbs. Pour butter mixture over casserole and bake uncovered at 400° for 35 minutes. Serve with drawn butter and lemon slices.

Incomparable Shrimp Curry   8-10 servings

6 tablespoons butter
6 tablespoons flour
3½ cups milk
1 7-ounce package
   shredded coconut or
   1 cup freshly grated
   coconut
1 large onion, chopped
1½ teaspoons freshly
   ground pepper
2 teaspoons salt
2 teaspoons paprika
1½ teaspoons powdered
   ginger
4 to 6 tablespoons
   imported Indian curry
   powder
Water
1 to 2 tablespoons
   domestic curry powder
3 pounds fresh, cooked
   medium shrimp

Melt butter in heavy skiliet over low heat. Stir in flour and blend well.

In a saucepan, combine milk and coconut and heat for about 15 minutes. Stir into butter and flour mixture. Add onion, pepper, salt, paprika and ginger.

In a small bowl, add water to imported curry powder to make a paste. Add domestic curry powder and blend well. Stir curry mixture into sauce. Add shrimp and simmer for about 5 minutes.

Cool and refrigerate overnight or for at least 12 hours. Reheat slowly over low heat for 1 hour. Serve over rice.

Serve with any of the optional condiments.

CONDIMENTS

Toasted coconut
Peanuts or cashews,
   chopped
Candied ginger, chopped
Mandarin oranges
Hard boiled eggs,
   chopped
Banana chips
Onions, chopped

Melon balls
Chutney
Raisins
Ripe olives
Cooked and crumbled
   bacon
Cucumber, chopped
Tomato, chopped
Dates, chopped

The best way not to overcook fish is to calculate 10 minutes per inch of thickness for whatever cooking method you are using.

270

Lemon Oriental Shrimp

8 servings

⅔ cup uncooked wild rice
2 tablespoons butter
1 cup chopped onion
2 cups chopped celery
1½ pounds large fresh
  shrimp, shelled and
  deveined
1 cup sliced fresh
  mushrooms
1 7-ounce package
  frozen pea pods **or**
  1 cup fresh snow peas
1 cup sliced water
  chestnuts

Cook rice according to package directions or for about 45 minutes.

In a large skillet, sauté onion and celery in butter.

Cut shrimp into bite-sized pieces and add along with mushrooms, pea pods and water chestnuts. Cook slowly over low heat for 5 minutes. Remove from heat.

Pour sauce over shrimp mixture and refrigerate until serving time. To serve, reheat for 20 minutes.

LEMON SAUCE I

2 chicken bouillon cubes
1 cup boiling water
2 tablespoons cornstarch
½ cup lemon juice
Dash soy sauce
1 tablespoon lemon rind,
  grated
1 garlic clove, minced

In a saucepan, dissolve bouillon in boiling water. Stir in cornstarch, lemon juice, soy sauce, lemon rind and garlic. Simmer until thick.

Always serve fresh lemon wedges with shellfish.

Thaw frozen fish in milk. The milk draws out the frozen taste and provides a fresh-caught flavor.

Creamy Crab Casserole   6 servings

16 ounces fresh crab
    meat
6 ounces fettuccine **or**
    linguine noodles
½ cup finely chopped
    onion
½ cup finely chopped
    celery
¼ cup finely chopped
    green pepper
1 large garlic clove,
    minced
5 tablespoons butter
1 cup sour cream
1 cup cottage cheese
1 cup grated sharp
    Cheddar cheese
¼ teaspoon salt
¼ cup minced parsley
⅛ teaspoon pepper
½ cup soft bread crumbs

Rinse crab meat and drain well. Set aside.

Cook noodles according to package directions. Drain and set aside.

In a skillet, sauté onion, celery, green pepper and garlic in **3 tablespoons** of the butter for 3 to 5 minutes.

In a large mixing bowl, combine sour cream, cottage cheese, Cheddar cheese, salt, parsley and pepper. Fold in crab, noodles and sautéed vegetables. Blend thoroughly. Pour mixture into a buttered 2-quart casserole.

In a small saucepan, melt remaining butter. Stir in bread crumbs. Sprinkle over casserole. Cover and bake at 350° for 35 minutes.

Curried Avocado and Crab Pie 1 9-inch pie

2 ripe avocados, peeled
2 tablespoons lime juice
    or lemon juice
1 tablespoon finely
    chopped green onion
1 tablespoon chopped
    fresh parsley
2 teaspoons curry
    powder
1 teaspoon salt
4 6-ounce packages
    frozen king crab meat
1 9-inch baked pie shell

In a bowl, mash **1** of the avocados. Add **1 teaspoon** of the lime juice and onion, parsley, curry powder and salt. Fold in crab. Pour into pie shell. Slice remaining avocado, brush with lime juice and arrange on top of crab.

To serve, spoon sauce over pie and serve immediately.

NOTE: Makes an excellent appetizer.

272

Curried Avocado and Crab Pie *(Continued)*

SAUCE

3 tablespoons butter
1 cup sliced apples, peeled
1 tablespoon grated onion
4 teaspoons curry powder
3 tablespoons flour
1 cup chicken broth
½ cup light cream

In a skillet, sauté apples and onion in butter. Stir in curry powder and cook for 1 minute. Blend in flour. Gradually stir in chicken broth and then cream. Continue stirring until sauce comes to a boil.

Snow Crab Mornay with Wild Rice

6-8 servings

2 pounds snow crab meat
1⅓ cups finely chopped celery
1 cup chopped green onion
4 garlic cloves, minced
4 tablespoons butter
6 tablespoons flour
1 teaspoon salt
Dash cayenne
Milk
4 tablespoons sherry
1 cup grated Swiss cheese
4 tablespoons chopped chives
Wild rice

Drain and slice crab, reserving liquid.

In a heavy skillet, sauté celery, onion and garlic in butter. Blend in flour, salt and cayenne.

Add enough milk to crab liquid to make 4½ cups. Stir mixture into vegetables. Stir in sherry.

Cook, stirring occasionally, until mixture thickens and bubbles. Add cheese and stir until melted. Fold in chives and crab. Serve over wild rice.

For many people, eating light now means eating fish.

Deviled Crab
6 servings

3 tablespoons butter
2 tablespoons chopped
  onion
3 tablespoons flour
1 teaspoon dry mustard
½ teaspoon paprika
¾ teaspoon salt
1 teaspoon
  Worcestershire sauce
Dash freshly ground
  pepper
1 cup milk
½ cup heavy cream
3 cups crab meat
½ cup buttered bread
  crumbs
½ cup grated cheese

In a heavy skillet, sauté onion in butter. Blend in flour and seasonings. Slowly add milk, stirring constantly over low heat until thickened. Add cream and stir well. Add crab and stir well.

Place crab mixture in 6 lightly buttered ramekins. Sprinkle with bread crumbs and cheese. Bake at 350° for 20 minutes.

Casserole Saint Jacques
6 servings

1 pound scallops
1 cup dry white wine
1 small onion, sliced
1 tablespoon chopped
  parsley
2 teaspoons lemon juice
½ teaspoon salt
5 tablespoons butter
6 tablespoons flour
1 cup light cream
2 ounces Gruyère cheese
Dash pepper
8 ounces fresh crab meat
6 ounces fresh shrimp,
  shelled and deveined
3 ounces fresh
  mushrooms, sliced
1½ cups bread crumbs

In a medium saucepan, combine scallops, wine, onion, parsley, lemon juice and salt. Heat to boiling, then simmer 5 minutes. Drain scallops and reserve 1 cup of the liquid.

In a medium saucepan, melt **4 tablespoons** of the butter. Stir in flour. Slowly add cream and reserved poaching liquid, stirring constantly until mixture thickens. Remove from heat.

Stir in cheese and pepper until cheese melts. Add scallop mixture, crab, shrimp and mushrooms. Spoon into ramekins.

In a small saucepan, melt remaining butter. Stir in bread crumbs. Sprinkle over top of ramekins and bake, uncovered, at 350° for 25 minutes.

Basque Clams

4-6 servings

3 to 4 pounds small butter clams, fresh
1 tablespoon cornmeal
Oil
1 garlic clove, minced
1 red chili pepper, crumbled
¾ cup chopped fresh parsley
2¼ cups soft white bread crumbs (3 slices)
2 chorizo sausages, cooked and crumbled, optional

Cover clams with salt water. Add cornmeal and soak. Rinse several times and drain.

In a large kettle, add oil to cover bottom of pan and sauté garlic for 5 minutes. Add clams and stir until shells open. Add chili pepper, parsley, bread crumbs and chorizos. Continue cooking for about 3 to 4 minutes, covered.

Adjust seasonings if needed.

Basque Rice and Clams

3-4 servings

36 to 48 butter clams
Cold water
½ cup cornmeal
1 cup white rice, rinsed
⅓ cup olive oil
¼ cup chopped fresh parsley
1 to 2 garlic cloves, minced
Salt
2½ to 3 cups water

Soak clams in **cold** water and cornmeal for 2 to 3 hours.

Scrub each clam under lukewarm running water.

In a large kettle, add all ingredients, adding clams last. Heat to boiling. Reduce heat. Cover and simmer for 20 to 25 minutes. Add more salt if necessary.

Serve in soup bowls and provide a dish for clam shells.

Truly fresh fish smell fresh like the ocean and are not slimy.

North Beach Cioppino

8-10 servings

2 dozen clams
3 cups red wine
¼ cup olive oil
4 tablespoons butter
3 celery stalks, chopped
2 onions, chopped
1 green pepper, chopped
4 garlic cloves, minced
10 green onions,
  chopped
1 15-ounce can tomato
  sauce
1 12-ounce can Italian
  plum tomatoes
2 bay leaves
1¼ teaspoons basil
1 teaspoon oregano
⅛ teaspoon paprika
2 tablespoons fresh
  lemon juice
2 pounds red snapper **or**
  halibut, cut into 1-inch
  pieces
2 dozen medium shrimp,
  shelled and deveined
½ pound scallops
2 pounds fresh crab,
  cracked and cleaned
½ cup chopped fresh
  parsley

In a saucepan, place clams and **1 cup** of the red wine. Cover and steam over medium heat 4 to 6 minutes or until clams open. Remove clams, discarding any that are not open. Strain stock and reserve.

In a large kettle, heat olive oil and butter. Sauté celery, onions, green pepper, garlic and green onions until tender, stirring often. Add reserved clam broth, remaining wine, tomato sauce, tomatoes, bay leaves, basil, oregano and paprika. Cover and simmer slowly for 1 hour.

Add lemon juice and snapper. Simmer 3 minutes. Add shrimp and scallops; simmer about 3 minutes more. Add clams and crab. Continue to simmer until heated through. Garnish with parsley.

NOTE: Have bowls available for discarded shells.

Poach fish in the same pan you serve it in – this removes the risk of breaking the fillets when moving from pan to platter.

Sautéed Oysters with Basil   2 servings

1 16-ounce jar oysters,
    drained
Flour
2 tablespoons butter
½ teaspoon basil
2 tablespoons dry white
    wine
Buttered noodles
Parmesan cheese

Gently pat oysters dry. Dredge with flour.

In a heavy skillet over high heat, melt butter. Add oysters and sprinkle with basil. Brown oysters lightly for about 2 minutes per side. Place oysters in 2 warm ramekins. Add wine to skillet to release browned particles and spoon over oysters.

Serve with buttered noodles tossed with Parmesan cheese.

Scalloped Oysters   4 servings

⅔ cup soft bread crumbs
1 cup fine saltine cracker
    crumbs
½ cup butter, melted
1½ pints small Eastern
    oysters, drained,
    reserving ⅓ cup liquid
¾ tablespoon salt
Coarsely ground pepper
    to taste
2 tablespoons chopped
    parsley
½ teaspoon
    Worcestershire sauce
3 tablespoons light
    cream

In a bowl, combine bread crumbs, cracker crumbs and butter. Put **half** the mixture into a greased 1-quart casserole. Add **half** the oysters and sprinkle with **half** the salt, pepper and parsley.

In a small bowl, combine reserved oyster liquid, Worcestershire sauce and cream. Pour over oysters. Layer remaining oysters in casserole. Sprinkle with remaining salt, pepper and parsley. Top with remaining bread crumbs. Bake at 350° for about 45 minutes.

When buying whole fish, look for red gills, scales close to the body, firm flesh and fresh, sweet odor.

Paëlla Valenciana

6 servings

6 chicken thighs and/or
  legs
½ cup olive oil
½ pound scallops
½ pound fresh fish (cod,
  perch or haddock) cut
  into 1-inch pieces
1 medium onion,
  chopped
2½ garlic cloves, minced
1 medium sweet red
  pepper, cut into ¼-inch
  strips
½ green pepper, cut into
  ¼-inch strips
2 large tomatoes, peeled
  and chopped
2 chorizos (or
  pepperoni), sliced
12 large raw shrimp, in
  shells
3 cups raw long grain
  rice
1 teaspoon salt
¼ teaspoon freshly
  ground pepper
½ teaspoon freshly
  ground saffron
6 cups boiling chicken
  broth
½ 10-ounce package
  frozen peas, thawed
15 small clams, washed
1 6-ounce jar artichoke
  hearts **or** 1 package
  frozen, cooked
¼ pound small shrimp
2 lemons, cut in wedges
Parsley

Pat chicken dry with paper towels and season with salt and pepper.

In a heavy skillet, heat **¼ cup** of the oil over high heat until a light haze forms. Brown chicken well and remove from pan.

Lower heat, add scallops and fish and cook for about 3 minutes. Remove from heat and discard all remaining fat.

Add remaining oil. Sauté onion, garlic, red and green peppers and tomatoes. Stirring constantly, cook until most of the liquid evaporates. Set aside.

In a skillet, brown chorizos quickly and place on paper towels to drain.

Shell and devein shrimp, leaving tails intact. Preheat oven to 400°.

In a paëlla pan (or wok), combine onion mixture with rice, salt, pepper and saffron. Pour in boiling broth and heat to boiling, stirring constantly. Adjust seasonings if necessary. Remove pan from heat. Stir in **some** of the scallops, fish, chorizos and peas. Place chicken, the **remaining** chorizos, scallops, and fish, and the large shrimp and clams on top. DO NOT STIR. Scatter peas over all.

Place pan in bottom of oven and bake covered for 20 minutes.

278

Bound to Please: The Pioneering Spirit

Beginning in 1840, thousands of pioneers followed the Oregon Trail to the west, often stopping to rest at Fort Hall and Fort Boise. Twenty years later, the region's first gold rush brought a new wave of fortune-seekers, and with them came the merchants and bankers who settled the first commercial centers of Idaho.

Today, pioneers of a different sort – major corporations such as Morrison-Knudsen, Albertson's, Simplot, Boise Cascade, Ore-Ida, Trus-Joist, and many others – still make their homes here, linking Idaho every day to the rest of the world.

Chicken & Turkey

Game Birds

Sauces

Paëlla Valenciana *(Continued)*

Add artichoke hearts and small shrimp. Bake uncovered for 10 minutes or until liquid has been absorbed and rice is tender. DO NOT STIR PAELLA ONCE IT IS PUT IN OVEN.

Remove from oven, drape a kitchen towel over the top for 5 minutes. Garnish with lemons and parsley and serve from pan.

OPTIONAL INGREDIENTS

Green stuffed olives
Asparagus
¼ pound diced ham
Mussels
Lobster
Octopus
Mushrooms
Squid
Snails

NOTE: Paëlla may be cooked covered on top of the stove. Clams may be steamed separately and added just before serving.

Tartare Sauce   2 cups

1 cup mayonnaise
¼ teaspoon grated onion
Dash salt
1 tablespoon white vinegar
⅓ cup sweet pickle relish
⅓ cup chopped green olives with pimiento
1 tablespoon chopped capers
1 teaspoon chopped parsley

In a medium bowl, combine all ingredients and refrigerate overnight.

NOTE: Will keep in refrigerator for about 2 weeks.

Cucumber Sauce
2 cups

1 cup sour cream
2 teaspoons fresh lemon juice
1 teaspoon prepared mustard
½ teaspoon dill weed
1 teaspoon finely minced onion
1 large cucumber, peeled, seeded and finely chopped
3 drops Tabasco sauce

Combine all ingredients in a small bowl. Blend well, cover and refrigerate overnight.

NOTE: Excellent served with cold poached salmon or as a topping for a crisp salad.

Seafood Filling for Just About Anything
8-10 servings

1 tablespoon butter
½ cup finely chopped onion
½ cup finely chopped celery
½ pound cooked shrimp
½ pound fresh crab meat
1 cup mayonnaise
2 tablespoons prepared mustard
2 teaspoons capers
¼ cup sherry
½ teaspoon curry powder
1 tablespoon parsley flakes
1 4-ounce can mushroom pieces, drained
1 8-ounce can sliced water chestnuts, drained

In a heavy skillet, sauté onion and celery in butter until limp.

In a saucepan, combine remaining ingredients and cook over medium heat for 10 to 15 minutes, stirring occasionally.

Serve over rice, in crêpes, puff pastry, phyllo leaves or on toast points.

NOTE: Reheats well.

280

Bon Bon Chicken Over Cold Noodles (Szechwan)

8 servings

4 chicken breasts
6 cups cooked Chinese
  wheat noodles
8 pre-soaked Chinese
  mushrooms, optional
½ cup soy sauce
1 tablespoon white wine
1 tablespoon sugar
4 eggs, lightly beaten
1 English cucumber,
  shredded
3 to 4 slices cooked ham,
  shredded

In a large kettle, heat 10 cups of water to boiling. Add chicken, lower heat and cook for 20 minutes. Remove chicken and cool. Bone and shred into 2-inch lengths and set aside.

Cook noodles according to package directions. Drain and set aside to cool.

In a medium saucepan, simmer mushrooms in soy sauce, white wine and sugar. Refrigerate for 2 hours, then shred.

Heat wok to medium and fry beaten eggs on both sides. Cool, shred and set aside.

Arrange chicken, mushrooms, eggs, cucumber and ham over cold noodles and chill for 1 hour.

To serve, pour sauce over all and serve immediately.

SAUCE

6 tablespoons peanut
  butter, creamy **or**
  crunchy
6 tablespoons soy sauce
3 tablespoons sugar
3 tablespoons sesame oil
3 tablespoons
  Worcestershire sauce
1 tablespoon MSG
2 tablespoons chopped
  green onion
2 tablespoons chopped
  garlic
2 tablespoons chopped
  ginger root

In a blender, combine all ingredients and blend until well mixed.

281

Thyme Chicken Breasts

4-6 servings

A nice dish to make ahead.

6 chicken breasts, boned
  and skinned
1 to 2 tablespoons whole
  thyme
1 cup fresh bread crumbs
Lemon pepper and salt to
  taste
2 eggs
1 tablespoon milk
6 tablespoons butter
6 tablespoons margarine
2 to 3 lemons, cut into
  wedges
Parsley

Taking one portion of breast at a time, lay meat on cutting board. Using a wooden meat mallet or the edge of a heavy saucer, pound each breast into a 5x3-inch round patty. Prepare all chicken breasts in the same manner.

With a mortar and pestle, grind thyme into a powder.

In a large bowl, mix bread crumbs, thyme powder, lemon pepper and salt.

In a small, shallow bowl, beat eggs and milk together. Carefully dip each chicken patty into egg mixture and then into crumb mixture, pressing crumbs into both sides of patty. Lay patties on waxed paper, stack on a plate and chill at least 1 hour.

In a large skillet, sauté patties in butter and margarine until light golden brown. Serve immediately with lemon wedges and parsley.

Chinese Chicken

2-4 servings

4 chicken breasts,
  skinned
⅓ cup soy sauce
⅔ cup vinegar
Pepper
Garlic powder
Brown sugar
Flour

Place chicken in a shallow baking pan. Combine soy sauce and vinegar, pour over chicken. Sprinkle with pepper, garlic powder, brown sugar and flour.

Bake uncovered at 350° for 1 hour, basting occasionally.

Italian Fried Chicken

6-8 servings

5 pounds fresh fryer
   chicken pieces
½ cup sifted flour
½ cup milk
3 eggs, beaten
¼ cup butter
5 tablespoons olive oil
1 ounce salt pork, diced
2 teaspoons minced
   fresh rosemary
½ teaspoon salt
½ teaspoon freshly
   ground pepper
Juice of 2 lemons

Pound chicken pieces lightly between
2 sheets of waxed paper. Sprinkle the
flattened pieces with flour, dip them
into milk, then into the flour again.
Shake off any excess flour and dip into
eggs.

Place butter, olive oil and salt pork in a
large heavy skillet and heat. Add
chicken pieces and brown slowly on
each side about 15 minutes. Sprinkle
with rosemary, salt and pepper. Cover
and cook about 15 minutes longer.
Test for doneness. Sprinkle with lemon
juice and serve.

Lemon Chicken

4 servings

1 pound boneless chicken
   breasts, cut into
   1½ x 1¼-inch pieces
2½ tablespoons peanut
   oil
1 teaspoon cornstarch
1 teaspoon salt
2 teaspoons finely grated
   lemon peel
⅓ cup chicken stock
½ pound snow peas,
   strings removed
¼ cup fresh mushrooms,
   sliced
2 teaspoons fresh lemon
   juice
½ tablespoon cornstarch
   mixed with ½
   tablespoon water
Pinch of white pepper
Salt

In a small bowl, combine chicken,
1 tablespoon of the oil and the
cornstarch; blend well.

Heat remaining oil with salt in wok or
skillet until very hot. Add chicken and
sauté until meat is white. Recipe can
be prepared ahead to this point.

Sprinkle with lemon peel. Add stock,
snow peas and mushrooms; cook an
additional minute.

Combine remaining ingredients and
pour over chicken. Continue cooking,
stirring constantly until sauce thickens.
Adjust seasoning with salt and white
pepper.

Transfer to chafing dish and serve
immediately.

Suggestion: Serve over rice.

283

Chicken and Pear Stir Fry

6 servings

2 medium unpeeled pears
3 tablespoons oil
4 chicken breasts
(approximately
2 pounds), skinned,
boned and cut into
2½ x ½-inch strips
2 garlic cloves, minced
2 celery stalks, thinly
sliced
3 green onions, sliced
diagonally into 2-inch
lengths
1 6-ounce can sliced
bamboo shoots,
drained
1 7-ounce package
frozen pea pods,
thawed
½ cup salted roasted
cashews

Quarter and core pears and cut into
½-inch thick slices.

Heat a wok or medium skillet over high
heat until hot. Add **2 tablespoons** of
the oil, swirl and heat for a few
seconds. Add chicken and garlic and
stir until lightly browned, about
4 minutes. Remove from pan with
slotted spoon. Add remaining oil,
celery, onions and bamboo shoots and
cook, stirring, 3 minutes.

Add pears, pea pods, chicken and
sauce. Stir until thickened. Serve
garnished with cashews.

SAUCE

4 teaspoons cornstarch
1 teaspoon sugar
2 teaspoons finely minced
fresh ginger **or**
½ teaspoon powdered
ginger
¾ teaspoon salt
2 tablespoons soy sauce
2 tablespoons sherry
¾ cup chicken broth

Combine ingredients and heat through.

It is easy to skin and bone chicken if slightly frozen.

284

Szechwan Hot Pepper Chicken 2 servings

Appealing appearance and texture.

2 chicken breasts, boned
   and skinned
1 to 2 dried **or** fresh red
   chili peppers
2 to 3 tablespoons
   peanut oil
1 tablespoon cornstarch
¼ cup cold water
½ cup chopped dry
   roasted peanuts
½ cup chopped green
   onions
Chinese cellophane
   noodles

Cut chicken into bite-sized pieces.
Toss chicken in marinade and let stand
at least 15 minutes.

Chop or crush red chili peppers.

In a wok or skillet, heat **1 tablespoon**
of the oil over high heat. Add peppers
and cook quickly. Drain chicken, add
to skillet and continue cooking over
high heat until tender, adding more oil if
necessary. Add sauce mixture and
continue cooking and stirring. Dissolve
cornstarch in water and add to sauce;
stir and simmer until thick and clear.

Arrange on serving platter and sprinkle
chopped peanuts and green onions in
the center. Serve immediately with
Chinese cellophane noodles.

MARINADE

2 tablespoons soy sauce
2 tablespoons dry sherry
1 tablespoon cornstarch
2 tablespoons cold water

In a medium bowl, mix ingredients in
order listed.

SAUCE

2 tablespoons dry sherry
1 tablespoon soy sauce
1 teaspoon MSG
1 teaspoon sesame oil
2 dashes Worcestershire
   sauce

In a small bowl, combine ingredients
and set aside.

Chicken with Broccoli and Walnuts

4 servings

2 large chicken breasts, boned and cut into small cubes
1 teaspoon salt
1 teaspoon ground ginger
2 tablespoons cornstarch
1 large egg white, lightly beaten
⅓ cup peanut oil
4 large, fresh broccoli spears, cut into small pieces
2 cups shelled walnut halves
1 cup sliced fresh mushrooms
1 teaspoon soft brown sugar
2 tablespoons soy sauce
3 tablespoons rice wine or dry sherry
¼ cup toasted sesame seeds

Rub the chicken pieces with salt and ginger and finally cornstarch. Place in a medium bowl and cover with egg white. Stir gently to coat all the pieces.

Heat the oil in a wok or large skillet. When very hot, add the chicken cubes and stir fry over moderately high heat for 3 minutes. Using a slotted spoon, transfer chicken to a plate and keep warm.

Add the broccoli pieces, walnuts, and mushrooms to the wok and stir fry for 3 minutes. Return chicken to the wok and stir fry for 1 minute or until well blended.

Stir in brown sugar, soy sauce and wine and cook for 1½ minutes. Transfer the mixture to a warmed serving bowl, sprinkle with sesame seeds and serve immediately.

Chicken in Beer

4 servings

1 3-pound chicken, cut up
½ cup flour
4 tablespoons butter
1 garlic clove, minced
½ cup sliced celery
2 bay leaves
2 teaspoons chopped parsley
1½ teaspoons salt
½ teaspoon pepper
2 cups beer

Coat chicken with flour and brown in butter in a large skillet over medium heat.

In a 2-quart casserole, combine remaining ingredients with chicken, cover and bake at 350° for 1½ hours.

Chicken Maria

3-4 servings

A "fancy" company dish.

4 chicken breasts, boned
  and skinned
3 eggs, beaten
1 cup dry bread crumbs
2 to 3 tablespoons butter
½ cup sliced mushrooms
2 tablespoons lemon
  juice
⅓ cup white wine
⅔ cup chicken broth
6 ¼-inch thick slices
  Monterey Jack **or**
  Muenster cheese

Soak chicken breasts in eggs at least
1 hour. Drain and roll chicken in bread
crumbs.

In a large skillet over medium heat,
brown in melted butter and place in an
8x8-inch baking dish.

In a medium bowl, mix mushrooms,
lemon juice, wine and broth. Pour
mixture over chicken. Top with slices
of cheese.

Cover dish with foil and bake at 350°
for 45 to 60 minutes or until tender.

Baked Chicken with Curried Peaches

4 servings

Easy to prepare, unique flavor.

1 2½ to 3-pound
  chicken, quartered
1 tablespoon flour
1 teaspoon curry powder
¾ teaspoon salt
⅛ teaspoon pepper
Dash cinnamon
Dash nutmeg
2 teaspoons butter **or**
  margarine
1 1-pound can sliced
  peaches, drained,
  reserving ½ cup of the
  syrup

Wash chicken under cold running
water, pat dry. Place in a shallow, foil-
lined baking pan.

Combine flour, **½ teaspoon** of the
curry powder, salt, pepper, cinnamon
and nutmeg. Sprinkle seasoned flour
over chicken, dot with butter. Bake
uncovered at 375° for 30 minutes.

Place peach slices around chicken,
sprinkle with remaining curry powder.
Spoon reserved syrup over chicken
and peaches. Return to oven and
continue baking for 25 to 30 minutes,
until tender.

To serve, arrange on heated platter.
Spoon any pan juices over all.

287

Elegant Chicken with Artichokes

4 servings

4 chicken breasts, boned
  and skinned
Salt and pepper
Flour
¼ cup butter
½ cup white wine
1 cup heavy cream
1 10-ounce package
  frozen artichokes,
  cooked and drained
1 cup halved pitted ripe
  olives
½ cup sliced green
  onions
Lemon wedges

Pound the chicken breasts between 2 sheets of waxed paper to ¼-inch thickness. Cut each breast into 3 pieces. Sprinkle with salt and pepper, coat lightly with flour.

Sauté chicken quickly in butter over medium-high heat, turning once, until golden brown. Remove to heated platter and keep warm.

Add wine and cream to pan juices and simmer until sauce thickens (4 to 5 minutes). Stir in artichokes, olives and green onions. Heat through and pour over chicken.

Serve immediately garnished with lemon wedges.

Shrimp 'N Chicken

6 servings

1 pint sour cream
1 envelope chicken gravy
  mix
¼ teaspoon salt
¼ cup butter
6 chicken breasts, boned
  and skinned
1 cup cornflakes,
  crumbled
1 cup cooked shrimp,
  coarsely chopped
¼ cup chopped ripe
  olives
3 tablespoons pimiento,
  chopped

Combine sour cream, gravy mix and salt; pour into two bowls and refrigerate one of the bowls.

Melt butter in shallow baking pan and set aside.

Coat chicken in **half** the sour cream mixture, roll in cornflakes. Arrange chicken in buttered pan and bake at 350° for 45 minutes. Turn and bake 20 minutes longer, until tender and brown.

Add shrimp, olives and pimiento to refrigerated sour cream and heat slowly. DO NOT ALLOW TO BOIL.

Serve sauce over chicken.

Chicken with Grapes and Pine Nuts

4 servings

1 4-pound chicken, skinned and cut in eighths
1 cup white wine
1 teaspoon salt
¼ teaspoon pepper
¼ teaspoon rosemary
¼ teaspoon savory
2 garlic cloves, minced
4 tablespoons olive oil **or** melted butter
4 ounces pine nuts, ground
½ cup bread crumbs
½ teaspoon salt
¼ teaspoon paprika
1 cup seedless green grapes

Rinse chicken in cold water, pat dry. In a large baking dish, marinate chicken for 1 to 2 hours in wine, salt, pepper, rosemary, savory and garlic, turning once.

Grease a large baking dish with **1-2 tablespoons** olive oil.

Combine pine nuts with bread crumbs, salt and paprika. Remove chicken from marinade (reserving marinade) and roll in seasoned crumb mixture and press into chicken to coat well.

Place chicken on greased baking dish. Drizzle with remaining oil.

Bake uncovered at 350° for 45 minutes. Pour reserved marinade over chicken, add grapes and bake 5 minutes longer.

If chicken is not brown enough, set oven at 400° or place 4 inches from broiler for 2 minutes.

Chicken is compatible with so many different seasonings and cooking methods that only lazy cooks risk turning out a boring chicken dish.

Lemon is a wonderful addition to most chicken dishes.

289

Chicken in Red Wine

6 servings

¼ pound bacon, chopped
1 cup chopped onion
¼ pound mushrooms,
   sliced
2 broiler-fryer chickens
   (1½-2 pounds each),
   cut up
4 tablespoons margarine
1 bay leaf
½ teaspoon tarragon,
   crumbled
4 peppercorns
Parsley sprigs
1 teaspoon salt
2 cups dry red wine
1 tablespoon flour
2 tablespoons chopped
   parsley

In a large skillet, cook bacon. Remove and drain. In remaining bacon drippings, sauté onions and mushrooms until soft. Remove, reserving drippings in skillet. Wash and thoroughly dry chicken pieces. Add **3 tablespoons** of the margarine to the drippings in the skillet. Add the chicken and brown. Return bacon, onion and mushrooms to skillet.

Tie bay leaf, tarragon, peppercorns and parsley in a small square of cheesecloth and add to skillet. Add salt to wine and pour over chicken. Simmer, covered, about 30 minutes or until tender. Remove cheesecloth bag. Blend flour and remaining margarine together and add to hot liquid, a little at a time, until sauce is thickened. Sprinkle with chopped parsley.

Serve on a large platter with sauce spooned over chicken. Rice makes a great side dish.

Chicken Oriental

4 servings

4 chicken breasts, boned
   and skinned
1 egg, slightly beaten
1 cup bread crumbs
1 teaspoon salt
¼ teaspoon ground
   thyme
¼ teaspoon ground
   marjoram
¼ teaspoon paprika
3 tablespoons butter

Dip chicken breasts in egg, then in mixture of bread crumbs and spices. Brown lightly in butter. Place in an ovenproof casserole, cover with sauce and bake uncovered at 350° for 1 hour.

Chicken Oriental *(Continued)*

SAUCE

2 cups pineapple juice
2 tablespoons cornstarch
2 teaspoons sugar
½ teaspoon curry
   powder
4 tablespoons lemon
   juice

Combine all ingredients and heat,
stirring constantly, until clear.

Chicken Boursin   4 servings

Nice combination, crispy outside, creamy inside. Unique flavor.

4 to 6 chicken breasts,
   boned and skinned
2 to 3 teaspoons lemon
   juice
Salt and pepper to taste
1 box Boursin cheese (an
   herb-spiced cheese
   spread, Alouette may
   also be used)
2 to 3 eggs, beaten
Italian seasoned bread
   crumbs
Flour
Butter **or** margarine
   (approximately
   4 tablespoons)

If chicken breasts are large, cut in half.
Pound each chicken breast with a
mallet to flatten, pour **½ teaspoon**
lemon juice over each, sprinkle with
salt and pepper to taste. Let stand
15 to 30 minutes.

Spread **1 to 2 tablespoons** Boursin
cheese on each chicken breast. Roll
chicken with cheese inside and secure
with toothpicks or string.

Dip each rolled chicken breast in egg
and seasoned crumbs, then roll in
flour.

In a large covered skillet, brown
chicken slowly in melted butter or
margarine 25 to 30 minutes, turning
frequently.

Serve immediately.

Soak toothpicks in water before inserting in chicken, thus eliminating swelling and difficulty of removal.

Chicken Royalle

6 servings

*A favorite banquet entrée at the HasBrouck House,
Nampa.*

3 whole chicken breasts
2 3-ounce packages
   cream cheese, softened
½ cup finely chopped
   chives
6 bacon slices, at room
   temperature
1 cup sliced fresh
   mushrooms
3 tablespoons butter
2 to 4 ounces white wine
5 cups rice pilaf **or**
   cooked rice

Split chicken breasts, remove skin and
bones and pound with a mallet to
flatten.

Mix cream cheese and chives, roll into
6 logs. Place 1 log on each flattened
chicken breast and wrap chicken
around cheese, tucking in ends. Wrap
one piece of bacon around each
chicken breast. Fasten with toothpicks
if necessary. Bake at 350° for
25 minutes.

While chicken is baking, sauté
mushrooms in butter until brown, add
wine and return to simmer. When
chicken is done, place on a bed of rice
pilaf (see index) and spoon hot
mushroom sauce over the top.

Tarragon 'N Thyme Chicken

6-8 servings

2 2½ to 3-pound
   chickens, cut up
2 teaspoons salt
¼ teaspoon pepper
2 teaspoons tarragon
½ teaspoon ground
   thyme
3 tablespoons lemon
   juice
2 tablespoons vinegar
2 tablespoons chopped
   parsley
Lemon slices

Rinse chicken in cold water, dry with
paper towels. Place chicken, skin side
up, in a shallow foil-lined baking pan.
Sprinkle with salt, pepper, tarragon,
thyme, lemon juice and vinegar.

Cover tightly with foil and bake at
375° for 40 minutes. Remove foil and
bake 20 to 25 minutes longer, until fork
tender.

To serve, remove chicken to heated
platter. Pour pan juices over, sprinkle
with chopped parsley, garnish with
lemon slices.

Italian Chicken

4 servings

*A favorite recipe from A Matter of Taste, Trail Creek
Village, Ketchum.*

4 whole chicken breasts
¾ pound ricotta cheese
½ pound fresh spinach,
** finely chopped**
1 small broccoli floweret,
** finely chopped**
A few pinches thyme,
** tarragon, parsley,**
** nutmeg**
Salt and pepper to taste
4 to 6 tablespoons butter
Grape leaves

Chicken breasts should be boned, but leave them in one whole piece, with the skin left on. Using a sharp knife, slit the skin on the chicken on one side, using your finger to lift the skin to form a pocket for stuffing.

In a bowl, combine ricotta, spinach, broccoli and seasonings. Stuff each chicken breast with enough of the ricotta-spinach mixture to form a pouch.

Place chicken in a shallow roasting pan with butter and enough water to cover the bottom of the pan and for steaming and basting. Place in a preheated 350° oven for 1 hour until chicken turns a summer gold and the cheese stuffing starts to ooze out.

May be served whole and hot, or refrigerate at least 2 hours or overnight (wrapped in foil). Slice and arrange on a bed of grape leaves. Garnish with pickled red cherries or other spicy fruit.

*The golden rule to remember when defrosting is "the
slower the better." This way the food will retain most of
its natural moisture.*

Crêpes with Chicken and Spinach Filling

6-8 servings

2 whole chicken breasts, poached, skinned and boned
¼ pound ground sausage
1 10-ounce package frozen leaf spinach, cooked, drained and squeezed dry
Salt and pepper to taste
½ teaspoon nutmeg
½ teaspoon ground cumin
Béchamel Sauce
Butter
1 cup tomato sauce
¼ cup freshly grated Gruyère cheese
¼ cup freshly grated Parmesan cheese

Dice chicken breasts. In a skillet, cook sausage, breaking it up with a fork, until lightly browned. Place chicken and sausage in the bowl of a food processor with steel blade and process 5 to 6 seconds, until well blended and chopped. Remove to a mixing bowl.

Process spinach in processor for 3 seconds until finely chopped. Combine spinach with chicken and sausage. Add seasonings and mix well. Add enough béchamel sauce to make a spreadable mixture.

Butter a 9x13-inch baking dish. Fill each crêpe with approximately ¼ **cup** of the chicken and spinach mixture, roll and place in baking dish. Spoon remaining béchamel sauce over all, covering with a thin layer. Pour tomato sauce over all, covering with a thin layer. Sprinkle with grated cheeses. Bake at 350° for 30 minutes.

BECHAMEL SAUCE I

4 tablespoons butter
4 tablespoons flour
1 cup chicken broth
⅔ cup milk
2 tablespoons light cream
¼ cup dry white wine
Salt and pepper to taste
Dash Tabasco sauce

In a saucepan over medium-high heat, combine butter and flour. Cook, stirring until blended. Gradually add broth and milk. Continue stirring until smooth and thickened. Stir in cream, wine, salt, pepper and Tabasco sauce. Simmer for 10 minutes.

Crêpes with Chicken
and Spinach Filling *(Continued)*

CREPES II

3 eggs
1 cup flour
½ cup chicken broth
½ cup milk
2 tablespoons butter,
   melted
Salt and pepper to taste
2 tablespoons brandy
Butter

Combine all ingredients, **except** butter, in a food processor and process until very smooth. Pour into a pitcher and chill at least 1 hour.

Heat a 6-inch crepe pan or skillet over high heat until water sizzles when dropped on the pan. Brush with a little melted butter and pour about **2 tablespoons** of the batter in the pan. Rotate pan, swirling batter so that it covers the bottom. As soon as the crepe is firm and golden brown, turn with a spatula. Cook other side ½ to 1 minute. Remove to a plate. Repeat until batter is used up, stacking crepes between squares of waxed paper. Makes approximately 24 crepes.

Maximum freezer storage for poultry and game birds is 6-8 months.

To slice cooked chicken breasts, have them well chilled (but not frozen). Carefully remove meat from bone (meat will split in half). Lay each piece flat on cutting board. Hold in place; with sharp knife, slice chicken breast length-wise parallel to board. You should get three thin slices from each half of the breast.

Swiss Chicken Enchiladas   6 servings

1 onion, chopped
2 tablespoons oil
1 garlic clove, minced
2 cups tomato puree
2 green chiles, chopped
2 cups diced cooked
   chicken
Salt
12 corn tortillas
Oil
3 cups light cream
6 chicken bouillon cubes
½ pound Monterey Jack
   or Swiss cheese,
   grated

GARNISHES

Avocado slices
Sliced hard boiled eggs
Sliced radishes
Green olives

In a medium skillet, sauté onion in the **2 tablespoons** oil. Add garlic, tomato puree, chiles and chicken. Season with salt. Simmer 10 minutes.

Meanwhile, in a small skillet, fry tortillas in 1 inch hot oil over medium heat. DO NOT CRISP.

Warm cream just enough to dissolve bouillon cubes. Dip each tortilla in cream mixture, place generous amount of chicken filling on center of each tortilla, roll and place in an 8x12-inch baking dish. Pour remaining cream mixture over tortillas. Top with cheese. Bake uncovered at 350° for 30 minutes.

Garnish to taste.

Marinades for Breast of Turkey

#1
½ cup oil
½ cup soy sauce
2 tablespoons honey
1 teaspoon fresh ginger,
   grated
2 teaspoons dry mustard
2 teaspoons MSG
2 cloves garlic, minced

#2
2 cups dry white wine
1 cup oil
1 cup soy sauce
1 teaspoon garlic powder

#3
¼ cup soy sauce
Grated rind of 1 lemon
Juice from 1 lemon

Place turkey in <u>one</u> of the above marinades for 12-24 hours. Grill or broil.

Turkey Tetrazzini

6-8 servings

Great with chicken, too.

6 tablespoons butter
6 tablespoons flour
1½ teaspoons salt
Dash nutmeg
2 cups milk
1 cup turkey stock **or** condensed chicken broth, undiluted
2 egg yolks
½ cup heavy cream
¼ cup dry sherry
½ pound spaghettini **or** vermicelli
3 cups diced leftover turkey or chicken
1 4-ounce can whole mushrooms, drained
1 cup grated Cheddar cheese

In a medium saucepan, melt butter over medium heat. Remove from heat, stir in flour, salt and nutmeg until smooth. Return to medium heat and gradually add milk and turkey stock. Heat to boiling, stirring constantly. Boil 2 minutes, or until slightly thickened.

In a small bowl, whisk together egg yolks and cream. Add a little of the hot mixture. Pour egg mixture into sauce. Cook over low heat, stirring constantly, until sauce is hot. DO NOT BOIL. Remove from heat, stir in sherry.

Cook spaghettini according to package directions. Drain and return to pan. Add **1 cup** of the sauce, toss until well combined. Place spaghettini in a 12x8-inch baking dish, arranging close to edges.

In a large bowl, combine **1 cup** of the sauce with turkey and mushrooms. Mix well. Spoon turkey mixture into center of baking dish. Reserve remaining sauce. Sprinkle cheese over spaghettini. Cover with foil, refrigerate 1 hour or overnight.

Bake covered at 350° for 45 minutes. Reheat remaining sauce and spoon over casserole before serving.

NOTE: May be frozen. Wrap in foil. Thaw 1 hour.

Pheasant and Lemon

6-8 servings

4 pheasants
Salt and pepper
½ cup flour
½ cup butter **or**
  margarine
8 ounces chicken broth,
  undiluted
1 chicken bouillon cube
1 lemon, thinly sliced
½ cup finely chopped
  parsley
½ cup white wine,
  optional

Cut each pheasant into 4 pieces. Generously salt and pepper the flour. Coat pheasant pieces with flour mixture.

In a large skillet over low heat, melt butter. Slowly brown pheasant on both sides. Add chicken broth and bouillon cube. Place lemon slices and parsley over pheasant pieces. Cover and simmer 1 hour or until tender. Baste occasionally with broth. Add white wine during last 10 minutes of cooking, if desired.

Hunter's Wife's Pheasant

6 servings

Wonderful served over wild rice.

2 pheasants, cut in
  serving pieces
½ cup butter
2 tablespoons brandy
2 tablespoons chopped
  green onion
2 tablespoons chopped
  parsley
1 cup sliced mushrooms
½ teaspoon thyme
1 teaspoon salt
Pepper to taste
2 tablespoons grated
  orange peel
2 tablespoons fresh
  orange juice
½ cup sauterne
½ cup light cream

Brown pheasant slowly in butter. Lower heat and continue cooking, uncovered, for 15 minutes turning occasionally. Pour in brandy and ignite. Shake pan until flame dies.

Add remaining ingredients **except** light cream. Mix well. Cover and simmer on very low heat until tender, about 45 minutes.

Cool and remove meat from bones if desired. Keep pieces in large chunks. Return to sauce. Recipe may be refrigerated or frozen at this point.

When ready to serve, heat through. Thicken sauce with a little flour mixed with cold water if necessary. Stirring constantly, gradually add cream. Thickness of sauce depends on how much cream is added.

Almond Pheasant Breast in Cream

6-8 servings

Delicious with rice and mushrooms.

4 whole pheasant
  breasts, skinned **or**
2 pheasants cut in
  pieces
1 cup flour
2 teaspoons salt
½ teaspoon lemon
  pepper
3 to 4 tablespoons butter
¼ cup water
1½ teaspoons cornstarch
1 cup light cream
¼ cup sherry
1 tablespoon lemon juice
1 teaspoon grated lemon
  peel
¼ cup sliced almonds
1 cup grated Swiss
  cheese

Shake pheasant in paper bag with flour, salt and lemon pepper. Sauté in butter on both sides until lightly browned. Add water and simmer, covered, 30 minutes, adding more water if necessary. Remove pheasant to a baking dish, reserving liquid.

Combine cornstarch with **¼ cup** of the cream and stir into pan juices. Cook slowly until thickened. Add remaining cream, sherry, lemon juice and peel, stirring constantly until thickened. Pour over pheasant. (May be refrigerated or frozen at this stage.) Top with almonds and bake at 300° for 1 to 1½ hours until tender. Top with cheese and return to oven just until cheese melts.

Chickens	*Broilers: ¼-½ lb. bird per serving*
	Fryers: ½-¾ lb. per serving
	Roasters: ½-¾ lb. per serving
	Stewers: ½ lb. per serving
Turkeys	*Under 12 lbs.: ¾ lb. per serving*
	Over 12 lbs.: ½ lb. per serving
Ducks	*3-5 lbs.: 1 lb. per serving*
Geese	*8-12 lbs.: ⅔ lb. per serving*

299

Pheasant and Sherry

8 servings

4 pheasants, quartered
Flour
½ cup butter **or**
  margarine
1 onion, chopped
½ cup raisins
1 cup chili sauce
½ cup water
½ cup brown sugar
2 tablespoons
  Worcestershire sauce
¼ teaspoon garlic
  powder
1 cup sherry
1 16-ounce can pitted
  dark sweet cherries,
  drained

Coat pheasant pieces with flour. In a heavy skillet, melt butter and brown birds thoroughly. Place pheasants in a deep casserole.

In the same skillet, combine onion, raisins, chili sauce, water, brown sugar, Worcestershire sauce and garlic powder. Heat to boiling, scraping bottom and sides of skillet. Pour over pheasants.

Bake covered at 325° for 1½ hours. Remove cover, add sherry and cherries. Continue baking 20 minutes longer.

Roast Pheasant with Brandy and Cream

3-6 servings

This pheasant stays moist and tender.

3 pheasants
6 bacon slices
8 shallots, thinly sliced
1 garlic clove, minced
4 tablespoons butter
½ cup brandy, heated
2 cups chicken stock
½ teaspoon freshly
  ground pepper
1 teaspoon salt
2 cups light cream
¼ cup prepared
  horseradish

Cover pheasants with bacon slices and tie securely to retain shape.

In a heavy skillet, brown birds in mixture of shallots, garlic and butter. Place in baking dish along with pan juices. Pour brandy over birds and ignite. When flame dies, add chicken stock, pepper and salt.

Roast uncovered at 375° for ½ hour, basting frequently. Add cream and horseradish to sauce and continue roasting 15 minutes, basting frequently.

Serve birds on a large heated platter covered with sauce.

Gamebird Casserole

4-6 servings

Breasts and legs of
  4 gamebirds, such as
  chukar, pheasant or
  sage hen
½ cup flour
Salt and pepper
¼ cup butter
½ pound mushrooms,
  sliced
1 10-ounce can cream of
  celery soup, undiluted
5 ounces water
5 ounces white wine
1 8-ounce can boiling
  onions, drained
2 tablespoons flour
½ cup light cream

Roll gamebird pieces in flour seasoned with salt and pepper. Melt **half** the butter in a skillet and brown the gamebirds. Remove and place in a large casserole.

Melt remaining butter in the same skillet and lightly sauté the mushrooms. Add soup, water, wine and onions. Stir well, thickening if necessary by combining the flour and cream and gradually adding the mixture to the sauce. Cook over medium heat, stirring until thickened.

Pour over gamebirds. Bake covered at 325° for 2 hours.

Wild Duck with Cumberland Sauce

6 servings

1 large apple, chopped
2 large oranges, chopped
1 medium onion, chopped
Salt
4 wild ducks
½ cup orange juice
1½ cups red wine

Combine the apple, oranges and onion. Salt the cavities and exteriors of ducks. Combine the orange juice and wine. Stuff cavities of birds with apple mixture. Make a "diaper" of heavy aluminum foil around each bird and pour the wine mixture over the birds; seal. Place in a preheated 475° oven. Bake for 30 minutes. Open foil and broil for 3 minutes. Serve with Cumberland Sauce.

CUMBERLAND SAUCE

2 cups

½ cup butter
1 cup currant jelly
½ cup chutney

In a small saucepan, combine ingredients and heat.

301

Mallard Duck

5 mallard ducks
Salt and pepper to taste
¼ cup lemon juice
10 tart apples
1 bunch watercress
1 cup red wine

Clean and rinse ducks. Remove all fat from inside. Rub generously with salt, pepper and lemon juice inside and out.

Core and quarter apples. Place apples and watercress in each duck. Sew up openings and place on rack in roasting pans.

Roast at 450° for 15 minutes to brown and bring out fat. Pour off fat. Roast at 350° basting with red wine until tender, about 1 to 1½ hours.

Serve ½ duck per person.

Sweet and Sour Duck

2 mallard ducks
2 quarts water
1 onion, chopped
2 celery stalks

Stew ducks in water, onion and celery for 3 hours. Drain, discard skin and remove bones. Cut meat into cubes. Add to sweet and sour sauce. Cook for 20 minutes.

SWEET AND SOUR
  SAUCE

¼ cup brown sugar
2 tablespoons cornstarch
¼ cup vinegar
2 to 3 tablespoons soy
  sauce
½ teaspoon salt
1 16-ounce can
  pineapple chunks,
  drained (reserving
  liquid)
1 small green pepper, cut
  into strips
¼ cup thinly sliced onion

Combine sugar and cornstarch. Add vinegar, soy sauce, salt and reserved pineapple liquid. Cook and stir until thickened. Add pineapple chunks, green pepper and onion.

India Duck

6 servings

Can also be served as an appetizer.

½ cup dry red wine
¼ cup soy sauce
½ teaspoon sugar
¼ teaspoon garlic salt
6 duck breasts, boned

Combine wine, soy sauce, sugar and garlic salt. Marinate breasts in the mixture at least 24 hours.

Broil 5 minutes on each side. Return to the marinade.

To serve, slice very thin and serve on crackers.

NOTE: Breasts will keep in marinade (after being cooked) in refrigerator for up to 2 weeks.

Super Duck

4-6 servings

Delicious – tastes like the most tender of steaks.

Breasts and legs from 2 to
    3 ducks
Bacon
½ cup olive oil
½ cup soy sauce
¼ cup butter, melted
¼ cup lemon juice

Cut each whole duck breast into quarters. Wrap each leg and piece of breast in bacon. Secure with toothpicks. Marinate for at least 1 hour in olive oil and soy sauce.

Barbecue over medium coals, turning often, until the bacon begins to crisp. Remove and dip into butter and lemon juice. Return to grill for a few minutes until medium rare.

NOTE: Marinade and lemon butter may have to be increased for additional ducks. Each duck yields 6 pieces of meat.

Barbecued Wild Goose

4 servings

1 wild goose, rinsed and
   patted dry
Salt

Salt goose inside and out. Prepare
barbecue sauce and baste goose
inside and out. Cover with foil and
place in roasting pan. Cook at 275°
about 8 hours, keeping goose well
basted.

HOT BARBECUE SAUCE

1 large onion, diced
3 large garlic cloves,
   minced
3 tablespoons oil
2 cups tomato sauce
½ teaspoon cayenne
Salt and pepper
1 tablespoon
   Worcestershire sauce
½ cup catsup
1 tablespoon vinegar

Sauté onion and garlic in oil. Add
remaining ingredients and simmer
1 hour.

Sherried Quail Casserole

4 servings

6 quail, quartered
¼ cup butter
½ cup chopped onion
½ cup chopped celery
1 tablespoon cornstarch
1 cup chicken broth
2 tablespoons dry sherry
2 tablespoons minced
   parsley

Sauté quail in butter for 10 minutes.
Remove quail with a slotted spoon and
sauté onion and celery in remaining
pan juices for 5 minutes.

Combine cornstarch and broth and
add to onion mixture; cook stirring
constantly until thickened. Add sherry
and parsley.

Arrange quail in a shallow casserole
and cover with sauce. Bake at 350°
for 15 minutes.

Quail in Grape Leaves

4-6 servings

12 large grape leaves,
  stems removed
12 whole quail,
  thoroughly cleaned
12 fresh sage leaves
Salt and freshly ground
  pepper
12 slices pancetta,* each
  about 1/16-inch thick
½ cup olive oil
2 small red onions,
  coarsely chopped
Salt and pepper to taste
1 cup dry white wine
1 cup chicken broth

*NOTE: Pancetta is Italian
  cured bacon, available from
  Italian specialty stores or
  through a butcher.

Soak grape leaves in cold water
(whether using fresh or preserved
leaves), for 30 minutes, changing the
water about every 5 minutes. Pat dry
thoroughly with paper towels.

Stuff each quail with a sage leaf, salt
and pepper. Wrap each bird in a grape
leaf, then unroll a slice of pancetta and
wrap around the bird. Tie with string to
hold together.

In a large skillet, heat oil and sauté
onions until translucent. Place quail in
pan, sprinkle with salt and pepper and
cook until light brown on all sides. Add
wine, cover pan loosely and simmer
until wine has evaporated, about
15 minutes.

Cook and add broth, a little at a time,
keeping lid on loosely, for about
25 minutes. Quail should be tender
when tested with a fork. Remove
strings carefully, place birds on serving
dish and cover with sauce. Serve
immediately.

Countryside Quail

4 servings

8 quail, halved lengthwise
2 tablespoons butter
½ cup chopped onion
¼ cup chopped celery
½ pound mushrooms,
  sliced
¼ teaspoon rosemary
½ cup dry white wine
1 10-ounce can cream of
  mushroom soup,
  undiluted

Brown quail in butter. Add remaining
ingredients and simmer covered over
low heat 45 minutes.

Dove Casserole

6 servings

6 bacon slices, chopped
24 doves
Flour
Salt and pepper
½ cup butter
¼ pound onions, sliced
¼ pound mushrooms,
   sliced
¼ cup chopped parsley
¼ teaspoon thyme
3 tablespoons flour
2 cups chicken broth
½ cup sherry
½ cup sliced stuffed
   green olives
Salt and pepper to taste

In a heavy skillet, fry bacon until crisp. Drain and set aside, reserving drippings.

Shake doves in bag of flour, salt and pepper. To reserved drippings, melt **¼ cup** of the butter over medium heat and brown doves on all sides. Remove to an ovenproof casserole.

In the same skillet, add remaining butter and sauté onions until soft. Add mushrooms, parsley and thyme and cook 3 minutes. Add the **3 tablespoons** flour and stir until well blended and bubbly. Lower heat, add broth and stir until sauce is smooth. Add sherry, bacon and olives, simmer another 2 minutes and correct seasonings.

Pour sauce over doves, cover and bake at 350° for 45 minutes or until tender.

NOTE: Serve doves over rice, passing extra sauce.

Wrap game birds in plastic wrap followed by heavy duty foil then freezer paper. Be sure to date the package.

Bound to Please: Ranges and Rodeos

In 1871, cowhands set out from Waco, Texas, to drive 1,500 head
of longhorns to Idaho to feed the miners. Less than twenty years
later, Idaho ranchers had developed a new industry, grazing
50,000 head of cattle on open rangeland.

The western tradition continues in Idaho in chuckwagon dinners,
in rodeos such as the early spring celebration at Riggins or the
week-long Snake River Stampede held each year at Nampa, in dis-
tant glimpses of a sheepherder's wagon, in county fairs all across
the state. In Idaho, the past is with us every day.

Mixed Grill with Herbs

Your choice

Amounts are not important with a mixed grill, just be ready with seconds.

Italian sausages entwined on skewers with sprigs of fresh rosemary
Lamb chops with bay leaves or fresh mint leaves
Skirt steaks with fresh tarragon sprigs

Cook foods about 6 inches above a solid bed of charcoal briquets, turning occasionally and brushing with oil as needed.

Sausages – 20 minutes
Lamb – 5 to 7 minutes per side
Steaks – 3 to 5 minutes per side

NOTE: For best flavor, be generous with the fresh herbs!

Basque-Style Leg of Lamb

6-8 servings

1 medium-sized leg of lamb
4 to 5 garlic cloves, thinly sliced
Salt and pepper
Flour
Bacon drippings, melted
1 cup water

Make small slits in lamb and insert garlic pieces. Season entire leg with salt, pepper and flour. Place lamb in a roasting pan and drizzle with bacon drippings. Oven brown in a preheated 450° oven for 15 to 20 minutes on each side. Add water to pan, cover and reduce heat to 300° and cook for 4 to 5 hours.

NOTE: The Basques often add peeled, quartered potatoes the last 45 minutes of cooking.

A shallow pan is better than a deep one for roasting because it allows heat to circulate around the roast.

Grilled Minted Leg of Lamb 8 servings

1 7 to 8 pound leg of
  lamb, butterflied
1 cup dry white wine
¼ cup finely chopped
  fresh mint leaves **or**
  2 teaspoons dried mint
  leaves
1 teaspoon salt
½ teaspoon coarsely
  ground pepper

Have butcher remove bone and flatten
the leg of lamb so it is roughly the
same thickness.

Combine wine, mint, salt and pepper in
a large shallow glass container. Place
lamb in marinade and refrigerate 3 to
4 hours, turning at least twice.

Remove lamb from marinade. Grill
4 inches from medium-hot coals about
15 minutes per side for medium
doneness. Brush with marinade. Slice
crosswise in ¼-inch thick slices.

Basque Lamb Chops 6 servings

12 lamb chops
Salt and pepper to taste
1 tablespoon olive oil
1 medium onion, chopped
1 green pepper, chopped
2 garlic cloves, minced
2 large tomatoes **or**
  1½ cups solid pack
  tomatoes, drained

Sprinkle lamb chops with salt and
pepper and brown well in hot oil.
Remove with a slotted spoon and
place in an ovenproof pan and keep
warm.

Combine onion, green pepper and
garlic and sauté in pan juices until
golden brown. Peel and chop
tomatoes; add to mixture and season
with additional salt and pepper.
Simmer gently 5 to 7 minutes.

Pour sauce over chops and cover.
Bake at 350° for 20 minutes.

*When broiling or barbecuing meat, slash the fat to
prevent curling.*

Lamb Chops with
Roquefort Cheese

4 servings

4 lamb chops, 1½ inches
  thick
4 tablespoons Roquefort
  cheese
4 tablespoons garlic
  vinegar
2 tablespoons heavy
  cream
2 slices bread, toasted
2 tablespoons chopped
  parsley

Place lamb chops on a broiler pan and
spoon mixture of cheese, vinegar and
cream over each chop. Broil to desired
doneness and serve on a toast
triangle. Garnish with parsley.

Lamb Shanks Madeira

6-8 servings

6 to 8 lamb shanks
Salt and pepper
¼ teaspoon thyme
¼ teaspoon oregano
¼ teaspoon marjoram
1½ tablespoons oil
2½ tablespoons flour
Water
4 tablespoons minced
  onion
2 garlic cloves, minced
1 teaspoon
  Worcestershire sauce
1 cup Madeira wine
Bouquet garni
  (2 cloves, 1 bay leaf,
  1 whole allspice,
  2 peppercorns, pinch
  of rosemary)
Flour
Water

Season lamb shanks with salt, pepper,
thyme, oregano and marjoram. Brown
on all sides in oil in a Dutch oven over
medium heat. Remove from pan and
set aside.

Blend flour with drippings and add
enough water to make a sauce the
consistency of heavy cream. Replace
shanks and add onion, garlic,
Worcestershire sauce, **½ cup** of the
Madeira and the bouquet garni.

Cover and bake at 325° for at least
3 hours, or until meat is very tender.

Remove shanks, make a roux of flour
and water and add along with the
remaining Madeira to make an
accompanying sauce.

309

India Curry

4-6 servings

¾ cup finely diced celery
1 tart green apple,
    peeled, cored and
    diced
½ cup chopped onion
1 garlic clove, minced
3 tablespoons butter
2 cups cubed cooked
    meat (lamb, chicken,
    veal, shrimp, beef)
1 tablespoon raisins
2 to 3 tablespoons curry
    powder, dissolved in
    ¼ cup cold water
1 tablespoon
    Worcestershire sauce
1 teaspoon salt
¼ teaspoon pepper
1 10-ounce can beef
    consommé, undiluted
1 egg
¼ cup heavy cream
Cooked rice

In a large skillet, sauté celery, apple, onion and garlic in butter until tender, but not brown. Add cubed meat, raisins, curry powder, Worcestershire sauce, salt, pepper and consommé. Cover and simmer about 30 minutes until most of the liquid has been absorbed.

Just before serving, beat egg and add to cream. Stir into curry mixture and heat through.

Serve over rice and sprinkle with choice of condiments.

CONDIMENTS

Chopped pecans **or**
    peanuts
Shredded coconut
Chutney
Bacon
Chopped hard boiled egg
Sliced green onions

Shish Kebab

4-6 servings

Half a large leg of lamb **or** equal amount of lamb shoulder
2 tablespoons olive oil
¾ cup red wine vinegar
¼ cup water
1 garlic clove, minced
Salt and freshly ground pepper
12 to 18 mushroom caps
Olive oil
12 bacon slices, halved
1 large green pepper, cut into 1½-inch squares
12 to 18 small white onions, whole
1 pint firm cherry tomatoes
6 cups cooked rice

Cut lamb into 2-inch square cubes, removing any fat, bone or gristle. Place in a large bowl and add the **2 tablespoons** olive oil, vinegar, water, garlic, salt and pepper. Marinate 2 to 3 hours or overnight.

Brush mushrooms with olive oil. Sauté green pepper squares in a small amount of olive oil until slightly soft. Parboil onions 5 to 8 minutes. Drain thoroughly and brush onions and tomatoes with olive oil.

Dry lamb with paper towels. Assemble the kebabs on skewers in the following order: mushroom caps, folded bacon square, lamb, folded bacon square, and so on, alternating the vegetables and lamb and bacon squares. Carefully push the ingredients close together and brush with olive oil.

Cook kebabs 5 minutes per side either under the broiler or on a barbecue. The meat should be pink in the middle and brown on the outside. Serve on a bed of hot rice.

To tenderize meats – marinate in vinegar and olive oil for at least 2 hours.

Whole garlic roasted in skin makes great accompaniment to grilled meats.

Idaho Finger Steaks

6-8 servings

Oil for deep frying
2 pounds sirloin **or** round
 steak, trimmed of all
 fat and cut in strips
 ½-inch wide and
 2 inches long

Heat oil to 375°. Dip steak strips in batter and deep fry 5 to 10 minutes or until golden brown. Drain briefly on paper towels and serve immediately with catsup, steak sauce and/or horseradish sauce.

BATTER

1 cup flour
1 teaspoon baking
 powder
1 teaspoon salt
Dash garlic salt
1 egg, beaten
¾ cup milk
1 tablespoon oil

Prepare batter by combining flour, baking powder, salt and garlic salt in a medium bowl. In a small bowl, beat egg, add milk and oil. Add liquid to dry mixture and mix well.

NOTE: Batter may also be used for onion rings.

Steak Benedictine

2 servings

2 cups heavy cream
¼ cup Scotch whiskey
¼ cup Benedictine
 liqueur
¼ cup sliced mushrooms
¼ cup sliced onions
1 large sirloin, 1½ to
 2 inches thick

In a large skillet, combine cream, Scotch and Benedictine. Sauté mushrooms and onions until tender. Remove vegetables with a slotted spoon and set aside. Liquid remaining in pan should measure ½ inch deep, add more if necessary.

Cook steak in same skillet, turning frequently, until done to taste. Remove to a large platter and spoon vegetables over top. Serve immediately.

Freeze extra pieces of bacon after crumbling for use as garnish.

Oyster Beef

1 flank steak,
  approximately 1 to
  1½ pounds
3 tablespoons cornstarch
1 tablespoon water
2 tablespoons sherry
2 tablespoons soy sauce
⅛ teaspoon MSG
2 cups fresh vegetables
  such as broccoli,
  asparagus or snow
  peas
2 tablespoons peanut oil
¼ cup oyster sauce
  (available in oriental
  food stores)
Steamed rice

Slice flank steak across grain in thin pieces 3 inches long.

In a medium bowl, combine cornstarch, water, sherry, soy sauce and MSG. Add flank steak and marinate several hours or overnight in refrigerator.

Slice vegetables and stir fry quickly in a wok or large skillet in **1 tablespoon** of the oil until the vegetables are barely tender. Remove with a slotted spoon.

In the same wok or skillet, stir fry the meat in remaining oil approximately 2 minutes, add vegetables and oyster sauce, heat through. Serve immediately over rice.

Marinated Flank Steak

¼ cup soy sauce
3 tablespoons honey
2 tablespoons vinegar
1½ teaspoons garlic
  powder
1½ teaspoons ground
  ginger
½ cup oil
2 green onions, finely
  chopped
1 flank steak,
  approximately 1 to
  1½ pounds

In a small bowl, combine all ingredients **except** flank steak; blend well. Pour over flank steak and allow to marinate, covered, at least 6 hours or overnight. Turn meat occasionally.

Barbecue or broil to desired doneness.

NOTE: If your steak has not been previously frozen, marinate as directed. Then place meat on a large piece of heavy duty foil. Pour marinade over and wrap securely. Freeze. You'll have a marinated steak ready when you need it. Simply thaw and barbecue or broil to desired doneness.

London Broil

4-6 servings

A great rendition of an old favorite from Jake's, Boise.

1 quart salad oil
²⁄₃ cup lemon juice
1 teaspoon salt
1 teaspoon coarsely
   ground black pepper
½ teaspoon garlic salt
3 pounds flank steak

Combine marinade ingredients and mix thoroughly. Add flank steak and marinate at least 24 hours. Char broil.

Sweet and Sour Beef

4 servings

2 pounds round steak, cut
   in strips
½ cup oil
1 teaspoon salt
1 tablespoon soy sauce
1 cup water
½ cup chopped onion
½ cup chopped celery
½ cup chopped green
   pepper
1 garlic clove, minced
1 tablespoon cornstarch
¼ cup cider vinegar
¼ cup sugar
1 tomato, peeled and
   chopped
1 8-ounce can pineapple
   chunks, undrained

In a large skillet (an electric frypan is preferred), brown beef in oil. Add salt, soy sauce and **½ cup** of the water. Cook over low heat 1 hour. Add onion, celery, green pepper and garlic. Cook another 30 minutes.

Combine cornstarch and remaining water and add to meat mixture, together with vinegar, sugar, tomato and pineapple, including liquid. Continue cooking over low heat (300°) until meat is tender. Excellent served over cooked rice.

Roast beef at any of the following temperatures:
200° – approximately 30-35 minutes per pound.
300° – approximately 15-18 minutes per pound.
325° – approximately 13-15 minutes per pound.

Carpetbagger Steaks

4 servings

4 beef tenderloins, cut
  2 inches thick
8 fresh oysters
¼ teaspoon salt
Freshly ground pepper
2 tablespoons butter
1 tablespoon oil
Melted butter, optional
1 tablespoon minced
  parsley, optional

One at a time, lay the steaks flat on a chopping board. With a long, sharp knife, cut a horizontal slit about 2 inches wide and 2½ to 3 inches deep into the side of each steak. Take care not to cut entirely through the steak.

Sprinkle oysters with salt and pepper and insert 2 oysters into each steak. Close the pockets with small skewers.

Pat the steaks completely dry with paper towels and sprinkle as much pepper on them as you like.

In a heavy skillet, melt butter with oil over high heat. Add steaks and brown them quickly for 1 to 2 minutes on each side, turning them with tongs to avoid piercing the meat. Then reduce the heat to moderate. Sauté the steaks, turning them every minute or two, so that the pepper does not form a crust on either side, for about 8 minutes if you like rare beef, or for about 10 minutes if you prefer medium rare.

Serve at once from a warmed platter. Just before serving, pour melted butter combined with chopped parsley over the steaks, if desired.

To prevent meat from scorching when roasting, place a pan of cold water in the oven.

Bistecca alla Diavola

4 servings

¼ cup olive oil
4 steaks (any good cut),
    ¾-inch thick
Salt and pepper to taste
½ cup dry Marsala wine
½ cup dry red wine
1½ teaspoons finely
    minced garlic
1 teaspoon fennel seeds
1 tablespoon tomato
    paste diluted in
    1 tablespoon water
¼ teaspoon Tabasco
    sauce or hot red
    pepper seeds
2 tablespoons minced
    parsley

Pour oil in a skillet large enough to hold all 4 steaks. Place over heat and tilt pan so bottom is well coated. When oil is hot, cook steaks on both sides to desired doneness. Remove steaks from pan and salt and pepper to taste.

Remove most of the oil from the pan and add the Marsala and red wine. On medium-high heat reduce the liquids slightly while scraping the sides and bottom of pan.

Add garlic, fennel seed, diluted tomato paste and Tabasco sauce. Cook and stir until the sauce is thick and syrupy, about 1 minute. Add the steaks just long enough to coat with sauce.

Transfer steaks to warm plates and top with remaining sauce and parsley and serve.

Prime Rib Supreme

6 servings

The leftovers are wonderful!

⅓ cup beef broth
¼ cup garlic salt
2 tablespoons curry
    powder
1 tablespoon coarsely
    ground pepper
1 5 to 6-pound standing
    rib roast (at least
    3 ribs)

Preheat oven to 500°. Combine broth and seasonings to form a paste. Apply paste to both ends and fat side of roast, pressing to adhere as much as possible.

Insert meat thermometer and place roast, rib side down, on a rack in a baking pan. Roast for 20 minutes. DO NOT OPEN DOOR.

Decrease temperature to 350° and roast for 1 to 1½ hours longer. Watch thermometer and remove at desired doneness.

Barbecued Brisket of Beef   6-8 servings

So tender it almost melts in your mouth.

1 2 to 2 ½-pound beef
   brisket, well trimmed
1 10-ounce bottle
   Worcestershire sauce
MSG
Garlic salt
Seasoned salt
Pepper
1½ to 3 ounces liquid
   smoke, depending on
   taste

In a large flat dish, sprinkle brisket with Worcestershire sauce, MSG, garlic salt, seasoned salt, pepper and liquid smoke. Marinate in refrigerator overnight. Drain.

Place brisket in a covered baking dish and bake at 275° for 5 hours. Uncover, spread with barbecue sauce (the amount depends on taste) and continue baking 1 hour. Serve hot or chilled.

BARBECUE SAUCE

3 cups catsup
1¼ cups brown sugar
3 tablespoons liquid
   smoke
½ teaspoon cayenne
1½ teaspoons celery
   seed

In a medium saucepan, combine all ingredients and simmer 45 minutes. Keeps indefinitely in refrigerator.

NOTE: Sauce is also good on chicken, pork, hamburgers, etc.

Roast Beef Teriyaki   8 servings

1 6-pound rolled rib roast
2 cups beef broth,
   undiluted
⅔ cup soy sauce
½ cup red wine
¼ cup chopped green
   onions
3 tablespoons brown
   sugar
2 tablespoons lemon
   juice
2 teaspoons ginger
2 garlic cloves, minced

Place roast in a deep bowl. Combine remaining ingredients and pour over meat. Refrigerate overnight.

Drain, reserving marinade. Roast meat at 325° for 3 to 4 hours, basting frequently with marinade. Let stand 20 minutes before serving. Heat remaining pan juices and marinade to serve alongside.

Spicy Pot Roast

4-6 servings

1 large chuck steak
2 teaspoons salt
½ teaspoon pepper
1 teaspoon allspice
3 tablespoons butter
¼ cup brandy
⅓ cup hot beef bouillon
2 medium onions, sliced
1½ teaspoons anchovy
   paste
2 bay leaves
2 tablespoons white
   vinegar
2 tablespoons molasses
2 cups heavy cream

Rub steak with salt, pepper and allspice. In a large skillet or Dutch oven, melt butter over medium heat. Add meat and brown on both sides. Pour on brandy and ignite.

Combine bouillon, onions, anchovy paste, bay leaves, vinegar and molasses. Pour over meat.

Cover and simmer slowly (or bake at 250°) for 2½ to 3 hours. Remove meat to hot platter.

Blend cream into gravy and heat through. Pour over meat and serve.

Rolled Beef España

4-6 servings

2 pounds beef chuck **or**
   round roast, cut 1-inch
   thick
½ cup slivered blanched
   almonds
½ cup green olives,
   pitted and chopped
Salt
1 teaspoon cinnamon
Olive oil
1 medium onion,
   quartered
1 medium tomato,
   quartered
1 garlic clove
1 cup dry red wine
1 cup beef stock
Pepper

Cut several horizontal pockets on one side of meat and fill with a mixture of the almonds, olives, salt and cinnamon. Roll the meat and tie securely. Brown in a heavy casserole in hot olive oil.

When evenly browned, add the onion, tomato, garlic, wine and stock. Liquid should just cover meat; if not, add more in equal parts. Season with pepper, cover and cook over very low heat until meat is tender (2-3 hours).

Slice and serve with strained sauce alongside or poured over meat.

Beef Roulades

3 pounds round steak,
  ¼-inch thick
¾ pound ground pork
1 teaspoon poultry
  seasoning
¾ teaspoon salt
½ garlic clove, minced
2 tablespoons finely
  chopped onion
¼ cup soft bread crumbs
6 bacon slices
3 tablespoons margarine
1½ pounds small white
  onions, peeled
⅓ cup flour
1 tablespoon beef flavor
  base (available in the
  spice section)
1 10-ounce can beef
  bouillon, undiluted
2½ cups red wine
1½ pounds fresh whole
  mushrooms
1 bay leaf
1 tablespoon chopped
  parsley

Wipe beef with damp paper towels and cut into 6 4x6-inch pieces.

In a large bowl, combine ground pork, poultry seasoning, salt, garlic, onion and bread crumbs. Toss to mix well. Place about ¼ **cup** of the mixture on each beef slice. Starting at the narrow end, roll each slice, wrap with bacon and tie with string.

In a Dutch oven, brown meat rolls on all sides in margarine over medium heat, removing as they brown.

Add onions to Dutch oven and brown on all sides.

Remove Dutch oven from heat. Stir in flour and beef flavor base. Gradually stir in bouillon and wine. Bring to a boil, stirring constantly. Return roulades to Dutch oven, add mushrooms and bay leaf.

Bake covered at 350° for 2 hours or until tender. If sauce is too thick, thin with more wine. Discard bay leaf.

To serve, remove string. Arrange roulades in center of large platter, surround with onions and mushrooms. Spoon some sauce over all. Sprinkle with parsley. Pass remaining sauce.

As a special sauce for browned meats – deglaze the pan with wine and whisk in some butter, a few herbs and cream.

Butcher Block Special

6 servings

3½ pounds chuck **or**
   round steak, cut into
   1-inch cubes
½ cup flour
2 tablespoons oil
1 large onion, chopped
½ pound fresh
   mushrooms, sliced
1½ teaspoons salt
½ teaspoon pepper
½ cup burgundy wine
1 teaspoon sugar
2 teaspoons lemon juice
1½ teaspoons
   Worcestershire sauce
½ cup water, if
   necessary

Roll beef in flour and brown in oil over medium heat in a large skillet. Add onions and continue browning. Add mushrooms, salt and pepper. Remove from heat.

In a medium bowl, combine wine, sugar, lemon juice and Worcestershire sauce. Add to meat mixture. Simmer covered 2 hours, adding more water or wine if necessary. Serve over rice or noodles.

Company at Six
Beef Stroganoff

4-6 servings

2½ pounds round steak,
   cut in ½-inch strips
¼ cup oil
1 teaspoon salt
½ teaspoon pepper
¼ cup dry red wine
1 cup sliced onion
2 cups mushrooms,
   quartered
¼ cup tomato paste
3 tablespoons flour
1 10-ounce can beef
   consommé, undiluted
1 bay leaf, crumbled
1 garlic clove, minced
½ cup sour cream

Brown meat quickly in hot oil and transfer with a slotted spoon to a 3-quart casserole. Reserve drippings. Add salt, pepper and wine to meat.

In the reserved drippings, sauté onion until golden brown, add mushrooms and cook 5 minutes. Combine tomato paste, flour and consommé; add to onion mixture along with bay leaf and garlic. Combine well and pour over meat.

Cover and bake at 350° for 1 hour. Remove from oven and slowly stir in sour cream. Serve over egg noodles or rice.

Beer Beef Curry

6-8 servings

2 pounds round steak, cut
in ½ x 2-inch strips
1 cup coarsely chopped
onion
4 tablespoons butter
1 teaspoon salt
1 12-ounce can beer
1 tablespoon curry
powder
½ cup chopped apple
½ cup shredded coconut
¼ cup chopped almonds
Steamed rice

In a large skillet, brown meat and onion in butter. Add salt, beer and curry powder. Simmer uncovered 45 minutes.

Add apple, coconut and almonds and cook 15 minutes longer. Serve on a bed of steamed rice.

Steak Fondue

6 servings

Nice change from fondue with oil, and less calories.

2 pounds sirloin steak
1½ cups red wine
1 10-ounce can beef
bouillon, undiluted
1 teaspoon salt
½ teaspoon pepper
½ teaspoon dried minced
onion
½ teaspoon dried
marjoram
½ bay leaf

Cut beef into ¾-inch cubes, removing all fat. Place in individual serving bowls. Refrigerate until serving time.

In a large saucepan, combine remaining ingredients. Heat to boiling. Transfer to fondue pot and keep at simmer during cooking process.

Let each person place 1 or 2 cubes of meat on skewer and cook his own meat in fondue. Serve with various sauces such as steak sauce, Worcestershire, mustard, horseradish, barbecue, teriyaki or soy sauce.

Don't forget chutney with meats or poultry, hot or cold. It can be just the thing to make a simple dinner sparkle.

321

Basque Tongue in Red Sauce   6 servings

1 beef tongue
    (approximately
    2¾ pounds)
Salt and pepper to taste
¼ cup + 2 tablespoons
    flour
1 egg
Oil for frying
1 large onion, chopped
Water
1 8-ounce can tomato
    sauce

Place whole tongue in pressure cooker and process for 1 hour and 15 minutes (or boil 3 to 4 hours in a deep kettle). Test for doneness, a fork should easily penetrate meat. Remove from container and peel off skin; wrap in plastic and refrigerate overnight. This **must** be done for easy slicing.

Slice ⅛-inch thick and salt and pepper to taste. Roll in **¼ cup** of the flour, dip in beaten egg and fry in oil. Remove and place on paper towels to drain any excess oil.

Sauté onion in pan juices until browned. Add remaining flour and enough water to make a thick gravy, stirring constantly. Add tomato sauce.

Place tongue slices in a 9x10-inch serving dish, pour gravy over all and bake covered at 350° for 1 hour.

Cabbage Rolls   8-10 servings

1 large cabbage
2 pounds ground beef
¼ pound sausage
1 onion, minced
¾ cup uncooked rice
1½ teaspoons salt
½ teaspoon pepper
2 eggs
Scant ½ cup catsup

Remove core of cabbage. Place in a large kettle, cover ¾ of cabbage with water and parboil 10 minutes only.

In a bowl, combine remaining ingredients. Drain cabbage and carefully peel off leaves. Fill each leaf with approximately **¼ cup** of the meat mixture. Roll and secure with toothpicks. Set aside.

Prepare sauce as directed and pour into a large kettle or Dutch oven. Carefully place rolls in sauce and simmer 1 hour.

Cabbage Rolls *(Continued)*

SAUCE

2 tablespoons brown
   sugar
1 quart canned tomatoes
1 6-ounce can tomato
   paste
1 cup water
2 teaspoons chili powder
2 beef bouillon cubes

Combine all ingredients.

Gourmet Meat Loaf
6-8 servings

1 pound ground lean
   chuck
½ pound ground lean
   veal
½ pound ground pork
   shoulder
2 tablespoons oil
1 medium onion, finely
   chopped
1 garlic clove, minced
2 slices day old white
   bread, crusts removed
¼ cup finely chopped
   parsley
¼ cup bourbon **or** cognac
1 egg, lightly beaten
1½ teaspoons salt
½ teaspoon pepper
¼ teaspoon allspice
½ teaspoon thyme
1 bay leaf
3 bacon slices

Bring meats to room temperature and combine. Preheat oven to 350°.

In a skillet, heat oil and sauté onion and garlic until soft. Remove from heat.

In a blender, crumble bread until fine. Sprinkle crumbs over meat and add onion mixture, parsley, bourbon, egg, salt, pepper, allspice and thyme. Mix well with your hands.

Place mixture in an oiled 1-quart loaf pan, top with bay leaf and cover with bacon slices. Bake on middle rack of oven for 1½ hours.

To avoid crumbling, wait 20 to 30 minutes before slicing.

Sweet and Sour Meat Loaf   6 servings

1 pound lean ground beef
1 medium onion, minced
12 saltine crackers,
  crushed
Dash pepper
½ teaspoon salt
1 8-ounce can tomato
  sauce
1 egg
2 tablespoons vinegar
¼ teaspoon dry mustard
2 tablespoons brown
  sugar
½ cup water

Combine ground beef, onion, crackers, pepper, salt, **half** of the tomato sauce and egg; mix lightly. Form into a loaf.

Mix together the remaining tomato sauce and the vinegar, mustard and brown sugar; pour over loaf. Pour water carefully around the base of the loaf (NOT over top). Bake at 350° for 1 hour. Serve with sauce from pan.

To keep bacon slices from sticking together, roll the package into a tube shape and secure with a rubber band before refrigerating.

Spicy Meatballs   4 servings

¾ pound ground beef
¼ pound ground pork
1 cup bread crumbs
½ cup grated Parmesan
  cheese
1 tablespoon minced
  parsley
2 garlic cloves, minced
½ cup milk
2 eggs, beaten
1½ teaspoons salt
⅛ teaspoon pepper
1 cup minced onion

Combine all ingredients, **except** minced onion, and shape into small balls.

In a large skillet, fry meatballs and onions in oil until browned. Add sauce and stir gently to combine.

Spicy Meatballs *(Continued)*

SAUCE

¼ cup minced onion
2 tablespoons butter
½ cup chili sauce
1 8-ounce can tomato
   sauce
1 teaspoon dry mustard
1 teaspoon prepared
   mustard
½ teaspoon
   Worcestershire sauce
1 teaspoon chili powder
1 4-ounce can chopped
   ripe olives
Dash Tabasco sauce

Cook onions slowly in butter. Stir in remaining ingredients and simmer for 10 minutes.

Tamale Pie
10-12 servings

Raisins give an unusual, slightly sweet taste.

3 pounds ground beef
2 large onions, chopped
6 garlic cloves, minced
2 teaspoons salt
4½ tablespoons chili
   powder
2 28-ounce cans
   tomatoes
2 cups chopped ripe
   olives
2 cups golden raisins
3 cups water
1 cup yellow cornmeal
1 to 2 cups grated
   Cheddar **or** Monterey
   Jack cheese

In a large skillet, sauté ground beef, onions, garlic, salt and **4 tablespoons** of the chili powder.

Purée tomatoes in blender and add to meat mixture. Add olives and raisins and simmer covered 1½ hours.

In a large saucepan, boil water and gradually add cornmeal, stirring constantly to prevent lumping. Add remaining chili powder. Cook and stir until mixture is thickened.

Spread meat mixture in a buttered 9x13-inch baking dish and spoon cornmeal mixture over top. Bake uncovered at 325° for 1 hour. Sprinkle with cheese during last 5 to 10 minutes of baking.

Enchilada Casserole

6-8 servings

1 dozen corn tortillas
2-4 tablespoons oil
3 tablespoons flour
½ teaspoon salt
¼ teaspoon paprika
1 10-ounce can mild
   enchilada sauce
1½ cups milk
1 cup grated Cheddar
   cheese
½ cup sliced ripe olives
1 pound ground beef
½ cup chopped onion
1 10-ounce can jalapeño
   bean dip
Salt and pepper to taste
1 large tomato, chopped

In a small skillet, gently fry tortillas in **1 tablespoon** of the oil, adding more oil as needed, drain on paper towels.

In a medium skillet, combine flour, salt and paprika and slowly stir in enchilada sauce until smooth. Add milk and cook over medium heat until bubbly. Add cheese and olives and continue cooking until cheese melts. Remove from heat.

In a large skillet, brown beef and onion, stir in bean dip and season with salt and pepper to taste.

Place **⅓ cup** of the meat mixture and a small amount of the tomato in the center of each tortilla and roll. Place rolled tortillas, seam side down, in a 9x13-inch baking dish. Pour cheese sauce over top and bake uncovered at 325° for 20 to 30 minutes, until bubbly.

Garnish with condiments.

CONDIMENTS

**Shredded lettuce
Tomatoes
Sliced avocados
Sliced ripe olives**

NOTE: Freezes well.

Beef liver will be especially tender if soaked in milk. Refrigerate about 2 hours, remove, dry thoroughly, bread and sauté.

Tacoritas

6 servings

A combination of tacos, tostadas and enchiladas.

1½ pounds ground beef
1 onion, chopped
2 tablespoons oil
½ to 1 pound fresh
  mushrooms, sliced
2 tablespoons butter **or**
  margarine
1 package taco
  seasoning
1 dozen small flour
  tortillas
½ head iceberg lettuce,
  shredded
1 to 2 tomatoes,
  chopped
1 pound Monterey Jack
  cheese, grated
1 pound Cheddar cheese,
  grated
3 10-ounce cans
  enchilada sauce

In a large skillet, brown ground beef and onion in hot oil.

In a medium skillet, sauté mushrooms in butter or margarine. Add to ground beef mixture.

Prepare taco seasoning according to package directions. Add to ground beef mixture.

Fill tortillas with ground beef, lettuce, tomatoes and cheeses, reserving 1 cup cheese. Roll tortillas.

In a 9x13-inch baking dish, spread 1 can enchilada sauce. Place rolled tortillas in dish, seam side down, pour remaining sauce over top. Sprinkle reserved cheese on top and bake uncovered at 350° for 30 minutes until bubbly.

Salt the meat only during the last 15 minutes of cooking time.

Instead of using a metal roasting rack, make a grid of carrot and celery sticks and place meat or poultry on it. The additional advantage – vegetables flavor the pan drippings.

Barbecued Spareribs

6 servings

3 pounds spareribs, cut in
serving-sized pieces
1 medium onion, chopped
2 tablespoons butter
2 tablespoons vinegar
2 tablespoons brown
sugar
¼ cup lemon juice
1 cup catsup
3 tablespoons
Worcestershire sauce
1 tablespoon prepared
mustard
1 cup water
½ cup chopped celery
Dash salt
Dash cayenne

In a large skillet, brown ribs evenly and remove from pan. Add onion and sauté in drippings until golden. Add remaining ingredients and cook slowly until flavors are blended, about 15 minutes.

Place ribs in an ovenproof dish. Pour sauce over meat, cover and bake at 350° 1½ to 2 hours.

Corn-Stuffed Pork Chops

6 servings

The pimiento, green pepper and corn make this a very colorful dish.

2 cups soft bread crumbs
2 eggs
½ cup sliced celery
1½ tablespoons chopped
pimiento
½ green pepper, chopped
½ small onion, chopped
½ teaspoon salt
¼ teaspoon pepper
¼ cup butter, melted
½ cup canned whole
kernel corn, drained
6 1-inch thick pork
chops, sliced in the
middle to form a
pocket

In a large bowl, combine all ingredients, **except** pork chops. Stuff pork chops with mixture.

Spread any remaining stuffing on the bottom of a 9x13-inch baking pan. Place pork chops on top of the stuffing and bake uncovered at 300° for 1½ hours, turning chops once.

Herbed-Stuffed Pork Chops   4 servings

8 ounces medium-sized
  mushrooms
⅓ cup chopped onion
⅓ cup chopped celery
½ cup butter
1 cup bread crumbs
¼ teaspoon ground sage
½ cup chopped parsley
4 double center loin pork
  chops sliced with
  horizontal pockets
½ teaspoon salt
¼ teaspoon pepper
½ cup apricots
1 cup dry white wine

Reserve 4 mushrooms for garnish and thinly slice the remainder. In a flameproof baking dish, sauté mushrooms, onion and celery in ¼ **cup** of the butter for 3 minutes. Add bread crumbs, sage and parsley and mix gently.

Sprinkle chops, inside and out, with salt and pepper. Reserve **4** of the apricots for garnish and chop the remainder. Add to mushroom mixture. Stuff the chops with this mixture and secure with toothpicks.

Scrape any remaining bits from baking dish and brown chops in remaining butter. Pour wine over and cover. Bake at 350° for 1 hour. Garnish with reserved apricots and mushrooms and serve.

Pork Roast in Sauerkraut   6-8 servings

A must for sauerkraut lovers.

1 4-5 pound well-
   trimmed pork roast,
   bone in
2 32-ounce jars
   sauerkraut, drained
⅓ cup brown sugar
4 tablespoons caraway
   seeds

In a Dutch oven or under the broiler, brown the pork roast.

In a bowl, combine sauerkraut, brown sugar and caraway seeds.

Place pork in a crockpot. Add sauerkraut mixture. Cover and cook on high 1 hour, reduce heat to low and continue cooking 7 hours.

Bean Chalupas with Pork

6-8 servings

1 pound dry pinto beans
1 3-pound pork roast
7 cups water
½ cup chopped onion
2 garlic cloves, minced
1 tablespoon salt
2 tablespoons chili
  powder
1 tablespoon cumin seed
1 teaspoon oregano
1 4-ounce can chopped
  green chiles
Corn chips

Soak beans in water overnight. Drain.

In a large kettle, place beans, pork, water, onion, garlic, salt, chili powder, cumin, oregano and chiles. Cover and simmer 5 hours or until pork shreds easily. Separate pork with fork and slightly mash beans. Remove bones (if any) and discard.

Continue simmering uncovered until thick, about 30 minutes longer.

Serve over corn chips and top with choice of condiments, depending on taste.

CONDIMENTS

Chopped tomatoes
Sliced avocado
Chopped onion
Shredded lettuce
Grated Cheddar cheese
Taco sauce

Marinated Pork Tenderloin

6 servings

½ cup soy sauce
½ teaspoon garlic
  powder
½ teaspoon MSG
¼ teaspoon salt
2 tablespoons catsup
1 pork tenderloin
¼ to ½ cup toasted
  sesame seeds

In a small bowl, combine soy sauce, garlic powder, MSG, salt and catsup. Pour over pork tenderloin and marinate in the refrigerator 24 hours. Drain.

Barbecue over medium heat or bake uncovered at 350° for 30 to 40 minutes per pound.

Roll in sesame seeds and slice thinly.

NOTE: Serve with additional sesame seeds and Chinese hot mustard.

Sausage-Filled Crêpes
16 crêpes

¼ cup chopped onions
Butter
1 pound ground sausage
½ cup grated Cheddar
  cheese
1 3-ounce package
  cream cheese,
  softened
¼ teaspoon marjoram

Cook onion in a small amount of butter until limp. Remove from pan and set aside.

In the same skillet, brown sausage. Drain.

In a saucepan, combine onions, sausage, cheeses and marjoram and heat until cheese melts. Place about **2 tablespoons** filling in the center of each crêpe. Roll up and place seam side down in a buttered 9x13-inch baking dish. Cover and chill.

Bake covered at 375° for 40 minutes. Spoon sauce over crêpes and bake uncovered 5 minutes longer.

CREPES

3 eggs, beaten
1 tablespoon oil
½ teaspoon salt
1 cup milk
1 cup flour

Combine ingredients and mix lightly. Cook in a buttered 6-inch pan using **2 tablespoons** batter for each crêpe.

SAUCE

½ cup sour cream
¼ cup butter, softened

Combine ingredients and mix well.

To keep hot fat from splattering, sprinkle a little salt or flour in the pan before frying.

Picnic Pizza

1 envelope active dry
  yeast
2 teaspoons salt
3 cups lukewarm water
4 tablespoons olive oil
8 to 9 cups unsifted
  all-purpose flour
3 pounds spinach,
  trimmed and washed
1 clove garlic, chopped
2 red onions, chopped
6 red or green bell
  peppers
1 pound Provolone
  cheese, thinly sliced
½ pound Cheddar
  cheese, thinly sliced
1 pound pastrami or
  Canadian bacon, thinly
  sliced
1 egg, well beaten

Mix the yeast, salt, water and
2 tablespoons of the oil, and stir until
the yeast is dissolved. Stir in enough
flour to make a stiff dough. Turn the
dough out on a floured surface and
knead until smooth and elastic.

Put the dough into a bowl, oil the top,
cover and let rise in a warm place until
double in bulk. Knead again.

Cut off 3 pieces, each the size of a
lemon. (Equals 3 small pieces and
1 larger piece of dough.) Roll out **2** of
the small pieces into 8-inch rounds and
put on cookie sheets. Prick with a fork
and bake at 400° for 10 to
15 minutes, or until lightly browned and
crisp. Cool.

Meanwhile, cook spinach for
5 minutes until wilted. Drain well,
pressing out all liquid.

Heat remaining oil; sauté garlic and
onions for 5 minutes. Mix with spinach.

Broil peppers until black on all sides,
then cover with foil and let stand for
20 minutes. Remove skins and seeds
and cut into quarters.

On a floured surface, roll out the **large**
piece of dough into an 18-inch round.
Put the dough into a greased 10-inch
springform pan, allowing it to hang
over the edge of the pan.

Picnic Pizza *(Continued)*

Divide the cheeses and pastrami into 6 portions. Place ⅙ of the cheese on the dough. Top with ⅙ of the pastrami, ⅓ of the spinach, 2 of the peppers, ⅙ of the pastrami, ⅙ of the cheeses, one layer of the baked, 8-inch round of dough, ⅙ of the cheeses, and ⅙ of the pastrami. Continue layering, ending with the pastrami and cheeses. Fold the overhanging dough over the top of the filling and brush edge with egg. Roll out the remaining small piece of dough into a 10-inch round and put it over the filling, pressing edges together. Cut slashes in the top and brush with beaten egg.

Put springform pan on a shallow pan to catch drips. Bake at 400° for 40 to 45 minutes. If the top browns too quickly, cover with foil.

The pizza will rise high above the pan during baking and will flatten somewhat as it cools. Cool thoroughly in pan.

When ready to serve, remove the sides and cut into wedges.

Italian Sausage and Vegetables with Green Sauce

6 servings

1 pound Italian link
   sausages
5 pounds fresh vegetables
   such as cauliflower,
   green beans, new
   potatoes, broccoli,
   zucchini or yellow
   squash, cut into bite-
   size pieces
¾ cup chicken broth
1 cup grated Parmesan
   cheese

Pierce sausages with a fork and cook in boiling water about 1 hour, or until cooked through. Cook vegetables separately until tender crisp. Drain and immerse in cold water to halt cooking.

Cut sausages into ½-inch thick slices. Pour broth into a casserole and place over low heat. Add vegetables, keeping them in separate piles. Sprinkle with all but **2 tablespoons** of the Parmesan cheese. Add sausage. Cook covered, over low heat, until vegetables are heated through. Place under broiler 2 minutes. Top with remaining cheese and serve hot with Italian green sauce on the side.

ITALIAN GREEN SAUCE

2 hard boiled eggs, finely
   chopped
Large bunch fresh parsley,
   finely chopped
2 anchovy fillets, mashed
¼ cup minced onion
1 tablespoon minced
   garlic
1½ tablespoons capers
¾ cup olive oil
½ cup red wine vinegar
Freshly ground black
   pepper

Combine eggs, parsley, anchovies, onion, garlic, and capers. Mix in oil and vinegar. Season with pepper.

Swiss Veal

4 servings

1 pound lean veal
2 tablespoons oil
1 medium onion, chopped
½ pound fresh
    mushrooms
1 tablespoon cornstarch
½ cup bouillon
½ cup white wine
½ teaspoon salt
⅛ teaspoon white
    pepper
4 tablespoons plain
    yogurt
1 teaspoon minced
    parsley
½ teaspoon paprika

Cut veal into thin strips across the grain. Heat oil in large skillet, add chopped onion and cook until transparent. Add meat and brown for 5 minutes. Add mushrooms, cut in half if they are large. Sauté a minute or two.

Blend cornstarch with a small amount of the bouillon and stir into the meat mixture. Add the rest of the bouillon and the wine. Stir constantly until the mixture is thick and bubbly. Season with salt and pepper. Gradually blend in yogurt. Heat through, but do not boil.

Arrange on a heated platter, garnish with parsley and paprika and serve hot.

Spice Parisienne

This French blend is nice in meat stews, wine sauces, and on fresh, steamed or sautéed vegetables:
5 tablespoons ground cloves
2 tablespoons ground white pepper
3 teaspoons ground nutmeg
3 teaspoons ground ginger
Mix all ingredients well and store in a tightly covered container.

Veal Sweetbreads

4-6 servings

A delicacy from The Shore Lodge, McCall.

3 pounds veal
   sweetbreads
1 small onion, coarsely
   chopped
3 celery stalks, coarsely
   chopped
2 carrots, coarsely
   chopped
2 bay leaves
3 whole cloves
½ teaspoon coarsely
   ground black pepper
2 garlic cloves, minced
1 teaspoon salt
Water
9 tablespoons butter
2 tablespoons tomato
   paste
3 tablespoons flour
½ cup red wine
1 cup sliced mushrooms
½ cup heavy cream
Seasoned salt
Chopped parsley

In a large pot, combine sweetbreads with onion, celery, carrots, bay leaves, cloves, pepper, garlic and salt. Add enough water to cover. Simmer over low heat for 30 minutes. Refrigerate overnight or at least 12 hours.

Strain stock from sweetbreads and reserve.

In a saucepan, melt **4 tablespoons** of the butter and brown lightly, stirring constantly. Add tomato paste and brown, stirring constantly. Add 2 cups of the reserved stock and heat to boiling.

Melt **4 tablespoons** of the butter and add flour to make a smooth paste. Add to boiling stock, stirring vigorously with a whisk. Heat to boiling. Reduce heat and simmer for 30 minutes.

Peel sweetbreads and cut into ½-inch slices.

In a skillet, melt remaining butter and brown very lightly. Add sweetbread slices and brown on both sides. Add wine and mushrooms and heat to boiling.

Combine sweetbreads with sauce and bring to simmer. Add cream, stir well and heat through. Add seasoned salt and garnish with a pinch of chopped parsley, if desired.

Serve immediately.

Layer and Bake Elk Steak   4-6 servings

1½ to 2 pounds elk steaks, cut ¾-inch thick, trimmed and cut into 2 to 3-inch pieces
¼ cup flour
2 tablespoons shortening
1 10-ounce can beef mushroom soup, undiluted
¼ cup white wine **or** sherry
4 tablespoons steak sauce
1 teaspoon minced parsley
1 teaspoon garlic salt
¼ teaspoon pepper
1 green pepper, cut in strips
½ onion, thinly sliced and separated into rings
2 tomatoes, cut in wedges, then in half
6 large mushrooms, sliced
1 cup grated Cheddar cheese

Coat steaks with flour and brown in shortening, 3 minutes per side. Place **half** the steaks in a baking dish.

Combine soup, wine, steak sauce, parsley, garlic salt and pepper and pour **half** of the mixture over the steaks. Layer **half** of the following: green pepper slices, onions, tomatoes, mushrooms and cheese. Repeat layers. Cover and bake at 250° for 1½ hours.

Rabbit "Hunterstyle"

4 servings

A delicacy from Peter Schott's Continental Restaurant.

2 small rabbits,
   2-3 pounds each **or**
   1 large rabbit,
   4-5 pounds
Bacon strips (slices cut in
   half crosswise)
Butcher twine
Salt and pepper
1 onion, sliced
1 carrot, sliced
2 stalks celery, sliced
1 teaspoon marjoram
2 bay leaves
1 teaspoon peppercorns
Salt to taste

Detach hind legs from rabbit with a boning knife. Be sure to remove pelvic bones. Using a butcher's cleaver, sever the rabbit in half just below the rib cage and again just above the already detached hind legs. The end result should be two pieces: a "saddle" squared off neatly at both ends, and the upper part of the body with rib cage and forelegs.

Using the cleaver, separate the neck and backbone from the ribs and forelegs, yielding two large pieces and a bare backbone with neck attached. Taking the saddles, run a sharp, thin fileting knife along one side of the backbone and remove the meat along its length. Repeat this on the other side. Put a half-slice of bacon on each filet and roll up lengthwise, tying in 3 places with butcher twine.

Salt and pepper the pieces well on all sides and place them in a deep casserole with the vegetables, marjoram, bay leaves and peppercorns. Cover with water and enough salt to make the water mildly salty.

Cover and bake in a 450° oven for 1½ hours (2 hours if the rabbits are very large). Remove from oven and let the pieces cool in the cooking stock.

To serve place rabbit pieces in a casserole and cover with the hunter sauce. Cover and place in a 300° oven until rabbits are thoroughly hot.

Rabbit "Hunterstyle" *(Continued)*

HUNTER SAUCE

¼ ounce dried **or** fresh
    morel mushrooms
1 pint red burgundy wine
1 tablespoon diced
    chopped shallots
2 cups beef bouillon **or**
    fresh brown veal stock
½ cup tomato paste
Salt and pepper
½ cup flour
¼ cup butter

Soak the morel mushrooms in the wine for about 2 hours. Pour wine off mushrooms into a 2-quart saucepan. Squeeze the remaining wine out of the mushrooms into the pan. Add shallots and place over high heat. Reduce by half its volume.

Add 2 cups of the rabbit cooking stock, the bouillon and tomato paste. Simmer, salt and pepper to taste.

Make a roux by blending flour into melted butter and add to sauce. Stir until thick and well blended.

Strain sauce into another saucepan. Chop mushrooms and add to sauce. Simmer until mushrooms are tender.

Chinese Venison
6 servings

1 venison roast, cooked
3 tablespoons dry
    mustard
1 tablespoon mayonnaise
White vinegar
Chinese hot mustard
1 2-ounce can sesame
    seeds, toasted

Slice roast into very thin slices.

Combine mustard, mayonnaise and vinegar (a little at a time, until desired consistency).

Serve on a platter with mustard and sesame seeds for dipping.

Venison in a Bag

6-8 servings

¼ cup flour
1 cup dry red wine
1 cup water
Salt and pepper
1 3 to 4-pound venison
   roast, cut 4 inches
   thick
2 tablespoons dried basil
1 large onion, chopped
2 bay leaves
2 garlic cloves, minced
1 16-ounce can
   tomatoes

Combine flour, wine and water in a
10x16-inch cooking bag and place in a
2-inch deep baking dish. Salt and
pepper the roast and place in bag with
remaining ingredients.

Close bag securely and make 6 small
(½ inch) slits in top. Bake in preheated
350° oven for 2 hours.

Venison Jerky

2 pounds

2 pounds venison flank
  steak, trimmed of
  excess fat
1 teaspoon liquid smoke
1 teaspoon MSG
⅓ teaspoon garlic
  powder
1 teaspoon onion powder
¼ cup Worcestershire
  sauce
¼ cup soy sauce

Cut venison into VERY THIN slices.
(Easy to do when meat is partially
frozen.) Combine remaining ingredients
and marinate meat overnight. Lay
strips of meat on rack in oven. Place
sheets of foil on bottom of oven to
catch drippings.

Bake at 150° for 8 to 12 hours. Keep
oven door slightly opened entire time.
Remove when desired consistency is
achieved.

Western Marinade for Steak   2 cups

1 cup red wine vinegar
½ cup oil
⅓ cup brown sugar
Few drops Tabasco sauce
¼ teaspoon salt
¼ teaspoon marjoram
¼ teaspoon rosemary
¾ cup chopped onion
1 garlic clove, minced

Combine all ingredients in a jar and shake well.

Marinade without Oil for Flank Steak   1½ cups

¼ cup garlic wine vinegar
1 cup soy sauce
1 garlic clove, minced
1 bay leaf
1 teaspoon sugar
Dash pepper

Combine ingredients. Marinate flank steak 4 to 5 hours after scoring meat diagonally. Marinade will keep in refrigerator and can be re-used.

Mushroom Onion Sauce   2 cups

Good over grilled steaks or beef patties.

¼ cup butter **or**
  margarine
½ pound mushrooms,
  sliced
¾ cup beef broth
¼ cup chopped green
  onions
1 teaspoon salt
¼ cup sauterne wine
1 tablespoon cornstarch

In a medium skillet, melt butter and sauté mushrooms over medium heat until tender, about 3 to 5 minutes, stirring occasionally. Stir in broth, onions and salt. Heat to boiling.

Meanwhile, in a cup, blend sauterne with cornstarch until smooth. Gradually add to the mushroom mixture. Continue cooking, stirring constantly until thickened.

341

Rib Sauce

1 quart

Delicious as a dip or basting sauce for all types of meat.

1 pound stewed tomatoes
1 cup water
1 large onion, chopped
1 teaspoon red pepper
  flakes
½ cup catsup
2 tablespoons brown
  sugar
1 garlic clove, minced
¼ teaspoon cayenne
¼ teaspoon Tabasco
  sauce
1 teaspoon pepper
2 bay leaves
1 cup butter
1 teaspoon prepared
  mustard
1 tablespoon mustard
  seed
Juice of 2 lemons
¼ cup red wine vinegar
2 teaspoons chili powder
1½ teaspoons salt

In a large kettle, combine all
ingredients and simmer, uncovered, for
½ hour or more if desired.

NOTE: Freezes well.

Horseradish Mustard

3 cups

½ cup sugar
¼ cup dry mustard
1 tablespoon flour
1 beef bouillon cube
½ cup very hot water
½ cup vinegar
3 egg yolks, beaten
¼ cup butter
½ cup horseradish, well
  drained

Combine sugar, dry mustard and flour.
In a double boiler dissolve bouillon
cube in water and add vinegar, egg
yolks and butter. Stir in dry ingredients
and horseradish.

Just Great Barbecue Sauce   1 generous cup

½ cup oil
½ cup dry sherry **or**
   bourbon
4 tablespoons soy sauce
2 teaspoons
   Worcestershire sauce
2 teaspoons garlic
   powder
Pepper

Combine all ingredients and marinate as follows:

Steaks – 4 hours
Chicken – 2 hours
Roasts – 8 hours

Chili Sauce   15-18 pints

30 pounds ripe tomatoes,
   peeled and chopped
8 large green peppers,
   chopped
4 large onions, chopped
1 bunch celery, chopped
½ cup salt
1 quart white vinegar
1 cup sugar
1 teaspoon pepper
1 teaspoon ground
   cloves
1 teaspoon allspice
1 teaspoon dry mustard
½ teaspoon cayenne
2 tablespoons cinnamon

In a large kettle or canner, heat tomatoes slowly until 1 quart of juice can be drained off. Discard juice.

Add all ingredients to the tomatoes, stirring well after the addition of the seasonings. Heat to boiling and simmer, uncovered, about 3½ hours or until thickened. Pour into pint jars, seal and process according to canning instructions. (Ten minutes at 10 pounds pressure.)

Hot Mustard

3 cups

1 4-ounce can dry
  mustard
1 cup cider vinegar
2 eggs, beaten
¾ cup sugar
1 teaspoon salt
1½ cups mayonnaise

In a small bowl, mix mustard and vinegar. Let stand overnight.

In a double boiler, combine eggs, sugar and salt. Stir in mustard mixture; cook until thick. Remove from heat, cool completely and add mayonnaise. Store covered in the refrigerator.

Cherry Pickles

1 quart

4 cups Bing **or** Lambert
  cherries, with stems
1 cup vinegar
1 tablespoon sugar
1 teaspoon salt
Water to fill jar

Wash cherries, cutting stems about halfway down. Pack in quart jar and cover with remaining ingredients. Seal and process according to canning instructions. Let stand 6 weeks before serving.

Serve with cold meats.

Lemon Pepper

This has become a popular seasoning for meat, fish and fowl.
4 tablespoons coarsely ground black pepper
2 tablespoons grated lemon rind
Shake together pepper and lemon rind in a tightly covered container and store in the refrigerator.

Bound to Please: The Spirits of Idaho

Lying along the same latitude as the great grape-growing regions of France, Idaho produced award-winning wines as early as the turn of the century. With the onset of Prohibition, the new industry faltered, but by the 1970s Idaho-produced wines were attracting national and international attention.

Nature has been bountiful to Idaho, providing the right amounts of sunshine, rainfall, cool nights, and perfect soils. The state's acres produce commercial quantities of barley and hops for beer, and vineyards can be seen along the hillsides. Even its mineral waters, bottled and named, are adding to Idaho's spirit.

Hot Beverages

Cold Beverages

Frozen Beverages

Liqueurs

Fireside Coffee

6½ cups powder

Here's one to have on hand for those long winter nights.

2 cups cocoa mix
2 cups instant non-dairy
   creamer
1 cup instant coffee
   (regular or decaf)
1½ cups powdered sugar
¾ teaspoon cinnamon
¾ teaspoon nutmeg

Using a large container with a lid, mix all ingredients. Stir well.

To serve, place 3 to 4 teaspoons of the mixture in a mug and fill with hot water.

Café Mexicano

2 cups

1½ ounces semisweet
   chocolate, broken into
   bits
1 cup milk
1 tablespoon sugar
¼ teaspoon almond
   extract
¼ teaspoon cinnamon
1 cup hot, strong coffee
¼ cup brandy
2 cinnamon sticks,
   optional

In a small saucepan, combine chocolate and milk. Heat gently over low heat, stirring constantly, just until chocolate melts and milk is hot but not boiling. Pour into blender. Add sugar, almond extract and ground cinnamon; blend for 15 seconds.

Pour chocolate mixture into 2 large mugs (should be half full). Add enough hot coffee (about ½ cup) to each mug to almost fill. Add **half** the brandy to each and garnish with a cinnamon stick, if desired.

Dessert coffees are very rich. Serve them in tall, tempered glasses.

Serbian Coffee

Perfect after an elegant dinner party and well worth the effort.

1 pound freshly roasted coffee (a desirable coffee mix is ¾ pound regular coffee and ¼ pound espresso)
⅛ teaspoon cinnamon
⅛ teaspoon allspice
⅛ teaspoon salt
15 cups water
1 quart milk
½ teaspoon orange extract
½ teaspoon vanilla
½ cup sugar
1 pint heavy cream, whipped
2 tablespoons Grand Marnier
2 tablespoons sugar
Rum
Shaved chocolate and/or nutmeg
Grated orange peel

Combine coffee, cinnamon, allspice and salt and brew using the 15 cups water in a medium-size coffee maker.

In a saucepan, heat milk, orange extract, vanilla and the **½ cup** sugar. Heat just to boiling and remove from heat.

To the whipped cream, add Grand Marnier and the **2 tablespoons** sugar and blend.

Pour approximately **⅓ cup** coffee, **⅔ cup** milk mixture and **1 jigger** of rum into each of 12 mugs. Top with whipped cream. Garnish with shaved chocolate and/or nutmeg and grated orange peel.

Café Marrakech

⅛ cup brandy
⅛ cup crème de cacao
Hot, freshly brewed coffee
Whipped cream, lightly sweetened
Bitter chocolate shavings

In a 6 to 8-ounce mug, pour brandy, crème de cacao and fill with coffee. Garnish with whipped cream and chocolate shavings.

Wassail

1 cup sugar
4 cinnamon sticks
3 lemon slices
¼ cup water
6 cups dry red wine
2 cups unsweetened
    pineapple juice
2 cups orange juice
1 cup dry sherry
Lemon slices

In a small saucepan, combine sugar, cinnamon sticks, lemon slices and water. Heat 3 to 5 minutes for sugar to dissolve. Stir frequently; strain and keep warm.

In a large kettle, combine wine, juices and sherry. Heat but DO NOT BOIL. Add sugar mixture and stir.

To serve, ladle into warm mugs and garnish with lemon slices.

English Wassail

Festive red color — just right for Christmas.

16 cloves
1 tablespoon whole
    allspice
6 cinnamon sticks
3 oranges, studded with
    more whole cloves
6 cups apple cider
1 pint cranberry juice
¼ cup sugar
½ teaspoon aromatic
    bitters
1 cup rum

Tie cloves, allspice and cinnamon sticks in a cheesecloth bag. In a large kettle, place all ingredients and simmer, uncovered, for 10 minutes. Serve immediately, in cups or mugs.

Avoid cracking cups by pouring hot drinks over metal spoon laid in cup.

Hot Spiced Cider

18 servings

4 quarts apple cider
1 cup orange juice
½ cup sugar
2 teaspoons grated
    orange peel
1 teaspoon whole
    allspice
½ teaspoon mace
¼ teaspoon salt
1 teaspoon coriander
    seed
2 teaspoons whole
    cloves
2 tablespoons cinnamon
    stick, broken into bits
1 cup pineapple juice,
    optional

In a large saucepan, combine all
ingredients. Cover and heat to boiling.
Reduce heat and simmer for
30 minutes. Strain and serve hot.

Hot Mulled Burgundy

15 servings

1 cup sugar
4 cups water
Peel of ½ lemon
18 whole cloves
2 fifths burgundy **or**
    claret
Cinnamon sticks
Lemon slices, optional

In a large kettle, heat sugar and water,
stir to dissolve. Add lemon peel and
cloves. Bring to boil and boil for
15 minutes. Strain. Add wine and heat
again gently. DO NOT BOIL.

Serve in mugs with cinnamon sticks as
stirrers or garnish with a lemon slice if
preferred.

*Wine adds delicious flavor to all foods. As it cooks, the
wine alcohol evaporates leaving a mellow taste.*

Traditional Tom and Jerrys   40 servings

Get out your largest mixing bowls as the volume is great and so are the Tom and Jerrys!

1 dozen eggs, separated
1 pound super-fine sugar
1 can sweetened
    condensed milk
1 pound powdered sugar
1 teaspoon cream of
    tartar
Bourbon **or** rum
Nutmeg

Using an electric mixer, beat yolks until thick. Add super-fine sugar, **1 tablespoon** at a time, beating constantly. Add sweetened condensed milk and mix thoroughly. Set aside.

In a large mixing bowl with clean beaters, beat egg whites until stiff. Add powdered sugar, **1 tablespoon** at a time, beating constantly. Add cream of tartar and mix. Fold egg mixtures together and store in airtight containers in refrigerator.

To serve, place a heaping tablespoonful of the batter in a mug, add 1 jigger bourbon or rum, fill with hot water and garnish with nutmeg.

Easy Tom and Jerrys   50 servings

1 dozen eggs, separated
1 pound butter, softened
3 pounds powdered sugar
2 teaspoons vanilla
Rum
Nutmeg

Using an electric mixer, beat egg whites until stiff peaks form; set aside. Beat yolks until light colored; set aside.

In a large bowl, cream butter and sugar. Add yolks; fold in whites and vanilla. Stir to mix. Store in refrigerator or freezer in an airtight container.

To serve, put 1 tablespoon batter in mug, add 1 jigger rum and fill with hot water. Garnish with nutmeg.

349

Hot Butter-Spiced Brandy   8 servings

1 quart apple cider
½ cup lemon juice
⅓ cup honey
½ teaspoon pumpkin pie
  spice
2 cups brandy
4 teaspoons butter
8 cinnamon sticks

In a medium saucepan, combine cider, lemon juice, honey and pumpkin pie spice; heat to boiling.

Pour ¼ **cup** brandy into each of 8 mugs; fill with cider mixture. Top each with ½ **teaspoon** butter and garnish with a cinnamon stick.

Hot Buttered Rum Balls   20 rum balls

1 pound dark brown sugar
½ teaspoon cinnamon
½ teaspoon nutmeg
½ teaspoon ground
  cloves
½ cup butter, melted
Rum
Nutmeg

In a medium bowl, combine sugar and spices. Add butter and mix well. Form into large walnut-sized balls and place on cookie sheet. Refrigerate until hardened, 1 to 2 hours. Store in airtight container in refrigerator.

For each serving, place 1 ball in mug, add 1 jigger of rum, fill with boiling water and stir. Garnish with nutmeg.

When preparing a punch, all ingredients should be <u>*cold.*</u> *The ice or ice ring will last longer if the punch is chilled.*

Eggnog for a Crowd

24 servings

1 dozen eggs, separated
1 pound powdered sugar
¼ cup real vanilla
4 to 6 cups dark rum,
　brandy **or** bourbon
8 cups evaporated milk
3 cups water
1 cup peach brandy
Nutmeg

Using a **large** bowl, beat egg yolks until light in color. Beat in powdered sugar gradually. Beating constantly, gradually add vanilla, **2 cups** of the liquor and let stand 1 hour. Beating constantly, add remaining **2 to 4 cups** of the liquor, the milk, water and peach brandy. Refrigerate, covered, for at least 3 hours or overnight.

Using an electric mixer, beat egg whites until stiff but not dry. Fold in lightly just before serving. Serve in a punch bowl; garnish with nutmeg.

The superb and interesting wines produced abroad and in this country can brighten your meals, bring new zest to your cooking, enhance your entertaining.

Hawaiian Iced Coffee

5 quarts/40 punch cups

1 pint **very** strong coffee
1 cup sugar
4 quarts milk
1½ pints half and half
Chocolate curls for
　garnish, optional

In a large round container, combine all ingredients. Freeze for 6 hours.

Unmold and place mixture in a punch bowl. Allow it to melt 20 minutes. Serve with a punch ladle and include some of the partially frozen mixture in each cup. Garnish with chocolate curls if desired.

Add fresh mint to white wine for a special touch.

Basque Sangria

12 servings

1 fifth dry red wine
1 cup orange juice
¼ cup Cointreau **or**
    orange-flavored liqueur
1 cup club soda
Ice cubes
Lemon and orange slices

In a large pitcher, combine wine, orange juice and Cointreau. Chill until serving. Add remaining ingredients and serve in wine glasses, putting some fruit in each glass.

Summer Party Wine

8 servings

This will enliven any party! Especially fun for the 4th of July celebrations.

1 watermelon
1 bottle berry wine
1 quart club soda
⅓ bottle gin
Lemon **or** lime slices
Raspberries

Slice top off watermelon making an oval opening. Scoop out fruit using a melon baller or spoon.

In a large pitcher or container, combine wine, club soda and gin. Gently stir in lemon or lime slices, raspberries and watermelon balls or chunks.

Chill 4 hours; pour into watermelon shell and chill another 2 to 3 hours.

Mock Champagne Punch

25 servings

1 fifth vodka
2½ quarts ginger ale
1½ cups Rose's Lime
    Juice
Cracked ice

In a large punch bowl, combine all ingredients and mix.

White Christmas Punch
6 servings

2 bottles champagne,
   chilled
1 cup vodka
½ cup Cointreau
½ cup Kirsch
12 strips of cucumber
   rind

Combine all ingredients. Pour over a
quart-sized ice ring in a large bowl.
Serve in chilled punch glasses.
Garnish with cucumber strips.

Cranberry Punch
16 servings

4 cups cranberry juice
½ cup sugar
4 cups pineapple juice
1 tablespoon almond
   extract
2 quarts ginger ale
1 fifth vodka

In a large glass container, combine
cranberry juice, sugar, pineapple juice
and almond extract. Stir until sugar is
dissolved. Chill until ready to serve.
Add ginger ale and vodka. Serve in a
large punch bowl.

Orange Almond Punch
35 servings

1 12-ounce can frozen
   lemonade
2 12-ounce cans frozen
   orange juice
2 cups sugar
2 cups water
1 gallon water
2 tablespoons almond
   extract
1 teaspoon vanilla
1 quart 7-Up

Combine all ingredients in a large
punch bowl.

Pineapple/Grapefruit Punch 42 servings

1 46-ounce can
  pineapple juice
1 46-ounce can
  grapefruit juice
1 12-ounce can frozen
  orange juice
  concentrate
1 cup sugar
2 quarts ginger ale

Combine all ingredients in a 1-gallon container and add water to fill. Freeze. Remove from freezer 20 minutes before serving. Add ginger ale.

Fruited Brandy Punch 6 servings

1 fifth brandy
1 teaspoon grenadine
1 teaspoon maraschino
  liqueur
1 32-ounce bottle club
  soda
2 cups mixed fresh fruit
Mint sprigs

Combine all ingredients **except** mint with ice or ice ring in chilled punch bowl. Ladle into mint-garnished goblets.

Tequila Punch 42 servings

1 16-ounce can
  pineapple chunks,
  drained
1 pint strawberries,
  stemmed and rinsed
1 fifth gold tequila
2 quarts 7-Up, chilled
2 quarts orange juice,
  chilled

Place pineapple and strawberries in ice cube trays or ring mold. Cover with water and freeze.

In a punch bowl, combine remaining ingredients, ice mold and serve.

Guava-Rum Punch
12 servings
---

1 12-ounce can guava
   nectar
3 cups pineapple juice
1½ cups light rum
¼ cup maraschino cherry
   syrup
½ cup lime **or** lemon juice

Mix all ingredients in a large glass container. Serve chilled; garnish with stemmed maraschino cherries or fresh strawberries and lime slices.

GARNISHES

Maraschino cherries
Strawberries
Lime slices

Rum Surprise
6 servings
---

6 ounces light rum
1 6-ounce can frozen
   limeade concentrate
1 12-ounce can beer
1 teaspoon orange flower
   water

Combine all ingredients. Place ½ of the mixture in blender, fill with ice cubes and process until smooth. Serve garnished with a lime slice. Repeat with other ½ of mixture.

Hawaiian Breeze
4 servings

A wonderful summer refresher.

4 ounces Kahlua
2 ounces vodka
2 ounces brandy
3 teaspoons coconut
   snow
½ cup milk
Ice

Put all ingredients in blender, fill with ice and process until very smooth.

355

Bloody Mary

1 serving

A spirited version from Jake's, Boise.

1¼ ounces vodka
Squeeze of lime
Dash Worcestershire
   sauce
Dash beef broth
Drop Tabasco sauce
3 to 4 shakes salt and
   pepper
Tomato juice
Celery salt
1 celery stalk
1 fat straw

Combine vodka, lime juice,
Worcestershire sauce, beef broth,
Tabasco sauce, salt and pepper in a
tall glass with ice cubes. Add tomato
juice to fill. Sprinkle with celery salt.
Add celery stalk and straw.

Piña Colada

2 servings

¼ cup cream of coconut
¼ cup unsweetened
   pineapple juice
⅓ cup rum
Crushed ice
2 fresh pineapple spears

In a blender, combine cream of
coconut, pineapple juice, rum and ice.
Process until smooth. Serve in
stemmed glasses with a pineapple
spear as garnish.

Cool Gin Fizz

6 servings

1 6-ounce can frozen
   limeade concentrate
1 6-ounce can gin or
   vodka
1 6-ounce can half and
   half
1 teaspoon orange flower
   water
Juice of ½ lime
Ice
Lime slices

Put all ingredients in blender, fill with
ice cubes and process until smooth.
Pour into wine glasses and garnish
with a lime slice.

356

Banana Daiquiri

2 servings

Crushed ice
1½ ounces light rum
2 tablespoons lime juice
½ large banana
2 tablespoons sugar
2 maraschino cherries
Lime slice for garnish,
   optional

Fill blender ⅓ full of crushed ice. Add remaining ingredients **except** lime slices and blend until it has a slushy consistency.

To serve, pour into champagne glasses and garnish with lime slice, if desired.

FRUIT OPTIONS

6 fresh strawberries
1 fresh peach
½ cup fresh pineapple

Frozen Margaritas

12 servings

1 pint tequila
1 pint triple sec
1 cup Rose's Lime Juice
2 12-ounce cans frozen
   lemonade concentrate
Ice cubes
Lime wedges
Coarse salt

In a large bowl or pitcher, mix tequila, triple sec, lime juice and lemonade concentrate.

In a blender, combine **1 cup** of the mixture and 3 cups ice cubes. Blend until smooth.

Serve in glasses after rubbing the rims with a lime wedge and dipping in salt.

Time cocktails to last about an hour before dinner is served. An endless cocktail hour can result in bored guests or those who have eaten so much that they ignore the delicious meal you have worked so hard to prepare.

Banana Crush
8 quarts

Great summer cooler.

4 cups sugar
6 cups water
1 quart pineapple juice
Juice of 5 oranges
Juice of 2 lemons
5 bananas, mashed
4 quarts 7-Up

Combine sugar and water. Heat to boiling until sugar dissolves.

In a large container, combine sugar and water with remaining ingredients, **except** 7-Up and freeze.

Remove from freezer 30 minutes before serving. Fill glasses ⅔ full with mixture, add 7-Up to fill glass. Serve with a straw and a spoon.

NOTE: May be frozen in smaller containers and removed from freezer when needed.

Pink Lassies
2½ cups

1 cup cranberry juice
¼ cup orange juice
1 cup vanilla ice cream

Put all ingredients into blender. Cover and process. Serve.

Orange Julius
3 cups

1 3-ounce can frozen orange juice concentrate, undiluted
½ cup milk
½ cup water
2 tablespoons sugar
½ teaspoon vanilla
5 to 6 ice cubes

Combine all ingredients in blender; process 30 seconds.

Tropical Smash   3½ cups

This is a great after-school treat, so quick, easy and healthy.

15 ice cubes
1 cup chilled crushed
    pineapple with juice
1 large ripe banana
1 egg
½ cup instant dry milk
¼ cup water
1 teaspoon lemon juice
1 tablespoon sugar

Using a blender, combine all ingredients and process until smooth.

Sunrise Fruit Smoothie   1 serving

Enjoy this healthful, quick breakfast or snack when you are on the run.

¾ cup orange juice
½ cup plain yogurt **or**
    ⅓ cup powdered milk
    and ⅔ cup very cold
    water
1 banana, fresh **or**
    frozen, cut in chunks
¼ cup raspberries **or**
    strawberries, fresh or
    frozen
1 egg, optional
Few ice cubes, if all fruits
    are fresh, not frozen

Using a blender, combine all ingredients and process until smooth.

Always remember to have sparkling water, tonic, fruit juices and soft drinks on hand for non-drinkers.

Amaretto

4 quarts

4 cups water
6 cups sugar
2 quarts 100 proof vodka
3 ounces almond extract
1 teaspoon vanilla
1 teaspoon caramel,
   optional

In a large kettle, combine water and sugar; boil for 2 minutes. Cool. Add vodka, almond extract, vanilla and caramel if desired; blend well. Bottle and age 30 days before serving.

The number of drinks consumed will depend on the time of day, type of drink, amount of food and season of the year.

Quick Kahlua

2 fifths

Incredibly good and requires no "sitting time."

2 cups water
2¾ cups sugar
6 tablespoons instant
   coffee crystals
½ cup warm water
2 teaspoons real vanilla
1 fifth vodka
2 teaspoons glycerine
   (available at pharmacy)

In a large saucepan, boil the **2 cups** water and the sugar for 3 to 4 minutes. Mix coffee with the **½ cup** warm water. Add all ingredients to sugar syrup, stirring to mix. Let cool and store in dark bottles.

One fifth of wine or champagne makes 5 drinks of 5 ounces each. One gallon of wine or champagne makes 26 drinks of 5 ounces each.

Bound to Please: The Gem State

The legend has endless variations, but in most of them Noah Kellogg's burro is credited with discovering in 1885 a rich vein of gold in what is now known as Idaho's Silver Valley. Miners had already been at work for more than two decades, and since the 1860s they have pulled from the earth 8.75 million troy ounces of gold and more than one billion troy ounces of silver.

Rich in minerals, Idaho is also a paradise for gem hunters. The Idaho Star Garnet, the state's official gemstone, is treasured by collectors everywhere, but within Idaho's borders can also be found agate, jasper, opal, amethyst, sapphires, rubies, aquamarines, topaz, tourmaline, malachite, diamonds, and other precious and semi-precious stones.

Mousses & Soufflés

Cakes & Cheesecakes

Pies & Pie Crusts

Fruit

Puddings

Cookies

Sauces & Miscellaneous

Mousse Amaretto   8 servings

5 eggs, separated
½ cup sugar
Pinch salt
1 teaspoon vanilla
1 cup milk
1 envelope unflavored
  gelatin
2 tablespoons cold water
1 pint heavy cream,
  whipped
2 to 3 ounces amaretto

In a bowl, beat egg yolks with sugar until mixture is light yellow. Add salt.

In a 2-quart saucepan, combine vanilla with milk and heat to boiling. Add hot milk to beaten yolks, mixing thoroughly. Heat mixture slowly, stirring constantly, but do not boil.

Soften gelatin in cold water. Add to milk mixture, stirring to blend well.

Cool mixture in a large bowl of ice, stirring constantly or it will be lumpy. Fold in whipped cream.

Beat egg whites until stiff but not dry. Fold into mixture. Add amaretto. Pour mixture into serving bowl or individual dessert dishes. Chill.

If desired, before serving float a tablespoon or two of amaretto on top of each portion.

Honey-Macaroon Mousse 8-10 small servings

1½ pints heavy cream
¼ cup powdered sugar
¼ cup honey
Dash salt
1½ cups crushed
  macaroons
Semisweet chocolate

Beat cream until light. Gradually beat in powdered sugar, then honey and add salt. Fold in crushed macaroons. Pour into mold, either 1 large mold or individual molds, and freeze. Thaw mousse slightly before serving. Top with shaved semisweet chocolate.

NOTE: Packaged macaroons usually do not have as tasty a flavor as homemade or bakery macaroons. The softer kinds have more coconut flavor, however, they should be dried or broken into small bits before mixing into cream.

Strawberry Mousse with Raspberry Sauce

6 cups

2 pints fresh strawberries
2 envelopes unflavored
  gelatin
1 cup water
1 cup sugar
Juice of 1 lemon
1 teaspoon vanilla
2 cups heavy cream
Dash salt

Wash strawberries. Dry on paper towels. Hull berries and purée in blender.

Sprinkle gelatin over cold water in saucepan. Place over low heat and stir constantly until dissolved, about 5 minutes. Remove from heat. Stir in sugar.

Combine mixture with berries. Stir in lemon juice and vanilla. Chill in freezer or refrigerator until mixture forms a ball when dropped from spoon.

Whip cream with salt until it forms stiff peaks. Fold berry mixture into cream. Pour into 6-cup mold and chill overnight. Serve with sauce.

SAUCE

1 10-ounce package
   frozen raspberries **or**
   1 pint fresh
   raspberries
1 tablespoon Kirsch,
   optional

Wash berries. Purée in blender until smooth. Strain to remove seeds. Stir in Kirsch, if desired.

Add a touch of dissolved unflavored gelatin or 1 beaten egg white to whipped cream to keep it from separating so you can make it ahead of time.

Frozen Soufflé with
Strawberry Sauce

12-14 servings

½ gallon vanilla ice cream
8 macaroon cookies,
  crumbled
6 tablespoons frozen
  orange juice, undiluted
1 tablespoon lemon juice
4 tablespoons Grand
  Marnier or Cointreau
1½ cups heavy cream,
  whipped
6 ounces sliced almonds,
  lightly toasted in
  butter
1 to 2 teaspoons
  powdered sugar
1 tablespoon Grand
  Marnier
Almonds

Soften ice cream. Add cookies, orange juice, lemon juice and the **4 tablespoons** Grand Marnier. Fold in whipped cream. Pour into a springform pan. Top with toasted almonds and sprinkle with powdered sugar. Freeze at least 5 hours.

To serve, pour **¼ cup** of the sauce over top of frozen soufflé. Pour the **1 tablespoon** Grand Marnier over top and flame. Cut into small wedges, serve with remaining sauce and garnish with almonds.

SAUCE

2 10-ounce packages
  frozen strawberries,
  thawed
6 teaspoons Grand
  Marnier **or** Cointreau
4 teaspoons frozen
  orange juice, undiluted
4 teaspoons lemon juice
1 teaspoon grated lemon
  rind
1 tablespoon sugar

In a saucepan, heat all ingredients until warm.

Chill bowl and beaters before whipping cream.

Grand Marnier Soufflé

6-8 servings

14 eggs, separated
(reserve 10 egg yolks)
¾ cup sugar
½ cup Grand Marnier
2 tablespoons grated
orange peel
½ teaspoon cream of
tartar
Butter
Sugar
Powdered sugar, sifted

In a double boiler, beat the **10 egg yolks** with a whisk until lemon colored. Gradually beat in sugar. Cook mixture over barely simmering water, stirring constantly. As soon as yolks have thickened, stir in Grand Marnier and orange peel. Transfer to a large bowl and set in ice water until mixture has chilled.

In a large mixing bowl, beat the **14 egg whites** and cream of tartar until whites form stiff peaks. Fold egg whites gradually into yolk mixture.

Pour batter into a 2-quart soufflé dish or mold which has been buttered and sugared. Tie a strip of waxed paper around mold so it makes a collar about 2 inches above rim, securing well. Butter inside of collar.

Bake at 450° for 15 to 20 minutes. Sprinkle top with sifted powdered sugar. Remove paper collar and serve immediately.

Amaretto Cheesecake

10-16 servings

CRUST

1 cup flour
¼ cup sugar
1 egg yolk
½ cup butter

Place ingredients in a bowl and cut with pastry cutter until mixture is crumbly. Pour into a 10-inch springform pan and press on bottom and up sides about 1 inch.

Amaretto Cheesecake *(Continued)*

FILLING

5 8-ounce packages
   cream cheese, softened
1½ cups sugar
¼ cup flour
¼ teaspoon salt
6 eggs
⅓ cup amaretto
2 tablespoons instant
   coffee

In a bowl beat cream cheese, 1 package at a time. Gradually add sugar, flour and salt until mixture is smooth.

Add eggs, 1 at a time, and beat until well mixed.

In a small bowl mix amaretto and coffee, stirring until well mixed. Gradually add liqueur/coffee mixture to cream cheese mixture. Beat until well blended. Pour mixture into crumb-lined pan. Pan will be full. Bake at 325° for 1 hour or until cake is set. Cool.

NOTE: Best when made the day ahead.

Ricotta Cheesecake   10-12 servings

A specialty from the Café Rose, Boise.

4 eggs
1 cup sugar
Grated peel of 1 lemon
1 pound ricotta cheese
4 ounces cream cheese,
   softened
4 tablespoons butter,
   melted
2 ounces honey, heated
1½ to 2 cups graham
   cracker crumbs

Beat eggs, sugar and lemon rind.

Beat ricotta cheese and cream cheese to a smooth consistency. Combine the above 2 mixtures and beat thoroughly. Set aside.

Combine butter and honey over low heat until mixed and warm. Pour into a mixing bowl. Add graham cracker crumbs and combine until thoroughly mixed. Press the crumb mixture into the bottom only of a 10-inch glass pie plate.

Pour filling over crust and bake at 300° for about 25 minutes or until filling is firm. Remove from oven and let cool before serving.

365

Kootenai Cheesecake

6-8 servings

¾ cup finely crushed
  graham cracker
  crumbs
3 tablespoons melted
  butter
2 tablespoons sugar
1 pint creamed small
  curd cottage cheese
1 8-ounce package
  cream cheese,
  softened
1 cup sugar
2 tablespoons flour
3 eggs
½ pint heavy cream
¼ teaspoon salt
1 teaspoon vanilla

Mix together graham cracker crumbs,
butter and the **2 tablespoons** sugar.
Pat into bottom and over seam of a
springform pan. Bake at 350° for
8 minutes.

With a wooden spoon, force cottage
cheese through a strainer.

In a large mixer bowl, beat cream
cheese, add cottage cheese and
gradually beat in the **1 cup** sugar
mixed with flour. Add eggs, 1 at a
time, beating until smooth. Mix in
cream, salt and vanilla; beat until
blended. Turn into baked crumb-lined
pan, and bake at 325° for 1 hour.

May be served with a fresh fruit
garnish such as sliced peaches or
strawberries.

Mom's Cheesecake

10 servings

2 cups graham cracker
  crumbs
¼ cup butter, melted
3 8-ounce packages
  cream cheese,
  softened
1¼ cups sugar
4 eggs
1½ teaspoons vanilla
¼ teaspoon almond
  extract
4 tablespoons lemon
  juice

Combine graham cracker crumbs and
butter. Press into a 9-inch deep dish
pie plate. Refrigerate until needed.

With a food processor, combine **half**
the cream cheese, gradually add
sugar, small amounts at a time, and
eggs, 1 at a time. Mix until smooth.

Add remaining ingredients in small
portions until all ingredients are well
mixed. Pour mixture into crust. Bake at
350° for 35 minutes. Turn off heat and
open door slightly, leaving cake in oven
for 1½ hours.

Pour topping over baked cheesecake
and bake in preheated 450° oven for
5 minutes.

366

Mom's Cheesecake *(Continued)*

TOPPING

1 pint sour cream
1 teaspoon vanilla
4 tablespoons sugar

Mix ingredients well.

Butter-Praline Cheesecake   8-10 servings

Recipe of Chef Chris Hudgens, The Kneadery, Ketchum.

3 8-ounce packages
   cream cheese, softened
2 cups brown sugar
4 eggs, lightly beaten
1 teaspoon vanilla
2 cups graham cracker
   crumbs
¼ cup sugar
⅓ cup butter, melted
½ cup butter, softened
¼ cup flour
½ cup coarsely chopped
   pecans
½ cup heavy cream,
   whipped

Beat cream cheese until fluffy. Add **1 cup** of the brown sugar and continue to beat for 3 minutes. Add eggs and beat until thoroughly blended. Add vanilla.

Meanwhile, in a 9½-inch springform pan, place graham cracker crumbs, sugar and **melted** butter. Mix thoroughly. Pat onto the sides and bottom of the pan.

Pour cheesecake mixture into crust.

In a small bowl, knead **softened** butter, remaining brown sugar, flour and pecans together. Drop lightly over top of cheesecake. Bake at 350° for 1 to 1¼ hours. Let cool completely. Top each piece with whipped cream.

Refrigerate cheesecake overnight for ease in cutting.

Custard-Filled Poppy Seed Cake

8-10 servings

½ cup poppy seeds
¾ cup milk
1½ cups sugar
¾ cup butter
3 cups flour
¼ teaspoon salt
3 teaspoons baking
  powder
4 egg whites
1 teaspoon vanilla

Soak poppy seeds in milk for 2 hours.

Cream sugar and butter. Add poppy seeds and milk mixture along with flour, salt and baking powder.

Beat egg whites until moderately stiff and fold into batter. Fold in vanilla.

Grease 3 8-inch round cake pans and lightly dust with flour. Divide batter evenly among pans and bake at 325° for 25 minutes. DO NOT OVERBAKE or cake will be dry.

When cake is cooled, spread filling between layers. Frost top and sides. Cake **must** be refrigerated.

FILLING

2 tablespoons flour
½ cup sugar
¼ teaspoon salt
3 tablespoons cornstarch
4 egg yolks, beaten
1½ cups hot milk
1 teaspoon vanilla
½ cup chopped walnuts

Mix flour, sugar, salt and cornstarch in a saucepan. Add yolks. Stir in hot milk and heat to boiling. Remove from heat, stir in vanilla and chopped walnuts. Cool.

FROSTING

1 8-ounce package cream
  cheese, softened
½ cup butter
1 pound powdered sugar
1 teaspoon vanilla

Beat all ingredients until creamy.

Poppy Seed Cake

10-12 servings

1 cup oil
3 eggs
2¼ cups sugar
3 cups flour
1½ teaspoons salt
1½ teaspoons baking powder
1½ cups milk
1½ teaspoons almond extract
1½ teaspoons butter extract
1 2-ounce can poppy seeds

Beat together oil, eggs and sugar. Sift flour, salt and baking powder. Add to sugar mixture alternately with milk and flavorings.

Pour batter into a well-greased Bundt pan. Bake at 350° for 1 hour. Cover with glaze while still hot.

GLAZE

¼ cup orange juice
½ teaspoon butter extract
½ teaspoon vanilla
½ teaspoon almond extract
½ cup sugar

Combine ingredients and mix well.

Fresh Coconut Cake

10 servings

2 cups sugar
1 fresh coconut, husked and grated
16 ounces sour cream
2 9-inch round yellow cake layers (may be made from a mix)

Combine sugar, coconut and sour cream; mix well.

Split cake layers in half, making 4 layers, and frost generously with entire coconut mixture. Cover and refrigerate at least 3 days to allow flavors to blend.

Hummingbird Cake

12 servings

3 cups flour
2 cups sugar
1 teaspoon salt
1 teaspoon baking soda
1½ teaspoons cinnamon
3 eggs, beaten
1½ cups oil
1½ teaspoons vanilla
1 8-ounce can crushed
   pineapple, undrained
1½ cups chopped nuts
2 cups chopped bananas
   (approximately
   3 bananas)

In a large bowl, combine dry ingredients. Add eggs and oil, stirring until moistened. DO NOT BEAT.

Stir in vanilla, pineapple, **1 cup** of the nuts and the bananas. Spoon batter into 3 greased and floured 9-inch round cake pans. Bake at 350° for 20 to 25 minutes.

Cool. Frost with Cream Cheese Frosting. Sprinkle with remaining nuts.

CREAM CHEESE FROSTING

1 8-ounce package cream
   cheese, softened
1 cup butter
2 pounds powdered sugar
   (approximately
   7½ cups)
2 teaspoons vanilla

With a mixer, beat cream cheese and butter until fluffy. Add powdered sugar and vanilla. Mix to a smooth spreading consistency.

Dust cake with cornstarch or flour before frosting and your frosting will not run off.

Butter and heat new cake pans in a moderate oven for 15 minutes before using.

Fresh Apple Cake

10-12 servings

2 teaspoons baking soda
4 cups diced apples
½ cup butter
2 cups sugar
2 eggs
2 teaspoons cinnamon
½ teaspoon salt
2 teaspoons vanilla
2 cups flour
1 cup raisins
1 cup chopped nuts

Sprinkle baking soda over diced apples.

In a large bowl, cream butter and sugar. Add eggs, beating well after each addition. Add cinnamon, salt and vanilla.

In another bowl, sift flour over raisins and nuts.

Add apples and nut/raisin mixture alternately to the batter. Mix very well, making sure that all the flour is absorbed. Mixture will be stiff.

Bake in a greased and floured Bundt pan at 350° for about 1 hour.

Cream Cheese Pound Cake

10-12 servings

3 cups sugar
1 8-ounce package cream cheese, softened
½ cup butter, softened
½ cup margarine, softened
6 eggs
3 cups cake flour
1 teaspoon vanilla

Cream sugar, cream cheese, butter and margarine until fluffy.

Beat in eggs, 2 at a time. Blend in flour and vanilla.

Pour batter into a well-greased Bundt pan. Start in COLD oven and bake at 300° for 1½ to 2 hours, or until golden brown. Top with powdered sugar, fruit or whipped cream if desired.

Sour Cream "Falling Down" Cake

20 servings

This cake will puff up, then fall.

1½ cups sugar
½ cup shortening
2 eggs
½ cup sour cream
1 teaspoon vanilla
1½ cups flour
1¼ teaspoons baking soda
1 teaspoon salt

Cream sugar and shortening. Add eggs, 1 at a time, beating well. Mix sour cream and vanilla together.

Sift flour, baking soda and salt. Alternating wet and dry mixtures, combine with sugar mixture, beating well after each addition.

Spread in a greased and floured 9x13-inch pan.

Sprinkle topping over batter. Bake at 350° for 40 to 60 minutes.

TOPPING

1 cup brown sugar
¼ cup butter
½ cup nuts, optional

Combine ingredients and mix well.

Grand Marnier Cake

8-10 servings

1 cup butter
1 cup sugar
3 eggs, separated
1 teaspoon Grand Marnier
2 cups flour
1 teaspoon baking powder
1 teaspoon baking soda
1½ cups sour cream
1 cup walnuts, chopped
Grated rind of 1 orange
Slivered almonds

Cream butter and sugar. Add egg yolks and Grand Marnier. Mix well.

Sift dry ingredients. Alternately add dry ingredients and sour cream to the creamed mixture beginning and ending with the flour. Add walnuts and orange rind. Beat egg whites until stiff and fold in.

Pour into a Bundt pan or a 9-inch tube pan and bake at 350° for 50 to 55 minutes. Drizzle glaze over cooled cake and top with slivered almonds.

Grand Marnier Cake *(Continued)*

GLAZE

½ cup sugar
1 cup orange juice
½ cup Grand Marnier

Combine all ingredients, and mix until smooth.

Hootenholler Whiskey Cake

1 9x5x3-inch loaf

½ cup butter
1 cup sugar
3 eggs, beaten
1 cup flour
½ teaspoon baking powder
¼ teaspoon salt
½ teaspoon nutmeg
¼ cup milk
¼ teaspoon baking soda
¼ cup molasses
1 pound raisins
2 cups chopped pecans
¼ cup bourbon

In a large bowl, cream butter with sugar and add eggs.

Combine flour, baking powder, salt and nutmeg. Add butter mixture and mix well. Add milk.

Combine baking soda and molasses. Mix well and add to batter. Stir in raisins, nuts and bourbon.

Pour batter into a greased and floured 9x5x3-inch loaf pan. Bake at 300° for 2 hours.

NOTE: This cake, wrapped in foil, keeps for weeks.

To keep the top of a cake from browning too quickly, put a pan of warm water on the rack above.

White Fruit Cake

7 small cakes

2 cups butter
2 cups sugar
10 eggs, well beaten
3 cups flour
1 teaspoon baking
   powder
1 pound golden raisins
1 pound candied
   pineapple
1 pound candied cherries
2 pounds dates, chopped
1 teaspoon vanilla
1 pound chopped nuts
1 cup coconut

Cream butter and sugar and add eggs.

Sift flour with baking powder. Coat fruit with flour. Add remainder of flour to butter mixture. Add vanilla, fruit, nuts and coconut. Bake in greased 3x5-inch loaf pans at 275° for 50 minutes.

Carrot Cake

12 servings

2 cups sugar
1¼ cups oil
4 eggs
2¼ cups flour
2 teaspoons cinnamon
½ teaspoon salt
1½ teaspoons baking
   soda
2½ cups grated carrots
½ cup chopped pecans or
   walnuts

Mix sugar and oil until well blended. Add eggs.

Sift dry ingredients. Combine with sugar mixture and beat well. Stir in carrots and nuts.

Pour into a greased and floured 9x13-inch pan. Bake at 325° for 50 to 55 minutes. When completely cooled, frost.

NOTE: This may also be baked in a Bundt pan at 350° for 1 hour and 10 minutes.

FROSTING

4½ tablespoons butter or
   margarine
6 ounces cream cheese
3½ cups powdered sugar
1½ teaspoons vanilla
½ cup chopped nuts

Cream butter and cream cheese. Add sugar and mix well. Add vanilla. Stir in nuts.

374

Almond-Potato Torte

12 servings

3 medium potatoes
10 eggs, separated
½ teaspoon cream of
   tartar
1 cup blanched, ground
   almonds
1 cup sugar
1 teaspoon almond
   extract
Fruit
Sweetened whipped
   cream, optional
Powdered sugar, optional

Peel and quarter potatoes and boil until just tender. Cool and grate coarsely. Measure out 2 cups and refrigerate.

Beat egg whites until frothy. Add cream of tartar and continue beating until stiff, but not dry. Beat egg yolks until thick and lemon colored. Beat in **¾ cup** of the almonds, the sugar and almond extract. Fold in the 2 cups potatoes. Fold about ¼ of the beaten whites into the yolk mixture. Gently fold in the rest of the whites.

Butter a 10-inch springform pan and dust the sides and bottom with the remaining almonds. Pour the batter into the prepared pan and bake at 350° for 1½ hours.

Remove the torte from the oven and cool before removing sides of pan. Torte will puff up during baking, but will fall slightly in middle and around sides when cool, giving it an irregular shape.

Garnish with seasonal fruits and top with sweetened whipped cream or dust with powdered sugar, if desired.

Place a paper doily on top of cake, dust with powdered sugar and lift off for intricate design.

Tarte aux Pommes

8-10 **servings**

A delicacy from A Matter of Taste, Trail Creek Village, Ketchum.

Puff pastry for a 12-inch tart pan
7 Golden Delicious apples
1 cup sweetened applesauce (see index, The Apple Who Got Sauced) or canned applesauce
Pinch nutmeg
½ cup finely chopped walnuts (if canned applesauce is used)
⅔ cup apricot preserves
Apricot liqueur or cognac

Place puff pastry in the tart pan and weight it with pastry weights. Bake at 375° about 30 minutes until golden brown. Remove pastry weights and bake another few minutes, being careful not to burn the edges.

Peel apples, cut in half and core. Cut each half into very, very thin slices, **while holding apple together.** Slip a knife under the sliced apple and place on a cookie sheet. Bake at 450° for 20 to 30 minutes, or until apple slices are tender, but still keep their shape.

Spread applesauce over the bottom of the puff pastry shell. Carefully season with a whisper of grated nutmeg (sprinkle with walnuts).

Lift the cooked apple slices using a knife and arrange them on top of the applesauce, curved sides up, making it look like a spiral. Use ALL the apples.

Spoon apricot preserves into a saucepan. Thin with liqueur or water and heat for a few minutes. Strain the mixture and glaze the tops of the apples.

Serve with thinly sliced wedges of sharp Cheddar cheese arranged on a serving plate with small clusters of green grapes.

Cranberry-Nut Pie

1 10-inch pie

1½ cups sugar
3 tablespoons cornstarch
½ cup water
3 heaping cups
   cranberries
   (1 12-ounce package)
2 tablespoons butter
⅛ teaspoon salt
½ cup pecans
1 10-inch pie shell,
   baked

In a saucepan blend sugar with cornstarch. Add water and stir until smooth. Add berries and cook until they pop open. Add butter, salt and nuts. Pour into baked pie shell.

Spoon meringue over pie. Broil until lightly browned, watching constantly.

MERINGUE

3 egg whites
¼ teaspoon cream of
   tartar
⅓ cup sugar

Beat all ingredients until stiff.

Special Pecan Pie

1 9-inch pie

3 eggs, beaten
⅔ cup brown sugar
Dash salt
1 cup dark corn syrup
⅓ cup butter, melted
1 cup pecans
1 cup raw cranberries,
   coarsely chopped
1 9-inch pie shell,
   unbaked

Combine eggs, sugar and salt, let stand 10 minutes.

Stir in corn syrup and butter. Add pecans and cranberries.

Pour into pie crust. Carefully cover edge of crust with a strip of foil. Bake at 350° for 25 minutes. Remove foil and bake 25 minutes longer.

377

Pecan-Peach Pie

1 9-inch pie

3 egg whites
1 cup sugar
12 saltine crackers
½ cup finely chopped
  pecans
¼ teaspoon baking
  powder
1 teaspoon vanilla
Dash salt
4 to 5 peaches, sliced
½ pint heavy cream,
  whipped and
  sweetened
	Beat egg whites until stiff peaks form.
	Gradually add sugar and beat well.
	
	Between 2 sheets of waxed paper,
	crush crackers finely with rolling pin.
	Add crackers to egg mixture. Add
	pecans, baking powder, vanilla and
	salt.
	
	Pour mixture into a buttered 9-inch pie
	pan. Bake at 325° for 30 minutes.
	Cool.
	
	To serve, cover pie with sliced
	peaches and top with whipped cream.

Brush unbaked pie crusts with beaten egg white before adding fruit fillings to keep from getting mushy.

Peaches and Cream Pie

1 9-inch pie

1 9-inch pie shell,
  unbaked
1 rounded cup sugar
4 tablespoons flour
¼ teaspoon cinnamon
4 or 5 fresh peaches,
  peeled and halved
½ pint heavy cream
	In a bowl, mix dry ingredients together
	and pour slightly less than half over
	the bottom of the pie shell.
	
	Place peach halves, cut side down, in
	pie shell making 1 layer of peaches.
	Pour remaining dry mixture evenly over
	peach halves.
	
	Pour cream evenly over peaches.
	Bake at 400° for 10 minutes, then at
	325° for 60 minutes.

378

French Pear Pie à La Crème   6-8 servings

1 29-ounce can pear
   halves
¼ cup flour
3 tablespoons brown
   sugar
¼ teaspoon nutmeg
2 tablespoons butter
1 8-inch pie shell with
   high fluted rim,
   unbaked

Turn pear halves into sieve to drain
well.

Combine flour, brown sugar and
nutmeg, stir to combine.

Cut butter into mixture to make coarse
crumbs. Set aside.

Pour half the filling into pie shell.
Arrange drained pears in shell and
pour remaining mixture over pears.
Sprinkle brown sugar crumbs over top.

Bake just below oven center at 400°
for 25 minutes, until filling is set. Cool
before cutting.

FILLING

1 egg, beaten
⅓ cup sugar
¼ teaspoon salt
⅛ teaspoon ginger
⅛ teaspoon nutmeg
½ teaspoon grated lemon
   peel
1 cup sour cream

Combine all ingredients and mix well.

Sour milk: 1 teaspoon vinegar to ½ cup milk.

Fresh Strawberry Cream Pie

1 9-inch pie

1 cup heavy cream
1 8-ounce package cream cheese, softened
½ cup sugar
1 teaspoon vanilla
1 baked 9-inch pie shell
4 cups fresh strawberries
½ cup water
½ cup sugar
⅛ teaspoon salt
1 tablespoon cornstarch
1 tablespoon water
1 teaspoon fresh lemon juice
½ teaspoon almond extract

Whip cream until stiff and set aside.

Using same beaters, beat cream cheese, sugar and vanilla until smooth. Fold in whipped cream. Turn mixture into pie shell and chill thoroughly.

Wash and hull strawberries. Slice enough to make **1½ cups** and place in saucepan with water, sugar and salt.

Heat mixture to boiling and cook 5 minutes, stirring to mash berries. Reserve juice and discard pulp. Return juice to saucepan.

Combine cornstarch and water. Stir into strawberry juice. Cook, stirring until thickened and clear. Remove from heat. Add lemon juice and almond extract. Cool.

About 1 hour before serving, arrange remaining whole strawberries over filling in pie shell. Spoon on cooled glaze. Return to refrigerator until served.

NOTE: Strawberries should be fresh and perfect.

Pumpkin-Almond Pie

6-8 servings

24 vanilla wafers
1 pint vanilla ice cream,
  softened
1 1-pound can pumpkin
1½ cups sugar
½ teaspoon salt
1 teaspoon cinnamon
½ teaspoon ginger
¼ teaspoon cloves
1 teaspoon vanilla
1 cup heavy cream

Line a 10-inch glass pie plate with whole wafers. Spread softened ice cream over cookies and freeze.

Mix pumpkin with sugar, salt, spices and vanilla.

Whip cream and fold into pumpkin mixture. Spoon over ice cream and freeze.

Sprinkle topping over pie.

NOTE: Remove pie from freezer 10 minutes before cutting.

TOPPING

¼ cup sugar
1 cup almonds

In a saucepan, cook sugar until brown and stir in almonds. Spread on waxed paper. When hardened, peel off paper and crumble.

Grasshopper Pie

8 servings

20 chocolate wafers,
  crushed
¼ cup butter, melted
25 large marshmallows
⅔ cup milk
¼ cup green crème de
  menthe
¼ cup white crème de
  cocoa
1 cup heavy cream,
  whipped

In a bowl, mix wafers with butter and press into a 10-inch pie plate. Chill 1 hour.

Melt marshmallows with milk over low heat. Add liqueurs and fold in whipped cream. Pour into chilled crust and freeze. If all the filling does not fit, allow it to settle in freezer and add rest later.

Remove from freezer to refrigerator 1 hour before serving.

NOTE: Pie may be topped with a dollop of whipped cream and chocolate shavings.

381

Easy Pie Crust

1 double crust

This is the perfect pie crust. No need to cut in shortening with a fork. Crust is always perfect; never seems to get soggy.

9-INCH

2 cups flour
1½ teaspoons salt
½ cup oil
5 tablespoons cold milk

Mix flour and salt together in a bowl. Mix oil and milk together in a measuring cup. Add oil mixture to flour mixture all at once. This will form a ball.

10-INCH

3 cups flour
2½ teaspoons salt
¾ cup oil
9 tablespoons cold milk

Wet counter and put a piece of waxed paper on counter. Place dough on waxed paper, cover with a second sheet of waxed paper and roll to desired size. Bake at 450° for 10 minutes.

Rich Pie Crust

1 10-inch crust

3 ounces cream cheese, softened
½ cup butter, softened
1 cup flour

Combine all ingredients and press into a 10-inch pie plate. Bake at 450° for 10 minutes.

Brush top crust of pie with milk before baking and sprinkle with sugar.

Green Grapes in Cognac 10 servings

6 tablespoons honey
3 tablespoons cognac
1½ teaspoons lemon
 juice
1 pound seedless green
 grapes
Sour cream

Combine honey, cognac and lemon juice. Marinate grapes in mixture for 5 to 6 hours. Stir occasionally.

Serve in individual bowls with a dollop of sour cream.

Strawberries Romanoff 6-8 servings

1 quart fresh strawberries
4 tablespoons powdered
 sugar
2 ounces Grand Marnier
½ pint heavy cream
1 teaspoon vanilla
Fresh mint

Clean berries the day before serving. Slice large berries in half and combine with **2 tablespoons** of the powdered sugar and the Grand Marnier. Allow to marinate overnight.

Before serving, whip cream until it starts to thicken. Add remaining sugar and the vanilla. Beat until cream forms stiff peaks.

Combine cream and strawberries. Mix thoroughly, crushing a few berries to give a slight pink color. Serve in stemmed glasses and garnish with fresh mint.

Strawberries à la Maison 4-6 servings

¼ cup port wine
¼ cup dry sherry
½ teaspoon vanilla
1 cup vanilla ice cream,
 softened
1 quart fresh
 strawberries, sliced or
 whole

Combine wines and vanilla. Blend into ice cream. Pour over berries in dessert goblets just before serving.

383

Bar-le-duc

2 8-ounce packages
cream cheese, softened
1 6 to 8-ounce jar red
currant jelly
Cream to thin

In a small bowl, blend ingredients until smooth. Place in freezer tray and freeze until firm.

To serve, let soften a bit, cut into small squares and serve on dessert plates with a few sweet crackers (Waverly or Ritz) and a butter knife.

NOTE: Should accompany fresh fruit when served as a dessert.

Apple Crisp

A special and so-easy favorite from Jake's, Boise.

½ cup sugar
1 teaspoon cinnamon
¼ teaspoon salt
3 tablespoons cornstarch
3 pounds sliced cooked
apples, well drained

Combine first 4 ingredients and mix well. Add apples and mix thoroughly. Put in a 9x9-inch square baking dish.

Sprinkle topping over apples and bake at 375° for 30 to 40 minutes or until nicely browned.

TOPPING

¼ cup butter, softened
⅔ cup flour
⅔ cup brown sugar

Combine and mix with pastry cutter or fork until crumbly.

The Apple Who Got Sauced

12 servings

This is the favorite applesauce recipe of Helcia Graf, A Matter of Taste, Trail Creek Village, Ketchum.

4 cups water
6 tablespoons lemon juice
12 Granny Smith apples
1 cup dry white wine (chablis)
1 cup sugar
½ cup currant jelly
3 cinnamon sticks
Grated rind of 2 lemons
1 cup walnuts, halved **or** finely chopped

In a bowl, mix **2 cups** of the water with **3 tablespoons** of the lemon juice. Peel, core and chop apples; drop into water and juice.

In a large saucepan, combine remaining water and lemon juice with wine and sugar. Drain apples, add to saucepan and simmer covered until they are just tender. **Do not overcook.**

With a slotted spoon, remove apples to a bowl and let them cool completely.

To the liquid, add jelly and cinnamon sticks and cook slowly until juice reduces a bit. Stir in grated lemon rind. Pour liquid over apples and toss in walnuts. (Walnuts should be finely chopped if applesauce is to be used in Tarte aux Pommes, see index). NOTE: Since this serves 12, you will have plenty left over, and it's a good thing, because it's so good!

Madai Saltzia (Pears in Wine Sauce)

6 servings

12 fresh pear halves
¾ cup sugar
3 cups red table wine
1 cup water
1 cinnamon stick

In a saucepan, combine ingredients and heat to boiling. Reduce heat and simmer 20 to 30 minutes, or until pears are tender.

Remove from heat and chill.

Cream in a Glass
6 servings

2 egg yolks
⅓ cup sugar
2 tablespoons lemon
  juice
¾ cup sour cream
¼ cup plain yogurt
1 cup heavy cream,
  whipped

In a double boiler over medium heat, combine egg yolks and sugar and beat well with a whisk. Add lemon juice and continue beating. Remove from heat and cool to room temperature. When cool add sour cream and yogurt.

Fold whipped cream into sour cream mixture. Pour into wine goblets and chill.

Persimmon Pudding with Sauce
8-10 servings

1 cup persimmon pulp
  (approximately
  2 persimmons)
1 cup flour
2 teaspoons soda
1 teaspoon cinnamon
1 cup sugar
½ cup milk
1 teaspoon vanilla
1 tablespoon butter
1 cup chopped walnuts
1 cup raisins

Combine all ingredients and beat well. Pour into a buttered pudding mold or 2-quart casserole. Place mold in a pan of water about 1-inch deep.

Steam pudding at 325° for 1 hour. Leave in oven to cool. To serve, spoon sauce over pudding.

SAUCE

6 tablespoons melted
  butter
⅓ cup brown sugar
⅓ cup sugar
¾ cup heavy cream

Mix all ingredients thoroughly and heat slowly. Do not allow mixture to boil or it will curdle.

Spanish Cream

2 envelopes unflavored
    gelatin
1 quart milk
4 eggs, separated
1 cup sugar
½ teaspoon almond
    extract **or** vanilla
Fruit, such as berries or
    pineapple, fresh or
    frozen and well drained
1 cup heavy cream,
    whipped
Sliced almonds

In a double boiler, soften gelatin in milk. Stir with whisk. Let stand a few minutes until gelatin is softened.

Heat milk mixture to 170°, but DO NOT BOIL.

In a small bowl, beat egg yolks with **½ cup** of the sugar. Put several teaspoons of hot milk slowly into sweetened yolks; stir and add warmed yolk mixture quickly to hot milk. Cook, stirring constantly, until custard coats the spoon or separates around the sides of the pan – about 5 minutes.

Beat egg whites until stiff. Add remaining sugar and the almond extract. Fold custard into whites and pour into a 1½-quart mold. Refrigerate for 2 hours or until set.

Unmold and garnish with fruit, whipped cream and almonds.

Almond Bavarois

1 quart milk
¾ cup sugar
3 ounces almond paste
¼ cup finely ground
    almonds
3 envelopes unflavored
    gelatin
½ cup cold water
1 pint heavy cream,
    whipped
2 tablespoons amaretto
Sliced almonds

In a saucepan combine milk, sugar, almond paste and **ground** almonds. Heat to boiling, remove from heat and let cool.

Sprinkle gelatin over water to soften.

In a double boiler heat gelatin over boiling water stirring frequently until dissolved. Stir gelatin mixture into almond mixture thoroughly and chill until thickened. Fold in whipped cream and amaretto.

Pour into a large mold and chill until firm. Unmold on a plate and garnish with **sliced** almonds.

387

Christmas Trifle

8-10 servings

Use an attractive, clear glass bowl. This shows the pretty layering of the dessert.

12 ladyfingers, sponge cake pieces **or** pieces of yellow cake

4 tablespoons rum, sherry or brandy

½ cup raspberry jam

½ cup slivered almonds

1 large package vanilla pudding, **not instant**

1 cup heavy cream, whipped

Place ladyfingers in one layer in a glass bowl. Sprinkle with rum. Cover with a thin layer of jam and slivered almonds, reserving a few almonds for topping.

Prepare pudding according to package directions, cool and spread in an even layer over almonds.

Spread whipped cream over pudding and sprinkle reserved almonds over top. Chill a few hours.

To serve, cut straight down through all layers for each serving.

Never-Fail Sabayon

5-6 servings

½ tablespoon unflavored gelatin (approximately ½ envelope)

¼ cup cold water

2 eggs, separated

½ + ⅓ cup sugar

¾ cup sherry

Soften gelatin in cold water.

In a double boiler, combine egg yolks, **½ cup** of the sugar and sherry. Cook over boiling water, stirring constantly until slightly thickened. Add softened gelatin to hot mixture and set aside to cool.

Beat egg whites until fluffy. Add remaining **⅓ cup** of the sugar and continue beating until well blended.

Fold cooled custard into egg whites. Pour into individual serving glasses. Chill until serving time.

388

Natillas (Basque Pudding)

6 servings

6 eggs, separated
1¼ cups sugar
1 quart milk
½ teaspoon cinnamon **or** nutmeg

Beat egg yolks, and add **1 cup** of the sugar, beating well. Add milk.

In a saucepan, heat mixture to boiling and cook 5 minutes. Remove from heat.

Beat egg whites and remaining sugar until soft peaks form. Fold into pudding. Cool and sprinkle with cinnamon.

Put plastic wrap on surface of custard to keep film from forming.

Lemon "Icebox" Dessert

6 servings

2 eggs, separated
8 tablespoons sugar
½ teaspoon lemon rind, grated
2 tablespoons lemon juice
⅔ cup heavy cream, whipped
12 to 14 vanilla wafers

In a double boiler, combine beaten egg yolks, **6 tablespoons** of the sugar, the lemon rind and juice. Cook 3 minutes, stirring constantly. Cool.

Beat egg whites until stiff, gradually adding remaining sugar. Fold stiffly beaten egg whites and whipped cream into egg mixture and chill.

Crush vanilla wafers with rolling pin. Cover bottom of shallow "ice box" tray or 7x11-inch pan with **half** the crumbs. Pour lemon filling into tray and cover with remaining crumbs. Freeze without stirring.

To serve, cut diagonally cross-wise to form pie-shaped wedges.

Avocado Sherbet

4-6 servings

Nice to serve with chocolate-dipped strawberries on the side.

1 teaspoon grated lemon rind
½ cup lemon juice
½ cup orange juice, freshly squeezed
1 cup sugar
1 cup mashed ripe avocado (approximately 3 medium avocados)
1 cup heavy cream, whipped

In a blender, combine lemon rind, juices, sugar and avocado. Blend until sugar dissolves. Pour mixture into a bowl and freeze about 20 minutes.

Remove avocado mixture from freezer and fold in whipped cream. Return to freezer in serving bowl or individual serving dishes until firm.

Pineapple Sherbet

1 quart

2 cups sugar
2 cups water
2 egg whites, stiffly beaten
1 medium can crushed pineapple, drained
Juice of 2 lemons **or** 4 tablespoons lemon juice
½ pint heavy cream
Chocolate sauce, optional (see index)

In a saucepan, boil sugar and water until sugar is dissolved; add egg whites. While mixture is still warm, add pineapple and lemon juice; stir well. Place in an ice cream freezer and begin freezing.

Add cream when mixture is half frozen. If this is impossible, it may be added with pineapple and lemon juice.

When frozen, pack in plastic container and place in freezer for at least 1 hour to set.

If desired, serve with chocolate sauce.

NOTE: This sherbet must be made in a dasher-type freezer; it will crystallize if done in storage freezer.

Syllabub
4½ cups

1 cup dry white wine ¼ cup sugar ¼ cup brandy 1 tablespoon lemon juice 2 cups heavy cream, whipped	Combine first 4 ingredients. Let stand until sugar is dissolved. Add whipped cream and spoon into stemmed dessert glasses. NOTE: May also be frozen and served as ice cream.

Caramel Sauce
1½ cups

This sauce keeps indefinitely in the refrigerator.

1½ cups brown sugar 4 tablespoons butter ¾ cup light corn syrup 1 cup evaporated milk	In a saucepan, bring brown sugar, butter and corn syrup to a boil and cook to soft ball stage. When cool, beat in evaporated milk.

Praline Sauce
1 cup

This sauce is especially good over ice cream alone. However, it is elegant poured over an ice cream-filled cream puff.

½ cup brown sugar 1 tablespoon cornstarch ¼ teaspoon salt ⅓ cup light cream ¼ cup water 2 tablespoons light corn syrup ½ cup coarsely chopped pecans 1 tablespoon butter or margarine 1 tablespoon praline liqueur, optional 1 quart ice cream, vanilla, chocolate, coffee or butter pecan	In a small, heavy saucepan, combine brown sugar, cornstarch and salt. Stir in cream, water and corn syrup. Cook and stir until thickened and bubbly. (Mixture may appear curdled.) Cook and stir 1 to 2 minutes longer. Remove from heat. Stir in pecans, butter and liqueur. Cover and cool slightly. Serve over ice cream.

391

The Perfect Sugar Cookie

4-5 dozen

½ cup butter
½ cup shortening
½ cup sugar
½ cup powdered sugar
1 egg
1½ teaspoons vanilla
½ teaspoon baking soda
½ teaspoon cream of
tartar
½ teaspoon salt
2¼ cups flour

Cream butter, shortening, sugar and powdered sugar. Beat in egg and vanilla.

Sift dry ingredients and add to creamed mixture. Mix well. Refrigerate for 30 minutes to 1 hour. Roll out on floured surface to ⅛-inch thickness and cut with cookie cutters.

Bake at 375° about 8 minutes until edges begin to brown. Watch closely as they burn easily.

Cool. Spread generously with frosting.

FROSTING

2 cups powdered sugar
4 tablespoons butter or
margarine, softened
1 egg yolk
Milk or light cream

In a mixing bowl, combine powdered sugar, butter and egg yolk; mix well. Gradually add enough milk to reach spreading consistency. Beat thoroughly.

Sunny Sugar Cookies

8 dozen

1 cup sugar
1 cup powdered sugar
2 eggs
1 cup butter
1 cup oil
1 teaspoon vanilla
1 teaspoon salt
1 teaspoon baking soda
1 teaspoon cream of
tartar
4 cups + 2 tablespoons
flour
Sugar

Cream sugars, eggs, butter and oil. Add vanilla. Add dry ingredients and mix thoroughly. Form into small balls, flatten and sprinkle with sugar. Bake at 350° for 8 to 10 minutes.

Salzburger Nockerl

4 servings

A favorite brought from Austria by Peter Schott for his Continental Restaurant.

⅛ cup soft butter
½ cup sugar
8 egg whites
⅓ cup sugar
4 egg yolks
½ teaspoon pure vanilla
1 teaspoon freshly grated lemon and orange zest, mixed together
Powdered sugar

Preheat oven to 425°. Rub a large platter with film of soft butter and cover with the **½ cup** sugar; pour off excess sugar. In a mixer bowl, whip the egg whites at high speed for 30 seconds. Add the **⅓ cup** sugar. Continue beating until semi-stiff peaks appear. The whites should shine like satin.

In a cup, mix the egg yolks, vanilla, and the lemon and orange zest. Stir well with a spoon. Pour the yolk mixture into the whites and fold in briskly and thoroughly with a spatula. Do not worry about hurting the egg whites.

Using a rubber spatula, make 4 even mounds of batter on the sugared platter. Shape each one like a little mountain range and place so that they **barely** touch each other on the sides.

Bake about 5 minutes or until golden brown. Liberally sprinkle with powdered sugar and serve on individual plates. Accompany with a sweet dessert wine such as a sauterne.

Snowballs

3 dozen cookies

1 cup butter
½ cup powdered sugar
2 teaspoons vanilla
2 cups sifted flour
½ teaspoon salt
1 cup chopped walnuts
  or pecans
Powdered sugar

With a mixer, cream butter, sugar and vanilla until fluffy. Sift flour and salt together and add to creamed mixture. Blend well. Stir in nuts.

Refrigerate until cool. Shape into 1-inch balls. Bake on lightly greased cookie sheet at 325° for about 20 minutes. Cool and dust with powdered sugar.

Filbert Christmas Fruit Cake Cookies

3 dozen

1 cup butter
2 cups brown sugar
2 eggs
3½ cups flour, sifted
1 teaspoon baking soda
1 teaspoon salt
½ cup sour cream
1½ cups candied cherries
  (red and green)
1 cup candied pineapple
1½ cups dates
2 cups filberts, chopped
1½ cups broken pecans

Cream butter and sugar. Add eggs. Add **3 cups** of the flour, the soda, salt and sour cream.

Cut up fruit and in a large bowl, mix with nuts and dredge with remaining flour. Add batter and mix well with a wooden spoon. Batter will be stiff.

Drop in small mounds with a teaspoon on a greased cookie sheet. Bake at 350° for 10 to 12 minutes.

German Almond Cookies   10 dozen cookies

These cookies are special at Christmas and freeze well.

1 pound unsalted butter, softened

1 pound powdered sugar (3¾ cups)

4 ounces blanched almonds, finely chopped

3¼ cups flour

1 tablespoon baker's ammonia, finely crushed (available from pharmacist or bakery)

1 teaspoon vanilla

Cream butter and sugar. Add almonds and continue to cream.

Sift flour with baker's ammonia. Gradually add flour mixture to creamed mixture. Add vanilla and mix until dough is crumbly. Form into 1-inch balls. Place balls on an ungreased cookie sheet 1 inch apart. Bake at 350° for 12 to 15 minutes, until lightly golden on bottom.

NOTE: The ammonia bakes out during the cooking process, do not breath the air as the oven door opens.

Flash freeze marshmallows, rebag, and keep in freezer to avoid staleness.

Norwegian Spritz   6 dozen cookies

1½ cups butter or margarine

1 cup sugar

1 egg

1 teaspoon vanilla

½ teaspoon almond extract

4 cups flour, sifted

1 teaspoon baking powder

Thoroughly cream butter and sugar. Add egg, vanilla and almond extract. Beat well.

Sift flour again with baking powder. Add to creamed mixture. Mix until smooth.

Force dough through cookie press, forming various shapes. Bake on an ungreased cookie sheet at 400° for 8 to 10 minutes. Cool.

395

Speculaas

8 dozen cookies

1 cup unsalted butter,
   softened
1 cup sugar
1 cup brown sugar
2 eggs
4 cups sifted flour
2 teaspoons cinnamon
1 teaspoon freshly grated
   nutmeg
½ teaspoon ground
   cloves
½ teaspoon allspice
Pinch cardamom,
   optional
1 teaspoon baking
   powder
¼ cup milk
½ cup coarsely chopped
   nuts

In a large bowl, cream butter and sugars until fluffy. Beat in eggs, 1 at a time.

Over the same bowl, resift flour with spices and baking powder. Stir with a fork to blend, then knead gently. Add milk as needed. Add nuts and knead to make a smooth cookie dough.

Chill 3 hours before rolling out on a floured board to ⅛-inch thickness. Cut out cookies of desired shape or press patterns into dough with floured mold.

Bake at 350° for 10 minutes.

DO NOT OVERBAKE or cookies will be hard.

Biscotti

4 dozen cookies

Traditional Italian cookies.

½ cup butter **or**
   shortening
1 cup sugar
3 eggs
3 cups flour
3 teaspoons baking
   powder
½ teaspoon salt
1 teaspoon anise
   flavoring
1 cup chopped almonds

Cream butter and sugar thoroughly. Add eggs, 1 at a time, and beat well. Sift flour, measure in baking powder and salt. Add creamed mixture. Stir in flavoring and nuts.

Turn mixture onto a lightly floured board and knead until smooth. Divide dough in half. Form into 2 rolls the length of a cookie sheet and approximately 1½ inches in diameter.

Bake at 350° for 30 minutes or until rolls are firm to touch. While still warm, cut rolls crosswise into slices ¾-inch thick. Lay cut side down, on cookie sheet and return to oven. Bake 10 minutes longer to toast and dry out.

396

Mini Blinis

42 blinis

2 1-pound loaves thin
   sliced white bread
2 8-ounce packages
   cream cheese, softened
½ cup sugar
2 egg yolks
1 cup butter **or**
   margarine, melted
2 teaspoons cinnamon
½ cup sugar

Remove crust from bread slices and **flatten** each with a rolling pin.

Beat cream cheese, sugar and egg yolks until smooth. Spread a thin layer on bread and roll up like a jelly roll. Dip rolls into butter and sprinkle with cinnamon mixed with sugar.

Arrange on a cookie sheet and bake at 400° for 8 to 10 minutes until lightly browned.

Kieflies

4 dozen cookies

1 pound butter, softened
½ pint heavy cream
5¾ cups flour
12 egg yolks
Powdered sugar

Combine ingredients and mix well. Divide dough into 4 sections and chill overnight.

Roll walnut-sized pieces of dough into very thin circles. Place an ample teaspoon of filling on each. Roll up and crimp ends. Bake at 350° for 15 minutes. Sprinkle with powdered sugar.

FILLING

12 egg whites
½ teaspoon lemon juice
1½ pounds walnuts,
   finely grated
1 pound powdered sugar
Cinnamon

Beat egg whites until stiff and add remaining ingredients.

Transport cookies in popcorn to keep from breaking.

397

Coconut-Pecan Squares   64 1-inch squares

CRUST

½ cup butter
½ cup dark brown sugar
1 cup flour

Cream butter with brown sugar and add flour. Mix well.

Press mixture into a greased 8x8-inch pan, spreading dough evenly into the corners. Bake at 350° for 20 minutes.

TOPPING

2 eggs
1 cup light brown sugar
1 cup coarsely chopped pecans
½ cup coconut, mixed with 2 tablespoons flour
1 teaspoon vanilla
Dash salt
Powdered sugar

Beat eggs well. Add brown sugar and beat until thick.

Stir in pecans and coconut. Add vanilla and salt. Mix well. Spread over crust. Bake at 350° for 20 minutes or until well browned. Sprinkle with powdered sugar and cool. Cut into 1-inch squares.

Add 1 tablespoon vinegar to baking soda for a moister cake.

Roll fruits and raisins in flour before adding to cakes to keep them from sinking to the bottom.

Finger Cheesecake Bars

4 dozen bars

CRUST

⅔ cup butter **or**
  margarine
1 cup brown sugar
2 cups flour
1 cup chopped nuts

Beat together butter and brown sugar until blended. Mix in flour and nuts. Set aside **2 cups** of the mixture.

Lightly press remaining mixture into a greased 9x13-inch baking pan. Bake at 325° for 15 minutes.

FILLING

2 8-ounce packages
   cream cheese
1 cup sugar
¼ cup milk
½ teaspoon grated lemon
  peel, optional
4 teaspoons lemon juice,
  optional
1 teaspoon vanilla
2 eggs

Beat together cream cheese and sugar until blended. Stir in milk, lemon peel, lemon juice, vanilla and eggs. Beat until smooth.

Pour mixture over crust. Sprinkle remaining crust mixture over top. Bake at 325° for 35 minutes, or until knife inserted in center comes out clean. Cool, cover and chill. Cut in 1x2-inch bars.

Spiced Walnuts

3 cups

1½ cups sugar
1 teaspoon light corn
  syrup
¼ teaspoon salt
½ cup orange juice
½ teaspoon nutmeg
½ teaspoon ground
  cloves
2 teaspoons cinnamon
3 cups walnut pieces

In a medium saucepan, cook all ingredients, **except** walnuts, to soft ball stage (238°). Add walnuts, remove from heat and stir until creamy.

Turn onto waxed paper and separate with a fork. When cool, store in airtight container.

399

Canutillos (Basque Pastry)

Delicious pastries filled with pudding.

½ cup oil
½ cup Muscatel wine
1 cup flour
2 egg whites
Oil for frying

Mix oil and wine. Add flour gradually, until well mixed. Turn onto a floured board and knead until elastic, but still moist. Using a rolling pin, roll thin, using extra flour as needed. Cut in appropriate rectangles for cannoli forms (available at specialty shops) and roll around each, sealing each with egg white.

Heat ¼ inch oil in a large skillet on high. Lower heat to medium and fry each canutillo until brown. Remove from oil. Allow to cool. Remove pastry from tube. Roll again with remaining dough and repeat until all pastry is used.

Using a pastry tube, fill canutillos with filling.

FILLING

1½ cups milk
¼ cup sugar
1½ tablespoons cornstarch
2 egg yolks, beaten
1 teaspoon vanilla

In a small heavy saucepan, slowly heat milk just until bubbles form around edge of pan.

Meanwhile, in a small bowl, combine sugar and cornstarch. Stir to mix well. Stir in hot milk all at once. Cook, stirring constantly, over medium heat, until mixture boils. Reduce heat and simmer 1 minute.

Canutillos *(Continued)*

Beat a small amount of the hot mixture into egg yolks. Add yolks to milk mixture and cook, stirring, over medium heat, until mixture boils and thickens. Stir in vanilla.

Cool with waxed paper directly on surface of filling to prevent film.

Basque Tostadas

2 dozen

3½ cups cold milk
¾ cup sugar
1¼ cups unbleached
  flour, unsifted
5 eggs, 4 whole and
  1 separated
2 large cinnamon sticks
Dash salt
1 teaspoon vanilla
Unbleached flour
Oil for frying
Cinnamon/sugar mixture

In a heavy saucepan, measure milk. Mix sugar and flour together in a bowl. With a wire whisk, add flour mixture to milk.

Beat 1 egg yolk and add to milk mixture with cinnamon sticks, salt and vanilla. Cook over medium heat until very thick, stirring constantly with a wooden spoon. Reduce heat if necessary. Remove cinnamon sticks.

Sprinkle cookie sheet with flour and spread mixture on sheet. Chill several hours or overnight.

Heat approximately 1 inch oil in a skillet to medium-high heat. Cut tostadas into 4-inch squares. Dip in flour, then in remaining eggs, beaten. Fry in oil until brown. Drain on paper towels and sprinkle with cinnamon/sugar mixture.

Baked Caramel Corn

2½ quarts

½ cup butter **or**
  margarine
1 cup brown sugar
¼ cup corn syrup
½ teaspoon salt
¼ teaspoon baking soda
½ teaspoon vanilla
3 quarts popped popcorn

In a 1½-quart saucepan melt butter, stir in brown sugar, corn syrup and salt. Heat to boiling, stirring constantly. Boil over medium heat for 5 minutes, without stirring. Remove from heat. Stir in baking soda and vanilla.

In a large bowl gradually pour hot syrup over popped corn, mixing well. Pour coated popcorn into a buttered 12x17-inch roasting pan. Bake uncovered at 300° for 30 minutes, stirring after 15 minutes. Remove from oven, cool completely in pan. Loosen popcorn with spatula and break into pieces.

Store in tightly covered container.

Popcorn Cake

2 cakes

This is so easy if you buy popped corn. Children love it.

½ cup butter
½ cup oil
1 pound miniature
  marshmallows
1 cup nuts (mixed, or of
  one kind)
1 8 to 10-ounce package
  small gum drops
6 quarts popped corn
  (unsalted, no grease)

Melt together the butter, oil and marshmallows.

In a large bowl, combine the nuts, the gum drops and popcorn. Pour the melted marshmallow mixture over all, mixing quickly and thoroughly.

Press into a buttered angel food cake pan. Depending on size of pan, this may make two large cakes. Let set up 10 or 15 minutes and pop out of pan.

NOTE: Any shape of pan could be used.

Bound to Please: Sawtooth Splendor

Already ten million years old, the Sawtooth Mountains are the youngest in Idaho, nestling within them rugged peaks, alpine lakes, and the headwaters of the Salmon, the "River of No Return." Captain B.L.E. Bonneville visited the North Fork of the Salmon in 1825, and there reportedly discovered "a cessation from toil, from hunger, and from alarm."

Today's backpackers, hunters, and hikers agree with Captain Bonneville's description, making the area a popular summer attraction. In 1972, Congress established the Sawtooth National Recreation Area to protect the region's history, wildlife, and pristine beauty.

Desserts

Candy & Confections

Pies

Cakes & Cheesecakes

Cookies & Bars

Sauces

Frostings

Jamoca Whizz

1 quart Jamoca ice cream
3 ounces brandy
3 ounces crème de cacao
Heavy cream **or** milk, if
  necessary
Bittersweet chocolate,
  optional

In a blender, mix ice cream, brandy and crème de cacao until smooth. (If possible, put ice cream in microwave at full power for 45 seconds so it is easier to blend.) A little cream or milk may be added to reach milkshake consistency.

Pour into stemmed glasses and chill. Garnish with shaved bittersweet chocolate if desired.

Délices au Chocolat

½ pound sweet
  chocolate
2 tablespoons butter
Hot water
¾ tablespoon unflavored
  gelatin, softened in
  cold water
1 cup hot milk
3 to 4 tablespoons sugar
Dash salt
½ pint heavy cream,
  stiffly beaten
Brandy
Grated unsweetened
  chocolate

In a double boiler, combine sweet chocolate, butter and a small amount of hot water. Stir until chocolate is dissolved. Coat the inside of small fluted paper cups with mixture. Refrigerate until firm.

Dissolve softened gelatin in hot milk. Add sugar and salt. Cool mixture. Add whipped cream and brandy to taste.

To serve, remove paper from chocolate cups. Pour filling into cups and top with grated chocolate.

Chocolate is a quick energy food that contains protein, carbohydrate and fat and several vitamins and minerals.

Million $$$ Mousse

12 servings

3 cups chocolate wafer
  crumbs
½ cup butter, melted
1 pound semisweet
  chocolate
6 eggs (4 of which are
  separated)
2 cups whipping cream
5 tablespoons powdered
  sugar

Combine crumbs and butter (a food processor works great). Press on bottom and sides (all the way up) of a 10-inch springform pan. Refrigerate or freeze until hard.

Melt chocolate carefully in top of double boiler. Let cool slightly. Add the **2 whole** eggs and mix well. Add the **4 egg yolks** and blend thoroughly. Beat cream with powdered sugar until soft peaks form.

Beat the **4 egg whites** until stiff, but not dry. Stir a little of the whipped cream into the chocolate mixture. Fold in remaining whipped cream and the beaten egg whites until completely combined (a whisk works best). Pour into crust and chill overnight.

Variation: Omit crust and put in individual wine glasses or a large soufflé dish.

The mousse may also be frozen and thawed several hours in refrigerator. Decorate with chocolate leaves after removing from springform pan.

CHOCOLATE LEAVES

4 ounces semisweet
  chocolate
½ tablespoon vegetable
  shortening
Waxy leaves (such as
  hoya, Oregon grape,
  camelia)

Melt chocolate and shortening in double boiler. Using a spoon, coat underside of leaves. Place on waxed paper and freeze. To separate, begin at stem end and gently pull apart.

To be sure the chocolate doesn't overcook, remove it from the heat a bit before it is completely melted.

Budino Amaro

2 cups milk
3 ounces unsweetened chocolate
3 ounces semisweet chocolate
3 egg yolks
3 tablespoons sugar
1 package unflavored gelatin
½ cup water
1½ teaspoons vanilla
½ teaspoon almond extract
½ teaspoon orange extract
4 tablespoons Drambuie or brandy
2 tablespoons strong coffee
½ cup heavy cream

Combine milk and chocolates in double boiler until melted and blended.

Cream yolks with sugar until pale.

Soften gelatin in water and add to chocolate. Stir in vanilla, almond and orange extracts along with Drambuie and coffee.

Slowly pour hot chocolate mixture into the yolks, beating constantly. Return to double boiler and stir until thickened. Cool. Refrigerate until begins to set.

Whip cream lightly and fold into chocolate mixture. Turn into serving bowl.

CREMA ZABAIONE

3 egg yolks
3 tablespoons sugar
½ cup Marsala
1 cup heavy cream
2 tablespoons powdered sugar

Beat yolks and sugar in top of double boiler. Slowly beat in Marsala. Beat until stiff, remove from heat and beat for 3 minutes. Let cool.

Whip the cream, add sugar, beat until thick. Fold into zabaione. Cover and refrigerate. Serve over budino.

Cocoa may be used in place of baking chocolate.
3 tablespoons of cocoa plus 1 tablespoon of shortening
or oil equals 1 ounce (1 square) of baking chocolate.

Classic Chocolate Soufflé
6 servings

3 tablespoons butter
2 tablespoons flour
1 cup milk
2½ ounces unsweetened chocolate, shaved
⅓ cup sugar
Pinch salt
4 eggs, separated
2 cups heavy cream, sweetened and whipped

In a saucepan, melt butter. Remove from heat, blend in flour, stirring until smooth. Gradually add milk, stirring until mixture begins to thicken.

Add shaved chocolate, sugar and salt. Cook over low heat about 5 minutes or until slightly thickened, stirring constantly. Remove from heat and cool slightly.

Beat egg yolks until thick and lemon colored. Gradually add chocolate mixture, stirring steadily.

Beat egg whites until stiff but not dry. Fold into chocolate mixture. Lightly butter a 1½-quart soufflé dish and sprinkle with sugar. Pour chocolate mixture into prepared dish, set dish in pan half-filled with water.

Bake in a preheated 400° oven for 15 minutes, reduce oven to 375° and bake for 20 minutes. Serve at once with well-chilled whipped cream.

French Mint Pies
50-60 miniature pies

The key to this recipe is to beat and beat and beat!

1 cup butter
2 heaping cups powdered sugar
4 squares unsweetened chocolate
4 eggs
1 teaspoon peppermint flavoring
2 teaspoons vanilla

Combine butter and sugar and beat thoroughly. Melt chocolate and cool. Add chocolate to butter mixture and mix well.

Add eggs, 1 at a time, and beat thoroughly after **each** addition. Add flavoring. Pour into fluted candy papers and freeze. Do not thaw before serving.

Chocolate Ring

8 servings

2½ cups milk
⅔ cup sugar
Dash salt
½ cup finely ground
  toasted almonds
4 teaspoons unflavored
  gelatin
1 teaspoon almond
  extract
1 cup heavy cream,
  whipped

In a double boiler, heat **2 cups** of the milk, the sugar and salt. When hot, add almonds. Cover and remove from heat allowing flavors to blend for 15 to 20 minutes.

Soak gelatin in remaining milk until softened and add to milk mixture. Heat until gelatin is dissolved. Cool and add flavoring.

When mixture begins to thicken, beat hard until fluffy. Fold whipped cream into mixture. Spoon into a 5-cup ring mold. Chill. When firm turn onto a platter or serving dish and coat with sauce.

SAUCE

1⅓ cups milk
3 squares unsweetened
  chocolate
Dash salt
⅓ cup sugar
2 teaspoons cornstarch
1 teaspoon vanilla
⅓ cup heavy cream

In a double boiler, heat milk, chocolate and salt. When chocolate is melted, add sugar and blend well. Heat until sugar is dissolved.

Stir cornstarch into a little cold water. Add to sauce and stir constantly until mixture is smooth and thick. Cool slightly and add vanilla. Thin sauce to the consistency of thick cream by adding cream, a little at a time.

If chocolate should stiffen when melting, you can salvage it by adding shortening such as Crisco, 1 teaspoon for each ounce of chocolate.

Chocolate-
Kahlua Cheesecake

10-12 servings

1¼ cups graham cracker
  crumbs
1 cup + 2 tablespoons
  sugar
¾ cup cocoa
⅓ cup butter **or**
  margarine, melted
2 8-ounce packages
  cream cheese,
  softened
2 eggs
¼ cup strong coffee
¼ cup Kahlua or other
  coffee-flavored liqueur
2 teaspoons vanilla
1 cup sour cream
6 to 8 chocolate curls,
  optional

Combine cracker crumbs, **¼ cup** of
the sugar, **¼ cup** of the cocoa and the
butter and mix well. Firmly press
mixture onto the bottom of a 9-inch
springform pan. Bake at 325° for
5 minutes. Cool.

Beat cream cheese with an electric
mixer until light and fluffy. Gradually
add **¾ cup** of the sugar, mixing well.
Beat in remaining cocoa. Add eggs,
1 at a time, beating well after each
addition. Stir in coffee, Kahlua and
1 teaspoon of the vanilla. Pour into
prepared pan. Bake at 375° for
25 minutes. Filling will be soft but will
firm up as cake stands.

Combine sour cream, remaining
2 tablespoons sugar, and remaining
vanilla. Spread over hot cheesecake.
Bake at 425° for 5 to 7 minutes. Let
cool to room temperature on a wire
rack. Chill 8 hours or overnight.
Remove sides of springform pan.

To garnish, place **3** chocolate curls in
center of cheesecake. Gently break
remaining chocolate curls, and sprinkle
over cheesecake, if desired.

*Chocolate should be stored where it is cool and dry and
the temperature is about 68 to 78 degrees.*

A Divine Cheesecake

2 8-ounce packages
  cream cheese, softened
¾ cup sugar
2 eggs
2 tablespoons Grand
  Marnier
1 teaspoon grated
  orange peel
¾ tablespoon sour cream
1 teaspoon vanilla
2 ounces unsweetened
  baking chocolate

With an electric mixer, beat cream cheese until softened. Beat in sugar. Add eggs, 1 at a time, beating well after each addition. Blend in Grand Marnier, orange peel, sour cream and vanilla.

In a double boiler melt chocolate. Add a generous teaspoon of cream cheese mixture to melted chocolate to loosen, then add chocolate to the cheese mixture. Stir to create a marbleized effect.

Pour mixture into crust. Bake at 350° for 45 minutes or until set.

Let cheesecake cool slightly. Spread topping over cheesecake and bake 15 minutes longer. Refrigerate until serving time. May be made the day ahead.

CRUST

1½ cups graham cracker
  crumbs
½ cup sugar
½ cup butter, melted

Combine cracker crumbs, sugar and butter in a bowl and mix well. Pat into bottom and sides of a 9-inch springform pan. Refrigerate until ready to use.

TOPPING

1 cup sour cream
2 tablespoons sugar
3 teaspoons vanilla

Combine sour cream, sugar and vanilla and blend well.

Use cocoa to dust pans for chocolate cake.

409

Soft-Hearted Chocolate Cake   12 servings

1 pound sweet dipping
  chocolate, light or dark
1 tablespoon sugar
1 tablespoon flour
⅔ cup butter, softened
4 eggs, separated
1 cup whipping cream,
  whipped and
  sweetened

Grease bottom of 8-inch springform pan.

In a double boiler, melt chocolate very slowly over warm water. Remove from heat. Add sugar, flour and butter, mixing thoroughly.

In a small bowl, lightly beat egg yolks. Add to chocolate mixture.

Beat egg whites until stiff but not dry and fold into chocolate mixture. Pour mixture into prepared pan and bake at 425° for exactly 18 minutes. NO LONGER!

Let cool completely (cake will sink in center as it cools). Chill or freeze.

Serve with whipped cream mounded in center of cake.

Gâteau Saint Germaine   8-10 servings

1 baked angel food cake
1 pint heavy cream,
  whipped and
  sweetened

Carefully remove middle of angel food cake by slicing off the top (about an inch) and set aside. Cut a trench around the center of the cake with a serrated knife, leaving a wall about ½ to ¾ inch thick. Fill center hole with some pieces of cake.

Pour filling into trench. Replace top. Frost entire cake with whipped cream. Refrigerate for 24 hours.

NOTE: If cake is prepared ahead and frozen, do not frost with whipped cream until ready to serve.

410

Gâteau Saint Germaine *(Continued)*

FILLING

6 egg yolks, beaten
1 cup sugar
1 cup butter, softened
4 ounces bitter chocolate,
   melted
4 egg whites, lightly
   beaten

Cream egg yolks and sugar. Add
butter and chocolate. Beat well to mix.
Gently fold in beaten egg whites.

Koffee Klatsch Cake   1 8-inch cake

A delicious recipe from the Koffee Klatsch, Boise.

1 cup prepared coffee,
   room temperature
¾ cup honey
½ cup corn oil
1 teaspoon vanilla
   extract
1 tablespoon vinegar
1½ cups all-purpose flour
¼ cup cocoa powder
½ teaspoon salt
¼ teaspoon ground
   allspice
¼ teaspoon ground
   cloves
1 teaspoon baking soda
Whipped cream

Preheat oven to 300°. Oil an 8-inch
square baking pan; set aside. In a
small bowl, combine coffee, honey, oil,
vanilla and vinegar. Stir to blend well.
Sift remaining dry ingredients into
medium bowl. Add coffee-honey
mixture, blend, and pour into prepared
pan. Bake in preheated oven 1 hour to
1 hour and 15 minutes or until top
springs back when lightly touched with
fingertips. Cool in pan on rack
5 minutes. Cut into squares and serve
warm topped with whipped cream.

Devil's Food-Potato Cake   1 3-layer cake

½ cup milk
3 squares unsweetened
  chocolate
1 cup hot, fresh mashed
  potatoes
1 cup shortening
2 cups sugar
4 eggs, separated
2 cups sifted cake flour
3 teaspoons baking
  powder
¼ teaspoon salt
1½ teaspoons vanilla

Heat milk and chocolate together. Stir until melted, add to potatoes, and blend well. Cream shortening and **1¾ cups** sugar until light and fluffy. Add to chocolate mixture. Add egg yolks and beat well.

Sift together flour, baking powder and salt. Stir into chocolate mixture slowly and add vanilla. Make a meringue by gradually beating remaining sugar into egg whites.

Fold meringue into cake batter and pour into 3 8-inch greased and floured layer cake pans. Bake in a preheated 350° oven for 25 to 30 minutes or until done.

When slightly cool, invert on rack and let cool. Frost with creamy vanilla frosting.

Chocolate-Chocolate Cake   1 Bundt cake

So easy the kids can make it. So rich all you true chocolate addicts will love it.

1 package chocolate
  fudge cake mix
1 6⅛-ounce package
  chocolate fudge
  instant pudding mix
1 12-ounce package
  semisweet chocolate
  chips
4 eggs
½ pint sour cream
½ cup warm water
½ cup oil
Powdered sugar

In a large bowl, beat all ingredients **except** powdered sugar together. Pour into greased and floured Bundt pan.

Bake at 350° for 45 minutes or until cake springs back when touched lightly on top.

Let cool 30 minutes in pan. Invert on platter and dust with powdered sugar.

412

Buttermilk-Sweet Chocolate Cake

1 13x15-inch cake or
1 11x17-inch cake

2 cups sugar
1 teaspoon baking soda
2 cups flour
½ teaspoon salt
1 cup margarine
4 tablespoons cocoa
1 cup water
½ cup buttermilk
1 teaspoon vanilla
2 eggs, lightly beaten

In a large mixing bowl, sift together sugar, soda, flour and salt.

In a small saucepan, melt margarine, add cocoa and water. Stir until well blended. Bring to a rapid boil and pour over dry ingredients, mixing well.

While hot, add buttermilk, vanilla and eggs. Mix well.

Grease and flour either a 13x15-inch or an 11x17-inch pan. Bake at 350° for 15-20 minutes. Pour icing over hot cake and spread evenly.

HOT BUTTERMILK ICING

1 cup margarine
4 tablespoons cocoa
6 tablespoons buttermilk
1 pound powdered sugar
  (approximately
  3¾ cups)
1 teaspoon vanilla
1 cup chopped nuts

In a saucepan, melt margarine. Add cocoa and buttermilk and stir until combined. Heat to boiling and remove from heat. Beat in powdered sugar, vanilla and nuts.

When you melt chocolate with no other ingredients, the container you melt it in and the tool you stir it with must be absolutely dry or the chocolate may become stiff and lumpy.

Chocolate

Outing Club Cake

8-10 servings

1 cup flour
2 teaspoons baking
   powder
½ teaspoon salt
¾ cup sugar
2 tablespoons cocoa
½ cup milk
1 teaspoon vanilla
2 tablespoons melted
   shortening
Ice cream
Chocolate syrup

In mixer, combine all ingredients **except** ice cream and chocolate syrup. Mix well and pour into a 9-inch greased metal ring mold. Pour topping over batter and bake at 350° for 40 to 45 minutes.

Before serving, warm cake in 300° oven for 15 minutes. Invert onto serving plate. Fill center with ice cream and top with chocolate syrup.

TOPPING

¾ cup brown sugar
¼ cup cocoa
¾ cup hot water

Combine all ingredients.

Sinful Chocolate

1 pie

A special treat for the chocolate addict.

7 ounces semisweet
   chocolate
1 cup sugar
1 cup butter
½ cup strong coffee
4 eggs
Whipped cream

Line the bottom of an 8-inch springform pan with buttered foil.

In a small pan over medium heat, melt chocolate, sugar, butter and coffee until well mixed. Cool.

Beat eggs into mixture. Pour into a springform pan and bake at 350° for 45 minutes or until it cracks around the sides. Remove from oven. Cool. Refrigerate overnight.

Unmold, invert onto plate, cover with unsweetened whipped cream.

414

Dobosch Torte

8-12 servings

Very fast, elegant and easy.

1 purchased loaf pound
cake, partially frozen
1 6-ounce package
semisweet chocolate
chips
¼ cup boiling water
4 egg yolks
1 teaspoon vanilla
¼ cup butter

Slice pound cake into 6 thin lengthwise layers.

Place chocolate chips in blender. Add boiling water and blend for about 50 seconds or until chips are completely melted. Add egg yolks and vanilla. Turn blender on low speed and add butter in small pieces.

Frost between layers of cake and also top and sides. Chill. Wrap cake in foil and freeze. Slice and serve.

Frozen Chocolate Torte

12 servings

1 7-ounce can almond
paste
1 tablespoon cocoa
5 eggs
6 ounces semisweet
chocolate
2 teaspoons instant
coffee
1 tablespoon brandy
2 tablespoons sugar
½ cup heavy cream,
whipped

Place almond paste, cocoa and 2 of the eggs in food processor or mixer and blend until smooth. Spread pastry into a greased and floured 8 or 9-inch springform pan. Bake at 375° for 15 minutes. Cool on wire rack.

Separate 2 of the eggs. Beat egg whites until foamy. Add sugar and beat until stiff, but still moist. In separate bowl, whip the cream. Set aside.

In a double boiler, melt chocolate.

In a large mixing bowl, beat yolks with remaining whole egg. Beat in coffee, brandy and melted chocolate.

Fold beaten egg whites into chocolate mixture then fold in whipped cream.

Spread filling over cooled crust and freeze. Thaw 15 minutes before serving.

415

Chocolate-Rum Torte

14 servings

1 6-ounce package semisweet chocolate chips
½ cup sour cream
½ cup powdered sugar
¼ teaspoon salt
1 teaspoon vanilla
1 10-inch angel food cake
3 tablespoons rum
1 cup heavy cream, whipped (use 2 cups for more generous frosting)
½ cup slivered almonds

In a double boiler, melt chocolate chips, stirring until smooth. Remove top of the double boiler from the water and blend in sour cream, powdered sugar, salt and vanilla. Beat until smooth.

Cut angel food cake crosswise into 4 layers. Sprinkle layers with rum. Spread layers with chocolate filling and reassemble. Frost top and sides with whipped cream and garnish with almonds.

NOTE: Use a serrated knife to slice. This cake may be frozen. Let stand at room temperature about 40 minutes before slicing.

Chocolate-Almond Torte

8 servings

½ cup butter
½ cup slivered almonds, chopped
1 cup flour
½ cup sugar
1 cup whipping cream, whipped
1 quart chocolate ice cream
¼ cup rum

In a skillet over medium heat, melt butter and add almonds. Toast, stirring constantly until almonds are golden brown.

Add flour and sugar to the almonds, stirring until mixture is golden and crumbly, about 6-8 minutes. Reserve ¾ cup of the crumb mixture.

Press mixture into bottom and sides of an 8-inch springform pan and freeze 2 hours.

Beat whipping cream into soft peaks and set aside. Soften ice cream; fold in rum and whipped cream. Spoon into crumb crust and freeze again until partially set. Sprinkle reserved crumb mixture over the top and return to freezer for at least 2 hours or until ready to serve.

416

Christmas Pie

1 12-ounce package semisweet chocolate chips
1 cup milk
¾ cup sugar
1 envelope unflavored gelatin
½ teaspoon salt
2 eggs, separated
¼ cup rum
1 cup heavy cream, whipped
2 tablespoons powdered sugar
1 9-inch pie shell, baked
1 3-ounce package cream cheese, softened

In a double boiler, combine chocolate chips, milk, **¼ cup** of the sugar, gelatin and salt over hot water. Heat until gelatin is dissolved and mixture is smooth.

Quickly beat in egg yolks and continue cooking for 2 minutes, stirring constantly.

Remove from heat, stir in rum. Refrigerate until completely cool and slightly thickened, about 1 hour.

In a small bowl, beat egg whites until frothy. Gradually beat in remaining sugar and continue beating until stiff, glossy peaks form. Fold into cooled chocolate mixture. Set aside.

In a small bowl, combine cream and powdered sugar. Beat until stiff peaks form.

Spread half the chocolate mixture into pie shell. Spread whipped cream over chocolate layer. Cover with remaining chocolate mixture.

Decorate with dollops of softened cream cheese or pipe through a pastry tube. Chill until firm, about 1 hour.

You can interchange semisweet chocolate pieces and semisweet chocolate squares.

German-Chocolate Pie
1 9-inch pie

A rich and delectable favorite from Nina Mae's, Boise.

4 ounces sweet chocolate
¼ cup butter
1 14-ounce can
  sweetened condensed
  milk
½ cup flour
1 teaspoon vanilla
⅛ teaspoon salt
2 eggs, beaten
1⅓ cups grated coconut
1 cup chopped pecans
1 9-inch unbaked pie
  shell

In a saucepan, melt chocolate and butter over low heat. Remove from heat and add condensed milk, flour, vanilla, salt and eggs. Mix well.

Reserve ¼ cup of the coconut for garnish. Stir remaining coconut and nuts into pie mixture. Pour into pie shell. Sprinkle reserved coconut over top. Bake at 350° for 40 to 50 minutes or until top is firm and coconut is lightly browned. Cool thoroughly before cutting.

Brandy-Black Bottom Pie
1 9-inch pie

1½ cups crushed graham
  crackers
4 tablespoons butter,
  melted
1 4-ounce bar German
  sweet chocolate
4 tablespoons hot water
3 eggs, separated
½ cup sugar
¾ cup milk
1 envelope unflavored
  gelatin
½ cup cold water
2 tablespoons brandy

Mix graham crackers with melted butter and press evenly over bottom and sides of a 9-inch pie pan. Melt chocolate with water and pour gently over bottom of crust.

Beat egg yolks and cook in a double boiler with sugar and milk until thick, stirring constantly. Remove from heat. Soften gelatin in cold water and add to mixture. Cool until it begins to set.

Beat egg whites until stiff. Stir brandy into cooled mixture and fold in egg whites. Pour into crust. Chill until firm. Spread with topping.

TOPPING

½ pint heavy cream
2 tablespoons sugar
2 tablespoons brandy

Whip cream with sugar and brandy until stiff.

418

Kahlua and Cream Pie

8-12 servings

½ cup butter
24 cream-filled chocolate
  cookies
1 cup sugar
1 envelope unflavored
  gelatin
Dash salt
2 eggs, separated
2 cups heavy cream
1 12-ounce package
  semisweet chocolate
  chips
½ cup Kahlua
1 teaspoon vanilla
Heavy cream, whipped,
  optional

In a saucepan, melt butter and mix with crushed cookies. Press onto bottom and sides of very deep pie plate or 10-inch springform pan. Chill.

Combine ¼ **cup** sugar, gelatin and salt in the top of a double boiler. Beat egg yolks with **1 cup** of the cream. Add to gelatin mixture. Cook until slightly thickened.

Add chocolate chips. Cook until melted. Cool. Stir in Kahlua.

Beat egg whites until foamy. Add ½ **cup** of the sugar and beat until stiff and glossy. Fold into chocolate mixture.

Whip remaining cream, vanilla and remaining sugar until partially whipped, enough to hold together and spread easily. Alternate white and chocolate layers in chilled cookie crust. Swirl with a knife to marble.

Chill several hours, preferably overnight. Cover with plastic wrap if overnight. Top with additional cream if desired.

Baking chocolate burns very easily – watch it carefully while it melts.

Pecan-Chocolate Chip Pie
1 9-inch pie

A wonderful and rich dessert from the HasBrouck House, Nampa.

2 eggs
1 cup sugar
½ cup flour
½ cup butter, melted and cooled
1 teaspoon rum flavoring or 3 tablespoons rum
1 cup milk chocolate chips
1 cup pecans
1 9-inch unbaked pie shell

Beat eggs until well mixed and frothy. Add ingredients in order, mixing well after each addition. Pour into pie shell and bake at 325° approximately 30 minutes.

Mile-High Ice Cream Pie
1 9-inch pie

1 baked 9-inch pie shell
1 pint French vanilla ice cream, softened
1 pint chocolate ice cream, softened
6 to 8 egg whites, room temperature
½ teaspoon vanilla
¼ teaspoon cream of tartar
1 cup sugar

In cooled pie crust, layer vanilla ice cream, then chocolate ice cream. Freeze.

Beat egg whites with vanilla and cream of tartar until soft peaks form. Gradually beat in sugar, **2 tablespoons** at a time, beating until stiff and glossy and sugar is dissolved.

Spread meringue over frozen pie to edges of pastry. Broil 30 seconds to 1 minute to brown meringue. Watch constantly! Freeze for several hours.

SAUCE

2 ounces German sweet chocolate
2 ounces unsweetened chocolate
½ cup heavy cream
¾ cup sugar

In a double boiler, combine all ingredients and cook until thick and smooth.

Drizzle sauce over each serving or pass sauce in a separate bowl.

420

Toffee-Mocha-Rum Pie

8 servings

½ 10-ounce package pie
   crust mix
¼ cup brown sugar
¾ cup finely chopped
   walnuts **or** almonds
1 square unsweetened
   chocolate, grated
1 tablespoon water
1 teaspoon vanilla
½ cup unsalted butter,
   softened
¾ cup sugar
1 square unsweetened
   chocolate, melted and
   cooled
3 tablespoons instant
   coffee
2 eggs
3 teaspoons rum extract
2 cups heavy cream
½ cup powdered sugar

Combine pie crust mix with brown sugar, walnuts and **grated** chocolate. Add water and vanilla; mix with a fork until well blended. Place in a well-buttered 9-inch pie plate, pressing against sides and bottom. Bake at 375° for 15 minutes. Cool.

Beat butter until creamy, gradually adding sugar. Blend in **melted** chocolate and **2 tablespoons** of the instant coffee. Add eggs, 1 at a time, beating for 5 minutes after each. Add **2 teaspoons** of the rum extract. Place chocolate mixture in pie shell and refrigerate covered overnight.

Combine cream with remaining coffee and the powdered sugar. Refrigerate covered for 1 hour. Beat until stiff, add remaining rum extract. Blend. Refrigerate for at least 2 hours. Spread over top of chocolate mixture in pie shell.

Garnish with grated chocolate or chocolate curls if desired.

Be sure to read chocolate labels carefully to make sure you are buying real and not artificial chocolate.

Frozen Champagne Cream in Chocolate Cups with Chocolate Sauce

8 servings

¾ cup brut champagne
½ cup sugar
5 egg yolks
1½ cups whipping cream

Combine ½ **cup** of the champagne and the sugar in saucepan. Bring to boil and continue boiling, without stirring, to soft ball stage.

Beat egg yolks until thick and lemon colored. Add syrup in thin stream, beating constantly, about 10 minutes. Gradually blend in the remaining champagne. Chill.

Whip cream in chilled bowl until stiff. Fold into champagne mixture. Cover, freeze overnight.

To serve, peel paper from chocolate cups. Spoon champagne cream into cups. Put 1 teaspoon champagne cream onto dessert plates; put chocolate cup on top to hold in place. Drizzle chocolate sauce over top.

CHOCOLATE CUPS

6 ounces semisweet real
  chocolate chips
8 paper cupcake liners
  (⅓ cup size)

Partially melt chocolate in top of double boiler. When melted, brush bottom and sides of paper cup liners with chocolate, building up sides thickly. Invert onto baking sheet and freeze.

CHOCOLATE SAUCE

6 tablespoons brut
  champagne
3 ounces (½ cup)
  semisweet real
  chocolate chips
1 tablespoon sugar
2 tablespoons butter

Combine all ingredients except butter until melted. Add butter and whisk until melted. Remove from heat. Keep warm.

422

Mud Pie
1 9-inch pie

22 (approximately)
chocolate wafers
¼ cup butter, melted
1 quart coffee ice cream
(vanilla may be used by
mixing softened ice
cream with
   1 tablespoon instant
   coffee dissolved in
   1 tablespoon boiling
   water)
1 4-ounce package
chopped almonds,
toasted
1 cup Chocolate Sauce –
Best in the World (see
index)
1 cup heavy cream,
whipped

Crush chocolate wafers. In a bowl,
add butter to wafers and mix well.
Press into a 9-inch pie plate. Bake at
375° for 8 minutes. Chill.

Fill crust with softened ice cream and
sprinkle with **half** the nuts. Freeze.

Spread chocolate sauce over pie and
return to freezer.

Top with whipped cream and remaining
nuts. Freeze.

Remove from freezer 15 minutes
before serving.

White Chocolate Ice Cream
1 quart

1 cup water
¾ cup sugar
6 egg yolks
1 tablespoon light rum
12 ounces white
chocolate*melted
2 cups whipping cream

*NOTE: Real white chocolate
must contain cocoa butter,
and a combination of sugar,
milk solids and vanilla.

Combine water and sugar in
saucepan. Cook over low heat until
sugar dissolves, stirring occasionally.
Bring mixture to a boil, and boil for
5 minutes.

Combine yolks and rum in the large
bowl of an electric mixer; beat at high
speed until light and fluffy, 8 minutes.
Slowly add hot syrup to yolk mixture,
beating constantly until thickened and
completely cool, 12 minutes.

Gradually add the white chocolate and
continue beating until cool, 8 minutes.
Stir in cream. Cover and freeze
overnight.

423

Chocolate-
Peppermint Freeze

8 servings

1¼ cups finely crushed
  vanilla wafers (about
  28)
4 tablespoons margarine,
  melted
1 quart peppermint ice
  cream, softened **or**
  vanilla ice cream
  flavored with
  peppermint extract
½ cup margarine
2 squares unsweetened
  chocolate
3 eggs, separated
1½ cups sifted powdered
  sugar
½ cup chopped nuts
1 teaspoon vanilla

Toss together the crumbs and melted margarine. Reserve ¼ **cup** crumb mixture. Press remaining mixture into a 9x9-inch pan.

Spread softened ice cream over crumb mixture and freeze.

Melt margarine and chocolate over low heat. Gradually stir chocolate mixture into well beaten egg yolks, alternating with powdered sugar, nuts and vanilla. Cool thoroughly.

Beat egg whites until stiff. Beat chocolate mixture until smooth. Fold in egg whites.

Spread chocolate mixture over ice cream. Top with reserved crumb mixture. Freeze. Cut into squares to serve.

Real white chocolate must contain cocoa butter and a combination of sugar, milk solids and vanilla – largely the same as those in milk chocolate, but without the chocolate liquor.

Sinful Strawberry Tart

8 servings

1 recipe Rich Pie Crust, baked and cooled in a 9-inch tart pan (see index)
1 6-ounce package semisweet real chocolate chips
2 tablespoons butter, melted
3 tablespoons Grand Marnier
¼ cup powdered sugar
1 tablespoon water
1½ pints fresh strawberries, rinsed, stemmed and dried

Melt chocolate in top of double boiler. Add butter and Grand Marnier and stir until smooth. Add powdered sugar and water, stirring until smooth. While still warm, pour into crust.

Place strawberries over chocolate filling. Brush strawberries with warm glaze.

Refrigerate tart about 2 hours before serving.

GLAZE

3 tablespoons red currant jelly
1 tablespoon Grand Marnier

Heat jelly and Grand Marnier slowly until of spreading consistency.

Chocolate-Dipped Strawberries with Orange Cream

24 servings

24 strawberries
Orange-flavored liqueur
8 ounces semisweet
chocolate
¾ cup heavy cream
1 tablespoon powdered
sugar
1 tablespoon orange-
flavored liqueur

With cooking injection needle, inject 24 unblemished strawberries, stems attached, with orange liqueur and let them stand at room temperature for 30 minutes.

In top of a double boiler, over warm water, melt chocolate. Stir constantly until candy thermometer reads 125°. Let chocolate cool to 85°, and keep at 85° by setting saucepan periodically over warm water.

Hold each strawberry by stem, and dip into chocolate, letting excess drip back into the pan. Place berries carefully on a baking sheet lined with buttered waxed paper and let chocolate harden.

In a bowl, beat cream with sugar until it forms stiff peaks. Fold in the **1 tablespoon** orange-flavored liqueur.

Arrange strawberries on dessert plates and serve with cream.

NOTE: Do not attempt chocolate dipping during humid, hot weather.

Chocolate covered fruits should be eaten within 24 hours.

Pretzel Cookies

3 dozen

Fun for children to make.

1 pound white chocolate*
1½ cups thin pretzel
   sticks, broken into
   thirds or less
1½ cups Spanish peanuts

*NOTE: Real white chocolate
   must contain cocoa butter,
   and a combination of sugar,
   milk solids and vanilla.

In a double boiler, melt chocolate slowly over hot, but not boiling, water. DO NOT COVER. Remove from heat and add pretzels and nuts. Drop by teaspoon on a foil-lined cookie sheet.

Chocolate-Mint Squares

20-24 bars

LAYER ONE

2 ounces unsweetened
   chocolate
½ cup butter
2 eggs
1 cup sugar
½ cup flour, sifted

Melt chocolate and butter.

Cream eggs and sugar. Add flour and chocolate mixture. Mix well.

Bake in an 8x8-inch pan at 350° for 20 minutes. Turn oven off and leave in oven for 5 more minutes. Cool.

LAYER TWO

1½ cups powdered sugar
3 tablespoons butter
2 to 3 tablespoons heavy
   cream
1 teaspoon peppermint
   extract
1 to 2 drops green food
   coloring, optional

Cream sugar and butter. Blend in cream, peppermint extract and food coloring if desired. Spread on first layer. Refrigerate until chilled.

LAYER THREE

3 ounces unsweetened
   chocolate
3 tablespoons butter

Melt chocolate and butter together and pour over peppermint layer. Chill. Cut into small squares.

427

Double Chocolate Jumbles

5½ dozen

1½ cups sugar
1 cup butter or
   margarine
1 egg
¼ cup water
1 teaspoon vanilla
1¼ cups unbleached
   flour
⅓ cup cocoa
½ teaspoon baking soda
¼ teaspoon salt
1½ cups oats
½ cup Grape-Nuts
½ cup raisins
1 6-ounce package
   semisweet chocolate
   chips

In a large mixing bowl, blend sugar and butter. Add egg, water and vanilla; beat well.

Gradually add flour, cocoa, baking soda and salt; blend until smooth. Stir in remaining ingredients.

Drop by rounded teaspoonfuls about 2 inches apart onto ungreased cookie sheets.

Bake at 350° for 10 minutes. Let cool one minute before removing from cookie sheet.

Frosted Chocolate Cookies

3 dozen

1 cup brown sugar
½ cup butter
1 egg
2 ounces unsweetened
   chocolate
1 tablespoon water
½ cup milk
1½ teaspoons vinegar or
   lemon juice
1½ cups flour
¼ teaspoon salt
¼ teaspoon baking soda
¼ teaspoon baking
   powder
1 cup chopped nuts

Cream brown sugar and butter together; beat in egg. Melt chocolate with water over double boiler. Cool. Add to butter mixture.

Add vinegar to milk and let stand a few minutes to sour. Add to chocolate mixture.

Sift dry ingredients together and blend into chocolate mixture. Beat well and stir in nuts.

Drop by spoonfuls onto greased cookie sheet and bake at 350° for 8 to 10 minutes or until cookies are soft to touch and a toothpick inserted in center comes out clean. Cool and spread frosting liberally on each cookie.

Frosted Chocolate Cookies   *(Continued)*

FUDGE FROSTING

1½ cups sugar
2 tablespoons cocoa
1½ tablespoons light
   corn syrup
½ cup evaporated milk
4 tablespoons butter
½ teaspoon vanilla

In a saucepan, combine sugar, cocoa, corn syrup and milk. Cook without stirring to soft ball stage. Remove from heat. Add butter and vanilla. Beat until creamy and thick.

Chocolate Turtles (Dinosaur Footprints)

5 dozen

Let your children help you bake these!

1 cup butter, softened
1½ cups sugar
4 eggs
½ cup cocoa
2 cups flour
½ teaspoon salt
1 teaspoon vanilla
Powdered sugar, optional

With an electric mixer, cream butter and sugar. Add eggs, **1** at a time, beating well after each addition.

Combine cocoa, flour and salt. Add to butter and mix well. Add vanilla and mix until blended.

Set waffle baker on high. Place **1 tablespoon** of the dough in each section. Cook 50 seconds, remove and immediately dust with powdered sugar or cool and frost with chocolate frosting.

CHOCOLATE FROSTING

3½ ounces cream cheese
6 tablespoons butter
1 cup powdered sugar
3 tablespoons cocoa
1 tablespoon vanilla

Cream all ingredients. Spread on cooled cookies.

Chocolate Thumbprints
2 dozen

½ cup butter
½ cup sugar
1 egg, separated
½ teaspoon vanilla
1 ounce semisweet
  chocolate, melted
1 cup flour
¼ teaspoon salt
¾ cup finely chopped
  pecans

Blend butter, sugar, egg yolk, vanilla and chocolate. Add flour and salt. Mix thoroughly.

Roll dough into little balls and dip into slightly beaten egg white. Roll in pecans. Place on cookie sheet and press thumb into each cookie. Bake at 350° for 10 to 12 minutes.

When cookies are cooled, fill thumbprint with filling.

FILLING

4 tablespoons butter
2 cups powdered sugar,
  sifted
1 egg
1 teaspoon vanilla
Milk, if needed

Beat butter until softened. Add powdered sugar. Beat in egg and vanilla. Add milk if necessary for spreading consistency.

Chocolate Squares
3½ dozen

½ cup shortening
¾ cup powdered sugar
2 ounces unsweetened
  chocolate, melted and
  cooled
1 egg
½ teaspoon vanilla
Dash salt
1¾ cups flour
40 (approximately)
  walnut halves

Cream shortening and powdered sugar. Add chocolate and continue to cream until mixed. Add egg and mix well. Add vanilla and salt. Gradually add flour, mixing until blended.

Press into a 7x11-inch pan. Press walnut halves into the dough, arranging in rows, leaving enough room to cut cookies after baking. Refrigerate for 2 hours.

Bake at 350° for 12 to 15 minutes. Cut into squares while warm. Cool, remove from pan.

The World's Best Chocolate Chip Cookies

6 dozen

¾ cup shortening
¾ cup butter, softened
1¼ cups sugar
1 cup firmly packed
  brown sugar
4 eggs
1 tablespoon vanilla
1 teaspoon lemon juice
2 teaspoons baking soda
1 teaspoon salt
1 teaspoon cinnamon **or**
  allspice
½ cup rolled oats
3 cups flour
2 12-ounce packages
  semisweet chocolate
  chips
2 cups chopped walnuts

In a large bowl, beat shortening, butter and both sugars until fluffy. Add eggs, beating well after each. Add vanilla and lemon juice; beat.

Combine soda, salt, cinnamon, oats and flour. Beat into creamed mixture until well combined. Stir in chocolate chips and nuts.

Drop on greased cookie sheets and bake at 350° for 10 to 12 minutes or until lightly browned. Cool on racks.

Chocolate-Peanut Butter Tarts

3½-4 dozen

1 cup chunky peanut
  butter
1 cup brown sugar
1 egg
1 teaspoon vanilla
1 package (box) miniature
  Reese's Peanut Butter
  Cups (candy)

Cream peanut butter and brown sugar. Add egg and vanilla and mix until combined.

Shape dough into balls using 1 teaspoon for each. Place balls in miniature muffin tins and bake at 350° for 10 to 12 minutes, until slightly browned.

While tarts are baking, unwrap the peanut butter cups. As soon as you remove the tarts from the oven, smash a cup in the center of each tart. Cool.

Store in refrigerator.

431

Chocolate Brownie Tarts

3 dozen

½ cup butter, softened
1 3-ounce package
 cream cheese,
 softened
1 cup flour
4 ounces semisweet
 chocolate
2 tablespoons butter
2 eggs, beaten
⅔ cup sugar
½ teaspoon vanilla
 extract
Dash salt
½ cup chopped walnuts

Cream butter and cream cheese until light and fluffy. Add the flour and continue mixing until well combined. Wrap pastry and refrigerate for 1 hour.

Melt chocolate and butter in top of double boiler. Remove from heat. Add remaining ingredients except nuts and mix well.

Preheat oven to 350°. Press a rounded teaspoon of pastry into bottom and sides of 1¾-inch small cupcake pans. Divide nuts evenly among pastry-lined cups. Spoon in chocolate mixture. Bake 30 minutes.

Remove from pan and cool on racks.

Frosted Brownies

8-10 servings

2 squares unsweetened
 chocolate
½ cup butter
2 eggs
1 cup sugar
½ cup flour
½ pound walnuts,
 chopped
¾ teaspoon vanilla
1 to 2 squares
 unsweetened
 chocolate, melted

In a saucepan, melt **2 squares** chocolate with butter.

Beat eggs with sugar. Add butter and chocolate mixture. Add flour, nuts and vanilla. Spread batter thinly on a 9x15-inch cookie sheet. Bake at 350° for 7 minutes.

Spread frosting on cooled brownies. Pour melted chocolate over frosting. Chill and cut into squares.

FROSTING

1½ cups powdered sugar
⅓ cup butter
½ cup heavy cream

Combine sugar, butter and cream in a saucepan and boil to soft ball stage. Whip mixture until creamy.

Elegant Espresso Truffles
40 truffles

12 ounces semisweet chocolate
4 ounces sweet butter, softened
2 egg yolks
4 tablespoons rum
½ cup heavy cream
40 espresso coffee beans
½ cup ground espresso coffee beans
¼ cup cocoa powder

Melt chocolate in top of double boiler. Remove from heat and beat in butter, 1 ounce at a time. Add yolks, rum and cream, beat until smooth.

Cover and refrigerate until hardened. Remove, using a teaspoon, make little mounds of chocolate, then roll into a 1-inch ball with your hands.

Force a whole espresso bean into the center using a toothpick. Fill in the hole with chocolate.

Sift together ground espresso and cocoa powder onto a plate. Roll each truffle in the mixture. Store in refrigerator.

Chocolate Truffles
24 truffles

¼ cup unsalted butter
2½ ounces semisweet chocolate
2 tablespoons dark rum
½ cup grated unsweetened chocolate or unsweetened cocoa

Melt butter and the **2½ ounces** chocolate in the top of a double boiler; stir to mix. Remove from heat and stir in rum. Refrigerate 30 to 40 minutes until firm.

Shape into small balls, using 1 teaspoonful of mixture for each. Roll balls in **grated** chocolate and put in foil or paper candy cups.

Refrigerate until served.

Chocolate deflates stiffly beaten egg white mixtures, so fold in carefully – just until blended.

433

Rocky Road

1½ pounds

1 pound sweet baking chocolate
3 to 4 ounces cocoa butter*
2 cups miniature marshmallows
1 cup chopped walnuts

*NOTE: Cocoa butter is available at pharmacies. Some stores keep it refrigerated, so you may have to ask for it.

In a double boiler or in the microwave, melt together the chocolate and cocoa butter. Remove top of double boiler and stir until blended. Let stand, at room temperature, until thickened, about 45 to 60 minutes, stirring occasionally. When thickened, fold in marshmallows and walnuts. Pour into a well-buttered 8x8-inch dish. Let harden completely before serving. Cut into 1-inch squares to serve.

Peanut Butter Cup Candy

1 9x13-inch pan

1 cup butter
1 cup extra crunchy peanut butter
3 cups powdered sugar
6 ounces semisweet chocolate chips

Melt butter and stir in peanut butter. Add powdered sugar and mix until of frosting consistency. Press into a 9x13-inch pan.

Melt chocolate chips and spread on top of peanut butter mixture. Refrigerate for 15 minutes to set chocolate. Remove from refrigerator and cut into bite-sized pieces.

NOTE: Do not leave in refrigerator longer than 15 minutes or chocolate will crumble when cut.

Pre-melted chocolate is not real chocolate, it is a combination of powdered cocoa and hydrogenated vegetable oil, thus giving it a less pronounced chocolate flavor.

Chocolate-Caramel Clusters   45 pieces

1 14-ounce package caramels
2 tablespoons butter
2 tablespoons water
1 teaspoon vanilla
3 cups broken walnuts or pecans
1 12-ounce package semisweet chocolate chips
½ block paraffin

Melt caramels, butter and water in top of double boiler. Remove from heat and add vanilla and nuts. Stir together well. Mixture will be stiff.

Drop by teaspoons onto buttered cookie sheet and let cool.

Melt chocolate chips and paraffin in top of double boiler.

Spear cooled candies from bottom with toothpick and dip in warm chocolate mixture (kept warm over hot water, but not on burner). Place right side up on sheet of waxed sheet to cool. Store in refrigerator when firm.

If your fudge turns to sugar, add 2 tablespoons of cream and stir over very low heat until it is warm and slightly softened. Should be creamier and smoother than before.

To make chocolate curls for garnish: Use a warm vegetable parer on room-temperature chocolate.

435

Double Whammy Frozen Chocolate Crêpes with Vanilla Sauce   12 crêpes

1 12-ounce package
    semisweet real
    chocolate chips
1 teaspoon vanilla
1½ cups whipping
    cream, heated to
    boiling
6 egg yolks

Combine chocolate and vanilla in blender or food processor, fitted with the steel knife, for a few seconds. Add boiling cream and continue processing until chocolate is completely melted (about 30 seconds). Add egg yolks and mix very briefly. Pour into a bowl and refrigerate until the consistency of pudding.

To serve, place about 2 tablespoons mousse into each crêpe and roll. Place seam side down on cookie sheet and freeze. Wrap and keep in freezer until serving time.

Serve **warm** vanilla sauce over frozen crêpes.

CHOCOLATE CREPES

1 cup milk
½ cup flour
¼ cup sugar
2 eggs
2 tablespoons cocoa
1 tablespoon butter,
    melted
1 teaspoon vanilla
Butter

In a blender combine all ingredients **except** butter and mix on low speed about ½ minute, until combined (do not overblend). Allow to stand in blender container 1 hour.

Brush a 7 or 8-inch crêpe pan with butter. Heat to high. When butter is sizzling, pour a little less than ¼ cup batter into pan. Lift off heat and swirl to coat bottom. Cook about 1 minute or until slightly dry on bottom (watch carefully as cocoa burns easily). Turn onto paper towel and repeat process, buttering each time if needed.

Double Whammy ... *(Continued)*

VANILLA SAUCE

4 egg yolks
½ cup sugar
1 vanilla bean, split
  (no substitutions)
1½ cups light cream

Combine yolks and sugar in medium bowl. Scrape the soft part of the vanilla bean into the mixture (reserving the pod). Beat mixture until fluffy. Bring the light cream and the vanilla pod to a boil. Beating constantly, pour the cream slowly into the yolk mixture. Pour into pan and cook over low heat about 20 minutes, stirring constantly, until mixture coats the back of a spoon.

Chocolate Roll

6-8 servings

7 eggs, separated
1 cup sugar
½ pound dark sweet
  chocolate
7 tablespoons strong
  coffee
Dash salt
Bitter cocoa
2 cups heavy cream
2 tablespoons rum

Place egg yolks in a small mixing bowl and whites in a large bowl.

Add sugar to yolks and beat until fluffy, light and creamy.

Over very low heat, melt chocolate and coffee. Cool slightly.

Beat egg whites with salt until stiff. Combine by folding whites, yolks and chocolate together.

Oil a 10x15-inch jelly-roll pan. Cover with buttered waxed paper.

Pour batter into pan and bake at 350° for 12 minutes. Remove and cool 5 minutes. Cover with a slightly damp cloth and cool completely at room temperature. Refrigerate for 1 hour. Remove cloth carefully and sprinkle top generously with cocoa. Turn onto waxed paper. Remove paper and spread with mixture of cream whipped with rum.

Roll up carefully and quickly like jelly-roll. This cake will crack as it rolls and resembles tree bark.

437

Chocolate-Filled Cream Puff   12 servings

1 cup water
½ cup butter, unsalted is
    best
1 teaspoon sugar
¼ teaspoon salt
1 cup flour
4 large eggs
Butter
Sliced almonds

Combine water, butter, sugar and salt in heavy saucepan. Heat to boiling.

Add flour all at once and beat with wooden spoon over low heat 1 minute or until mixture leaves sides of pan and forms a ball which does not separate. Remove from heat and beat about 2 minutes to cool mixture slightly.

Add eggs, 1 at a time, beating after each addition until mixture has a satin finish.

Butter a 9-inch circle on a cookie sheet. Drop cream puff paste by ¼-cup measures inside circumference of circle to form a ring. Bake in preheated 400° oven for 40 minutes or until puffed and well browned. Cool on rack.

Several hours before serving, slice ring crosswise and lift off top. Fill with chocolate filling and replace top. Drizzle with chocolate glaze and sprinkle with almonds. Chill before serving. Serve with whipped cream, if desired.

CHOCOLATE FILLING

1 cup butter, softened
1 cup sugar
4 ounces unsweetened
    chocolate, melted and
    cooled
2 teaspoons vanilla
1 teaspoon almond
    extract
6 eggs

Cream butter and sugar until light and fluffy. Beat in chocolate, vanilla and almond extract. Add eggs, 1 at a time, beating 2 minutes after each addition. Continue beating until sugar is dissolved. Chill.

438

Chocolate-Filled Cream Puff *(Continued)*

CHOCOLATE GLAZE

2 ounces semisweet chocolate 2 tablespoons butter	In top of double boiler, over hot (not boiling) water, melt chocolate and butter. Stir to combine.

Mocha Log   10 servings

4 eggs
¾ cup sugar
½ teaspoon vanilla
¼ cup flour, sifted
¼ cup cocoa
¼ teaspoon baking powder
¼ teaspoon salt

Beat eggs in a medium bowl. Beat in sugar gradually until mixture is thick. Stir in vanilla.

Sift dry ingredients and fold into egg mixture. Pour into a well-greased, waxed paper-lined jelly-roll pan. Bake at 350° for 25 minutes or until top springs back when lightly touched.

Turn cake onto a clean towel sprinkled with powdered sugar. Peel off waxed paper. Roll up cake. Wrap in towel and let cool.

Unroll cake carefully and spread evenly with **half** the filling. Reroll. Frost roll with remaining filling. Sprinkle with chocolate curls. Chill roll for 1 hour or until serving time. Slice in 1-inch slices.

NOTE: To make chocolate curls, warm square of chocolate until slightly soft. Shave thin slices with a vegetable parer.

FILLING

2 cups heavy cream
¼ cup powdered sugar
4 teaspoons instant coffee
1 teaspoon vanilla

Beat cream with sugar, coffee and vanilla until stiff.

439

Real Chocolate Sauce
1 cup

When poured over ice cream, this sauce will harden and is delightfully rich.

1 6-ounce package
  semisweet chocolate
  chips
4 tablespoons butter
  (do not substitute)
1 to 2 tablespoons milk

In a double boiler, melt chocolate chips and butter. Stir. Add milk and stir until smooth. Sauce may also be made in a microwave by heating until melted.

Chocolate Sauce – Best In The World
5 cups

1 13-ounce can
  evaporated milk
1 pound caramels
1 cup butter
12 ounces semisweet
  chocolate chips or
  1 12-ounce chocolate
  bar

In top of double boiler, combine milk, caramels, butter and chocolate. Stir until smooth and cook for 30 minutes, stirring frequently.

Remove from heat and beat 3 minutes with electric mixer. Serve warm or refrigerate.

Bound to Please: The Marvelous Appaloosa

The spotted Appaloosa was far from its Chinese origins by the time the Nez Perce Indians began breeding it for transportation, hunting, racing, and war. In 1877, Chief Joseph and the Nez Perce eluded the U.S. Army for six months, but in the end the tribe was sent to a reservation and its sturdy mounts – the Appaloosa among them – scattered.

Today the Appaloosa is Idaho's official state horse, restored by breeders as an animal for both pleasure and show. And each year the flight of the Nez Perce is commemorated by riders who re-trace a part of the journey, bringing a bit of Idaho's past to the forefront again.

The Junior League of Boise would like to thank our members and friends who contributed their favorite recipes for our book . . .

Recipe Contributors

JULIANA ALDAPE
DELPHINE ALDECOA
JEAN ALLAN
SALLY ALLRED
CAROLE ALMOND
WINNIE AMBROSE
LODY ANDERSEN
GENIE ANDREWS
CONSTANCE ARANA
LUCY ARTIS
PETRA ASUMENDI
JUDY AYRE
CHERIE BABBITT
PATTY BACKUS
BARBARA BARNEY
SUE BAXTER
BARBARA BEATTY
SUSAN BECKMAN
ARLENE BELL
LENETTE BENDIO
CAROL BERGER
JAN BERGESEN
KATIE BERGQUIST
CAROL BETTIS
DIANE BEVIS
BARBARA BILLS
LINDA BILOW
VIRGINIA BIRNEY
BUTCH BISHOP
SHERRY BITHELL
LORNA BOARD
BETH BOWLER
DEL BOWMAN
JEANNENE BOYD
LOUANN BOYD
ISABEL BRASSEY
SHELLEY BRAZIER
KATHY BROMSTEAD
BARBARA BROOKOVER
ANNE BROWN
BRADFORD BROWN
FRANCES BRUTON
MIRIAM BURNS
HAMMET BURROUGHS
JUDY BURROUGHS
JANE BUSER
LAURA BUSHNELL
SUSAN CAGEN
ROSA CAMPBELL
MARY CANTRELL
GAIL CHALOUPKA
SUSAN CHALOUPKA
THERESA CHANEY
CHRISTY CHAPMAN
HELEN CHASTAIN
SHIRLEY CHETWOOD
MARY CLEMONS
BETTY CLIFFORD

DARLENE CODE
MARCIA COGSWELL
MIMI COPSEY
CONNIE CROOKSTON
DORIS CRUZEN
NATALIE CUMMINGS
GAYLE D'ALESSANDRO
JANE DALY
KAREN DALOS
CATHY DATER
MARJORIE DAVIDSON
PATRICIA DAVIES
MARGARET DECKER
BEVERLY DECORE
BARBARA DERBY
JOLENE DeWALD
JOAN DILLON
KATHLEEN DODSON
NANCY DONALD
BETTY LOU DONNELLY
MARCIA DONNELLY
PHYLLIS EDMUNDSON
GINNY EIDEN
CAROL ELLIOTT
DARLENE ENNIS
MARY LOU ENNIS
VERLA ENNIS
TAMA EVERETT
LOLA EVANS
ANITA FALK
KAREN FALK
PENNY FALKNER
GERIDEE FARLEY
JANE FERGUSON
JO ANN FISHER
JUNE FITZGERALD
SHARON FOWLER
ROBERTA FREDERICKS
PAM FREI
KATHY FRENCH
CHERYL FROBENIUS
CE CE GADDA
PEG GILBERTSON
CAROLE GILL
ALLEE GIVENS
PATTY GLAISYER
MARCIA GLENN
VICKI GLERUM
SUSAN GOODMAN-SMITH
ANNE MOREE GOSS
LINDA GOSSETT
JEAN GRAEBER
ELOISE GRAVES
AGNES GRAY
LINDY GREENE
ROBIN GREENFIELD
SUSAN GREY
JANICE CRUZEN GRIFFITH

REBECCA GROVER
MARILEE GROSS
BETSY GUDMUNDSEN
MARY LOU GUERCABETTIA
ROSE MARIE GUERCABETTIA
TONYA HALL
PAM HALLVICK
RUTH MARIE HAMERSLEY
DOROTHY HANFORD
BEV HARAD
KAY HARDY
JANA HARRIS
SUSAN HART
ANGELA HARTLEY
KIT HARVEY
BARBARA HAWLEY
JANET HAYES
KANDY HEARNE
POLLY HEDEMARK
PAT HENDERSON
MERLYN HENDREN
ARDIS HEWITT
RAMONA HIGER
LINDY HIGH
MARY JANE HILL
ROSEMARY HILL
VICKI HOLSINGER
ANN HOLTON
ROMAINE HON
FRAN HOPPER
BETTY JEAN HOUSTON
BONNIE HOVENCAMP
RUTH HOWARD
CATHY HULL
LINDA HURLBUTT
BONNIE HUTCHINSON
MARILYN HUTCHINSON
CHRISTINA ILETT
SUSAN INSINGER
JESSE LOIS IRVIN
MARY ANN JACKSON
DIANE JACOBSEN
DONNA JACOBSEN
MARY JARDINE
JUDY JAUREGUI
MARGARET JOHNSON
VESTA JOHNSON
TERESA JONES
ROY KAPICKA
CHARLENE KAUFMAN
HELEN KAUFMAN
ELAINE KEMPTON
SUSAN E. KETNER
NORMA KIESEL
CAROLYN KIEFER
JEANNE KING
JO KING
KAYE KNIGHT

MARIE KNOX
BETTE KRUEGER
MARY KRUZICH
DOROTHY KURATLI
CANDY LAMBUTH
SUSAN LAMBUTH
PAM LANDON
BECKY LANGHUS
KAREN LANSING
MARGARET LEMOYNE
SYLVIA LEMOYNE
HELEN LEROY
JERRY LILLGE
SHEILA LINCOLN
MARLIS LINDBLOOM
ROBERT LINK
MARGARET LINVILLE
TRUDY LITTMAN
JULIANA LLITERAS
CAROLYN LOCANDER
LORI LODGE
JUDY LUTZ
JODY MABE
JANE MACK
KAREN MARMILLION
PEGGY MARSHALL
DOREEN MARTIN
GRETCHEN MASSMAN
DONNA MATLOCK
KRIS McARTHUR
SALLY McCLURE
LYN McCOLLUM
JANET McCULLOCH
NANCY McDANIEL
SHARON McEWAN
ELSIE LEE McKLVEEN
GILMORE McLEAN
LISA McMURRAY
MIKEL McMURRAY
VIRGINIA McMURRAY
NANCY MEADOWS
DOROTHY MELVILLE
SUSAN MEULEMAN
JO MILLER
JO ANNE MINNICK
DONNA MOORE
BEVERLY MORGAN
CAROLE MORGAN
RUTHIE MOSER
BARBARA MOSSMAN
KATHY MOYER
ANN MURDOCH
BRUCE MURDOCH
RUTH MURDOCH

TERRY MURDOCH
KERRIE MURRAY
MARIAN MURRELL
BARBARA NAGEL
SHARYN NEGUS
GLENVA NEWHOUSE
BLANCHE NICHOLSON
SHARON NIELSEN
ANNE OPPENHEIMER
JANE OPPENHEIMER
JEAN OSBORNE
DAMA OVERSTREET
ANNETTE PARK
KATHY PARKER
VICKI PARKINSON
MARTY PEARSON
SUZI PEARSON
JUDY PEAVEY
JANIS PERRY
ANNE PETERSON
JEANNE PIDGEON
PATRICIA PIEROSE
DIANE PLASTINO
CHRISTINE POOLE
JULIE PRINCE
JAN RAEDER
CAROL REAGAN
NANCY REDFORD
CHAR REED
SUE REENTS
BETTY LOU REIFSCHNEIDER
PENNY RICE
PHYLLIS RICHARDSON
DEBBIE RICHEY
VICKI RISCH
JANET RISHEL
DIANNE ROBERTSON
DOROTHY ROBINSON
SHEILA ROBINSON
VICKI ROBINSON
JO ROTHCHILD
OLGA ROTHCHILD
CYNDY SALLADAY
HELMI SCHADE
CAROLE SCHROEDER
KIM SCHUH
BETTY SHEILS
MARTHA SHELLWORTH
THERESA SHINN
CLAIRE SIMI
CLAUDIA SIMPLOT
EMMA LUCY SIRHALL
JANE SLATTERY
JULIE SLEE

JEAN SMITH
JUNE SMITH
SANDY SMITH
SUSAN SMITH
LINDA SQUYRES
CATHERINE STEIN
KATIE STEIN
MARGARET STEVENS
ALICE STEWART
JUDY STOKES
VICKIE STOPPELLO
TANYA STORTI
JEAN SULLIVAN
JOAN SULLIVAN
SUE SULLIVAN
LINDA SWANSON
JULIE TAYLOR
MAUREEN THOMAS
CYNTHIA THORESON
WANDALEE TIMM
PATRICIA TONEY
BARBARA TROXELL
TERRI TURPIN
BETSY TWILEGAR
SUE TYLER
JENA VASCONCELLOS
MARY ELLEN VOSHELL
MARY LOU WAGNER
BONNIE WALKER
PAT WALLIN
NANCY WARD
ALICE WEAVER
MARY JANE WEBB
CATHERINE WEICK
CONNIE WERNER
JOYCE WHITE
STEPHANIE WHITE
JUDY WITT
MARY GLYNN WILFORD
CHEROL WILLIAMS
HELEN WILLIAMS
EVE WILLIAMSON
ALLEN WILLIS
BENEDICTA WILSON
PATSY WILSON
PETER WILSON
MARCHIA WINZELER
SUSAN WORCHESTER
CONNIE YOUNG
JUANITA YRIBAR
LIZ ZEMLICKA

. . . and hope we haven't inadvertently left anyone's name off.

Selected recipes from *Boise's Best,* 1973; *Favorite File of Brunches, Lunches, Munches, Punches,* 1963; and *The Junior League of Boise Cookbook,* 1930 (published by The Junior League of Boise) have been included in this book.

About the indexing ...

Use this index along with the chapter dividers. The chapter dividers list all recipes by title that appear in a specific chapter. This index lists recipes by name or main ingredient.

Index

~~~ **C** ~~~

Index

Index

Index

Index

Index

I

J

K

L

Index

Index

Index

Index

~~~ **Q** ~~~

~~~ **R** ~~~

Index

~~~ **S** ~~~

Index

Index

Index

~~~ U - V ~~~

~~~ W ~~~

Index

BOUND TO PLEASE   **COOKBOOK ORDER FORM**

A Collection of Recipes From The Junior League of Boise, Inc.
P.O. Box 6126, Boise, Idaho 83707

Please send ____copies of BOUND TO PLEASE @ $14.95 each $ _____

Add postage and handling @ $ 2.00 each $ _____

Add sales tax for delivery in Idaho @ $ .75 each $ _____

If desired, add gift wrap @ $ 1.50 each $ _____

Allow 2-4 weeks for delivery.   TOTAL ENCLOSED $ _____

Make check payable (in U.S. funds) to: BOUND TO PLEASE

☐ Visa

☐ Mastercard

Signature _____ Exp. Date _____

Name _____

Address _____
      STREET   CITY   STATE   ZIP

MAILING LABEL – PLEASE PRINT

FROM: Junior League of Boise, Inc.
          P.O. Box 6126, Boise, Idaho 83707

MAIL: Name _____

           Address _____

BOUND TO PLEASE   **COOKBOOK ORDER FORM**

A Collection of Recipes From The Junior League of Boise, Inc.
P.O. Box 6126, Boise, Idaho 83707

Please send ____copies of BOUND TO PLEASE @ $14.95 each $ _____

Add postage and handling @ $ 2.00 each $ _____

Add sales tax for delivery in Idaho @ $ .75 each $ _____

If desired, add gift wrap @ $ 1.50 each $ _____

Allow 2-4 weeks for delivery.   TOTAL ENCLOSED $ _____

Make check payable (in U.S. funds) to: BOUND TO PLEASE

☐ Visa

☐ Mastercard

Signature _____ Exp. Date _____

Name _____

Address _____
      STREET   CITY   STATE   ZIP

MAILING LABEL – PLEASE PRINT

FROM: Junior League of Boise, Inc.
          P.O. Box 6126, Boise, Idaho 83707

MAIL: Name _____

           Address _____

BOUND TO PLEASE   **COOKBOOK ORDER FORM**

A Collection of Recipes From The Junior League of Boise, Inc.
P.O. Box 6126, Boise, Idaho 83707

Please send ____copies of BOUND TO PLEASE @ $14.95 each $ _____

Add postage and handling @ $ 2.00 each $ _____

Add sales tax for delivery in Idaho @ $ .75 each $ _____

If desired, add gift wrap @ $ 1.50 each $ _____

Allow 2-4 weeks for delivery.   TOTAL ENCLOSED $ _____

Make check payable (in U.S. funds) to: BOUND TO PLEASE

☐ Visa

☐ Mastercard

Signature _____ Exp. Date _____

Name _____

Address _____
         STREET   CITY   STATE   ZIP

MAILING LABEL – PLEASE PRINT

FROM: Junior League of Boise, Inc.
       P.O. Box 6126, Boise, Idaho 83707

MAIL: Name _____

       Address _____

       _____

BOUND TO PLEASE   **COOKBOOK ORDER FORM**

A Collection of Recipes From The Junior League of Boise, Inc.
P.O. Box 6126, Boise, Idaho 83707

Please send ____copies of BOUND TO PLEASE @ $14.95 each $ _____

Add postage and handling @ $ 2.00 each $ _____

Add sales tax for delivery in Idaho @ $ .75 each $ _____

If desired, add gift wrap @ $ 1.50 each $ _____

Allow 2-4 weeks for delivery.   TOTAL ENCLOSED $ _____

Make check payable (in U.S. funds) to: BOUND TO PLEASE

☐ Visa

☐ Mastercard

Signature _____ Exp. Date _____

Name _____

Address _____
         STREET   CITY   STATE   ZIP

MAILING LABEL – PLEASE PRINT

FROM: Junior League of Boise, Inc.
       P.O. Box 6126, Boise, Idaho 83707

MAIL: Name _____

       Address _____

       _____